The Psychological and Social Impact of Disability

Robert P. Marinelli, EdD, CRC is Professor and Coordinator of Rehabilitation Counselor Education in the Department of Counseling Psychology and Rehabilitation at West Virginia University. He received his masters and doctoral degrees in Rehabilitation Counseling from the Pennsylvania State University, the latter in 1971. A licensed psychologist and counselor, he has served on the faculties at Penn State and Boston University, as a consultant to rehabilitation agencies, mental health centers, and the Social Security Administration, and as a rehabilitation counselor. His professional activities have included national, regional, and state offices in rehabilitation associations and editorial board service to a variety of rehabilitation journals. His scholarly activities focus primarily on the psychological and career impact of disability and include authoring or coauthoring three textbooks, and numerous book chapters and articles. He and Dr. Dell Orto are currently co-editing the *Encyclopedia of the Rehabilitation of Persons with Disabilities* to be published in 1993.

Authur E. Dell Orto, PhD, CRC, is a professor and chairperson of the Department of Rehabilitation Counseling at Sargent College of Allied Health Professions, Boston University. He received his masters in Rehabilitation Counseling from Seton Hall University, and his doctorate from Michigan State University in 1970. Professionally, Dr. Dell Orto has worked in a variety of settings, both as a rehabilitation consultant and as a licensed psychologist. He is the coauthor of five books: *The Psychological and Social Impact of Physical Disability*, with Robert P. Marinelli; *Group Counseling and Physical Disability* with Robert Lasky; *Role of the Family in the Rehabilitation of the Physically Disabled* with Paul Power and *Family Intervention Throughout Chronic Illness and Disability* with Paul Power and Martha Gibbons.

The Psychological and Social Impact of Disability

Third Edition

Robert P. Marinelli, EdD
Arthur E. Dell Orto, PhD
Editors

Foreword by Irving Kenneth Zola, PhD

SPRINGER PUBLISHING COMPANY, New York

This book is dedicated to Irving Kenneth Zola whose writings, teachings, and life style validate all people and remind us that we are only temporarily able-bodied.

Springer Publishing Company, Inc.
536 Broadway
New York, N.Y. 10012

96 97 98 99 00 / 10 9 8 7 6

Library of Congress Cataloging-in-Publication Data

The psychological and social impact of disability / Robert P. Marinelli, Arthur E. Dell Orto, editors; foreword by Irving Kenneth Zola. — 3rd ed.
    p. cm.
    Includes bibliographical references and index
    ISBN 0-8261-2212-4
    1. Handicapped—United States—Psychology. 2. Handicapped—Rehabilitation—United States. 3. Handicapped—United States Family relationships.
    4. Handicapped—United States—Sexual behavior. 5. Handicapped—United States—Public opinion. 6. Public opinion—United States. I. Marinelli, Robert P., 1942– . II. Dell Orto, Arthur E., 1943– .
    [DNLM: 1. Handicapped—United States. 2. Rehabilitation—United States. HV 1553. P974]
HV1553.P75 1991
155.9'16—dc2O
DNLM/DLC
for Library of Congress   91-4809
                                                                                                                            CIP

Printed in the United States of America

CONTENTS

FOREWORD

It has been nearly eight years since I wrote a foreword to the second edition of this book. Then the United Nation's International Decade of the Disabled was just beginning. Now it is nearly over. The decade has been a time of mixed blessings, particularly in the United States. The 1980's introduced drastic cuts and changes in benefit eligibility for people with disabilities. The philosophical underpinnings of the Reagan era presaged a general retrenchment in benefits and services. The economic downturn of the late 1980's and early 1990's has only reinforced this trend. As a result there was great fear that the gains in civil liberties promulgated by Section 504 of the Rehabilitation Act of 1973 would be undercut and the Independent Living Movement which grew in its wake would flounder. But the doomsayers were wrong. Section 504 proved to be a consciousness turning point in the lives and minds of people with disabilities. By 1986, a national Louis Harris poll showed that we were beginning to identify with other oppressed minority groups. We began to realize that disability was not merely a personal problem to be solved by individual effort. Disability was as much a social problem created and reinforced by social attitudes and prejudices whose solution would require governmental resources, protections, and interventions.

While Independent Living Centers staffed and run by people with disabilities have become a mainstream addition to our service delivery systems, disability rights have moved onto the national agenda. While the courts, in decision after decision, seemed to limit the scope of Section 504 (after all, only fifty words in a more omnibus bill), the legislative efforts have been outstanding. Setbacks in the courts have been met by gains in the legislatures culminating in 1990 with the federal passage of the Americans with Disabilities Act—a law which clarifies and strengthens (though not perfectly) much of what has been merely alluded to and interpreted from previous acts. But this time there is recognition that this landmark legislation marks just a beginning, not an end.

Our issues have become everyone's issues, our rhetoric more and more an accepted reality. The term TAB's (temporarily able-bodied) has become more than a slogan as analysis after analysis shows that the number of people with a chronic disease or disability is increasing steadily, with even the oft cited figure of 43 million now considered by some statisticians to be conservative. Coalition building has become once again a reality as common agendas are shared between people with disabilities, people who are aging, and people with AIDS. Personal assistance systems pioneered by Centers of Independent Living twenty years ago are becoming models for other forms of home health care as well as part of new national policy initiatives dealing with family assistance, parental leave, and long-term care. Quality of life has become a criteria of care in the 1990's and at the center of ethical debates on such disparate issues as reproductive technology/genetic testing and right to die/assisted suicide (e.g., the celebrated Cruzan case).

This book addresses, though appropriately does not solve, all such issues. While we welcome all political rhetoric to integrate us into the mainstream, we need again and again to remind everyone that we are the mainstream. What is done in the name of disability today affects all our tomorrows.

Irving Kenneth Zola
Mortimer Gryzmish Professor of Human Relations:
Department of Sociology, Brandeis University

PREFACE TO THE THIRD EDITION

THE CHALLENGE OF DISABILITY

Disability is a challenge. It challenges one's resources, creates opportunity, and often presents a harsh reality. However, life's journey with a disability does not necessarily have to be better or worse than it would be without one. Unfortunately this journey is often made more difficult by the existence of negative forces that can often frustrate the goals of self-actualization and rehabilitation. While these forces such as ignorance, prejudice, negativism, and insensitivity exist in 1991, significant progress toward their eradication has been made. The goal of this edition is to present that progress and create a perspective that is meaningful and relevant to all those challenged directly or indirectly by the disability experience.

The exploration and understanding of disability in light of its psychological and social impact continues as the main focus of this book. The dramatic changes in rehabilitation since the publication of the first and second editions, in 1977 and 1984 respectively, have resulted in most of this edition being totally new. Many factors account for this change. New concepts of disability and directions in rehabilitation have resulted in the evolution of rehabilitation from a historical perspective to a futuristic one. This evolution is documented throughout this book. Part VII, New Directions, has been added to reflect the changing nature of our field from the perspective of individuals served, critical issues, and rehabilitation models.

The developmental and social context in which disability occurs has received more emphasis in this edition, a reflection of increased emphasis in our society. It is also recognized by us and by many others, that persons with physical and mental disabilities share similar challenges, needs, and aspirations. This acknowledgment has resulted in a significant broadening of this volume to encompass the psychological and social issues impacting all persons with disabilities; whether those disabilities be physical, intellectual, or emotional.

The assumption that guided the earlier editions—that disability affects different facets of a person's life—continues in this edition. Over the last several years available literature in our field has broadened due to the establishment of many new and innovative journals; this made our task of selecting readings more challenging as well as more rewarding. As in the past, practicality and utility for service providers as well as innovation have been used as benchmarks for selecting readings.

Other persons are the primary contributors to this edition, as they were to the first two editions. We thank the authors and their publishers for permission to reprint their work. A special acknowledgment is given to Dr. Hanoch Livneh of

Portland State University, who contributed three major chapters to this edition and Irving Kenneth Zola of Brandeis University whose vision and writings have guided us throughout this project and to whom this book is dedicated. We would like also to acknowledge the support of our colleagues in the Department of Counseling Psychology and Rehabilitation at West Virginia University and the Department of Rehabilitation Counseling at Boston University for their encouragement and support, especially William Anthony and Shari Thurer who contributed articles and Robert Lasky who helped conceptualize the Disability Awareness Exercises.

We would also like to thank members of our staff—Candy Long, Vicki Bennett, Rosemary Hess, Linda Fletcher, Ana Maria Garcia, Joanne Wu, and Susan Cannata—for their clerical help, as well as Ken Paruti for his organizational skills and support during the project. A special acknowledgment is made to June C. Holt, Library Director at the Massachusetts Rehabilitation Library, and Assistant Librarians David Cain and Maya De, without whose assistance this project would have been most difficult. We also gratefully acknowledge Dr. Ursula Springer, Kathleen O'Malley, and all others at Springer Publishing Company who contributed their invaluable expertise and assistance.

RPM
ADO
1991

CONTRIBUTORS

Constance Anderson, Ph.D.
National Medical Center
Washington, DC

William A Anthony, Ph.D.
Boston University
Boston, Massachusetts

Andrew I. Batavia, J.D., M.S.
Georgetown University
School of Medicine
Washington, DC

Karen Berger, M.S.W.
National Medical Center
Washington, DC

George F. Bills, Ph.D.
Abarex Rehabilitation Facility
Parkersburg, West Virginia

Laura Blankertz, Ph.D.
Horizon House
Philadelphia, Pennsylvania

Robert Bogdan, Ph.D.
Syracuse University
Syracuse, New York

Martha Wingerd Bristor, Ph.D.
Michigan State University
East Lansing, Michigan

Daniel Callahan, Ph.D.
Hastings Center
Briarcliff, New York

Ram A. Cnaan, Ph.D.
Tel Aviv University
Tel Aviv, Israel

Sandra S. Cole, AASECT, CSE
University of Michigan Medical
School
Ann Arbor, Michigan

Sherry E. Davis, Ph.D.
National Medical Center
Washington, DC

Patricia E. Deegan, Ph.D.
Northeast Independent Living
Program
Lawrence, Massachusetts

Gerben DeJong, Ph.D.
National Rehabilitation Hospital
Washington, DC

Arthur E. Dell Orto, Ph.D., C.R.C.
Boston University
Boston, Massachusetts

Stanley Ducharme, Ph.D.
Boston University School of Medicine
Boston, Massachusetts

Marc W. Eaton, Ph.D.
Private Practice
Waycross, Georgia

Carl F. Feinstein
National Medical Center
Washington, DC

Jerome R. Gardner, M.S.W.
Horizon House
Philadelphia, Pennsylvania

Kathleen M. Gill, Ph.D.
McLean Hospital
Belmont, Massachusetts

Harlan Hahn, Ph.D
University of Southern California
Los Angeles, California

David B. Hershenson, Ph.D., C.R.C.
University of Maryland
College Park, Maryland

H. Ronald Hulnick, Ph.D.
University of Santa Monica
Santa Monica, California

Mary R. Hulnick, Ph.D.
University of Santa Monica
Santa Monica, California

Helen Q. Kivnick, Ph.D.
Hospital of the University of
 Pennsylvania
Philadelphia, Pennsylvania

Peter T. Knoepfler, M.D.
Private Practice
Bellevue, Washington

Robert Lasky, Ph.D.
Mercy Hospital
Springfield, Massachusetts

Donald C. Linkowski, Ph.D., C.R.C.
George Washington University
Washington, DC

Hanock Livneh
Portland State University
Portland, Oregon

Robert P. Marinelli, Ed.D., C.R.C.
West Virginia University
Morgantown, West Virginia

William A. McDowell, Ph.D.
Marshall University
Huntington, West Virginia

Karlyn W. Messinger
Horizon House
Philadelphia, Pennsylvania

Richard I. Naugle, Ph.D.
Cleveland Clinic Foundation
Cleveland, Ohio

Paul W. Power, Sc.D., C.R.C.
University of Maryland
College Park, Maryland

Ruth B. Purtilo, Ph.D., P.T.
Massachusetts General Hospital
Boston, Massachusetts

Nancy K. Schlossberg, Ph.D.
University of Maryland
College Park, Maryland

Franklin C. Shontz, Ph.D.
University of Kansas
Lawrence, Kansas

William B. Stafford, Ph.D.
Lehigh University
Bethlehem, Pennsylvania

Joseph Stubbins, Ph.D.
California State University
Los Angeles, California

Steven J. Taylor, Ph.D.
Syracuse University
Syracuse, New York

Shari L. Thurer, Sc.D., C.R.C.
Boston University
Boston, Massachusetts

Jean Vanier
l'Arch Movement
Oise, France

Janet M. Williams, Ph.D.
University of Kansas
Lawrence, Kansas

R. Jane Williams
Lehigh University
Bethlehem, Pennsylvania

Irving Kenneth Zola, Ph.D.
Brandeis University
Waltham, Massachusetts

Part I

Perspective on Disability

The consequences of disability can have an impact at many levels. At the personal level, various life functions are frequently affected. At the interpersonal level, relationships with other individuals often change. Responses to disability at the social and cultural levels often result in legislative change and improved services and rights. The effects of disability—personal, interpersonal, and cultural—therefore have significant implications for persons with disabilities, rehabilitation workers, the rehabilitation system, and our society. The purpose of Part I is to sensitize the reader to these issues by providing both professional and consumer perspectives about disability.

In a moving presentation concerning an international application of a self help group, L'Arche Movement, Vanier, in Chapter 1, focuses on the contribution that persons with handicaps make to humanity. His firsthand experience as founder of the movement, which now encompasses worldwide communities of people who are physically and mentally challenged, has provided Vanier with a philosophy of life that he sensitively and emotionally shares with the reader.

In Chapter 2, Stubbins examines rehabilitation psychology from a perspective extending beyond the focus of individual characteristics and dynamics to those that emphasize civil rights and environmental obstacles. His more inclusive interdisciplinary perspective of disability, which draws on formulations from political science, economics, sociology, linguistics, and social-science philosophy, may enable the reader to better understand the complexity of issues confronting persons with handicaps.

Hahn, in Chapter 3, contrasts the "functional limitations" and the "minority group" models and continues to broaden our perspective of disability as well as its individual and social consequences. His analysis examines life or death questions from the perspective of a person with disability who has chosen to identify with the disability rights movement and "minority group" paradigm. The contrasting theoretical, moral, and practical ramifications of these two models are presented with the hope that traditional clinical disciplines will develop an increased recognition of and respect for the values implied by the "minority group" viewpoint.

In "Ethical Issues in Teamwork," Purtilo focuses on discussing the interdisciplinary moral and ethical issues arising from the workings of the rehabilitation "team." In her discussion, time-held traditions and philosophic positions relating to the concepts of autonomy, paternalism, and beneficence are synthesized into guidelines for a morally responsible approach for team-based rehabilitation.

In Chapter 5, Thurer examines several critical rehabilitation issues from a woman's perspective. In the discussion of employment issues, psychological concerns, sexual exploitation, and motherhood, she identifies the needs of women that must be considered in maximizing their rehabilitation potential.

Bridging the gap between psychiatric and physical rehabilitation is Anthony's major focus in Chapter 6. He thoughtfully identifies the major dimensions of physical rehabilitation and provides a direct application between these constructs and the evolving field of psychiatric rehabilitation.

In our final chapter in Part I, Deegan provides a further example of the parallel between physical and psychiatric disability through her moving first-person account of recovery as lived by a man and woman challenged respectively by physical and psychiatric disability. She provides excellent recommendations for creating rehabilitation environments conducive to the recovery process.

1

The Contribution of the Physically and Mentally Handicapped to Development

Jean Vanier

Those who live close to wounded people become rather accustomed to hearing talks about how so-called "normal" people should help their unfortunate brothers and sisters. We rarely ask what handicapped people can bring to others. The very thought rarely comes to mind; it seems so remote and farfetched.

And yet I feel deeply that handicapped people have an important part to play in the development of the world, in helping it to find its equilibrium. They can ensure that development is not just a development of mind and matter, but a development of the total human person, who is certainly intelligence and creativity, activity and productivity, but who is also a heart, capable of love, a seeker of peace, hope, light, and trust, striving to assume the reality of suffering and of death.

I have had the grace and joy to live with mentally handicapped adults over the last ten years. With friends, we have been able to create some forty-five small homes for men and women who were either roaming the streets, locked up in asylums, or just living idly—though frequently in a state of aggression or depression—with families who did not know how to cope with them. These homes of l'Arche are in France, Canada, the United States, England, Scotland, Belgium, and Denmark, as well as in Calcutta and Bangalore in India; our first home in West Africa is just beginning in the Ivory Coast. Each of these homes welcomes and finds work for eight to ten handicapped men and women and for their helpers or assistants. They try to be communities of reconciliation where everyone can grow in activity, creativity, love, and hope. Some of the handicapped people leave us and find total autonomy; others, who are more severely handicapped, will stay with us always.

Published in *"Development and Participation—Operational Implications for Social Welfare"*: *Proceedings of the XVIIth International Conference on Social Welfare*, Nairobi, Kenya, 290–297. (Published 1975 for the International Council on Social Welfare by Columbia University Press, New York & London.) Reprinted by permission.

It is this experience of daily living, working, and sharing with my handicapped brothers and sisters that has made me so sensitive to the question of their contribution to the development of our world. A man or woman can only find peace of heart and grow in motivation and creativity if he or she finds a meaning to life. If they are there only to be helped and can bring nothing to others, then they are condemned to a life of simply receiving, of being the last, the most inferior. This will necessarily bring them to depression and a lack of confidence in themselves. This in turn will push them into anguish and make them aggressive towards themselves and others. For them to find real meaning in life, they must find people who sense their utility, their capacity for growth, and their place in the community and in the world.

The tragedy of humanity is not primarily the lack of development of peoples, or even poverty. It is the oppression, the despisal, and the rejection of those who are weak and in want. It is the horrible and disastrous inequality of wealth and opportunity and lack of sharing. The tragedy of man is his hardness of heart, which makes individuals and nations endowed with the riches of this world despise and consider as inferior those who are poor and handicapped. They not only refuse to help them, they tend also to reject and exploit them.

The tragedy of mankind is the collective national or religious prejudices and pride that close nations and peoples upon themselves, making them think and act as if they were the elected ones and the others enemies to be rejected and hurt, whose development and expansion should be checked. Our world today, with its terrible divisions and hatred, with its continual sounds of war, with its vast budgets being poured into armaments instead of into works for love and justice, is the result of these prejudices and fears.

The tragedy of our world today is that man is still afraid of man. Far from seeing other individuals and peoples as collaborators in the mystery of universal human growth, we see them as enemies of our own growth and development.

It is of course terribly important that misery and starvation be erased from our earth. It is of course terribly important that everyone has access to social and medical benefits. But it is even more important that the hearts of all men open up to universal love and to the understanding of others, to gentle service to mankind and especially to its weaker members. For if we do not work together to create a world of fraternity and of peace, we will sink in wars, economic crises, and national disasters.

There is a continual struggle in all our countries between traditional religious and moral values, lived through family ties, and economic and industrial development. Highly industralized countries offer a certain financial prosperity, but so frequently this prosperity has been achieved at the cost of the values of community. Competition and the desire for wealth, individual leisure, and liberty have tended to crush compassion and understanding. So it is that we find old people lingering in homes for the aged, handicapped people in large institutions, and a mass of marginal and suffering people unable to work because of alcoholism, drugs, and social ills. We find thousands of children abandoned and given over to social agencies, a frightening rise in delinquency, and prisons that offer only punishment instead of reeducation and so cause the high rise in recidivism. We find mental disease rampant, because in our search for efficiency we have lost our acceptance of "the other" and prefer to label people "mad" rather than to understand them. We condemn more and more people to live like strangers, in terrible loneliness, in our large urban conglomerations. The growing population of our cities, our disastrous housing, and inhuman working conditions bring a real disequilibrium of the human heart in its quest for love, peace, and truth.

In the small villages of Africa and India, or in rural areas of North America and Europe, there are still sturdy people living simply off the land and artisans bound closely to the matter with which they work. There is deep love and commitment among families. There is a spirit of gentleness and openness, sharing and welcome for the stranger, which has often been lost in the big cities. Certainly this is a generalization, for there are also tribal warfares and social injustices and individual anguishes. But we must not forget the values of fraternity and community held by simple people, which are so often crushed with the coming of economic development. We can see the gradual breakdown of these values as the desire for material possessions is stimulated, as the attractions of big-city leisure activities become stronger, and the older generation and its ways are rejected.

Of course, it is essential that people should develop and find the benefits of greater wealth and security. But it is even more essential that this development take place in a human context that safeguards and strengthens the forces of sharing, participation, and responsibility. Where economic development coincides with the breakdown of cultural and ethnic ties, where villages are destroyed; where children are displaced and men obliged to leave their homes for far-off lands, the situation is extremely serious: It can gradually cause the destruction of what makes a human a person.

In each of us there is a mixture of weakness and strength. Each of us is born in weakness, unable to fend for ourselves, to find nourishment, to clothe ourselves, or to walk. The growth to autonomy is long and slow, and demands many years of loving education. The period of strength and capacity, during adolescence and manhood, the period during which we are able to act efficaciously and to defend ourselves, to struggle against the forces of nature and environment, is in fact short. After it, we all enter a period of weakness, when our bodies become tired and sick, when we are hurt by the trials and sufferings inherent in human life. And all of us are then called to the last and final poverty of death.

The child in his weakness has all the potential of activity that must grow in him. The strongest of men is inherently weak, because he has a mortal body, and also because he is called to love and is vulnerable to the sufferings of love and of infidelity in friendship; he is weak because he is capable of depression and sadness, drowning in the vicissitudes of life.

The society that encourages only the strong and the intelligent tends to forget that man is essentially weak. We are all potentially handicapped, and we are all created to suffer and to die. So often the search for riches, or hyperactivity in work, is a flight from these essential realities which we must all face one day. What is the meaning of our life, and of suffering, and of death? Are we called simply to be active and to gather wealth, or does man find peace of heart, interior liberty, and happiness in the growth of love? Is it not in service to others, sharing, and mutual understanding—which is not mere sentimentality—that we find this inner peace and human fulfillment?

If people do not refind this energy of love and acceptance of their own intrinsic poverty, if they do not discover that joy comes more in giving then in taking, we are heading for more conflict. If we do not grow in the desire to give our lives rather than to exploit and take the lives of others, than we are all doomed to destruction.

In all societies there are vast numbers of weaker brothers and sisters: those who are aged or depressed, those who have been struck by sickness while young and cannot take on a working life. Are these people just misfits who must be gradually eliminated? Are they just people we must try to reeducate so that they become active members of society? Or have they a special place and role in the development of our society? This is the question we must ask ourselves.

My experience of living with the wounded, the weak, is that they have very precious values that must be conserved for the full development of society. Their experience of rejection, their experience of suffering, which is a taste of death, has brought them closer to certain realities that others who have not suffered flee and pretend do not exist.

Handicapped people have all the rights of other men: the right to life, to medical and social help, and to work. They are able, when this is recognized, to develop in so many ways. With the right educational and work techniques, many can find their place in the world of work and become totally integrated in that world. I have seen men who at the age of six were judged incapable of any growth, working in a factory at the age of twenty and living quite autonomously. Others who were condemned to asylums, to beggary, or to total inactivity are now finding fulfillment as artisans and enjoying life in the community. With care, loving attention, and the right kind of technical help, many can find their place in society.

Handicapped people, and particularly those who are less "able," are frequently endowed with qualities of heart that serve to remind so-called "normal" people that their own hearts are closed. Their simplicity frequently serves to reveal our own duplicity, untruthfulness, and hypocrisy. Their acceptance of their own situation and their humility frequently reveal our pride and our refusal to accept others as they are.

I had occasion once to appear on television with Helen and some others. Helen has cerebral palsy. She cannot talk, she cannot walk, she cannot eat by herself. She is condemned to a wheelchair for the rest of her life. Her only means of communication is through a typewriter, on which she laboriously expresses her thoughts with two fingers. But Helen has the most beautiful smile. She gives herself through her smile. At one moment in the program, someone asked her if she was happy. She broke out into a big smile and typed: "I wouldn't change my life for anything in the world." Her smile got even bigger, and as the program closed, the camera picked up the last word she was writing: "Alleluia!"

Helen, who has nothing except her joy and her love, revealed to me, and to so many who possess the goods of this earth, that fulfillment does not come from material riches but from some inner strength and liberty. Through her acceptance of herself and her condition, she showed how poor we are, in all our petty quarrels, pride, and desires.

At a weekly meeting with some two hundred people, there was a handicapped man called Glen. He could not use his legs, and he lay on the floor. During the last day, there was a period when each person could express what he felt about the week's activity. Glen propped himself up and just said: "I have only one thing to tell you: I love you all so much." His simple words broke down the barriers of convention and of fear in many of us. He wasn't afraid to talk of love.

So often "normal" people have interior barriers that prevent them from relating with others in a simple way. All of us have deep needs to love and to be loved. All of us are in the conflict of our fear of death and of our own poverty. We so quickly pretend we are more clever, more intelligent, and more powerful than we actually are. So often we flee reality by throwing ourselves into activity, culture, and the struggle for power and prestige. We lose contact with our deep inner selves. Handicapped people do not always have these barriers. In their poverty, they are more simple and loving, and thus they reveal to us the poverty of our riches.

The weaker members of society are total human persons, children of God. They are not misfits or objects of charity. Their weaknesses and special needs demand deep attention, real concern, and continuing support. If we listen to their call and to their needs, they will flourish and grow. If we do not, they will sink into depression, sadness, inward revolt, and a form of spiritual suicide. And we who carry responsibilities will have closed our beings to love and to a strength that comes from God and which is hidden in the smallest and the weakest.

Those who take time to listen to them, who have the inner peace and patience to respond to their silent call, will hear crying in them the great cry of all humanity for love and for peace. A great Dutch psychiatrist has written of the schizophrenic that he is not insane, not made of wood, but is "the loudspeaker from whom the sufferings of our time ring perhaps most clearly" (Foundraine, 1974). The same can be said for all weak and handicapped people who cannot fend for themselves.

If we listen to them, then we, the so-called "normal" people, will be healed of our unconscious egoisms, our hardness of heart, our search for power and for dissipating leisure. We will discover that love, communion, presence, community, and deep interior liberty and peace are realities to be found and lived. We will discover that these can become the inspiration for all men. We will realize more fully that men are not machines or objects to be used, exploited, tyrannized, and manipulated by law and by organizations, but that each one is beautiful and precious, that each one in his uniqueness is like a flower that should find its place in the garden of humanity for the fulfillment and beauty of all mankind.

If each one of us who holds a responsible place in society pays attention to the heartbeats of the smallest, the weakest, and the companionless, then gradually we will make of our countries not lands of competition, which favor the strong and powerful, but lands of justice, peace, and fraternity where all men unite and cooperate for the good of every man.

Then nations will no longer rival each other in their search for power, prestige, and wealth, but will work together. They will turn from fear and from group prejudices and from the creation of large and horribly expensive armies. They will use their intelligence, strength, wealth, and natural resources for the growth of all men throughout the world, and especially for the smallest, the weakest, and the companionless. Mankind will then, through the heart of the poor and those crucified in their flesh, refind the road to unity and universal love, where all can be themselves without fear, growing together in love and in the peace of God, our beloved Father.

REFERENCE

Foundraine, J. (1974). *Not made of wood.* London: Quartet Books.

2

The Interdisciplinary Status of Rehabilitation Psychology

Joseph Stubbins

Most practitioners and researchers concede that clinical and behavioral psychology by itself provides a limited perspective on disability problems and that other perspectives are needed for an integral holistic picture of a person with a disability. Economics, sociology, history, anthropology, and politics—each ascribes meanings to disability that differ from those which prevail among rehabilitation psychologists. Some of these varied meanings of disability are beginning to appear in *Rehabilitation Psychology*, but are not representative of the corpus of social science on disability problems. An interdisciplinary approach has remained a distant ideal, evidencing little vitality. Avenues to career advancement, funding for research, collegial recognition, and other factors are not supportive of interdisciplinary approaches (Stubbins, 1985).

This chapter surveys perspectives and realities current among other social sciences and so indicates the limitations of the individualism that prevails in rehabilitation psychology as well as among other practitioners of psychosocial rehabilitation. Rehabilitation's client population is increasingly restive with the status quo. Consumerism, civil rights activities, the beginnings of an adversarial relationship between professional providers and clients, and the emergence of independent lay spokespersons at legislative hearings are some of the indications that rehabilitation psychologists, like other providers in the health fields, can no longer be insulated and protected by their professional privilege. The appeal of an interdisciplinary approach, then, is to engage in more radical ways of trying to understand and reconcile the realities that separate rehabilitation psychologists and other social science practitioners from consumers of their services.

This critique of the limitations of clinical practice proceeds by examining the meanings of disability current among other social science disciplines. These varied meanings reflect significant differences about what should count as science and how funds for disabled persons should be allocated.

LANGUAGE, THOUGHT, AND REALITY

Philosophers of social science have increasingly turned their attention to the analysis of language (Derrida, 1982; Spender, 1980) and how metaphors structure reality and cognition (Schwartz, 1981). Psychologists are sensitive to the ways in which language perpetuates bias and to the need to change terms that carry stigma and prejudice about gender, ethnic origin, and disability (Guidelines, 1987; Spender, 1980). However, little research has been done on how psychological and medical language have structured and dominated the meanings of disability.

Many people who are disabled think of their handicaps as inhering in their *medically controlled label* rather than in the stigma of being cut off from the opportunity structure and in the ways in which they are socially disadvantaged by conditions common across numerous disablements. Clearly, technical language has played an important role in structuring the experience and cognition of disability.

The shadow cast by technical terms on rehabilitation needs to be "deconstructed" (Derrida, 1976; Gergen, 1986) so as to reveal their biases. A number of writers (e.g., Cornes, 1984; Hahn, 1983, 1986; Finkelstein, 1980; Stubbins, 1982) have begun this task. As clinicians, rehabilitation psychologists have at hand innumerable technical terms for describing individual psychological deficits and problems faced by persons with disabilities but a relatively meager repertoire to describe the social pathology that provides alternative explanations (Davis, 1961). The sociological literature on deviance is one source of such explanations. In addition, research could draw on linguistics, semantics, history, and genealogical and archaeological methods employed by Foucault (Dreyfus & Rabinow, 1982).

IMPAIRMENT IN THE TECHNOLOGICAL AGE

After 30 years of advances in the technical training of rehabilitation professionals, unemployment among disabled people is at a very high level. It is time to seek alternatives to individual methods of analysis and to coaching disabled clients to present themselves more effectively to employers. In spite of widespread knowledge of the impact of the internationalization of the major industries, of U.S. trade, monetary, and labor policies in generating the high levels of unemployment, the majority of unemployed individuals with disabilities still attribute their economic misfortune to their impairments. It is time to consider whether refined technical modalities of vocational rehabilitation can overcome the economic policies creating unemployment.

Our *de facto* national employment policy for citizens with impairments is to improve their competitiveness in the labor market. According to this policy, disability means a deficit that is to be redressed by professional services. Those who remain unemployed after being through the sieve of services are regarded as unsolved problems for future clinical research. Psychologists should assume some responsibility for this masking of the social, economic, and political ingredients of unemployment.

DISABILITY AND REDUCTIONISM

Various modes of conceptualizing disability do not arise randomly but are related to special interests that gain or lose when one or another meaning is ascendant. An insurance carrier, lawyer, physician, judge, sociologist, economist, an injured party in a tort case—each brings a different perspective to reality. There is no ultimate reality of disability independent of the meanings men and women in diverse circumstances bring to it. What professionals focus on, what they ignore, the data they collect, what they research, write about—all these reflect a particular perspective. These perspectives have been variously referred to as paradigms (Kuhn, 1970), rationalities (Shweder, 1986), models (Wimsatt, 1986), world views (Converse, 1986), subcultures (Bledstein, 1976), special interests (Habermas, 1971), and ontologies (Gergen, 1986).

Most social scientists concerned with disability problems pursue their special interests (disciplines) with little attention to competing perspectives that could lead to discovering alternative truths. Should we not specify the limitations of regarding the individual and his or her disability as primarily something that can be measured, manipulated, and changed, very much as natural phenomena are? Even social forces are reduced to individual psychological dimensions as when institutional and cultural influences are treated as epiphenomena. Sampson (1977) has dubbed the self-contained individual as "the greatest intervention of American psychology."

Rehabilitation psychologists (as well as other kinds of rehabilitationists) have, in effect, constructed a world consisting of a disabled person whose environment is either a constant or is only marginally relevant to the particular individual's problems. This disabled person does not resemble many in real life. He or she is a static entity with a functional deficit that could be dealt with more competently, a person who needs advice and training in the business of finding a sympathetic employer, and counseling in how to break out of social isolation.

This reduction of the problematics of disability to what exists inside the skin is a pervasive characteristic of rehabilitation science and inherent in positivistic social science generally. Reductionism may or may not be useful and productive; that depends on the outcomes and on who validates them. In the field of rehabilitation psychology, disability problems that do not respond to reductionist assumptions (e.g., clients in receipt of Supplemental Security Income) are ignored, as mentioned in the next section.

Interdisciplinary methods would require working beyond the current rules of the psychology game; to be specific, it means redefining the needed facts and the methods of study currently in vogue. For example, when laymen and consumers of disability services become involved in professional affairs, they often seek to reorder the priorities established by the professional providers.

THE COST OF DISABILITY

Injuries and disabilities constitute social costs, as in Social Security Disability Insurance, workers' compensation, the state–federal programs of vocational rehabilitation, recovery through tort actions, and so on. All these costs constitute a significant sector of the total economy and they are a major drain on national resources. Any measures that could reduce these costs would add to the wealth of the country.

Evidence exists that funds earmarked for persons with injuries are not cost-effective. Here are some examples: administrative costs, duplicated medical examinations, legal fees, etc., consume the largest share of employers' premiums for workers' compensation. Personal injury redress covered by other forms of insurance (such as auto insurance) are similarly unconscionably inefficient except in those states with no-fault insurance. An insignificant number of persons on Social Security Disability Insurance, and on Supplemental Security Income, are rehabilitated, despite the earlier infusion of large sums of federal money to raise the level of professional training in vocational rehabilitation. Though many of the stubborn problems faced by rehabilitationists are spin-offs of these inefficiencies, they concern few practitioners and researchers in our field.

It may be that the whole system has remained relatively immune from critical examination because the best-informed professionals are truly its beneficiaries while its victims are powerless and unorganized. The various professionals who earn their living in these systems are not inconvenienced by the inequities and inefficiencies. It is left to public-spirited laymen to sort out the usual conjunction of self-serving and public good that occurs in the disability industry.

Economists keep reminding us that resources are limited and therefore public and private funds devoted to disabled persons exist at the expense of alternative investments in human development, and other goods and services. If successfully rehabilitating a severely disabled person means putting an able-bodied person out of work, rehabilitation may not be justified. In a free-enterprise system, an unemployed disabled person is simply part of the price of having a free and competitive market.

The programs in the Western European countries that employ a better balance between treating the individual and treating the system are a source of inspiration for socioeconomic macro approaches (Burkhauser, 1986; Haveman, Halberstadt, & Burkhauser, 1984).

DISABILITY AS PHYSIOLOGICAL DEFICIT

Anyone concerned with workers' compensation or personal injury litigation is aware of the dominance of medical testimony in resolving these claims. Physicians' testimonies typically consist of diagnoses detailing loss of function. Opposing experts interpret objective findings differently, but they rarely disagree about whether medical findings are, so to speak, the independent variable in the disputed issue. Disputes center on how much damage has been done to the bio-physical system.

DISABILITY AS BEHAVIORAL PROBLEMS

Bodily insults and developmental abnormalities make heavy adaptive and coping demands, for which individual and small group methods are the preferred treatment. Psychology's successes in this area are clear to the readers of rehabilitation psychology literature.

The kinds of advances associated with the infusion of other social science disciplines can be seen in the progress of mental retardation during the last 40 years. Advocates in this arena have effectively exploited legislative, public media, and other multifaceted approaches to improving the quality of living of citizens with intellectual limitations. Probably no other disability category has made comparable progress. Far from limiting the opportunities for psychologists, the infusion of pluralistic perspectives has greatly enhanced the attractiveness of working with such individuals.

Psychologists and similar professionals who deal in motivation, traits, dynamisms, learning, and cognitive styles could benefit from coordinating with the insights of those concerned with larger social units and the macro social sciences (Stubbins, 1984).

DISABILITY AS SOCIOLOGICAL ISSUES

It is difficult to interest psychologists in sociological approaches to disability (Albrecht, 1976; Stubbins & Albee, 1984). The university departments in which they are educated do not foster sociological formulations. Concepts such as sick role, prejudice, normalization, institution, the social order, the power elite, and how these concepts shed understanding on issues in disability are regarded as interesting but deemed only marginal in clinical practice. In fact, the few who attempt to implement functional aspects of sociological formulations find themselves in conflict with their agency policies. The concept of normalization (Wolfensberger & Tullman, 1982) is used to illustrate this point.

Normalization is advanced by means of public education that focuses on securing civil rights, promoting self-help groups, putting pressures on vulnerable employers to hire people handicapped by disabilities, fostering linguistic changes that break down stereotypes, striving for the reform of institutions to implement the goals of normalization, and encouraging grass roots coalitions to advance needed legislation.

Mental retardation has engaged a broad band of disciplines. With all the superior resources and pluralistic modalities that benefit citizens with this disability, these individuals still face stubborn problems that can be better addressed by one discipline than another. For instance, efforts aimed at opening up employment opportunities can succeed only so far without preparing job applicants for responsibility and a degree of independence, tasks for which counseling psychologists and rehabilitation counselors are well prepared. Housing for group living has encountered neighborhood opposition, a problem that draws on the expertise of those skilled in community organization. The flexibility in exploiting a wide band of theoretical and pragmatic methods would not have been possible without the political leverage shown by advocates in mental retardation. That is our next consideration.

THE POLITICS OF DISABILITY

While other disability constituencies have recently emulated mental retardation and the veterans' lobby, disabled persons across types have little power. A number of writers have emphasized powerlessness (Anspach, 1979; Finkelstein, 1980; Hahn, 1983; Stubbins, 1988). These writers assert that such persons constitute a stigmatized and disadvantaged group whose members for the most part are unaware of their common interests; they would reformulate disability problems into sociopolitical issues.

The political perspective regards disability as a power relationship between persons with an impairment, on the one hand, and those who control the environment, on the other. In this relationship, the able-bodied (especially professionals) are superordinate; they define and choose critical concepts that pose the problems of disability, and determine the kinds of remedial services needed. To phrase it differently, able-bodied people are in charge of resources and their allocation. It is hardly possible to overemphasize how critical this perspective can be in the evolution of the consciousness of persons disadvantaged by impairments.

Defining disability as a power issue is not a common-sense approach as its validity is not supported by daily feedback. The media is increasingly presenting handicapped persons in a favorable light; legislation at the national, state, and local levels seeks to ameliorate the effects of disability; and large sums are contributed to private organizations on behalf of persons with disabilities. To put it simply: Is anyone against those having disabilities? The average citizen's image of power politics conjures up giant corporations, political action committees, and so on. Yet the common-sense view hardly jibes with the existence of stigma and avoidance. It helps to transcend this contradiction by recalling that Foucault (1963) noted that power is not necessarily wielded visibly and openly in the modern democratic state (Dreyfus & Rabinow, 1982). For instance, the workers in a small town are suddenly thrown out of work because an industry has closed down; property values are depressed; alcoholism increases and family life deteriorates. The decision to close the plant was not a plot to produce the resulting social pathology but a consequence of impersonal market forces. Those affected were powerless to influence the course of events. The fact that collections might be taken up to alleviate the resulting damage hardly changes the power dimension of the phenomenon.

Professionals do not intend to aggravate problems of which they are sometimes accused. What they do is sanctioned by custom and legal permission (Larson, 1977). The search for the bad guys only obscures the issues and certainly lowers the level of communicative integrity. These points are convincingly made by Foucault and Habermas (Ingram, 1987; McCarthy, 1978).

Foucault and Habermas have shown that one of the prime characteristics of the modern state is its substitution of refined subtle technological methods of control for police methods. The principal instrument of modern control is superior knowledge. Knowledge is power (Gordon, 1980). Government offices are filled with records about claimants seeking various forms of assistance. But these persons know very little about the bureaucratic operations of agencies. An early step in their changed consciousness is to repair this lack. Knowing how to trigger the political process is clearly an advantage to any disability group, and for that matter, to any group of citizens with common interests. But first it is essential to cope with centrifugal forces that obscure vital common interests.

In a competitive society, most of us are both victims and wielders of power. If this is kept in mind, we are more likely to admit morality into the scientific attitude. The game does not go on only in Washington, the state and country capitals, and City Hall. It infiltrates all aspects of our lives. The implications of conceptualizing disability as an issue in resource accessibility and allocation are far-reaching.

THE PHENOMENOLOGY OF DISABILITY

The developing reconciliation between philosophy and psychology raises the hope that the relevance of phenomenology to our theme would be evident. The value of this critical method of analysis might be difficult to convey to those readers unfamiliar with idealist traditions, with their emphasis on the structuring properties of the mind. The ways of experiencing disability vary according to one's role and angle of involvement, and the resulting perceptions may be called diverse realities (Shweder, 1986; Converse, 1986). Phenomenology has the merit of making us aware of the subjective character of knowledge formation. Such a reflexive effort by psychologists would mean attending more rigorously to the raw experience of persons with impairments while withholding prejudgments—as, for instance, occurred in the reformulation of the phantom limb experience.

Phenomenology is not a philosophic school, cosmology, religion, or anti-intellectual indulgence. In the context of this chapter, phenomenology would examine knowledge and technology and test them against alternatives grounded on other interests and perceptions. Scientific knowledge is power that is unevenly distributed and sometimes subject to abuse. Objectivity and subjectivity are not opposites but close relatives. Phenomenology asks us to regard scientific facts in that light and to trace their origins to special interests and examine their relevance for the majority of disabled citizens.

SUMMARY

The great diversity of functions, roles, and viewpoints among rehabilitation psychologists was not addressed within the scope of this chapter and perhaps leaves the impression of having stereotyped them. Their diversity, however, may be helpful in discovering fresh approaches to the place of psychology in the field of disability.

The inferior life quality experienced by most handicapped persons can be understood better than it is today. Their marginal status is not accidental, random, and unpredictable; nor do the individual personal life dimensions with which psychologists are primarily concerned account for more than a small part of their marginality. Disabled persons are aware of this. In taking on the challenge of becoming more relevant to the essential nature of disability as a societal phenomenon, rehabilitation psychology should consider incorporating more of the insights and perspectives of the other social sciences.

REFERENCES

Albrecht, G. L. (Ed.). (1976). *The sociology of physical disability and rehabilitation*. Pittsburgh: University of Pittsburgh Press.

Anspach, R. (1979). From stigma to identity politics: Political activism among the physically disabled and former mental patients. *Social Science & Medicine, 13A*, 765-773.

Bledstein, B. J. (1976). *The culture of professionalism*. New York: W. W. Norton.

Burkhauser, R. V. (1986). Disability policy in the United States, Sweden, and the Netherlands. In M. Berkowitz & M. A. Hill (Eds.), *Disability and the labor market: Economic problems, policies, and programs* (pp. 262-284). Ithaca, NY: ILR Press, Cornell University.

Converse, P. E. (1986). Generalization and the social psychology of "other worlds." In D. W. Fiske & R. A. Shweder (Eds.), *Metatheory in social science* (pp. 42-60). Chicago: University of Chicago Press.

Cornes, P. (1984). *The future of work for people with disabilities: A view from Great Britain*. New York: World Rehabilitation Fund.

Davis, F. (1961). Deviance disavowal: The management of strained interaction by the visibly handicapped. *Social Problems, 9*(2), 121-132.

Derrida, J. (1976). *Of grammatology*. Baltimore: Johns Hopkins University Press.

Derrida, J. (1982). *Margins of philosophy*. Chicago: University of Chicago Press.

Dreyfus, H. L. & Rabinow, P. (1982). *Michel Foucault: Beyond structuralism and hermeneutics*. Chicago: University of Chicago Press.

Finkelstein, V. (1980). *Attitudes and disabled people*. Monograph #5. New York: World Rehabilitation Fund.

Foucault, M. (1963, English translation, 1973). *The birth of the clinic*. New York: Vintage Books.

Gergen, K. J. (1986). Correspondence versus autonomy in the language of understanding human action. In D. W. Fiske & R. A. Shweder (Eds.), *Metatheory in social science* (pp. 136-162). Chicago: University of Chicago Press.

Gordon, C. (Ed.). (1980). *Power/knowledge: Selected interviews and other writings by Michel Foucault*. New York: Pantheon Books.

Guidelines to contributors. (1987). *Rehabilitation Psychology, 32*(3), 193.

Habermas, J. (1971). *Knowledge and human interests*. Boston: Beacon Press.

Hahn, H. (1983). Paternalism and public policy, *Society, 20*, 36-46.

Hahn, H. (1986). Public support for rehabilitation programs: The analysis of US disability policy. *Disability, Handicap & Society, 1*(2), 121-137.

Haveman, R. H., Halberstadt, V., & Burkhauser, R. V. (1984). *Public policy toward disabled workers: Cross-national analyses of economic impacts.* Ithaca, NY: Cornell University Press.

Ingram, D. (1987). *Habermas and the dialectic of reason.* New Haven, CT: Yale University Press.

Kuhn, T. S. (1970). *The structure of scientific revolutions.* (2nd ed.). Chicago: University of Chicago Press.

Larson, M. (1977). *The rise of professionalism: A sociological analysis.* Berkeley, CA: University of California Press.

McCarthy, T. (1978). *The critical theory of Jurgen Habermas.* Cambridge, MA: MIT Press.

Sampson, E. E. (1977). Psychology and the American ideal. *Journal of Personality and Social Psychology, 35,* 767-782.

Schwartz, B. (1981). *Vertical classification: A study in structuralism and the sociology of knowledge.* Chicago: University of Chicago Press.

Shweder, R. A. (1986). Divergent rationalities. In D. W. Fiske & R. A. Shweder (Eds.), *Metatheory in social science* (pp. 163-196). Chicago: University of Chicago Press.

Spender, D. (1980). *Man made language.* London: Routledge & Kegan Paul.

Stubbins, J. (1982). *The clinical attitude in rehabilitation: A cross-cultural view.* New York: World Rehabilitation Fund.

Stubbins, J. (1984). (Editor). Social science perspectives on vocational rehabilitation: A symposium. *Rehabilitation Literature, 45*(11-12), 339-380.

Stubbins, J. (1985). Some obstacles to policy studies in rehabilitation. *American Behavioral Scientist. 28*(3), 387-395.

Stubbins, J. (1988). The politics of disability. In H. Yuker (Ed.), *Attitudes towards persons with disabilities* (pp. 22-23). New York: Springer Publishing Company.

Stubbins, J., & Albee, G. (1984). Ideologies of clinical and ecological models. *Rehabilitation Literature, 45*(11-12), 349-353.

Wimsatt, W. C. (1986). Heuristics and the study of human behavior. In D. W. Fiske & R. A. Shweder (Eds.), *Metatheory in social science: Pluralisms and subjectivities* (pp. 293-314). Chicago: University of Chicago Press.

Wolfensberger, W., & Tullman, S. (1982). A brief outline of the principle of normalization. *Rehabilitation Psychology, 27,* 131-146.

3

Theories and Values: Ethics and Contrasting Perspectives on Disability

Harlan Hahn

The sharp conflict between health professionals and persons with disabilities that emerged during the symposium sponsored by Rehabilitation International, the World Institute on Disability, and the World Rehabilitation Fund at the 1989 annual meeting of the Society for Disability Studies in Denver, Colorado, seemed to reflect the complex interaction between intellectual, personal, and ethical issues as well as the formidable problem of securing a hearing for new ideas. The controversy essentially revolved about divergent perceptions of the amount of attention to be focused on the contrasting theoretical implications of the "minority-group" and the "functional-limitations" models that have been struggling to gain ascendancy as the dominant paradigm for the study of disability. That normative and empirical concerns cannot be totally separated is indicated by the fact that each of these orientations is based on ethical values derived from dissimilar personal experiences. Moreover, because the traditional "functional-limitations" model, which has provided a theoretical foundation for research in medicine and rehabilitation, is more familiar than the relatively recent "minority-group" model, this analysis examined life-or-death questions from the perspective of a disabled person who has chosen to identify with the disability-rights movement and from the vantage point of the "minority-group" paradigm.

FUNCTIONAL-LIMITATIONS MODEL

From the perspective of the "functional-limitations" model, disability is located within the individual. As a result, public attitudes and the stigma imposed by others on disabled women and men are excluded from consideration. It is assumed that the benevolent desire to help or to improve the condition of disabled persons exhausts the conscious or unconscious feelings that professionals or others may harbor toward disability. No attention is devoted to the possibility that the external influence of negative perceptions is the primary source of the problems that people with disabilities encounter.

Hence neither is there any mention of the unfavorable attitudes that have made disabled women and men a deprived and disadvantaged minority facing one of the highest rates of poverty, unemployment, and welfare dependency as well as a pattern of segregation in education, transportation, housing, and public accommodations that parallels the practice of apartheid. These are the problems that must be solved to enable disabled people to lead a satisfying life; but the assumption that disability resides in the individual and the corresponding tendency to exclude exterior considerations from the field of analysis have prevented investigators from engaging in a serious examination of the ethical implications of these issues.

No one has openly suggested that children or adults should be exterminated in modern times because of the difficulties that they may confront on the basis of skin color, gender, or sexual preference; but these recommendations have been widely accepted with regard to individuals with disabilities. Even though relatively few persons are able to achieve an ideal level of physical functioning, limitations labeled as disabilities have been viewed from this perspective as pathological conditions to be eradicated or remedied to the maximum extent possible. Rather these limitations could be viewed simply as additional manifestations of the diversity of human attributes which may become a source of prejudice in a culture that imposes a high degree of conformity on the characteristics of its members. And little consideration is given to the possibility that professionals working with disabled persons might share some of the negative attitudes about disability pervasive in society or that their feelings may be influenced by the failure of their intervention to restore such individuals to a desired level of functional capacities.

DISABILITY AS A SOURCE OF DIGNITY

The "functional-limitations" paradigm seems to imply that the only means of adjusting to a disability involve prevention, which suggests the futile hope that such differences might eventually be abolished; normalization, or the effort to approximate the state of the nondisabled majority; and dissociation, or the attempt to reduce the importance of disability on a person's life. No provision is made for the possibility that some disabled women and men might actually wish to identify with disability as a source of dignity and pride. The ethical principles derived from the "functional-limitations" model reflect the faulty premise that all disabled persons would wish to eliminate their disabilities and that no one might conceivably choose to live with a disability as a matter of preference.

Perhaps most significantly, this orientation promotes a total denial of the positive experience to be gained from life with a disability. It tends to reject alternative personal values that can be fully realized when the penalties of social discrimination have been abolished. In the immediate aftermath of a disability, for example, people are required to grapple with two of the most difficult questions that can be posed to any human being; namely, why? and why me? Answers obviously vary but one consequence seems certain: after a disability, people experience the world differently. And that difference is a source of creativity that can become the basis of empowerment.

Furthermore, these individuals have an unusual opportunity to join the disability rights movement in an historic struggle to extend and expand the definition of human rights, which can provide an invaluable sense of meaning and purpose in life. As a result, it is imperative both that newly disabled citizens should have an opportunity to learn about these and similar perspectives derived from the lived experience of other disabled adults and that theoretical assumptions should not permit nondisabled professionals to ignore such alternatives. Moreover, the conclusion seems inescapable that the reluctance of these professionals to consider values supported by the disability-rights movement can be ascribed to pervasive public fears and negative feelings about disability. Hence by neglecting these viewpoints and by suggesting that death could be an appropriate solution to the problem of disability, these professionals appear to convey an oblique and almost imperceptible but terrifying message about prevalent conscious or unconscious feelings concerning the remainder of the disabled community. Consequently, many disabled women and men fear that one possible solution to the problems posed by disability might eventually become *the* solution to the problem.

MINORITY-GROUP PARADIGM

By contrast, the "minority-group" paradigm is based on a sociopolitical definition of disability as a product of the interaction between the individual and the environment. From this perspective, the principal difficulties confronting persons can be traced to the exterior force of a disabling environment, which imposes severe restrictions on various types of abilities, rather than to supposed personal defects or deficiencies. Fundamentally these external influences reflect social attitudes that have shaped public policies which, in turn, determine both the physical capacities required to master the built environment and the segregating barriers imposed on various segments of the population.

The "minority-group" perspective is predicated on the belief that prejudical attitudes can be altered primarily through the modification of institutions and behavior to facilitate equal-status contacts between disadvantaged and dominant portions of society. As a result, the inequality of the disabled minority can be remedied principally through legal and political action. Perhaps most significantly, this orientation points out that disabled citizens are exactly what the term implies: a minority group. Women and men with disabilities might appear to lack both a subcultural heritage and a sense of generational continuity, but they share with other oppressed minorities a realistic fear that the narcissistic propensities of the dominant majority to favor the predominant appearance of people like themselves could prompt a corresponding drive to eliminate the presence of others with deviant or supposedly undesirable physical characteristics.

From the vantage point of the "minority-group" model, therefore, the ethical values represented by the suggestion that death could conceivably be an appropriate solution to the problem of disability may be interpreted as a step toward genocide, or the eventual elimination of people who are designated as different from the majority of the population.

CONFLICTS FROM OPPOSING PARADIGMS

Hence the emotional conflict over the notion that physicians might assist in the suicide of a newly disabled citizen becomes understandable in the context of the radically dissimilar ethical implications of the opposing theoretical paradigms. From the viewpoint of nondisabled health professionals who have never had any personal or educational exposure to the positive values of life with a disability, death could be mistakenly treated as a supposedly humane option to the underlying frustration engendered when all of their techniques for restoring the functional abilities of the individual have been exhausted. By contrast for many of those who believe that people with disabilities form a disadvantaged minority group, the danger of genocide only comprises the most extreme manifestation of aversion based on public attitudes that reflect the tendency to shun and to segregate those who are perceived as different.

Even though the precise basis of the egocentric proclivity of the dominant majority to prefer persons who are similar to themselves and to avoid others on the basis of skin color, gender, age, or disability has not been fully discovered as yet, such an explanation is not necessary to comprehend the justifiable fear experienced by women and men who have chosen to identify with their disabilities, the very trait that some members of the nondisabled group may be seeking to eliminate. Thus personal and theoretical concerns are joined in the position of many disabled people that regards the idea of death as a plausible response to disability as both morally reprehensible and personally threatening.

NEED TO MODIFY EDUCATIONAL CURRICULA

The "minority-group" perspective, which is founded on the lived experiences of disabled adults as well as on research in the social sciences instead of clinical disciplines, encompasses ethical values that cannot be totally ignored by health professionals and others in vocations that involve extensive work with disabled clients. Although these issues may be less familiar to researchers responsible for training students in these careers than other topics, a lack of knowledge cannot be considered an adequate excuse for the failure to assess the moral ramifications of this new approach.

In fact, there is a pressing need to modify educational curricula to acquaint students preparing for these occupations with the ethical dimensions of the "minority-group" paradigm and perhaps even to enable them to enhance their clinical skills by preparing for roles as advocates and monitors of laws protecting the civil rights of people with disabilities. Eventually this new orientation might even modify the relationship between clients and professionals by making them joint participants in the social as well as the personal struggle to improve the lives of people with disabilities.

At this moment in the history of the disability-rights movement and the development of public policy, however, major priority might appropriately be assigned to the development of an expanded dialogue about the moral principles embedded in these contrasting theoretical perspectives. And perhaps the most crucial prerequisite for this sort of increased discussion is for professionals trained in traditional clinical disciplines to display an increased recognition of—and respect for—the ethical values implied by the "minority-group" paradigm.

4

Ethical Issues in Teamwork:
The Context of Rehabilitation

Ruth B. Purtilo

"Teamwork" as an approach to the provision of health care services is a relatively modern phenomenon. Only during and after World War II has the notion gained wide acceptance. Today almost no health professional can imagine what it would be like to work outside of some type of team structure (Brown, 1982).

The purpose of this chapter is to evaluate the extent to which one type of health care team, the medical rehabilitation team, has succeeded in promoting the well-being of patients. It is impossible to evaluate fully the success of rehabilitation teams in helping rehabilitation patients receive better care than they would have received without the team approach. Nonetheless, one can subject the team approach to two basic criteria of good patient care: (1) technically competent care, and (2) personalized care, that is, care tailored to the individual patient (Naji, 1975). We will examine how well rehabilitation teams fare in meeting these challenges.

REHABILITATION TEAMS AND THE PROVISION OF TECHNICALLY COMPETENT CARE

Licensure, standardized examinations, and other mechanisms have been implemented to define standards of technical competence among health professionals and enforce sanctions against persons who fail to uphold them.

Competent care requires that each component team member skillfully applies his or her professional skills. At first blush, the plurality of the team suggests that checks and balances will be assured simply by virtue of the fact that each team member feels responsible for patient outcome, and will attempt to weed out weak, incompetent colleagues whose contributions may compromise an optimum outcome.

However, history is laced with accounts of health care providers who have protected incompetent colleagues well beyond any defensible moral limits of loyalty to fellow professionals. Part of the psychology of teams is that members experience their membership on a team as entailing "team loyalty"—a moral obligation of loyalty to other team members and to the team itself (Naji, 1975). They may believe that they have voluntarily committed themselves to a type of "social contract," one that requires a good team member to protect team secrets, thereby promoting a tendency for cover-ups or protection of weaker members (Erde, 1982). A troubling moral conflict arises when one's moral obligation of faithfulness to one's colleagues does battle with one's moral obligations to patients. Therefore, holding peers accountable for incompetence may be made more difficult by the team ideal and team rhetoric. It cannot be assumed that competent interventions are fostered by the team approach.

REHABILITATION TEAMS AND THE CANDIDATES' WELFARE

Despite the importance of technical competence, neither the writings about health care providers in general, nor those about rehabilitation groups in particular, judge it as the sole criterion of good health care. Health professionals must also fulfill the stringent requirement of tailoring care to suit the individual who receives it. This requirement is adduced from the pervasive moral ideal of "respect for persons" in principle I of the 1981 American Medical Association *Principles of Medical Ethics*. A good intervention must fit within the context of the patient's needs, hopes, and fears. For example, following a shoulder disarticulation for cancer, a person who is well qualified medically to be fitted with an upper extremity prosthesis may be opposed to it on esthetic, financial, or religious grounds. Assuming that the individual understands the ramifications of each option, withholding the prosthesis would be judged the morally good course of action, despite the technical advantages of the prosthesis. Thus, the patient's or candidate's well-being becomes the reference point for judging whether the person is being treated with respect, and for ultimately determining the moral worth of the treatment program.

No other group of health professionals takes this highly personalized approach to treatment more seriously than rehabilitation specialists. Rehabilitation is explicitly designed to enable each individual to attain his or her highest possible level of functional independence given the constraints imposed by illness or injury. Goals rest on the ideal that maximal functioning will enable the person to engage in appropriate forms of interdependence with peers, employers, family members, and other social groups (Rothberg, 1985). Rehabilitation teams may be distinguished in part from other health care teams by their explicit commitment to psychologic, social, and vocational outcomes, as well as medical outcomes. Rehabilitation team members are prized according to their willingness and capability to foster these more broadly defined outcomes in whatever form deemed fitting for an individual patient.

There is widespread agreement today that a necessary (although not always sufficient) requirement for assuring a good patient care outcome is to honor the patient's wishes or autonomy. The President's Commission for the Study of Ethical Problems in Medicine and Biomedical and Behavioral Research concluded that, even in decisions with consequences so serious that death will ensue, the competent patient's wishes should guide health care decisions (President's Commission, 1983). The doctrine of informed consent, a governing concept in health care, is designed to enhance patient autonomy. How does patient autonomy fare within the rehabilitation team context? A vague idea of autonomy combined with team pressures may (although not inevitably will) compromise autonomy.

AUTONOMY AND THE REHABILITATION PROCESS

While the notion of "autonomy" is often invoked in discussions about good patient care, only a loose (if any) definition of the concept usually is offered. As Beauchamp and Childress observe, such diverse philosophers as Kant, Mill, Sartre, Nietzche, and Hare have developed dissimilar views of autonomy and its role in morality. One emphasizes freedom of choice, while another focuses on the creation of one's own moral position, acceptance of responsibility for one's views, or the task of reconciling the tension between individual freedom and social and political constraints on one's own actions (Beauchamp & Childress, 1979). Beauchamp and Childress point out the important contributions of Kant and Mill to the development of the concept of autonomy as it is applied in the health professions today. Kant emphasizes the role of self-determination, being-in-control, making one's own choices in accord with principles that could be willed to be valid for everyone. His main contribution to a theory of autonomy probably is his emphasis on the importance of giving the right reasons for choice of a course of action. Conversely, Mill focuses on freedom of action, arguing that an individual's actions are legitimately constricted only when necessary to prevent harm to other individuals. Otherwise, each person should be permitted to act according to his or her own desires. Mill highlights the social-political context of action.

Rehabilitation team members have several means of expressing their commitment to the general ideal of patient autonomy, but none is more formal and explicit than the process of setting rehabilitation goals. Kant's interpretation of autonomy, entailing the ideal that we ought to respect an individual "as ... rightfully a rational determiner of his or her own destiny," (Beauchamp & Childress, 1979) is precisely the message conveyed to a candidate as he or she begins discussion with the rehabilitation team when the goal setting process is initiated. The patient-candidate (a role transition not always made easily) is encouraged to take a more active, participatory role in developing himself or herself and is told outright that rehabilitation goals ultimately must be guided by the personal goals of the candidate (and, when present, the candidate's family). Most candidates initially are eager to take advantage of this "new lease on life." An individual who may have been a passive observer during the acute treatment phase of an injury or debilitating illness now is charged with "taking control."

The stage is set. While the intentions of all are to work together, disenchantment sometimes ensues because of a misunderstanding of how much self-determination the candidate really will have in the process of rehabilitation. The candidate may believe that his/her choices (hopes, desires, fears, and dreams) will dominate the direction of the rehabilitation program. At the same time, team members leave the initial goal-setting session eager to establish treatment priorities that will enable the candidate to make an appropriate adjustment to the disability. Writers in the independent living movement have observed that rehabilitation professionals focus their efforts on molding the individual candidate to cope with constraints engendered by disability in an able-bodied society (DeJong, 1980). Professionals define autonomy as limited by structural and environmental barriers. This interpretation of autonomy is akin to Mill's conception, in which freedom of action is the key to autonomy. Although respect for the person's choices governs the goal-setting process, an actual rehabilitation plan is fashioned with an emphasis on the constrictions that will have to be accommodated by the candidate. Rehabilitation professionals, who themselves may wish that the candidate could live life more fully in harmony with his or her desires, usually rationalize their emphasis on adjustment by drawing on the experience of other candidates: It is almost always inevitable that the affected person will have to make many accommodations. Therefore, in many cases, the two conceptions of autonomy lead to differing expectations and the envisioning of different treatment programs by candidate and rehabilitation team.

After the initial weeks or months of rehabilitation, the situation sometimes becomes yet more stultifying for all involved. Table 1 summarizes six structural factors that act as barriers to candidates' attempts to stay involved in setting the direction of their rehabilitation. All but the first directly relate to team-organized approaches to treatment.

This summary highlights explanations for how the locus of authority progressively shifts from the individual candidate to the team. To be sure, team members may act as important checks and balances on each other by using their ongoing perceptions of the candidate's desires or needs as guides (e.g., "He told me ..."; "Well, yesterday he said ...."), but these attempts by individual members to honor a candidate's self-determination may be insufficient to offset the shift in the direction of the team's collective judgments. Furthermore, it is possible that the candidate may tell members what he thinks each of them wants to hear; in such circumstances, self-determination has given way to the crying need for acceptance by team members. At this point even a Millsian ideal of autonomy—action carried out within constraints viewed by the larger society as necessary—is compromised. Desiring the security which requires that he depend on the team's judgment, and believing himself largely unknowing and impotent, the candidate is in danger of losing sight of what he or she wants.

Consider again the phenomenon of "adjustment to disability." We have implied that rehabilitation teamwork may lead to a compromise, even at times an op-

Table 1. *Barriers to Rehabilitation Candidates' Autonomy*

Factors	Candidate is:
1. "Can't turn back now"	Too invested to back out or change course of action.
2. Fatigue	Too engaged with multiple activities and team members to envision, or seek, alternatives.
3. Anxiety	Too anxious to risk new approaches, especially since so many team members appear largely in agreement about the course of action.
4. Gratitude	Too grateful for this opportunity or "gift" from the team to reject it, even though it may not seem completely suitable.
5. "Reasonable expectation"	Too convinced that the team demands the candidate's cooperation to risk engendering their hostility.
6. Team numbers	Too outnumbered to experience having any power to change the course of events.

probrious compromise, of the candidate's desires, hopes, and dreams. But we have also hinted that the team's emphasis on the necessity of helping the candidate "adjust" is a perspicacious approach to the candidate's actual dilemma. As Haas indicates, "judgment calls" by the team usually are based on their experience with many like-situated candidates (Haas, 1988). For instance, rehabilitation team members observe time and time again that just as all persons alter their goals as time and events intervene, so much more must persons who have faced the exigencies of serious illness or injury do so. Candidates are faced with profound changes in the way their bodies look, work, and feel; they may encounter intense, negative responses of friends and loved ones as they lose the ability to carry out previously cherished mental or physical activities (Purtilo, 1981). These factors may require that the rehabilitation team adopt an approach not guided entirely by the candidate's opinions; his or her cataclysm may bar a clear vision of who he or she will become in the future. Religious conceptions of death and resurrection may be apt in trying to assess what happens to a candidate during the rehabilitation process. Sometimes a "new" person seems to emerge from the old. To the extent that this occurs, the initial act of setting rehabilitation goals is but an exercise in the blind hope that the shadow which falls between the dream and the reality will not destroy the dream. More important, to the extent that the truly desired ends are not initially knowable by either the rehabilitation candidate or team members, the candidate's autonomy does fail to be reliable as the governing moral guide.

In summary, the ideal of autonomy as a guide for setting the course of action by the rehabilitation team is challenged throughout the treatment process. One might conclude that the rehabilitation team approach is able to uphold the highest moral values of health care only in the rare situations in which team and candidate are in complete agreement from the start. Another way to view the issue, however, is to propose that autonomy may be appropriate, but not the supreme or sole standard by which to judge the moral value of rehabilitation team practices.

BENEFICENCE AND PATERNALISM IN THE REHABILITATION PROCESS

A richer portrayal includes the principle of "beneficence" as an appropriate moral standard to judge the extent to which a rehabilitation team's practices contribute to and support a morally good form of health care. Beneficence long has been held to include acts that contribute positively to the welfare of others, as well as acts intended to prevent or remove harm. While not always ascribed the moral stringency of a "duty" within philosophical thought, beneficence has been treated as a duty by others, including many writing in medical ethics. Those writers sometimes suggest that beneficence is realized largely by honoring patient preferences; being beneficent actually places the rehabilitation team members squarely back into the lap of being guided by the candidate's wishes, hopes, and desires! But even the most competent person can make poor choices under conditions of disequilibrium and high uncertainty, such as those characteristic of rehabilitation candidates' situations. Philosophers long have argued that fundamental respect for persons may—in carefully prescribed situations—require that the agent not be guided entirely by an individual's desires or wants. The rehabilitation team's judgment of what is optimum for the candidate indicates that team members act as if they hold such a belief. Having decided that it is beneficial to alter the outcomes articulated by the patient, team members act paternalistically.

Paternalism, a complex, much misunderstood, and much debated concept, presumes that beneficence and autonomy can be incompatible, and in some cases beneficence should dominate (Mill, 1859). Paternalistic behavior is justified by the conviction that an individual's wishes may be overruled in the name of more fully benefitting or preventing harm to the person. This differs from coercion, which is the practice of overruling an individual's wishes without the intent to more fully benefit or prevent harm to the person.

In the context of the rehabilitation team, paternalistic behavior poses a moral challenge by its presumption that the team's judgment should (in some cases) take precedence over the candidate's. Coercion never is justified. The rehabilitation team shifts from a position in which respect for the person is expressed by honoring his wishes to one in which respect is expressed by making an independent judgment regarding his welfare (Jameton, 1984).

Paternalism is thought to encourage candidates into avenues that they would want to pursue. The rehabilitation team has the moral responsibility to deliberate thoughtfully and thoroughly about the person's welfare, regardless of patient desires. Specifically in situations of high uncertainty, limited paternalism (a term employed by some philosophers to express the importance of balancing beneficence with a respect for autonomy) may be useful for fostering a desirable outcome. Limited paternalism assumes that the person acting on the candidate's behalf has made the following assessments:

> ... the patient has some defect, encumberance, or limitation in deciding, willing, or acting; there is probability of harm to the patient apart from intervention; [and] the probable good effects of the intervention outweigh the probable bad effects of the intervention and alternative modes of action and non-action ... (Childress, 1984)

An additional insight into paternalistic interventions by rehabilitation team members is offered by Cross and Churchill (1982). They suggest that "paternalism with permission" is defensible in high uncertainty situations. That is, they argue that when a patient acknowledges that the health professional is in a better position to decide on a course of action, a patient may actually exercise autonomy by appointing the health professional as decision maker. The patient must explicitly acknowledge that he/she chooses to follow the professional's judgment.

Finally, Childress (1984) observes that paternalistic behavior is justified only when "the least restrictive, least humiliating, and least insulting alternative has been selected. Paternalistic conduct by a team that failed to hold these rigorous guidelines no longer could be judged as beneficial for the candidate.

Obviously, teams might unintentionally or intentionally limit a candidate's choices for reasons other than considerations of the patient's welfare. Does the rehabilitation team arrangement have checks and balances to prevent coercion of the candidate or punishment of a disliked one? James Groves' study of "the hateful patient" revealed that some types of patients, including those who are not in agreement with the judgment of professionals, are capable of evoking deep-seated feelings of revenge, anger, and repugnance among health professionals (Groves, 1978). The rehabilitation candidate, treated in the health care setting for a long period while intensely interacting with health care providers, is more at risk than most types of patients of feeling indirect or direct repercussions should his conduct be unacceptable to the team. To prevent harmful conduct toward "errant" candidates, team members must be vigilant and bold, calling attention to teammates who are acting in a revengeful manner toward candidates. Failure to try to stop this conduct by team members is a regrettable instance of how neglect can become complicity.

Viewing the situation optimistically, one can point to the character traits of many rehabilitation team members: often they have chosen rehabilitation careers from a genuine commitment to improving the welfare of persons struggling under the weight of severe illness or injury. A team including several such persons can be "leavened" by their influence, increasing the candidate's likelihood of benefitting, compared to treatment conducted by one person or a less caring group. Public documents and policies in rehabilitation medicine (e.g., the Commission on the Accreditation of Rehabilitation Facilities, 1986), moreover, emphasize the necessity of the team expending considerable energies to ascertain rehabilitation goals appropriate for an individual candidate.

In summary, where, then, does this discussion of autonomy, beneficence, paternalism, and the challenges of each take us in our search to determine the degree of team success in fostering rehabilitation outcomes? At the very least, it highlights that although autonomy is a valid moral standard for good rehabilitation outcomes, it is not a sufficient one. Constraints on autonomy must be guided by thoughtful concern for the candidate's welfare, rather than distorted by conflicting interests. The morally responsible approach is for the team to synthesize several moral principles.

An expression of respect for persons by the rehabilitation team involves both respect for their welfare as reflected in their choices and, in rare instances, for their welfare instead of their choices (Caplan, 1988). In the challenge of seeking the best interest of the patient, the team approach can either hinder or enhance a morally good rehabilitation outcome. Part of the team's moral responsibility is to develop habits and procedures that best enable a morally good outcome for each candidate.

Comprehensive health care requires the collaboration of several health care disciplines and perspectives. Physical medicine and rehabilitation, with its explicit emphasis on the candidate's physical, psychosocial, and emotional well-being, understandably has depended on a team arrangement from its very beginnings. In spite of its shortcomings, there are ample opportunities for the rehabilitation candidate's best interests to be served by a team that utilizes workable moral policies.

Because team-based rehabilitation is a promising ideal, we must attempt to improve the team model. Mechanic and Aikin (1982) systematically assess problem areas as they attempt to work out a cooperative agenda for medicine and nursing. Spitzer and Roberts (1980) rigorously analyze areas of discord in physician teams. A helpful set of suggestions for the "moral education" of interdisciplinary teams is offered by Thomasma (1982), who maintains that in order "to bring about a concert of moral interests within a team" several steps are necessary: (1) the team must develop a common moral language for discussion of moral issues, (2) team members must have cognitive and practical training in how to rationally articulate their feelings about issues, (3) value-clarification exercises are needed, (4) the team must have common experiences upon which to base workable moral policies, and (5) the team must develop a moral decision-making method for all to use (Thomasma, 1982). These authors create optimism about constructive steps that may further refine the rehabilitation team's concept, roles, and functions as a means of fostering positive rehabilitation outcomes.

REFERENCES

Beauchamp, T. L., Childress, J. F. (1979). *Principles of biomedical ethics* (pp. 56-59). Oxford: Oxford University Press.

Brown, T. (1982). An historical view of health care teams. In G. Agich (Ed.). *Responsibility in health care* (pp. 603-778). Boston: Reidell.

Caplan, A. L. (1988). Informed consent and provider-patient relationships in rehabilitation medicine. *Arch Phys Med Rehabil* **69**:312-317.

Childress, J. F. (1984). Ensuring care, respect, and fairness for elderly. *Hastings Center Report* **14**:27-31.

Commission on Accreditation of Rehabilitation Facilities: Standards Manual. (1986). Tucson: CARF.

Cross, A. W., Churchill, L. R. (1982). Ethical and cultural dimensions of informed consent: case study and analyses. *Ann Intern Med* **96**:110-113.

DeJong, G. (1980). The historical and current realities of independent living: implications for administrative planning. *Workshop Proceedings: Policy Planning and Development in Independent Living, University Center for International Rehabilitation* (pp. 2-6). Ann Arbor, Michigan State University Press.

Erde, E. (1982). Logical confusions and moral dilemmas in health care teams and team talk. In G. Agich (Ed.). *Responsibility in health care* (pp. 193-214). Boston, Reidell.

Groves, J. E. (1978). Taking care of the hateful patient. *N Engl J Med* **298**:883-887.

Haas, J. F. (1988). Admission to rehabilitation centers: selection of patients. *Arch Phys Med Rehabil* **69**:329-332.

Jameton, A. (1984). *Nursing practice: Ethical issues* (p. 126). Englewood Cliffs, NJ:Prentice-Hall.

Mechanic, D., Aiken, L. H. (1982). Cooperative agenda for medicine and nursing. *N Engl J Med* **307**:747-750.

Mill, J. S. (1859). *On liberty* . Reprinted in *Essential Works of J. S. Mill.* New York: Bantam Books, 1961.

Naji, S. (1975). Teamwork in health care in United States: sociological perspective. *Milbank Mem Fund Quar* **54**:75-91.

President's Commission for Study of Ethical Problems in Medicine and Biomedical and Behavioral Research: Introduction and summary. (1983). In *Deciding to forego life-sustaining treatment: Report on ethical, medical, and legal issues in treatment decisions* (pp. 1-12). Washington, DC: United States Government Printing Office.

Purtilo, R. (1981). Loneliness, the need for solitude and compliance. In D. Withersty (Ed.), *Communication and compliance in the hospital setting* (pp. 91-115). Springfield, IL:Charles C Thomas Publishers.

Rothberg, J. S. (1985). Rehabilitation team practice. In P. J. Lecca, J. S. McNeil (Eds.), *Interdisciplinary team practices, issues and trends* (pp. 23-24). New York:Praeger Publishers.

Spitzer, W. O., Roberts, R. F. (1980). Twelve questions about teams in health services. *J Community Health* **6**:1-5, Fall.

Thomasma, D. (1982). Moral education in interdisciplinary teams. *Surg Technologist* **2**:17.

5

Women and Rehabilitation

Shari L. Thurer

The occurrence of disability is a jolt. To assert that it is more devastating for one gender than another begs the issue: It is a psychosocial shock for most persons. But the fact that the pain of disability is sex-blind does not imply that the issues are the same for males and females. Nor does it imply that rehabilitation service is equitable. To date, there has been very little attention paid to the concerns of disabled women. Public disability policy was originally designed to address the needs of males in the labor force; scientific inquiry into the psychology of disability, especially that concerning sexuality, is most frequently from a male point of view; the special needs of women have not been recognized. This dearth of literature, in itself, suggests a certain bias. The following, then, is an attempt to partially redress this lack of attention by highlighting some of the areas of special concern to disabled women.

EMPLOYMENT

Disabled women are much less likely to have paid employment than men (Bird, 1979). Levitan and Taggart (1977) found that 60% of men with disabilities have paying jobs, compared to only 29% of women with disabilities. While the weekly wage of employed disabled males averaged 79% that of nondisabled males, the ratio for females was lower—74% of nondisabled women (Levitan & Taggart, 1977). Although relatively fewer disabled women seek jobs, these data imply that such women are at a double disadvantage. Employers may be reluctant to hire them because of their disability *and* their gender. Moreover, these statistics suggest that the whole may be greater than the sum of its parts: that disabled women face *more* employer resistance than the combination of the factors of gender plus disability

From *Rehabilitation Literature, 43*(7-8) (1982), 194-197. Reprinted with permission. Published by the National Easter Seal Society, 2023 W. Ogden, Chicago, IL 60612.

I wish to extend thanks to Janna Zwerner, counselor, Boston Self-Help, and Sanda Wiper, Student at Boston University, for sharing their ideas with me; and to the staff of the Massachusetts Rehabilitation Commission for aid in research.

can account for. While 70% of disabled males who had been working in the year before the onset of their condition were employed in 1966, only 44% of formerly working women had returned to work (German & Collins, 1974).

Even a cursory observation of the current employment situation confirms the implications of these figures. Disabled women are not meaningfully present in the work place. The leaders of the disabled rights movement are, more often than not, male; the rehabilitation establishment is dominated by men. When women with disabilities are trained for jobs, they are frequently trained for less skilled jobs because they are female (Bird, 1979).

BENEFITS

Disability policy in the United States was originally tailored to the needs of formerly working males. Only later were individuals with more tenuous ties to the labor market (i.e., females) included. Even today, women receive not only fewer but also less generous benefits from the major programs—disability insurance, supplemental security income, workers' compensation, and vocational rehabilitation (Kutza, 1983). Because eligibility for benefits includes participation in the labor force for a prescribed period of time, and because disability insurance benefits correlate with earnings, women in a sense are punished for having been unpaid homemakers prior to the onset of disability. Conversely, women are overrepresented under supplemental security income, which is a public assistance program that supports disabled individuals *below* the poverty level.

One of the most glaring inequities in service delivery to disabled men and women is found in the vocational rehabilitation program, especially with respect to the nature of rehabilitation outcome (i.e., work status and occupation) and its correlate, weekly earnings at closure. Hence, in fiscal year 1976, one woman in three was in a nonwage-earning activity at rehabilitation closure (homemaking and unpaid family work), compared to only one man in 15. The mean weekly wage at rehabilitation closure was $63 for women and $112 for men. Only 2.1% of the women, compared to 10.3% of the men, were earning $200 or more per week at closure. Also, vocational rehabilitation services may be underutilized by women in the first place—only 47% of referrals are female (Sachs, 1978), and the "typical" client that the Division of Vocational Rehabilitation sends for a work evaluation is male (Task Force No. 1, 1975).

These data do not incontrovertibly prove sex discrimination, but it is clear that a woman is less likely than a man to receive most kinds of training. As Sachs (1978) has written:

> ...while one woman in three is rehabilitated as a non-wage-earner nationally, it is safe to assume that this proportion is higher in some agencies. These agencies, in particular, should review their placement policies for female clients. Surely, two questions to

be answered from such a review would be, "Was the homemaker closure really what the client wanted?" and "Was this closure appropriate to the situation?"

Ironically, women may have a greater need for disability benefits. Kutza examined the Social Security Administration's 1972 *Survey of Disabled and Nondisabled* (Krute & Burdette, 1978) and found that women represent a greater proportion of persons in the population who report experiencing one or more chronic conditions or impairments. They are more likely than men to be limited or prevented from working because of their disability, and are likely to experience a higher degree of work disability at an earlier age than men. Analyzing data in the Office for Handicapped Individuals' 1979 *Digest* (DHEW, 1979), Kutza (1983) found, in addition, that disabled women are more likely to be without a spouse than disabled men. Such a situation naturally deprives them of the benefits that may accrue from the presence of a husband, such as greater income and perhaps greater attention to personal care needs. In short, women with disabilities may tend to be worse off than men with disabilities, and receive fewer benefits. Clearly, disabled women require a more responsive public policy.

THE PSYCHOLOGY OF WOMEN WITH DISABILITIES

That men and women respond differently to disease is rarely questioned, but almost never examined. To be sure, there are isolated studies available, such as one suggesting that injury or deformity that mars aesthetic quality of the body is likely to have more serious significance for a woman than a man. He is more likely to be affected by any chronic illness which enforces dependence on others and interferes with capacity for work (Lipowski, 1975). Another study indicates that women are more concerned than men with the effects of their disability on their personal relationships (Kutner & Kutner, 1979). But these findings, while important, do not go far enough toward providing a thoroughgoing and rigorous understanding of the interaction of gender and handicap.

The issues beg consideration. It is commonly acknowledged that there is a cultural expectation for women to be passive and dependent, and that there are similar expectations for individuals with disabilities. Faced with compound pressure for compliance and docility, how do women with disabilities cope? How may they avoid being psychologically undermined? Recently, the Task Force on Concerns of Physically Disabled Women (1978) reported some of the experiences of women with disabilities. These included issues of body image, dependence, social and sexual vulnerability, intimacy, relationships with parents—all areas special to the experience of being female (Task Force on Concerns of Physically Disabled Women, 1978). Unfortunately, there appears to be very little empirical data to shed light on these areas.

Sexuality is a case in point. The literature is replete with studies of the sexuality of males with spinal cord injury. But only very recently have researchers addressed the female response (Becker, 1978; Bregman, 1975). To date, we have only very imperfect advice to offer disabled women on sexual exploration, orgasm, family planning, menstruation, menopause, and similar important aspects of being female. Indeed, numerous women have reported instances of gross insensitivity by medical staff regarding these matters (Task Force on Concerns of Physically Disabled Women, 1978).

SEXUAL EXPLOITATION

Public lack of awareness notwithstanding, there seems to be an alarming incidence of women with disabilities who suffer from sexual abuse—specifically, harassment, molestation, incest, and rape. While there is almost no attention paid to these matters in the professional or even popular media, they are issues of great concern to disabled women themselves. Recently, women have been voicing their distress at various conferences across America, such as at the workshop entitled "The Disabled Person and Sexual Assault," held at Minnesota's Southwest State University in the spring of 1980 (Stuart, 1980); the Eighth Annual Conference on Feminist Psychology, held in Boston in March, 1981; and the Third Annual Symposium on Sexuality and Disability at New York University in June, 1981. Visually impaired women complain of unwanted and objectionable looks as well as contact by men who may deem them unconscious of these acts and/or vulnerable. Mobility-impaired women have spoken of encounters with men who are perversely attracted to their prostheses. Numerous reports of sexual abuse by caregivers are offered by physically and developmentally disabled women and their associates. Sanford, author of *The Silent Children*, indicated that the use of disabled children in pornographic films is becoming more common (Sanford, 1980).

Just why there has been no popular acknowledgment of these issues is speculative. Disabled individuals are often stereotyped as asexual, so perhaps the public does not readily associate them with sexual acts. Law enforcement officials typically do not record whether the victim of sexual abuse is disabled or not. Probably more cases go unreported anyway. Seemingly, the only available data documenting these problems are contained in a startling report by the Developmental Disabilities Project of Seattle Rape Relief. This project recorded over 300 incidents involving sexual exploitation of physically or mentally disabled persons between July, 1977, and December, 1979. These cases include both adult and child victims of rape, incest, and indecent liberties in the Seattle/King County regions of Washington. The study contains speculation that only 25 to 30% of all disabled victims report the event, and its authors also estimate that up to 30,000 cases of sexual exploitation involving disabled persons occur each year in Washington state alone (Developmental Disabilities Project, 1979).

Project data also indicate that only 1% of reported cases involve sex offenders who are strangers to the disabled victim. Most persons with disabilities are exploited by "friends," acquaintances, or relatives. These offenders include neighbors, boyfriends, staff persons in residential facilities, bus drivers, aides, fathers, and foster fathers. Frequently the victim is in a position of dependency upon the sexual offender (Developmental Disabilities Project, 1979). There appears to be a great need for consciousness-raising in this area among both rehabilitation professionals and individuals with disabilities, as well as in the community at large.

MOTHERS

While not readily thought a "women's issue," or even an issue at all, the difficult situation of mothers of individuals with disabilities should be examined. These women often struggle with a relentless grind of caring for an individual who may require feeding, dressing, toileting, frequent medical treatment, and constant supervision. Of course men may be involved in these tasks, but typically it is the female parent who is in charge of vigilantly overseeing the child's care. Sometimes, these mothers have no respite.

Medical and rehabilitation professionals have compounded the deinstitutionalization and mainstreaming movements, they have inadvertently reinforced a moral climate suggesting that individuals with disabilities—no matter what their nursing and personal care needs—are best served in the home. This implies care by one's mother; after all, mothers are culturally designated to be at home and do the caretaking. While the deinstitutionalization movement is highly praiseworthy, it may place an undue burden on individual women. Even when deinstitutionalization has not been put into practice and when residential care continues to be publicly provided, the cultural notion that this case is "less good" may be highly guilt-inducing for the mother involved. If and when the child is returned home, the mother may be faced with a life of unremitting servitude. Certainly such a choice should be hers and not the government's.

Ironically, the mother of an individual with disabilities endures not only the pain of loss and the burdens of caretaking, but she is often seen as the cause of the disability. Perhaps she sipped a glass of wine during pregnancy or underwent natural childbirth; or perhaps she did *not* undergo natural childbirth, or averted her eyes for a moment as her child turned on the stove. Mothers of children with emotional disorders may be especially vulnerable to blame. Theories abound which imply that mothers cause mental disease, such as schizophrenia ("the mother herself must have been schizophrenic"), and autism ("the mother is probably cold, humorless, and perfectionistic"). Scientific proof, in these cases, is nonexistent.

Finally, mothers are expected to oversee a treatment plan, no matter how unrealistic in terms of time, energy, money, and the demands on the rest of the family. Sometimes she is expected to do so with little outside support, much conflicting advice from other professionals, and little promise of success—and when things do not proceed smoothly, she is blamed! Should she discourage her child from unnecessary risks, she may be deemed "overprotective"; should she encourage independence, she may be deemed "neglectful" or "rejecting"; should she demur from following any professional advice, she may be called a "saboteur." Featherstone movingly captures the frustrations of the mother's predicament. When told by a well-intentioned nurse to brush her disabled child's teeth three times a day, for five minutes, with an electric toothbrush, this was the mother's response:

> Although I tried to sound reasonable on the phone, this new demand appalled me. I rehearsed angry, self-justifying speeches in my head. Jody, I thought, is blind, cerebral-palsied, and retarded. We do this physical therapy daily and work with him on sounds and communication. We feed him each meal on our laps, bottle him, change him, bathe him, dry him, put him in a body cast to sleep, launder his bed linens daily, and go through a variety of routines designed to minimize his miseries and enhance his joys and his development. (All this in addition to trying to care for and enjoy our other young children and making time for each other and our careers.) Now you tell me that I should spend fifteen minutes every day on something that Jody will hate, an activity that will not help him to walk or even defecate, but one that is directed at the health of his gums. This activity is not for a finite time but forever. It is not guaranteed to help, "it can't hurt." And it won't make the overgrowth go away but may retard it. Well, it's too much. Where is that fifteen minutes going to come from? What am I supposed to give up? Taking the kids to the park? Reading a bedtime story to my eldest? Washing the breakfast dishes? Sorting the laundry? Grading students' papers? Sleeping? Because there is no time in my life that hasn't been spoken for, and for every fifteen-minute activity that is added, one has to be taken away. (Featherstone, 1980, p. 77)

Mothers of individuals with disabilities need a reprieve. In the frustrating business of trying to rehabilitate seriously disabled individuals, professionals must stop over-identifying with the patient and projecting blame onto the mother. She is entitled to her rage and sadness, even her shortcomings. She needs emotional support, guidance, and consistency, and—probably most of all—actual physical help in caretaking.

That the special needs of women with disabilities and mothers of persons with disabilities have been overlooked is not surprising. Such an oversight is merely part of a larger male-oriented world view. But, as this bias is being corrected in other spheres—literature, media, history, religion—it is time we did the same in the field of rehabilitation. Both women and individuals with disabilities have been demanding and attaining equal rights in recent years. We are now ready for women who themselves have disabilities to receive the same. As rehabilitation professionals we must become more sensitive to the needs of women and to the needs of mothers; we must advocate for affirmative action to assure equal employment and equal benefits, and to eradicate sexual harassment. We are long overdue for consciousness-raising. Sexism in rehabilitation should become a *non sequitur*.

REFERENCES

Becker, E. F. *Female Sexuality Following Spinal Cord Injury*. Bloomington, IL: Cheever Pub., 1978.

Bird, C. *What Women Want*. New York: Simon & Schuster, 1979.

Bregman, S. *Sexuality and the Spinal Cord Injured Woman*. Minneapolis, MN: Sister Kenny Institute, 1975.

Department of Health, Education, and Welfare. Office for Handicapped Individuals. *Digest of Data on Persons with Disabilities*. Washington, DC: U.S. Government Printing Office, 1979.

Developmental Disabilities Project. *Information Concerning Sexual Exploitation of Mentally and Physically Handicapped Individuals*. Seattle, WA: Seattle Rape Relief, 1979.

Featherstone, H. *A Difference in the Family: Life with a Disabled Child*. New York: Basic Books, 1980.

German, P. S., & Collins, J. W. Disability and Work Adjustment. *Social Security Survey of the Disabled*, Report No. 24. Washington, DC: U.S. Department of Health, Education, and Welfare, Social Security Administration, 1974.

Krute, A., & Burdette, M. E. 1972 Survey of Disabled and Non-Disabled Adults: Chronic Disease, Injury, and Work Disability. *Social Security Bul.* 1978. 41:4:3–7.

Kutner, N. G., & Kutner, M. H. Race and Sex as Variables Affecting Reactions to Disability. *Arch. Phys. Medicine & Rehab.* 1979. 60:62–66.

Kutza, E. Benefits for the Disabled: How Beneficial for Women? *Sociol. and Social Welfare*, 1983.

Levitan, S., & Taggart, R. *Jobs for the Disabled*. Baltimore, MD : Johns Hopkins University Press, 1977.

Lipowski, Z. Physical Illness, the Patient and His Environment. In: S. Arieti (ed.) *American Handbook of Psychiatry, 2nd ed.* New York: Basic Books, 1975.

Sachs, F. *Information Memorandum*, RSA-JM-78-62, U.S. Department of Health, Education, and Welfare, Office of Human Development, Rehabilitation Services Administration, 1978.

Sanford, L. *The Silent Children*. New York: Doubleday, 1980.

Stuart, V. W. *Sexuality and Sexual Assault: Disabled Perspective*. Marshall, MN: Health and Rehabilitation Services Program, Southwest State University, 1980.

Task Force No. 1. Vocational Evaluation Services in the Human Services Delivery System. *Voc. Evaluation and Work Adjustment*. 1975. 8:7–48.

Task Force on Concerns of Physically Disabled Women. *Toward Intimacy: Family Planning and Sexuality Concerns of Physically Disabled Women*. New York: Human Sciences Press, 1978.

6

Explaining "Psychiatric Rehabilitation" by an Analogy to "Physical Rehabilitation"

William A. Anthony

The problems of rehabilitating the severely psychiatrically disabled client are well known, by the treatment professional, the client, and the public (Pardes & Pincus, 1980). In many people's minds the nightmare of institutionalization has now been replaced by the horrors of deinstitutionalization. However, regardless of whether the treatment setting is in the community or the hospital, the treatment professional's goal remains the same—to provide the severely disabled person with effective care based on a humane and responsive treatment philosophy.

Out of the pursuit of this elusive goal has evolved the practice of psychiatric rehabilitation. Unfortunately, many mental health professionals do not understand what is involved in the principles and practices of psychiatric rehabilitation, because it is a new concept for them. Many think of rehabilitation as only vocationally oriented; others think of rehabilitation as something that is done to old houses or as something that was done in the prison system that never seemed to work. Thus it behooves psychiatric rehabilitation practitioners to be able to explain the rehabilitation approach to uninitiated mental health practitioners in a way they can appreciate and understand.

I have found that the concept of psychiatric rehabilitation can be meaningfully explained by drawing an analogy between the psychiatric rehabilitation approach and the approach used in physical medicine and rehabilitation. Severely physically disabled clients are less stigmatized than psychiatrically disabled clients, their disabilities seem more understandable, and the treatment processes seem more legitimate. Demonstrating parallels in both philosophy and practice between psychiatric and physical rehabilitation can help clarify the concept of psychiatric rehabilitation.

From *Psychosocial Rehabilitation Journal, 5*(1) (1982), 61–65. Reprinted by permission.

This chapter is based in part on a presentation made at a conference entitled "Assessing Treatment Efficacy and Outcome of Schizophrenics and the Chronically Mentally Ill," sponsored by the National Institute of Mental Health, October 8–10, 1980, Portsmouth, New Hampshire.

THE FIELD OF PHYSICAL MEDICINE AND REHABILITATION

While the strong emphasis on rehabilitating the psychiatrically disabled is a relatively new focus within the mental health field (Anthony, 1977), practitioners of physical medicine and rehabilitation have for many years been attempting to rehabilitate a severely disabled population, out of a long-standing concern for the medical, psychological, and vocational implications of chronic physical disability (Dembo et al., 1956; Kessler, 1935; Rusk & Taylor, 1949; Wright, 1980). Out of the traditions of physical medicine and rehabilitation has emerged a treatment philosophy that can serve as a model for the practice of rehabilitating the severely or chronically disabled psychiatric patient.

The practitioners of physical medicine have a successful history of wanting to serve and of serving the more severely disabled, such as those afflicted with blindness, deafness, hemiplegia, quadriplegia, and other severe conditions. In so doing practitioners in the field have developed a philosophy and expertise in helping persons whose residual disabilities impair role performance, who need a range of services, and who often need long-term and frequent care. Their successes in this regard have been notable: As an example, the Rehabilitation Services Administration reports that between 1973 and 1977 the number of spinal-cord-injured persons vocationally rehabilitated increased nearly 400%. Such success has not been the case in the mental health field. During the same time period there was a 3% decrease in the number of persons with the primary disability of mental illness who were successfully rehabilitated (Skelley, 1980).

Such comparisons may remind us of the obvious differences between persons with severe psychiatric disabilities and those with severe physical disabilities, but they can also point out the meaningful similarity between the two disability groups. Both groups of patients require a wide range of services, they exhibit impairment of role performance, and they may be involved for a long time in the caregiving system. As a reflection of this similarity in patient needs, the array and duration of services provided to the psychiatrically disabled by mental health practitioners are becoming more rehabilitation oriented.

THE GOALS AND TREATMENT APPROACHES
OF REHABILITATION

All the definitions of physical rehabilitation essentially converge around the idea that the client should achieve the best life adjustment possible in his or her environment, be it social, vocational, recreational, or educational (Wright, 1980). It is of course quite possible to adapt this goal of physical rehabilitation to arrive at a useful definition of the goal of psychiatric rehabilitation: to help assure that the psychiatrically disabled person possesses the physical, intellectual, and emotional abilities needed to live, learn, and/or work in his or her particular community (Anthony, 1977).

Flowing from this rehabilitation goal are the two primary treatment approaches of physical medicine and rehabilitation that can also be applied to psychiatric rehabilitation: (1) developing the client's skills and (2) modifying the environment in order to maximize the client's present skill level. For example, the techniques of physical therapy do not attempt to probe for or remove the cause of hemiplegia; rather, the physical therapist focuses on rebuilding the patient's damaged skills, on teaching the patient new skills, or on adapting the environment to better accommodate the patient's skill level (Anthony, 1980). Similarly, the interventions needed to achieve psychiatric rehabilitation involve teaching clients the skills they need to function in the community and/or modifying the community to accommodate or strengthen the clients' present level of functioning. The psychiatric rehabilitation treatment approach is directly analogous to the treatment approach used in physical medicine and rehabilitation.

REHABILITATION OUTCOME IS ENVIRONMENTALLY SPECIFIC

The field of physical rehabilitation teaches us that measures of client outcome must be specific to the environment. Rehabilitation treatment focuses on the client's ability to perform certain tasks within certain environments, and the physical rehabilitation specialist needs to know the type of environment for which the person is being rehabilitated. For example, treatment outcome for a blind person is not just the learning of mobility skills; it is also the application of these mobility skills in certain environments of need (home, work, and so on). Thus the outcome is tied into an environment. Likewise, the psychiatric rehabilitation specialist must not just work toward improving, say, conversational skills, but must do so with respect to the conversational demands of the specific environment in which the client is presently or will be functioning.

SKILL TRAINING MUST ENSURE SKILL GENERALIZATION

One of the main treatment approaches of psychiatric rehabilitation is skill training, although practitioners who attempt to teach their clients the skills they need to function in specific environments have often failed to help the clients transfer those skills to the environment of need (Hersen & Bellack, 1976). Newly learned skill behaviors are usually situation specific: Occupational skills learned in a hospital setting, for example, are not readily used in the community (Anthony, 1979).

Practitioners of physical rehabilitation have understood this principle of situation specificity. They know that the ability to learn to transfer from a wheelchair to a hospital bed does not guarantee a successful wheelchair-to-bed transfer in one's own home. The practitioner must teach directly toward that application goal and understand the specific skill demands of the home environment, including the possibility of conducting training in the home environment.

In order to ensure skill generalization, psychiatric rehabilitation training programs must become less contrived and simulated. Efforts need to be made to arrange for training in the environment of need, or at least in more natural environments than a hospital or clinic. Psychiatric rehabilitation must operate, as physical rehabilitation does, on the principle that generalization does not just occur, it must be programmed.

THE NECESSITY OF AN INDIVIDUALIZED REHABILITATION DIAGNOSIS

A rehabilitation diagnosis ensures that the actual skills being taught to the clients are the skills they will most need in their environment. There seems to be a tendency in mental health settings to teach all clients the same skills because those are the skills practitioners teach best, rather than teaching clients the skills they most need. Thus, for example, all schizophrenics in a day treatment center are taught assertiveness skills, seemingly independent of whether assertiveness is their most critical skill need. A similar practice in physical rehabilitation might be to teach all physically disabled clients, including the spinal-cord-injured, the deaf, and the blind, how to use a guide dog!

The important rehabilitation principle is that skill needs must be diagnosed and skill training must be tailored to those diagnosed skill needs. Without such an individual diagnosis, any outcome benefits of skill training are problematic at best.

UNDERSTANDING THE CONCEPT OF LEAST RESTRICTIVE ENVIRONMENT

The treatment of the psychiatrically disabled person seems to be based on a concept of least restrictive environment that is totally different from the intent of this concept in rehabilitation practice. Bachrach has correctly pointed out the error in the present application of this concept (Bachrach, 1980), arguing that the restrictiveness of an environment is not just a function of the environment but a function of the unique needs of the patient within that environment. An environment that is unduly restrictive for one patient may be ideal for another patient. The quality of restrictiveness does not reside totally outside the patient and exclusively in the environment.

Bachrach's argument accurately reflects the philosophy of physical medicine and rehabilitation with respect to the concept of least restrictive environment. Physical medicine and rehabilitation practitioners realize that environments cannot be graded in terms of their restrictiveness without taking into account the needs and abilities of the client who functions in that environment. For example, a quadriplegic might find his or her premorbid home setting (theoretically the least restrictive) much more limiting than an architecturally modified center for independent living. Similarly, a blind person who has not yet learned mobility skills will find a busy street corner much more restrictive than the hospital corridor.

An effective rehabilitation philosophy replaces the concept of least restrictive environment with the principle of *most facilitative environment*, in which no unnecessary restrictions are placed on the client's functioning but in which the client's present abilities are accommodated. And, yes, this means that for some clients at certain points in time a humane and responsively run inpatient setting may be the most facilitative environment.

THE IMPORTANCE OF THE CLIENT–PRACTITIONER RELATIONSHIP

In the practice of physical medicine and rehabilitation the value of an understanding and respectful relationship between client and practitioner is rarely underestimated. As a matter of fact, it is routinely viewed as a source of treatment effect. A rehabilitation program is not done *to* a client, it is done *with* a client. The success of a rehabilitation practitioner in helping clients learn new skills or function in new environments is affected in part by the relationship that exists between the client and the practitioner. It is the potency of this human relationship that may account for similar therapeutic outcomes of seemingly disparate rehabilitation practices. For example, the treatment of some injuries with ice now accomplishes what in the past appeared to be helped by the administration of heat. Perhaps it is doing something apparently helpful with somebody that is the common source of treatment effect.

Several research studies have reaffirmed the importance of the relationship between rehabilitation outcome and the relationship or interpersonal skills of the practitioner. Bozarth and Rubin (1975) found a significant relationship between the rehabilitation counselor's interpersonal skills and the client's vocational gain. In an inpatient setting for alcoholics, Valle (1982) found that the level of interpersonal skills of the alcoholism counselors related to client relapse rate at follow-up periods of 6, 12, 18, and 24 months.

The critical rehabilitation principle is that the human element is always a part of the rehabilitation equation. Not only do the relationship skills of the practitioner correlate with rehabilitation outcome, these skills also ensure a more decent, humane rehabilitation process for the client (Anthony, 1979).

THE SOMETIMES EQUIVOCAL RELATIONSHIP BETWEEN TREATMENT PROCESS AND TREATMENT OUTCOME

It is appealing to our scientific values to be able to identify the exact process that achieved a particular outcome. Unfortunately, from a scientific standpoint, client rehabilitation outcome can seemingly be achieved without an awareness of the specific elements that account for the outcome. For example, a physically disabled client may obtain a job even though the client never accurately applied his or her newly learned job-interviewing skills as they were taught by the rehabilitation practitioner. Or in a slightly different vein, a client may benefit from the rehabilitation process without actually succeeding in achieving the immediate goal of the process, as in the case of a client who fails in her attempts to learn to walk, yet still profits from the attempt by developing a willingness to return to school, even though she is now confined to a wheelchair.

What then can account for this apparent independence of successful process from successful outcome? One explanation may be that the very process of an intense skill-training experience, in the context of a supportive human relationship, may change the client's values, expectations, or attitude toward the meaning of his or her life, even though it doesn't achieve the desired skill change. Physical rehabilitation practitioners have long recognized the importance of these changes in personal values and meanings that accompany a rehabilitation intervention (Wright, 1960). Phrases such as "enlarging the scope of one's values," "minimizing the spread of disability," and "coping with disability rather than succumbing" are used to describe those personal changes so often experienced by the rehabilitation client.

Psychiatric rehabilitation practitioners are also aware that clients can still reap benefits from a rehabilitation intervention even though the targeted skills were neither completely acquired nor accurately applied. The very process of rehabilitation appears to have an unexplained impact on outcome, an impact that is perhaps mediated by value changes that are stimulated and encouraged by involvement in the rehabilitation process. Because the potential of the rehabilitation process cannot be accurately predicted even as the process is occurring, every severely disabled client should be allowed to participate in rehabilitation programs. The process itself may trigger certain changes that bring about benefits the professional could neither predict nor scientifically explain.

DEPENDENCY AS A REHABILITATION VALUE

It seems that in some mental health treatment programs client independence has become so valued that client dependence has become devalued. Yet, from a rehabilitation perspective, "dependency" is not a dirty word. Rehabilitation interventions with the physically disabled often encourage dependency on persons or things in one environment so the client can function more effectively in another environment. Dependency in one area of functioning can set a client free in another area. For example, a quadriplegic's dependence on a personal-care attendant for help in dressing for work may allow him or her to hold a full-time job. Dependency in a physical rehabilitation client is a matter of degree, varying naturally between and within environments.

Psychiatric rehabilitation interventions also recognize the value of dependency. The technology of rehabilitation is limited in its ability to achieve maximal client independence. Furthermore, dependence on people or things is a normal state of affairs. Interventions that allow for a certain degree of dependency at certain times, such as through the use of "enablers" or aides, may in fact maximize the client's functioning in other environments at other times (Weinman & Kleiner, 1978).

CLIENT BENEFITS AS THE ULTIMATE CRITERIA FOR REHABILITATION OUTCOME

There are a number of ways in which treatment success can be calculated. Measures of cost, family burden, or other indices of societal effort or impact are often suggested. Yet, from a rehabilitation perspective, the crucial impact variables are assessments of client gain in specific environments of need (Anthony & Farkas, 1982). The old saw "The operation was a success but the patient died" has no quarter in the practice of rehabilitation. If the client's functioning in a particular environment has not improved, then no rehabilitation benefits have accured.

Physically disabled clients must ask of the physical rehabilitation process: Will the process improve my chances of walking, talking, or working? Why should I go through the pain, put forth the effort, and take the time to be involved in a rehabilitation program?

Severely disabled psychiatric patients rarely ask this benefit question so strongly or directly. If asked to participate in a rehabilitation program they either submit to treatment or drop out (Freeman et al., 1980; Stickney et al., 1980). However, other people are beginning to ask the benefit question in the clients' stead. Clients' families, taxpayers, politicians, and ex-patient groups are beginning to ask the question more vociferously. Just as physical medicine and rehabilitation has had to do, the field of psychiatric rehabilitation has to provide answers to clients asking what is in it for them. As in the case of the physically disabled client, psychiatrically disabled clients should be able to expect answers in terms lay people can understand and appreciate.

SUMMARY

The analogy between physical rehabilitation and psychiatric rehabilitation is by no means perfect, but this chapter has presented many parallels between the two fields for the purpose of more clearly explaining the practices of psychiatric rehabilitation. An additional benefit of such an analogy is that it can help legitimize the need for a rehabilitation approach to the psychiatrically disabled.

REFERENCES

Anthony, W. A. Psychological rehabilitation: A concept in need of a method. *American Psychologist,* 1977, 32, 658-662.

Anthony, W. A. *Principles of psychiatric rehabilitation.* Baltimore: University Park Press, 1979.

Anthony, W. A. A Rehabilitation model for rehabilitating the psychiatrically disabled. *Rehabilitation Counseling Bulletin,* 1980, 24, 6-21.

Anthony, W. A., & Farkas, M. A client outcome planning model for assessing psychiatric rehabilitation intervention. *Schizophrenia Bulletin,* March, 1982.

Bachrach, L. L. Is the least restrictive environment always the best? Sociological and semantic implications. *Hospital and Community Psychiatry,* 1980, 31, 97-103.

Bozarth, J. D., & Rubin, S. E. Empirical observation of rehabilitation counselor performance and outcome: Some implications. *Rehabilitation Counseling Bulletin,* 1975, 19, 294-298.

Dembo, T., Leviton, G. L., & Wright, B. A. Adjustment to misfortune—a problem of social psychological rehabilitation. *Artificial Limbs*, 1956, 3, 4-62.

Freeman, S. J., Fischer, L., & Sheldon, A. An agency model for developing and coordinating psychiatric aftercare. *Hospital and Community Psychiatry*, 1980, 31, 768-771.

Hersen, M., & Bellack, A. Social skills training for chronic psychiatric patients: Rationale, research findings and future directions. *Comprehensive Psychiatry*, 1976, 17, 559-580.

Kessler, H. H. *The crippled and the disabled: Rehabilitation of the physically handicapped in the United States*. New York: Columbia University Press, 1935.

Pardes, H., & Pincus, H. A. Treatment in the seventies: A decade of refinement. *Hospital and Community Psychiatry*, 1980, 31, 535-542.

Rusk, H. A. & Taylor, E. J. *New hope for the handicapped: The rehabilitation of the disabled from bed to job*. New York: Harper, 1949.

Skelley, T. National developments in rehabilitation: A rehabilitation services administration perspective. *Rehabilitation Counseling Bulletin*, 1980, 24, 22-23.

Stickney, S. K., Hall, R. C., & Gardner, E. R. The effect of referral procedures on aftercare compliance. *Hospital and Community Psychiatry*, 1980, 31, 567-569.

Valle, S. Alcoholism counselor interpersonal functioning and patient outcome. *Journal of Alcohol Studies*, 1982.

Weinman, B., & Kleiner, R. J. The impact of community living and community member intervention on the adjustment of the chronic psychotic patient. In *Alternatives to mental hospital treatment*, ed. L. Stein and M. Test. New York: Plenum Press, 1978, 139-150.

Wright, B. A. *Physical disability: A psychological approach*. New York: Harper, 1960.

Wright, G. *Total Rehabilitation*. Boston: Little, Brown, 1980.

7

Recovery: The Lived Experience of Rehabilitation

Patricia E. Deegan

The application of rehabilitation approaches and technologies to psychiatrically disabled adults is a relatively new and exciting development in our field. The discovery and application of rehabilitation models allow us to think about this population in new and exciting ways. Of significance is the fact that, from the perspective of the rehabilitation approach, it is no longer necessary to isolate the psychiatrically disabled as totally different from other groups of persons with disabilities. Today, artificial boundaries between groups of disabled persons can be bridged through the understanding that most disabled people share the same fundamental needs and aspirations: The need is to meet the challenge of the disability and to reestablish a new and valued sense of integrity and purpose within and beyond the limits of the disability; the aspiration is to live, work, and love in a community in which one makes a significant contribution.

It is important to understand that persons with a disability do not "get rehabilitated" in the sense that cars "get" tuned up or televisions "get repaired." Disabled persons are not passive recipients of rehabilitation services. Rather, they experience themselves as *recovering* a new sense of self and of purpose within and beyond the limits of the disability. This distinction between rehabilitation and recovery is important. Rehabilitation refers to the services and technologies that are made available to disabled persons so that they might learn to adapt to their world. Recovery refers to the lived or real life experience of persons as they accept and overcome the challenge of the disability. We might say that rehabilitation refers to the "world pole" and that recovery refers to the "self pole" of the same phenomenon.

The recovery process is the foundation on which rehabilitation services build. This is most evidenced in the simple observation that we can make the finest and most advanced rehabilitation services available to the psychiatrically disabled and still fail to help them. Something more than just "good services" is needed, for example, the person must get out of bed, shake off the mind-numbing exhaustion of the neuroleptics, get dressed, overcome the fear of the crowded and unfriendly bus to arrive at the program, and face the fear of failure in the rehabilitation program. In essence, disabled persons must be active and courageous participants in their own rehabilitation project or that project will fail. It is through the process of recovery that disabled persons become active and courageous participants in their own rehabilitation project.

We see then that recovery is an important and fundamental phenomenon on which rehabilitation efforts depend. It is therefore surprising that very little has been written in our professional and scientific journals regarding it. Perhaps the phenomenon is elusive precisely because it is so fundamental. Perhaps it is because the recovery process cannot be completely described with traditional scientific, psychiatric, or psychological language. Although the phenomenon will not fit neatly into natural scientific paradigms, those of us who have been disabled know that recovery is real because we have lived it. At a recent conference that brought together persons with diverse disabilities, I had the pleasure of talking with a man who was paraplegic. We shared our stories of recovery.

THE EXPERIENCE OF RECOVERY

At a young age we had both experienced a catastrophic shattering of our world, hopes, and dreams. He had broken his neck and was paralyzed and I was diagnosed as being schizophrenic. We recalled the impact of those first days following the onset of our disabilities. He was an athlete and dreamed of becoming a professional in the sports world. I was a high school athlete and had applied to college to become a gym teacher. Just days earlier we knew ourselves as young people with exciting futures, and then everything collapsed around us. As teenagers, we were told that we had an incurable malady and that we would be "sick" or "disabled" for the rest of our lives. We were told that if we continued with recommended treatments and therapies, we could learn to "adjust" and "cope" from day to day.

Needless to day, we didn't believe our doctors and social workers. In fact, we adamantly denied and raged against these bleak prophesies for our lives. We felt it was all just a mistake, a bad dream, a temporary set-back in our lives. We just knew that in a week or two, things would get back to normal again. We felt our teenage world was still there, just waiting for us to return to it. Our denial was an important stage in our recovery. It was a normal reaction to an overwhelming situation. It was our way of surviving those first awful months.

The weeks passed us by but we did not get better. It became harder and harder to believe we would ever be the same again. What initially had seemed like a fleeting bad dream transformed into a deepening nightmare from which we could not awake. We felt like ships floating on a black sea with no course or bearings. We found ourselves drifting farther and farther away from the young, carefree people we had been. He lay horizontal and in traction while his friends were selected to play ball for prestigious colleges. I stood drugged and stiff in the hallways of a mental hospital while my classmates went off to their first year of college.

We experienced time as a betrayer. Time did not heal us. Our pasts deserted us and we could not return to who we had been. Our futures appeared to us to be barren, lifeless places in which no dream could be planted and grow into a reality. As for the present, it was a numbing succession of meaningless days and nights in a world in which we had no place, no use, and no reason to be. Boredom and wishfulness became our only refuge (Knowles, 1986).

Our denial gave way to despair and anguish. We both gave up. Giving up was a solution for us. It numbed the pain of our despair because we stopped asking "why and how will I go on?" (Harrison, 1984). Giving up meant that for 14 years he sat in the day rooms of institutions gazing at soap operas, watching others live their lives. For months I sat in a chair in my family's living room, smoking cigarettes and waiting until it was 8:00 P.M. so I could go back to bed. At this time even the simplest of tasks were overwhelming. I remember being asked to come into the kitchen to help knead some bread dough. I got up, went into the kitchen, and looked at the dough for what seemed an eternity. Then I walked back to my chair and wept. The task seemed overwhelming to me. Later I learned the reason for this: when one lives without hope, (when one has given up) the willingness to "do" is paralyzed as well.

All of us who have experienced catastrophic illness and disability know this experience of anguish and despair. It is living in darkness without hope, without a past or a future. It is self-pity. It is hatred of everything that is good and life giving. It is rage turned inward. It is a wound with no mouth, a wound that is so deep that no cry can emanate from it. Anguish is a death from which there appears to be no resurrection. It is inertia which paralyzes the will to do and to accomplish because there is no hope. It is being truly disabled, not by a disease or injury, but by despair. This part of the recovery process is a dark night in which even God was felt to have abandoned us. For some of us this dark night lasts moments, days, or months. For others it lasts for years. For others, the despair and anguish may never end.

Neither the paralyzed man nor I could remember a specific moment when the small and fragile flame of hope and courage illuminated the darkness of our despair. We do remember that even when we had given up, there were those who loved us and did not give up. They did not abandon us. They were powerless to change us and they could not make us better. They could not climb this mountain for us but they were willing to suffer with us. They did not overwhelm us with *their* optimistic plans for *our* futures but they remained hopeful despite the odds. Their love for us was like a constant invitation, calling us forth to be something more than all of this self-pity and despair. The miracle was that gradually the paralyzed man and I began to hear and respond to this loving invitation.

For 14 years the paralyzed man slouched in front of the television in the hell of his own despair and anguish. For months I sat and smoked cigarettes until it was time to collapse back into a drugged and dreamless sleep. But one day, something changed in us. A tiny, fragile spark of hope appeared and promised that there could be something more than all of this darkness. This is the third phase of recovery. This is the mystery. This is the grace. This is the birth of hope called forth by the possibility of being loved. All of the polemic and technology of psychiatry, psychology, social work, and science cannot account for this phenomenon of hope. But those of us who have recovered know that this grace is real. We lived it. It is our shared secret.

It is important to understand that for most of us recovery is not a sudden conversion experience. Hope does not come to us as a sudden bolt of lightning that jolts us into a whole new way of being. Hope is the turning point that must quickly be followed by the willingness to act. The paralyzed man and I began in little ways with small triumphs and simple acts of courage: He shaved, he attempted to read a book, and he talked with a counselor; I rode in the car, I shopped on Wednesdays, and I talked to a friend for a few minutes. He applied for benefits, he got a van and learned to drive; I took responsibility for my medications, took a part-time job, and had my own money. He went to college so he could work professionally with other disabled people; I went to school to become a psychologist so I could work with disabled people. One day at a time, with multiple setbacks, we rebuilt our lives. We rebuilt our lives on the three cornerstones of recovery—hope, willingness, and responsible action. We learned to say: "I am hopeful"; "I am willing to try"; and "I discover that I can do" (Knowles, 1986). This is the process of recovery that is the ground from which springs effective use of rehabilitation services.

Recovery does not refer to an end product or result. It does not mean that the paralyzed man and I were "cured." In fact, our recovery is marked by an ever-deepening acceptance of our limitations. But now, rather than being an occasion for despair, we find that our personal limitations are the ground from which spring our own unique possibilities. This is the paradox of recovery, that is, that in accepting what we cannot do or be, we begin to discover who we can be and what we can do.

Recovery does not refer to an absence of pain or struggle. Rather, recovery is marked by the transition from anguish to suffering. In anguish the paralyzed man and I lived without hope. We experienced anguish as futile pain, pain that revolved in circles, pain that bore no possibility other than more pain, and pain that led nowhere. However, when we became hopeful, our anguish was transformed into true suffering. True suffering is marked by an inner peace, that is, although we still felt great pain, we also experienced a peace in knowing that this pain was leading us forward into a new future. A biologist who is handicapped with spina bifida captures this spirit of true suffering in recovery when she writes: "Suffering is peaceful. You know the pain may kill you, but it won't destroy you. In a very risky way, you are safe" (Harrison, 1984).

For many of us who are disabled, recovery is a process, a way of life, an attitude, and a way of approaching the day's challenges. It is not a perfectly linear process. At times our course is erratic and we falter, slide back, re-group and start again. Our experience of recovery is similar to that described by the poet Roethke (1948/1975) who was himself afflicted with major mental illness:

CUTTINGS
... One nub of growth
Nudges a sand-crumb loose,
Pokes through a musty sheath
Its pale tendrilous horn.

CUTTINGS
(later)
This urge, wrestle, resurrection of dry sticks,
Cut stems struggling to put down feet,
What saint strained so much,
Rose on such lopped limbs to a new life?... (p. 35)

Recovery is the urge, the wrestle, and the resurrection. Recovery is a matter of rising on lopped limbs to a new life. As professionals we would like nothing more than to somehow manufacture the spirit of recovery and give it to each of our program participants. But this is impossible. We cannot force recovery to happen in our rehabilitation programs. Essential aspects of the recovery process are a matter of grace and, therefore, cannot be willed. However, we can create environments in which the recovery process can be nurtured like a tender and precious seedling. Some of the principles for creating such environments in rehabilitation programs are given below.

RECOVERY IN REHABILITATION PROGRAMS

As we have seen, recovery is not a linear process marked by successive accomplishments. The recovery process is more accurately described as a series of small beginnings and very small steps. To recover, psychiatrically disabled persons must be willing to try and fail, and try again. Too often, rehabilitation programs are structured in such a way as to work against this process of recovery. These programs tend to have rigid guidelines for acceptance. They tend to have linear program designs in which a person must enter at point "A" and move through a series of consecutive steps to arrive at point "B." Failure at any point along the way will require that participants return to entry level. Finally, some of these programs define failure in absolute terms, for example, a program participant dropped from a vocational placement for failing to attend work for X number of days is simultaneously dropped from the program and must completely reapply to the program when ready to accept the program's rules and expectations. In all of these ways, the design and structure of rehabilitation programming can work against the process of recovery.

Rehabilitation programs can be environments that nurture recovery if they are structured to embrace, and indeed expect, the approach/avoid, try/fail dynamic that is the recovery process. This means that rehabilitation programs must have very flexible entry criteria and easy accessibility. The design of rehabilitation programming must be nonlinear, that is, with multiple points of entry and levels of entry into programming. The real challenge of rehabilitation programs is to create fail-proof program models. A program is fail-proof when participants are always able to come back, pick-up where they left off, and try again. In a fail-proof environment where one is welcomed, valued, and wanted, recovering persons can make the most effective use of rehabilitation services.

A second point regarding the establishment of rehabilitation environments conducive to the recovery process derives from the understanding that each person's journey of recovery is unique. Of course, there are certain fundamental constituents of the process of recovery that are similar in all persons with a disability, for example, the experience of despair and the transition to hope, willingness, and responsible action. However, disabled people are, above all, individuals and will find their own special formula for what promotes their recovery and what does not. Therefore, it is important to offer recovering persons a wide variety of rehabilitation program options from which to choose, for example, supported work programs, social clubs, transitional employment programs, consumer-run drop-in centers and businesses, workshops, skill training programs, and college support programs.

Consumer-run self-help groups, self-help networks and advocacy/lobbyist groups can also be important resources for recovering persons and should be available as options. Of course, these important resources can only be established and maintained by persons recovering from psychiatric disability. Creating these resources, as well as linking with other groups of disabled persons and sharing existing resources, is one of the greatest challenges that face those of us who are recovering.

Additionally, if we truly hope to offer a wide variety of rehabilitation programs to the psychiatrically disabled, then it is important to examine the values on which so much of our programming is based. Too often we project traditional "American" values on disabled people, for example, rugged individualism, competition, personal achievement, and self-sufficiency. Too often our program models have tacitly adopted these, and only these, values. We might ask ourselves: Are all of our local area's vocational rehabilitation programs built on a competitive model in which individual achievement is stressed more than cooperative group efforts? Are our residential rehabilitation programs all geared toward preparing people to live independently?

For some psychiatrically disabled people, especially those who relapse frequently, these traditional values of competition, individual achievement, independence, and self-sufficiency are oppressive. Programs that are tacitly built on these values are invitations to failure for many recovering persons. For these persons, "independent living" amounts to the loneliness of four walls in the corner of some rooming house. For these persons, "individual vocational achievement" amounts to failing one vocational program after another until they come to believe they are worthless human beings with nothing to contribute. For these persons, an alternative type of rehabilitation program, and even lifestyle, should be available as an option. Instead of competitive vocational training based on individual achievement, a cooperative work setting stressing group achievement could be established. The value here is cooperation in the achievement of work goals and the sharing of responsibility for work production so that the group or work community can compensate for the individual during periods of relapse. Residential program options should include the possibility for communal living situations such as the L'Arche communities pioneered by Jean Vanier (Dunne, 1986; Vanier & Wolfensberger, 1974). When these types of options are made available and exist alongside rehabilitation programs based on more traditional values, then we can feel confident that we are offering a truly comprehensive network of services from which recovering persons can choose their own course of rehabilitation.

The third recommendation for creating programs that enhance recovery involves recognition of the gift that disabled people have to give to each other. This gift is their hope, strength, and experience as lived in the recovery process. In this sense, disabled persons can become role models for each other. During that dark night of anguish and despair when disabled persons live without hope, the presence of other recovering persons can challenge that despair through example. It becomes very difficult to continue to convince oneself that there is no hope when one is surrounded by other equally disabled persons who are making strides in their recovery!

Hope is contagious and that is why it is so important to hire disabled people in rehabilitation programs. Because recovery is a phenomenon that is similar for all disabled people, it can be very effective to have persons with divergent disabilities act as role models for one another. Additionally, a person need not be "fully recovered" in order to serve as a role model. Very often a disabled person who is only a few "steps" ahead of another person can be more effective than one whose achievements seem overly impressive and distanced.

Finally, and perhaps most fundamentally, staff attitudes are very important in shaping rehabilitation environments. There are a number of common staff attitudes that are particularly unhelpful to recovering persons. For instance, too often staff attitudes reflect the implicit supposition that there is the "world of the abnormal" and the "world of the normal." The task facing the staff is to somehow get the people in the "abnormal world" to fit into the "normal world." This creates an us/them dichotomy wherein "they" (the disabled) are expected to do all of the changing and growing. Such an attitude places staff in a very safe position in which they can maintain the illusion that they are not disabled, that they are not wounded in any way, and that they have no need to live the spirit of recovery in their own lives. Indeed, when the us/them attitude prevails, "staff" and "clients" are truly worlds apart. Such an environment is oppressive to those disabled persons who are struggling with their own recovery.

If a rehabilitation program is to be a dynamic setting that promotes and nurtures the recovery process, then the rigid walls separating the "world of the disabled" and the "world of the normal" must be torn down. Staff members must be helped to recognize the ways in which they, too, are deeply wounded. Perhaps they have experienced anguish in their lives or perhaps they have known personal tragedy or struggle. To embrace and accept our own woundedness and vulnerability is the first step toward understanding the experience of the disabled. In so doing we discover that we share a common humanity with the disabled and that we are not "worlds apart."

A dynamic rehabilitation environment is one in which staff members are vitally involved in their own personal growth and/or recovery. Therefore, they empathize deeply with the woundedness and vulnerability that the disabled experience. They understand that in some mysterious way to be human means that all of us must "rise on lopped limbs" to a new life.

REFERENCES

Dunne, J. (1986). *Sense of community in L'Arche and in the writings of Jean Vanier: Daybreak monograph 20*. Richmond Hill, Ontario: Daybreak Publications.

Harrison, V. (1984). A biologist's view of pain, suffering and marginal life. In F. Dougherty (Ed.), *The deprived, the disabled and the fullness of life*. Delaware: Michael Glazier.

Knowles, R. T. (1986). *Human development and human possibility: Erikson in the light of Heidegger*. Lanham: University Press of America.

Roethke, T. (1948/1975). The lost son and other poems. In *The collected poems of Theodore Roethke*. New York: Anchor Press/ Doubleday.

Vanier, J., & Wolfensberger, W. (1974). *Growing together: Daybreak monograph 2*. Richmond Hill, Ontario: Daybreak Publications.

Part I: *Perspective on Disability— Study Questions and Disability Awareness Exercise*

1. Has the development of the medical rehabilitation team been beneficial to the consumer? Why? Why not?
2. Discuss how a patient's well-being can be compromised for the well-being of the health professional.
3. Discuss the role of autonomy in the rehabilitation process. Is this role similar for all people coping with disability?
4. Discuss autonomy in rehabilitation from the perspective of people challenged by:

   a. Spinal cord injury
   b. Head trauma
   c. AIDS
   d. Chronic mental illness
   e. Alzheimer's disease
   f. Substance abuse
   g. Mental retardation

5. Identify the barriers to rehabilitation candidates' autonomy and discuss how they can be reduced.
6. Discuss the "common ground" between psychiatric and physical rehabilitation.
7. What are the unique problems faced by a person having both a chronic mental as well as a chronic physical disability?
8. Compare the benefits/deficits for persons who are disabled when they are viewed from the perspective of the "minority group" versus the "functional limits" model.
9. Discuss how the world view of people experiencing disabilites reflects each particular society's value system.
10. Identify and discuss the similarities and differences between women and men living the disability experience. Discuss the same topic considering persons who are members of ethnic and racial minorities.

11. Should women with severe disabilities be encouraged not to have children?
12. Are the goals of recovery compatible with the goals of rehabilitation for people experiencing a physical disability? A psychiatric disability?

WELCOME BACK

The following exercise is designed to sensitize participants to the impact of a disabling condition.

Goals

1. To raise the awareness of participants to the qualitative dimensions of disability.
2. To enable participants to evaluate the differential impact of a disabling condition on their interpersonal relationships.
3. To explore with participants the most helpful approaches in dealing with disability.
4. To list the most devastating disabilities that could occur in participants' lives.
5. Consider how participants' lives would be altered if a traumatic disability occurred early or later in life, that is age 5, 10, 15, 20, 30, 40, 50, 60, 70.

Procedure

1. Participants are asked to list the three most important people in their lives.
2. Each member is asked to list three specific disabilities that he or she would least want to experience personally.
3. Participants write a brief statement about each disability focusing on why they would not want it.
4. The leader then asks the group members to take the most undesirable disability and list five specific ways in which it would affect their relationship with each person listed if they were hospitalized and away from that person for one year.
5. The group leader asks the participants to verbalize their feelings and discuss what they have written.
6. The leader asks who would be most supportive and why.
7. The leader asks group members what would be most helpful to facilitate their integration back into the community.
8. Group is asked to select the age they would prefer the disability to occur.
9. Leader stresses the point that disability can occur any time during the life span.

Part II

Developmental and Family Issues in Disability

Disabilities may be present congenitally, or they may be acquired at any time during the life span of a person. Part II focuses on the impact of disability on lifelong human development. In doing so, the response of the family to the birth of a child with a handicap and the impact of disability during adolescence, midlife, and old age, are essential topics that are considered.

The birth of a child with a handicap results in family members experiencing significant loss. Bristor presents a six-phase wholistic framework for grieving this loss with the intent of assisting the family members in understanding and facilitating the grieving process so that growth may be experienced. Her model represents grief as a normal process that requires time and energy to achieve resolution.

In Chapter 9, Davis and her colleagues focus on the developmental tasks and transitions of adolescents with disabilities. Their intent is to educate professionals in understanding the impact that chronic illnesses and disabilities have on development and the mastery of important psychosocial tasks of adolescents. The authors provide valuable suggestions for assisting adolescents to establish their identity as self-accepting persons who happen to have a disability.

Passing through midlife is an important and inevitable transition with significant psychosocial changes. For the person with a disability this experience may be intensified. In Chapter 10, Power, Hershenson, and Schlossberg provide an overview of this topic with selected implications for persons with disabilities. They provide thoughtful suggestions to facilitate midlife passage and to assist clients with participation in the rehabilitation process.

Disability is typically an integral part of old age. Kivnick, in Chapter 11, considers the ways that physical disabilities influence psychosocial development in old age and the influences that psychosocial factors may have on the older person's experience of disability. She further provides a theoretical rationale and suggests psychosocial interventions to assist older persons in drawing on lifelong strengths to prevent impairments from becoming disabilities and disabilities from becoming handicaps.

8

The Birth of a Handicapped Child—
A Wholistic Model for Grieving

Martha Wingerd Bristor

Loss is part of our everyday life. However, the potential for loss is rarely anticipated in having a child. The birth of a baby is usually thought of with great expectation by the parents and family members. Most family members develop certain expectations, wishes, and fantasies during the course of the pregnancy, and these dreams embody their hopes for the future. The possibility of this anticipated relationship is abruptly terminated with the birth of a handicapped child.

In the United States a major malformation occurs in 2 of every 100 births (Klaus & Kennell, 1976). The birth of a child with congenital malformations presents complex challenges to the family. Yet despite the relatively large number of infants with anomalies, understanding of the grieving process and the development of parental attachment to the malformed infant remains incomplete.

During the course of a normal pregnancy, the parents develop a mental picture of their baby. The imagined baby is a composite of impressions and desires derived from the parents' own experiences. Although the degree of concreteness varies greatly, each has an idea about the sex, complexion, personality, and other important features. One of the early tasks of parenting is to resolve the discrepancy between this idealized image of the infant and the actual appearance of the real infant (Solnit & Stark, 1961). If the baby is born with a malformation, the discrepancy is much greater and the parents must grieve the loss of the "dreamed-of infant" to make the necessary adjustments to begin the process of attachment.

The birth of a handicapped child often precipitates a major family crisis. The strength and character of the parent–infant attachment will influence the quality of the child's bonds with other individuals in the future (Klaus & Kennell, 1976, 1981). The long-term goal for the child is best described by Bettelheim (1972): "Children can learn to live with a disability. But they cannot live well without the conviction that their parents find them utterly loveable. . . If parents, knowing about his (the child's) defect, love him now, he can believe that others will love him in the future" (p. 34).

THE NATURE OF LOSS

According to Schneider (1983), the nature of loss has four important aspects that affect an individual's reaction to loss. The first is the degree of attachment established by a mother during pregnancy and through the delivery of the infant. Following the nine months when a woman may be intensely involved in the pregnancy, the sense of failure at the birth of a handicapped child will probably affect her more deeply than the man because of her increased emotional attachment.

The second aspect that affects an individual's reaction to a loss is the change the loss causes in the day-to-day routine. The realization of how much an individual's life will change by the loss is usually an impact that cannot be fully comprehended in the initial stages of grief. This is especially true at the birth of a handicapped infant because the degree of incapacitation of the handicapping condition varies from mild to severe and is often difficult to fully assess at birth. Further, the potential for individual growth and development of the child is unknown because of individual differences and developmental patterns.

A third aspect that influences an individual's reaction to loss is the manner in which stress is normally handled and the individual's ability to cope. As Tanner (1976) noted, the reaction to loss in adulthood is grounded in how the individual handled losses in childhood. Some of the coping mechanisms from childhood no longer work, and the magnitude of the present loss encountered causes added stress for the individual. That is why in grieving a loss there is no "script," for everyone copes in his/her own way. There is no prescribed way to mourn the birth of a child who has special problems. Such a loss has different dimensions than any previous losses encountered.

A fourth aspect that influences a reaction to loss and the grieving process is the individual's support system. The support of family and friends gives the individual the permission and freedom to grieve. Support helps the individual get on with the necessary grieving when external pressures for acceptance of the child may push the mother to stop her grieving prematurely. Gendlin (1964) found that growth occurs within an ongoing, supportive relationship. In the case of a handicapped infant's birth, the individual who lacks guiding support and/or permission for the grieving process can easily block or interrupt the grieving process leading to unresolved grief. Unresolved grief becomes a major stressor in life consuming energy needed to care for the child.

According to Klaus and Kennell (1976), the reaction of the parents and the degree of their future attachment difficulties depend largely on questions revolving around issues regarding the properties of the malformation and whether it is correctable or noncorrectable, visable or nonvisable. The questions include: Does the malformation affect the central nervous system and is the condition life-threatening? Does the condition affect the eyes? Is the malformation single or multiple? Will the condition have an effect on the future development of the child?

Is the malformation familial? Will there be a need for repeated doctor visits or hospitalization? Initial reactions of the parents depend on the answers to these questions and the supportive attitudes present or not present in those answering these crucial questions.

Despite a wide variation among infants' malformations, generally, the parents could recall the events surrounding the birth and their reactions in great detail (Drotar, Baskiewicz, Irvin, Kennell, & Klaus, 1975). The loss did involve pain. Losing a belief (perfect child) is especially disappointing and often quite frightening. A mother especially questions the belief in herself as a competent person after experiencing the birth of a less than perfect child. She also questions the issue of her ability to have control over the outcome of events. A significant loss also forces her to look at the issue of her own helplessness with the future unknown. She not only feels helpless to control what she lost (perfect child), but also experiences the thoughts of the possibility of losing everything else including her life. Thus, according to Schneider (1983), such a loss forces into awareness her own mortality and the fragility of life.

The "stages" of grief are largely reflections of trying to deal with the loss and subsequent grief. Parents defend against the reality and subsequent feelings of vulnerability by trying to insist that loss is manageable. The stages of grief, then, are best understood as a result of trying to handle the loss and to maintain the illusions of omnipotence in the face of lack of control. General stages provide a useful framework for recognition of means of coping, but within the stages of a framework, individuality creates tremendous variability. However, the sequence of stages reflects the natural course of reactions in the usual order of occurrence.

UNDERSTANDING THE NATURE OF THE GRIEVING PROCESS

Schneider (1983) has postulated a wholistic model of the grief process that differs from other existing models (Bowlby, 1973; Engel, 1971; Kübler-Ross, 1968; Lindemann, 1944; Parkes, 1972). This model involves a more inclusive definition of significant losses, which makes it more generalizable in application to all life circumstances. Other authors have developed models with special populations. For example, Lindemann based his model on the reactions of the survivors of an unexpected catastrophe. Kübler-Ross based her model on observations of the terminally ill. Bowlby based his writings on loss and infant separation. Engel wrote observations of the chronically ill, and Parkes wrote of widows.

Most existing models of the grieving process recognize the physical and emotional aspects. A few models define some behavioral manifestations. The wholistic model by Schneider (1983) provides a framework that offers a systematic study of how grief affects not only the biological, emotional, and behavioral aspects of the individual, but also the intellectual and spiritual or attitudinal (in terms of attitudes and values) aspects. The model also incorporates phases that include awareness and growth as part of the total grief process.

The focus of application of other grief models is on the more traumatic and overwhelming loss events, and does not include the growth potential from grief. These models have presented peaceful acceptance as the ending. Some models have acknowledged some growth potential (Marris, 1974), but Schneider's model attempts to integrate motivation for growth into the resolution of grief. An interdependence and interrelatedness among the five aspects of the model is also suggested by the Schneider model.

The stages of grief included in the wholistic model with application to the mother and family at the birth of a handicapped child are:

1. *Initial awareness.* This is the stage in which a definable loss first becomes a reality to the individual. Manifestations include shock, loss of balance, and increased vulnerability with lowered resistance to infection.

In the initial awareness stage, the family, especially the mother, may be literally stunned. The mother may be still subject to the effects of medications from the delivery that may enhance a feeling of being more like a spectator in a drama and feeling that what is occurring is not real. An effort to fully understand what is happening may be overwhelming at this time. Guilt feelings are perhaps the most demanding, erratic, and difficult to cope with. Panic may set in with the overburdening of emotions at a time when the body is already physically tired from the delivery and vulnerable. At such a stressful time, she is unable to command her usual resources to cope with the immediate situation.

Such emotional stress may affect the mother's physical well-being. Headache, intestinal upsets, dizziness, delayed healing of surgical wounds, and insomnia may be the body's response to the shock of the loss involved at the birth of a malformed child.

2. *Strategies to overcome loss.* This stage includes two very different strategies of coping. The adaptive defenses of the individual include holding on and letting go of the object of concern. This occurs when the loss may be a threat because the total extent of the loss cannot be fully assessed at the time that one becomes aware of it. This strategy seems to be more prominent around issues of ambiguous loss (Schneider, 1983) and is especially applicable in the case of a child with a disability.

The significant loss to the family at the birth of a handicapped child is difficult to fully comprehend. The ambiguity of the outcome of the child's developmental potential contributes to this uncertainty. The extent of the care that will be required, and the disruption to the family system are other issues around which ambiguity exists. So much uncertainty about the reality of caring for a child with a handicap destroys the illusion of control over events that the mother and family may have.

The ambiguity of the situation for the mother and family lends itself to the utilization of the strategies for coping, which vacillate with feelings of holding on to the image of the perfect child and a normal family routine to letting go of that image and dealing with the inevitable changes that must ensue. In her holding on process the mother may think, after all, the baby may not be that different from the others in the nursery, and someone may have made a mistake in diagnosis.

In this stage, conflicting emotions are common, especially with a situation in which there cannot be specific answers regarding the outcome of the child. The uncertain outcome may range from fear of imminent death of the infant, living with severe medical problems accompanied by frequent surgeries and brushes with death, to less severe conditions that will be only mildly disruptive to the individual and the family. Conflicting emotions are common in situations of not knowing the extent to which life will be changed.

Other conflict centers around not knowing whether to allow oneself to attach to an infant who may not even live beyond a few days. Can the mother in such a state of confusion and vulnerability utilize her energy to foster attachment to her newborn?

3. *Awareness of loss.* The purpose of this phase of grieving is the extensive and intensive exploration of the extent of the loss and its present implications. This particular phase requires much energy resulting in feelings of exhaustion and lowered resistance to infections. Physical self-neglect is often present.

As a result of the exhaustion and lowered resistance the mother agonizes over simple decisions that she used to accomplish with ease. She may state: "I cannot get through this day, so how will I ever manage the rest of my life?"

Resentment and cynicism are emotional states caused by frustration and are a natural part of the grief process, along with the closely related feelings of sadness and anger. The mother may question why she is angry at everyone around her, including family members, doctors, and nurses. At the same time she fails to recognize and accept her feelings as part of the natural grief process. Anger at self is also a common reaction. The mother believes other people seem to manage so well. What could be wrong with her?

This phase also is a very introspective time and loneliness is a prominent feeling. Cynicism accompanies the questioning of beliefs and ability to control. During the intensive exploration of ideals many ideas and beliefs are questioned and reevaluated. It is a time of reassessing priorities and requires time to be alone.

During this phase the mother and family members may spend time appearing to stare off into space, escaping from the pressing urgency of the situation. Cynicism is part of the thought process. The mother may reason that she had avoided the pitfalls and mistakes she had seen others make, and followed the doctor's orders to ensure that this child would be healthy and a joyful addition to a happy family. She may think, "What has gone wrong? I cannot do anything right. I failed at producing a healthy baby, why should I try to do anything more? I am a failure."

4. *Completions.* The fourth phase of grieving has three separate functions and/or benefits: healing, acceptance of loss, and resolution. The major purpose and benefit of the completion phase is to free the grieving individual from the energy invested in the loss so this energy can be utilized in coping with present issues and attachment to the infant.

In this phase, the parents grieving the loss continue to feel loneliness. They also believe that no one can comprehend the depths of their despair or understand the importance of the loss. What does emerge from this "loss-centered" phase is the beginning of healing and acceptance. Time becomes a valuable friend. The sadness that was interminable along with the relentless pain begins to pass. The tears still come, but with less intensity and frequency. The process of healing proceeds slowly and requires not only time but patient understanding of self.

5. *Resolution and reformulations.* In this phase, an enhanced sense of personal power often occurs for the individual, especially in areas where he/she might have lacked balance prior to the loss. An example of this can be illustrated by persons who overemphasized responsibility and commitment prior to a loss and now are more likely to explore activities that are limited in responsibility and commitment.

In this stage, continued healing occurs and the mother and family who have suffered a loss begin to show interest in outside activities. Recovery, healing, and a new sense of power emerge. The language of the individual reflects this change. Conversational speech changes from "I can't" to "Perhaps I can do this" or "Maybe this is an option." Acceptance of the present situation allows the mother to cope better with the demands of her situation and provide care for the handicapped member. However, a variety of situations may trigger anger and a previous stage of grief. Examples would be watching a perfect child at play, conversation regarding the child's limitations, or exclusion of the child from something because of less than perfect development.

The mother spends little time now looking for reasons for the imperfections of the child she bore, and no longer feels the necessity to blame. Out of acceptance comes the recognition of some joys in the situation. Resentment and cynicism have lessened because feelings of resolution have replaced frustration and inability to cope. Resolution is usually an ongoing, often lifetime process as new developments and situations occur. Over the life cycle many changes occur in both the individual's and family's needs. Further, new members may be added to the family causing a reevaluation of roles, coping mechanisms, and resolutions.

6. *Transcending loss.* In this phase, the growth of the individual is no longer bound by the power of what was lost. Its purpose is to develop the capacity of the individual to extend beyond the grief and loss to a wholistic balance in life activities. During this time growth occurs. Energies freed from grieving may be directed to new activities.

The grieving individuals now may begin to feel a serenity without passivity. The parents now begin to see more options both for themselves and for the child. They begin to realize for the first time the potential for enjoyment in living. Once again they begin trusting themselves and their judgments and begin assuming more care and responsibility for their child.

SUMMARY

Within this wholistic model the following important issues are dealt with. The handicapped infant is a complete distortion of the dreamed of and planned for infant. The parents must grieve the loss of this infant—a process that usually takes many months or longer—before they can become fully attached to the living and less-than-perfect infant. Along with the grieving process is a large component of guilt that can take many forms (such as unremitting dedication to the care of the infant to the exclusion of others) and must be recognized and worked through. Resentment and anger are signs of grief and probably will be present and directed to those trying to facilitate the grieving and subsequent attachment between parents and child.

CASE STUDY

A young couple eagerly awaited the birth of their first child. After an extended and difficult labor, Mrs. A. delivered a 6 pound boy. The infant had an obvious deformity on the left arm with the digits lacking total development. She gave this account of some of her feelings around the birth of her son.

> When my son was born I was so eager to see him and hold him. The doctors and nurses seemed to give me many vague answers, but did not bring me my baby. When I did get him he was tightly wrapped in blankets, and I was told he needed to be that way to keep warm. He was quickly taken away. Later I was told my son had a problem with his left arm. I was concerned, but did not see my baby again for several hours.
>
> Finally my pediatrician brought the baby to me and unwrapped him for me to see. I was stunned (Initial Awareness). This was not my perfect baby! I was still tired from my delivery, and I felt like a spectator in a dream. I just knew I would wake up and everything would be all right. I could not take this baby when I was uncertain that it was mine. I felt panic. How could I ever cope? What would this mean for our perfect family? What would my husband think?
>
> I watched in amazement as everyone seemed to be going about as if nothing had happened. There were always people around, but there was no one to share my feelings. Nobody understood what I was feeling. I tried to talk with my husband but he seemed unable to respond. I had many conflicting emotions (Holding on/Letting go). I felt so confused. I asked questions and felt I received very few answers. I didn't even feel as if this baby was mine. People kept telling me I was lucky he was so healthy, but he did not seem to move his left arm. What did this mean? Will he ever be able to use his arm? Will surgery help? There must be some mistake. Just bring me *my* baby (Holding on). This all happened so fast. I want to run away (Letting go).
>
> After sleepless nights and restless days I began to realize that this was my baby (Awareness of Loss), and I must cope. I was very tired. I could not make decisions, and I felt overwhelmed by trying to decide how to feed or care for my baby. I felt very lonely. Even my husband seemed distant. All I wanted to do was to be alone and stare out the window. I had tried to do everything right while I was pregnant, and I did follow the doctor's orders. What did I do wrong? I cannot do anything right!

After a couple of days, I felt pressured by the staff to take my baby but I was still unable to cope with even the simplest of care. I dissolved in tears. Through encouragement from several understanding nurses, I began to see my baby's beautiful face. One nurse just sat with me in the room holding and talking to my baby. I began to see the baby respond to her talking, and saw for the first time his beautiful face. I wanted to hold him (The beginning of completions).

As time passed I finally began to accept my child. I was able to talk with my baby and look at him. Caring for the baby became easier. I began to feel as if I could make decisions (Resolution and reformulations). I was able to talk with the pediatrician about what the future may be for my son and what medical treatment would be necessary.

I still get angry and have many questions, but I am able to hold my son, bathe him, and call him by name. I am looking forward to going home and learning to do what I can to help him develop his arm (Transcending Loss). My husband can now hold our son too. We realize we cannot change what has happened, but we can make plans for the best care we can get. We'll make it!

As can be seen, this young woman and her husband were able to move through part of their grieving so that they could effectively begin caring for their infant and form an attachment to him. They even began making plans for his future. Resentment and anger will probably still continue to crop up as part of the ongoing grieving process, but Mr. and Mrs. A. were able to get through enough of their grieving to establish a positive relationship with their son.

IMPLICATIONS

Using the model described, professionals can better understand and support families at the birth of a handicapped child. Facilitating the grief process of adults and other children in the family can help with the resolution of the loss. Through the resolution of the loss experience of having a handicapped child, the family members, and especially the mother, can redirect their energies to care for the child and realize positive gains from the experience.

Grieving individuals need to be able to do more than simply acknowledge their feelings. They need help to understand the cause. When an individual is hurting desperately, acknowledgement is not sufficient. People deserve to be allowed to explore what is causing the feelings and grow through their pain in order to be able to cope with present and future situations.

The following guidelines are offered to professionals to help the understanding and facilitation of the grief process with mothers and families of handicapped children.

1. *Initial awareness.* The person needs to "tell the story" as it was experienced to a significant person. This has been demonstrated to be an effective means of decathecting the loss (Gendlin, 1964). Incidents of importance to the griever usually must be told before one can proceed in the grieving process.

2. *Accept emotions.* Significant losses cause pain. Emotions are a natural re-

sponse to the significant loss experienced at the birth of a handicapped child. Reactions are varied and contradictory. Under the circumstances, such a range of emotions is normal.

Trying to cope with guilt feelings is very demanding, erratic, and difficult. The feelings of guilt are common but will not change the situation. Everyone errs, and to forgive, especially the self, is most difficult.

3. *Express feelings.* The recognition of conflicting emotions is not enough. Emotions must be expressed and dealt with openly. Special support needs to be provided for parents in expressing anger and sadness, because there are social/sexual sanctions associated with the expression of these feelings.

Every individual has the right to cry. Crying is a natural expression of grief for men as well as women and children. Do not encourage stoicism or self-control when the appropriate thing to do is cry. Encourage appropriate outlets for pent up feelings.

Tranquilizers and alcohol cannot do the grief work for an individual. Drugs only delay the mourning process. There are no detours for the pain of loss.

4. *Include children in the grieving process.* Other children in the family need to share in the process. They cannot be shielded from the loss. The family needs to be encouraged to share the crisis together. Silence and secrecy leave much to the fertile imaginations of children, and lack of sharing deprives them of an opportunity for growth.

Often children feel parents are angry with them when they are excluded from sharing their concerns. There is no "right" or "proper" way to explain loss. Let parents know that what is said is significant, but how it is said will have a greater bearing on whether children develop unnecessary fears or are able to accept, within their ability, the reality of loss.

Parents need to know that they are the most important source of security for their children. Encourage them to hug their children and be close to them when words fail. Reaching out physically is the clearest communication of reassurance and comfort.

5. *Friends are important.* A common denominator of grief is loneliness. Encourage individuals to maintain friendships and share feelings. People in grief have a tendency to avoid bothering anyone with their problems. Encourage them to reach out. Martyrdom is not a necessary part of the grief process.

6. *Support groups are helpful.* Self-help groups often are successful in providing necessary emotional support. Especially helpful is the sharing of how to cope with the multiple hurdles of learning to care for a handicapped member. Members of the support group share in the frustrations of trying to deal with the day in, day out chores of coping. They help with ideas and listen without changing the subject because they really understand.

7. *Allow time for self.* Encourage self-care, for only by caring for physical and emotional needs can parents give fully to a demanding schedule.

8. *Counseling may be beneficial.* Sorrow leaves an imprint on the healthiest

personalities. Individuals who seem to experience difficulty over an extended period of time may benefit from counseling.

CONCLUSION

The loss and grief experienced at the birth of a handicapped child have been explored within a wholistic framework. The six phases of the model have been discussed with application of the loss experienced. People can stop at any point in the grieving process and not proceed any further. They do not go through stages in a nice, neat orderly fashion. People go back and forth, often grieving parts of losses but not others. When individuals experience the pain of awareness, they sometimes become frightened and want to give up.

The proposed model attempts to represent grief as a process—one that is normal and may take a large segment of a person's life to totally resolve. While phases of grief are proposed, they are seen as dynamic, repetitive and varying in terms of their length and intensity.

The model is within a wholistic framework, based on the view that grieving has important biological, intellectual, emotional, behavioral, and spiritual aspects. Focusing on only one of the components, as many do, limits the understanding of the growth potential of grief.

Finally, the model attempts to put grief in the context of developing a growth potential for those who are able to use their losses as a motivation to do so. Thus, the model includes phases that go beyond grief and represent changes in the individual's thinking and ability to redirect both physical and emotional energies that would otherwise be involved in grieving.

Recognition of the stages of grief offered here represents an attempt to understand the grief reaction of parents at the birth of a handicapped child. Beginning the grieving process and resolution of loss enhances the person's willingness and ability to relate to the infant and form attachments needed to accept and care for the child. Helping the grieving individual understand the grief process permits the bereaved to associate their experiences to their loss. This helps enhance the predictability of their behavior and reduces their fears of lack of control. Understanding of grief can also convey hope that something positive can occur through the painful experience. These stages of grieving are offered as guidelines for understanding and facilitating the grief process so that the possibility of growth may be experienced.

REFERENCES

Bettelheim, B. How do you help a child who has a physical handicap? *Ladies Home Journal,* 1922, 89, 34–35.

Bowlby, J. *Attachment and loss: Separation.* New York: Basic Books, 1973.

Drotar, D., Baskiewicz, A., Irvin, N., Kennell, J. H., & Klaus, M. H. The adaptation of parents to the birth of an infant with a congenital malformation: A hypothetical model. *Pediatrics,* 1975, 56, 710–717.

Engel, G. L. Sudden and rapid death during psychological stress. *Annals of Internal Medicine,* 1971, 74, 771–782.

Gendlin, E. A theory of personality change. In P. Worchel & D. Byrne (Eds.), *Personality change.* New York: John Wiley and Sons, 1964.

Klaus, M., & Kennell, J. *Maternal infant bonding.* St. Louis: C. V. Mosby, 1976.

Klaus, M., & Kennell, J. *Parent–infant bonding.* St. Louis: C. V. Mosby, 1981.

Kübler-Ross, E. *On death and dying.* New York: Macmillan, 1968.

Lindemann, E. Symptomatology and management of acute grief. *American Journal of Psychiatry,* 1944, 101, 141–148.

Marris, P. *Loss and change.* New York: Pantheon Books, 1974.

Parkes, C. M. *Bereavement: Studies of grief in adult life.* New York: International Universities Press, 1972.

Schneider, J. *The nature of loss, the nature of grief: A comprehensive model for facilitation and understanding.* Baltimore: University Park Press, 1983.

Solnit, A. J., & Stark, M. H. Mourning and the birth of a defective child. *Psychoanalytical study of the child,* 1961, 16, 523–537.

Tanner, I. J. *The gift of grief.* New York: Hawthorne Books, 1976.

9

Developmental Tasks and Transitions of Adolescents With Chronic Illnesses and Disabilities

Sherry E. Davis   Karen Berger
Constance Anderson   Carl F. Feinstein
Donald C. Linkowski

Adolescents who are chronically ill or disabled present a major challenge to health, education, and rehabilitation professionals. Several investigators have noted that by the time disabled children reach adolescence, many aspects of their rehabilitation have been complicated by the immense practical and emotional stress their conditions place on them, their parents, and teachers (Levy & Nir 1980; Pless & Pinkerton, 1975). Although it is clear that psychosocial factors greatly add to the difficulties of adjustment and adaptation of disabled adolescents, disabled teenagers and their parents receive insufficient support and guidance from all varieties of care providers (Minde, 1978).

Adolescence is a stage of life when the individual is undergoing rapid, enormous physiological and psychological changes that transform the child into an adult. Personality development proceeds along the lines of increasing responsibility, morality, and independence. Failure to achieve mastery of the developmental tasks that confront all adolescents may have grave, potentially lifelong consequences both for the individual and for society. Achievement of a clearer understanding of the impact that a chronic illness or disability has on adolescent development necessitates an exploration of how the illness or disability may affect the adolescent's ability to master certain psychosocial tasks that are crucial to leading a productive, psychologically healthy life. These psychosocial tasks include an

This chapter was written under the auspices of the George Washington University Rehabilitation Research and Training Center (Grant #G008300123–02), which has been recently established by the National Institute of Handicapped Research to investigate and improve the psychosocial environment of individuals with chronic illnesses and disabilities.

adjustment to physical and physiological changes of puberty and the accompanying flood of emotions, the establishment of effective social and working relationships between same- and opposite-sex peers, achievement of independence from primary caretakers, preparation for a vocation, and movement toward a sense of values and a sense of definable identity (Conger, 1973; Siegel, 1982).

PHYSIOLOGICAL CHANGES AND BODY IMAGERY

During early adolescence, the individual must adjust to the physical and physiological changes that are associated with puberty (e.g., increased growth in extremities, development of secondary sex characteristics). These bodily changes have profound psychological consequences, particularly because body image is at the core of the overall self-image (Siegel, 1982). Physical characteristics receive particular attention and examination during adolescence, and several investigators have noted that most early adolescents are more concerned about their physical appearance than about any other aspect of themselves (Jersild, 1952; Simmons & Rosenberg, 1975). The early adolescent wants to avoid being "different" at all costs, particularly because physical appearance, body image, and peer-group conformity are important derivatives of self-esteem (Hofman, 1975). Indeed, undesirable physical characteristics make the adolescent susceptible to teasing, ridicule, and exclusion (Berscheid, Walster, & Bohrnstedt, 1973).

Several investigators have found that chronically ill and disabled adolescents are more likely to be dissatisfied with their physical appearance than are their physically healthy and able-bodied counterparts, particularly if their conditions are very conspicuous or visible. Adsett (1963) and Kellerman and Katz (1977) observed that individuals who were disfigured from cancer therapy (e.g., facial disfigurement, loss of limb) had a greater fear of unacceptability and isolation secondary to their disfigurement than of death itself or of a recurrence of the illness. Anderson and Klarke (1982) and Skellarn (1979) found an exaggerated self-consciousness and "obsession" associated with physical appearance among adolescents with cerebral palsy.

Adolescents with relatively nonvisible conditions are also likely to have impaired body images because some conditions may result in delays in physical growth and in the appearance of secondary sexual characteristics. These adolescents may seem younger looking than their physically healthy peers, which can result in feelings of psychological and emotional distress. McCracken (1985) observed that at a time when adolescents become increasingly interested in their bodies and appearance, the adolescent with cystic fibrosis spends much energy attempting to hide the physical stigmata of the disease (e.g., delayed growth). Poorly controlled juvenile diabetes may lead to slowed growth and delayed onset of puberty, and several investigators have found that diabetic adolescents have significant alterations in their body images (e.g., feeling that their bodies are damaged, feeling that internal organs are missing) (Kaufman & Hersher, 1971; Sullivan, 1979).

Although individuals reach sexual maturation during adolescence, the area of psychosexual development in chronically ill and disabled adolescents has received scant attention in the literature. Beliefs that disabled individuals are asexual beings who are unable to engage in sexual activity and, furthermore, have no need for sexual expression are perpetuated by society in general and by the medical, educational, and rehabilitation professions in particular (Anderson & Cole, 1975; Blum, 1985; Diamond, 1974).

Health care professionals and parents tend to avoid the issue of sexuality among chronically ill and disabled adolescents, although concerns about sexuality and fertility are particularly important for the late adolescent. Mid- and late-adolescents typically are concerned with dating, developing satisfactory, intimate relationships with their peers, and with issues of procreation. Thus, adolescents whose conditions have resulted in delays in physical growth and in the onset of puberty may feel inadequate or self-conscious about their sexuality. Blum (1983) argued that conceptualizations of sexuality among disabled teenagers should include physical maturation and body image, attitudes about sex-role socialization, and social relationships.

PEER RELATIONS

Although the importance of peers in the socialization process does not begin with puberty and adolescence, peers do play a more important role in adolescence than in childhood. During adolescence, relationships between both same- and opposite-sex peers come closer to serving as prototypes for later adult relationships in both social and professional relationships (Conger, 1973). The peer group is also important during adolescence because ties with parents have become progressively looser as greater independence is achieved.

The role of the peer group in helping the adolescent to define his or her identity assumes particular importance during adolescence. At no other stage of development is the individual's sense of identity so fluid: The adolescent is no longer a child but is not yet fully accepted as an adult (Conger, 1973; Siegel, 1982). The adolescent has to prepare, with few guidelines, to meet society's demands for social independence, vocational competence, the role as a citizen, intimate relationships, and a workable philosophy of life. All of this is occurring as the adolescent is struggling to discover, interpret, and control a self that is changing rapidly, both physiologically and psychologically (Erikson, 1968; Siegel, 1982).

The few studies in which the peer relationships of chronically ill or disabled adolescents have been examined suggest that these adolescents express great concerns about their social relationships. Blum (1983), Dorner (1976), and Schloss (1973) have found loneliness and a sense of isolation to be prevalent among adolescents with spina bifida. Minde (1978) and Podeanu-Czehofski (1975) observed social isolation and peer-group rejection in adolescents with cerebral palsy. Boyle, di Sant Agnese, Sack, Millican, and Kulczycki (1976) and McCollum and Gibson (1970) determined that retardation in growth and sexual development contributed to peer-group rejection of adolescents with cystic fibrosis.

The chronically ill or disabled teenager frequently faces a dilemma of which peer group to associate with—other disabled individuals or their able-bodied peers. Adolescents with disabilities may attempt to dissociate themselves from other disabled persons to avoid potential rejection from peers because disabled teenagers do not want to be identified as being different. This may be particularly true of adolescents with nonvisible conditions, and their decision to disclose that they have a chronic illness or disabling condition may be closely associated with their subjective perception of whether they are disabled.

INDEPENDENCE AND AUTONOMOUS FUNCTIONING

Although the peer group assumes heightened importance during adolescence, the adolescent also is faced with the challenge of relinquishing parental ties and childhood identifications while still maintaining the continuity of parental and familial relationships (Siegel, 1982). The development of independence from parents is a critical psychosocial task that adolescents must achieve if they are to become autonomous, self-sufficient, productive, and competent adults.

The impact of chronic illness or disability on the achievement of independence from parents is contingent on many factors. These include the quality of the parent–child relationship, the nature and severity of the illness or disabling condition, and the degree of acceptance of the condition by all family members.

Numerous studies have confirmed the importance of the parent–child relationship to the achievement of independence by both able-bodied and disabled adolescents. Parental love, support, and acceptance nurture in the child and adolescent the ability to form positive relationships and develop positive self-esteem, a confident sense of identity, and successful separation and autonomous functioning (Coopersmith, 1967; Elder, 1968; Mussen, Conger, & Kagan, 1969; Pinkerton, 1971; Reuter, 1969). The restrictive, controlling, or overly protective parent impedes the achievement of these skills. Safilios-Rothschild (1970) pointed out the importance of the role of the parents or significant others in influencing the disabled person's perception of what can and cannot be done and also in promoting the development of independence. Restrictive or overly protective parents may thus be a crucial impediment to the development of independence and self-sufficiency in their disabled teenagers.

The nature and severity of the illness or disabling condition also affects the autonomous functioning of the chronically ill or disabled adolescent. Parents may feel particularly overprotective toward their teenager if past attempts at independent functioning (e.g., participation in sports activities) have resulted in exacerbations of the illness or disability. When the chronic illness or disability has a fluctuating or progressive course, it may be particularly difficult for both the family and the teenager to foresee that the adolescent will be able to live independently outside of the family constellation. It is critical, however, that both the family and teenager learn to understand and accept that some restriction in activities (e.g., mobility, diet) does not translate into total dependence on others in activities of daily living.

The development of a sense of autonomy is closely related to the parents' and adolescent's acceptance of the chronic illness or disabling condition. Acceptance of disability is linked to mastery of many of the developmental tasks of adolescence. For example, research findings indicate a link between acceptance of disability and self-esteem (Linkowski & Dunn, 1974), which in turn is related to adolescents' perceptions of their body images and of their abilities to function in an autonomous manner (Rosenberg, 1979). Thus, if the adolescent does not ultimately resolve the conflict between a continuing, potentially regressive dependence and the newer demands and privileges of independence, he or she will encounter difficulties in other areas (e.g., social relationships, pursuit of a vocation, and a sense of identity) (Conger, 1973).

Preparation for a Vocation

One of the major developmental tasks of adolescence is to become increasingly aware of the need to acquire skills, behaviors, training, and education in preparation for a vocation. Employment, more than any other accomplishment, conveys self-sufficiency and autonomy.

Empirical research supports the notion of a steady but gradual maturation of the average young person's vocational thinking during the adolescent years (O'Hara & Tiedeman, 1959). For an adolescent with a chronic illness or disability, the difficulties of achieving the pervasive tasks of adolescence can be easily exacerbated by the manifestations of the illness or disability.

The particular nature of the additional stress associated with an illness or disability varies with each condition. Overs (1975) speculated that the type of disability and age of onset are important variables in vocational development, whereas others (Davidson, 1975; Lacey, 1975) have contended that some disabled or chronically ill persons may lack vocational maturity because of restricted experiences and opportunities. The adolescent with an illness or disability, however, may be limited not so much by his or her condition as by opportunities and early experiences imposed by certain conditions. For example, school or other experiences crucial to development and maturation may be interrupted for treatment, or exposure to certain experiences may be limited by the condition itself.

Another problem for disabled teenagers is that medical and allied health practitioners, as well as parents, often become so concerned and preoccupied with the disabling condition that they forget that these youngsters must simultaneously deal with the physical limitations of the disability but also with how these limitations affect their vocational interests and the development of vocational skills.

Vocational maturity and subsequent vocational readiness are critical to the achievement of the developmental tasks of adolescence. Vocational maturity consists of one's repertoire of coping behaviors compared with that of one's peers (Super, 1974). Additional factors thought to influence vocational maturity are emotional autonomy, adaptive skills, interests, decision-making skills, and values (Bresnicks, Woodcock, Weatherman, & Hill, 1984; Herr & Cramer, 1979). These factors are viewed as precursors that influence later vocational choice, self-sufficiency, and autonomy.

Brolin (1980) stated that vocational maturity in disabled or chronically ill adolescents is largely contingent on the efforts of parents, school personnel, rehabilitation professionals, and vocational counselors. In efforts to nurture vocational maturity in disabled and chronically ill adolescents, the thrust is currently toward awareness and attention to their developmental needs. When dealing with adolescents and aiding in their preparation for transition from school to the work world, it is important to focus on rehabilitation, or returning the individual to a former level of functioning. Equally important is a focus on fostering development and ensuring that the progress of this development is as close as possible to that of their age mates (Eisenberg, Sutkin, & Jansen, 1984).

Fostering development of vocational maturity to help ill or disabled adolescents in their achievement of vocational self-sufficiency and autonomy requires programs and settings that address their educational, social, and developmental needs. The goals of interdisciplinary professional teams must involve the provision of vocational preparation programs, counseling, and education that foster development, increase the adolescent's feelings of autonomy, promote transition from the school environment to the work world, and enhance the chances for the disabled or ill adolescent to prepare for and pursue vocations in a way that is comparable to that of their able-bodied peers.

VALUES AND IDENTITY

The adolescent with a disability must ponder a wide range of personal questions, including those of self-confidence, competence, and esteem. Included as an integral part of the identity process of adolescents with chronic illnesses or disabilities are the value questions associated with acceptance of the physical impairment (Dembo, Leviton, & Wright, 1956; Wright, 1983). There are wide variations in reactions of adolescents to particular impairments. Wright (1983) emphasized the importance of the meaning a disability has for an individual, rather than the fact of a disability per se.

Because of the heightened concern with physique and body functions, adolescents with disabilities may tend to place a high level of importance on those areas that are affected most by the disability and as a result tend to suffer more and have lower self-esteem than do those who do not place such importance on the affected body part. Similarly, adolescents who are chronically ill or disabled must develop a wide range of interests and values, must learn about their disabilities or chronic illnesses to contain the "spread" of their effects beyond the life areas actually limited. Furthermore, they must learn to appreciate their personal assets and avoid comparing themselves to others in ways that emphasize their shortcomings. In coming to terms with these issues, the adolescent will tend to adopt values associated with the acceptance of disability, increased self-worth, and a strong sense of personal competence.

Research has demonstrated repeatedly that there is a close relationship between acceptance of disability and self-esteem among adolescents with disabilities (Heinemann & Shontz, 1982; Linkowski & Dunn, 1974; Starr & Heiserman, 1977). Significant relationships between acceptance of disability and measures of personal competence have also been found. These measures include acceptance of disability being associated with an internal rather than an external locus of control (Mazzula, 1982), a higher level of education (Thomas, Davis, & Hochman, 1976; Trainor, 1980; Woodrich, 1981), assertion skills (Morgan & Leung, 1980), and leadership in self-help organizations (LaBorwit, 1980; Trainor, 1980).

The acceptance of disability also seems to be closely tied to sexual identity. Heinemann and Shontz (1982) found that the acceptance of disability was significantly related to masculinity, but not androgyny, of both male and female adolescents. The association between acceptance of disability and masculine identity may be due to the socially defined values of independence, active involvement, and emphasis on ability, which these two constructs have in common.

Adolescence as a time of transition is also characterized by "overlapping situations." The youngster, who at times acts like a child and at other times acts like an adult, is frequently confronted by demands for both dependent and independent behavior. Furthermore, a person with a disability may deal with situations by sometimes acting like a disabled person and at other times acting like a nondisabled person (Wright, 1983). For example, an adolescent with a disability may choose either to be exempt from a game in gym class because he or she uses a wheelchair or to participate (with modification, if necessary) along with the other members of the class. In both situations the disability is considered, but in the latter, the youngster chooses to act more like the "normal kids." The adolescent typically tries out various roles to work through these situational conflicts and needs role models to help establish his or her identity as a self-accepting person with a disability.

RECOMMENDATIONS FOR REHABILITATION COUNSELORS

The literature suggests that adolescents with chronic illnesses or disabilities have more to cope with than do other adolescents because of their impairments. Thus, they may need more help in life planning than does the able-bodied adolescent.

They must come to terms with their disability during a time when so many changes are occurring in their lives. Consequently, the rehabilitation and vocational process dictates a holistic approach to counseling adolescents with disabilities.

To ensure maximum opportunity and experience for a teenager with a disabling condition, counselors must initiate and plan the vocational process so that disabled students may participate in the work force to the greatest extent possible. Early vocational planning, certainly while the adolescent is still in high school, is critical. This early planning may be particularly important for adolescents who are not going to attend institutions of higher learning. Rehabilitation counselors can facilitate this process by working cooperatively with educators and parents to identify and foster the development of prevocational skills and vocational interests in these youngsters.

The development of prevocational interests and skills in teenagers with disabling conditions requires that they be helped not only to understand and accept their disability—and the accompanying alterations in their activities that may be necessary—but also to identify and build on strengths in their behavioral repertoire. Thus, the adolescent who is totally blind may not be able to become a surgeon, but he or she may become a psychiatrist; the adolescent who is a wheelchair user may not become a fashion model, but he or she may be able to work in fashion design. The disabled teenager also needs role models who have disabling conditions and who are functioning successfully and independently in a variety of careers. Role models can be particularly helpful in the context of a mentoring relationship with the disabled teenager.

The rehabilitation counselor must also consider how the teenager and parents are grappling with the normative developmental tasks of adolescence when helping the teenager in the rehabilitation and vocational process. Disabled teenagers who have low self-esteem and who do not accept their disability are likely to fail in the vocational planning process because they probably do not view themselves as independent, effective, and productive individuals. Overprotective parents may impede the planning process by fostering age-inappropriate dependence in their teenager. The rehabilitation counselor must identify problem areas within the family and provide interventions (e.g., consultation or counseling) when necessary.

To meet fully the needs of youth in transition, rehabilitation personnel must work in a more consistent and integrated fashion with other professionals. Efforts must be made to close the gaps through which adolescents may easily fall in crossing the bridge from school to work. High school counselors, parents, university preservice counselors, and in-service training personnel must play a central role in meeting this critical initiative.

REFERENCES

Adsett, C. A. (1963). Emotional reactions to disfigurement from cancer therapy. *Canadian Medical Association Journal, 89,* 385–391.

Anderson, E. M., & Klarke, L. (1982). *Disability in adolescence* (B. Spain, collaborator). London: Methuen.

Anderson, T., & Cole, T. (1975). Sexual counseling of the physically disabled. *Postgraduate Medicine, 58*, 117-123.

Berscheid, E., Walster, E., & Bohrnstedt, G. (1973). The happy American body: A survey report. *Psychology Today, 7*(6), 119-131.

Blum, R. W. (1983). The adolescent with spina bifida. *Clinical Pediatrics, 22*, 331-335.

Blum, R. W. (1985). Sexual health needs of the physically and intellectually impaired adolescent. In R. W. Blum (Ed.), *Chronic illness and disabilities in childhood and adolescence* (pp. 127-141). Orlando, FL: Grune & Stratton.

Blumberg, B. D., Lewis, M. J., & Susman, E. J. (1984). Adolescence: A time of transition. In M. G. Eisenberg, L. C. Sitkin, & M. A. Jansen (Eds.), *Chronic illness and disability through the life span* (pp. 133-149). New York: Springer Publishing Co.

Boyle, I. R., di Sant Agnese, P., Sack, S., Millican, F., & Kulczycki, L. (1976). Emotional adjustment of adolescents and young adults with cystic fibrosis. *Journal of Pediatrics, 88*, 318-326.

Bresnicks, R., Woodcock, R., Weatherman, R., & Hill, B. (1984). *Scales of Independent Behavior.* Allen, TX: Developmental Learning Materials.

Brolin, D. E. (1980). *Vocational preparation of persons with handicaps* (2nd ed.). Columbus, OH: Merrill.

Conger, J. J. (1973). *Adolescence and youth: Psychological development in a changing world.* New York: Harper & Row.

Coopersmith, S. (1967). *The antecedents of self-esteem.* San Francisco: Freeman.

Davidson, T. M. (1975). The vocational development and success of visually impaired adolescents. *New Outlook for the Blind, 69*, 314-316.

Dembo, T., Leviton, G. L., & Wright, B. A. (1956). Adjustment to misfortune—A problem in social psychological rehabilitation. *Artificial Limbs, 3*, 4-62.

Diamond, M. (1974). Sexuality and the handicapped. *Rehabilitation Literature, 35*, 34-40.

Dorner, S. (1976). Adolescents with spina bifida: How they see their situation. *Archives of the Diseases of Children, 51*, 437.

Elder, G. H., Jr. (1968). *Adolescent socialization and personality development.* Chicago: Rand McNally.

Eisenberg, M. G., Sutkin, L. C., & Jansen, M. A. (1984). *Chronic illness and disability through the life span.* New York: Springer Publishing Co.

Erikson, E. H. (1968). *Identity: Youth and crisis.* New York: Norton.

Heinemann, A. W., & Shontz, F. D. (1982). Acceptance of disability, self-esteem, sex role identity, and reading aptitude in deaf adolescents. *Rehabilitation Counseling Bulletin, 25*, 197-203.

Herr, E. L., & Cramer, S. H. (1979). *Career guidance through the life-span: Systematic approaches.* Boston: Little, Brown.

Hofman, A. D. (1975). The impact of illness in adolescence and coping behavior. *Acta Paediatrica Scandinavica Supplement, 256*, 29-33.

Jersild, A. T. (1952). *In search of self.* New York: Columbia University, Bureau of Publications, Teachers College.

Kaufman, R. V., & Hersher, B. (1971). Body image changes in teenage diabetics. *Pediatrics, 48*, 123-128.

Kellerman, J., & Katz, E. R. (1977). The adolescent with cancer: Theoretical, clinical, and research issues. *Journal of Pediatric Psychology, 2*, 127-131.

LaBorwit, L. J. (1980). *Cross-validation of the Knowledge of Laryngectomy Inventory.* Paper presented at the 18th Congress of the International Association of Logopedics Phoniatrics, Washington, D.C.

Lacey, D. (1975). Career behavior of deaf persons: Current status and future trends. In J. S. Picou & R. E. Campbell (Eds.), *Career behavior of special groups.* Columbus, OH: Merrill.

Levinson, D. J., Darrow, C. N., Klein, E. B., Levinson, M. H., & McKee, B. (1978). *The seasons of a man's life.* New York: Knopf.

Levy, A. M., & Nir, Y. (1980). Chronic illness in children. In S. Bemporad (Ed.), *Child development in normality and psychopathology* (pp. 337-361). New York: Brunner/Mazel.

Linkowski, D. C. (1969). *A study of the relationship between acceptance of disability and response to rehabilitation.* Unpublished doctoral dissertation, State University of New York at Buffalo.

Linkowski, D. C. (1971). A scale to measure acceptance of disability. *Rehabilitation Counseling Bulletin, 14,* 236-244.

Linkowski, D. C., & Dunn, M. A. (1974). Self-concept and acceptance of disability. *Rehabilitation Counseling Bulletin, 14,* 28-32.

Mazulla, J. R. (1982). *The relationship of locus of control expectancy, and acceptance of acquired traumatic spinal cord injury.* Unpublished master's thesis, East Carolina University, Greenville.

McCollum, A. T., & Gibson, L. E. (1970). Family adaptation to the child with cystic fibrosis. *Journal of Pediatrics, 4,* 571-578.

McCracken, M. J. (1985). The disabled and chronically ill adolescent: Cystic fibrosis in adolescence. In R. W. Blum (Ed.), *Chronic illness and disabilities in children and adolescence* (pp. 397-411). Orlando, FL: Grune & Stratton.

Minde, K. K. (1978). Coping styles of 34 adolescents with cerebral palsy. *American Journal of Psychiatry, 135,* 1344-1349.

Morgan, B., & Leung, P. (1980). Effects of assertion training on acceptance of disability by physically disabled college students. *Journal of Counseling Psychology, 27,* 209-212.

Mussen, P. H., Conger, J. J., & Kagan, J. (1969). *Child development and personality* (3rd ed.). New York: Harper & Row.

O'Hara, R. P., & Tiedeman, O. V. (1959). Vocational self-concept in adolescence. *Journal of Counseling Psychology, 6,* 292-301.

Overs, R. P. (1975). Career behavior of the physically and mentally handicapped. In J. S. Picou & R. E. Campbell (Eds.), *Career behavior of special groups* (pp. 59-73). Columbus, OH: Merrill.

Pinkerton, P. (1971). The psychosomatic approach in child psychiatry. In J. G. Howells (Ed.), *Modern perspectives in child psychiatry* (Vol. 1, pp. 306-335). New York: Brunner/Mazel.

Pless, I. B., & Pinkerton, P. (1975). *Chronic childhood disorder: Promoting patterns of adjustment.* Chicago: Year Book Medical Publishers.

Podeanu-Czehofski, I. (1975). Is it only a child's guilt? Aspects of family life of cerebral palsied children. *Rehabilitation Literature, 36,* 308-311.

Reuter, M. W. (1969). The father-son relationship and the personality adjustment of the late adolescent male. *Dissertation International Abstracts, 70,* 5327.

Rosenberg, M. (1979). *Conceiving the self.* New York: Basic Books.

Safilios-Rothschild, C. (1970). *The sociology and social psychology of disability.* New York: Random House.

Schlenoff, D. (1975). A theory of career development for the quadriplegic. *Journal of Applied Rehabilitation Counseling, 6,* 3-11.

Schloss, A. L. (1973). The adolescent with myelomeningocele. *Developmental Medicine and Child Neurology, 15*(Suppl. 29).

Siegel, O. (1982). Personality development in adolescence. In B. B. Wolman (Ed.), *The handbook of developmental psychology* (pp. 537-548). Englewood Cliffs, NJ: Prentice-Hall.

Simmons, R., & Rosenberg, M. (1975). Sex, sex roles, and self-image. *Journal of Youth and Adolescence, 4,* 229-258.

Skellarn, J. (1979). The self-concept of children and adolescents and the effects of physical disability. *Austrialian Nurses' Journal, 8*(6), 36-38.

Smits, S. (1965). The reaction of self and others to the obviousness and severity of physical disability. *Rehabilitation Counseling Bulletin, 5,* 56-60.

Starr, P., & Heiserman, K. (1977). Acceptance of disability by teenagers with oral-facial clefts. *Rehabilitation Counseling Bulletin, 20,* 198–202.

Sullivan, B. J. (1979). Adjustment in diabetic adolescent girls: I. Development of the diabetic adjustment scale; II. Adjustment, self-esteem, and depression in diabetic girls. *Psychosomatic Medicine, 41,* 119–138.

Super, D. E. (1974). *Measuring vocational maturity for counseling and evaluation.* Washington, DC: National Vocational Guidance Association.

Thomas, K. R., Davis, R. M., & Hochman, M. E. (1976). Correlates of disability acceptance in amputees. *Rehabilitation Counseling Bulletin, 19,* 508–511.

Trainor, M. A. (1980). *Acceptance of ostomy and the visitor's role in a self-help group for ostomy patients.* Unpublished doctoral dissertation, The Catholic University of America, Washington, DC.

Turosak, F. H. (1974). *Self-concept, acceptance of disability, and work identity in spinal cord injured Vietnam era veterans.* Unpublished master's thesis, George Washington University, Washington, DC.

Wissel, E. A. (1981). *Analysis of self-concept and acceptance of disability with the traumatic spinal cord injured.* Unpublished doctoral dissertation, The Catholic University of America, Washington, DC.

Woodrich, F. (1981). *Demographic and disability related variables which influence acceptance of disability in spinal cord injured men and women.* Unpublished doctoral dissertation, Florida State University, Tallahassee.

Wright, B. A. (1983). *Physical disability: A psychosocial approach.* New York: Harper & Row.

10

Midlife Transition and Disability

Paul W. Power
David B. Hershenson
Nancy K. Schlossberg

During the past 10 years considerable attention has been devoted in the literature to the changes that are experienced in midlife. These changes are referred to by some authors as a "crisis" and by other writers simply as a "transition." There is evidence of a midlife transition of men, there are now many studies that identify a less well-defined but equally stressful phase for women (Gilligan, 1982; Lowenthal, Thurnher, & Chiriboga, 1975; Neugarten, 1968). There is, however, little available evidence on whether disability makes any difference in coping with reported midlife changes for those who enter the midlife period with a disability or who become disabled in midlife.

In this article we provide a brief overview of the theoretical perspectives of the midlife stage of adult development, with selected implications for the disabled. We also suggest a model for the midlife disabled person, which includes the midlife issues that usually have an impact on the individual. Using this model, we discuss implications for vocational rehabilitation intervention with this disabled population.

MIDLIFE ADULT DEVELOPMENT OVERVIEW

Midlife is one of several important and inevitable transitions occurring during the life cycle (Norman & Scaramella, 1980; Schlossberg, 1984; Sheehy, 1974; Sze, 1975). The theoretical perspectives on adult development and on what influences the middle transition are many and varied. Such theorists as Erikson (1975); Gould (1978); Levinson, Darrow, Klein, Levinson, and McKee (1978); and Vaillant (1977) conceptualized the life span by stages, with each stage having certain themes and specific tasks to be mastered. Other writers have emphasized the role of life or marker events as pivotal for individual development (Baltes & Danish, 1980; Brim & Ryff, 1980). These include marriage, birth of children, children leaving home, and retirement. These events also give shape and direction to the various aspects of each individual life (Schlossberg, 1984). A few authors, moreover, identify either individual timing or sex differences as essential ingredients in understanding adult development (Lowenthal, Thurnher, & Chiriboga, 1975). Differences in behavior and maturity that are assigned to men and women on the basis of their sex roles are often more significant than stage differences (Schlossberg, 1984).

Of particular interest is Cytrynbaum and Patrick's (1979) proposal on understanding the midlife period. They believe there are many precipitators of this period in a person's life, such as biological changes and decline, a life-threatening illness, the death and illness of significant others, and cultural and social structural transitions (i.e., early retirement, status loss, or the "empty nest"). Once these precipitators occur, then a series of three developmental phases begins. In the first phase, reassessment, the individual realizes that the process of change that is taking place cannot be reversed, and there is a reevaluation of current identity and life structures. In the second phase, reintegration, the individual becomes aware of other emerging aspects of personality and defense structures are modified toward allowing new, differentiated patterns of behavior and experiencing. In the third phase, behavioral and role change, the individual recommits, modifies, or dramatically changes behavior or relationships to family or work systems. In each phase there are issues to be negotiated, but a person who successfully tackles the transition emerges not only with more individuality but also with greater self-confidence and self-knowledge than before.

Although the state of research and theory on adult development is one of healthy disagreement (Wortley & Amatea, 1982), there are some common assumptions held by major theorists regarding the kinds of tasks, roles, and attitudinal changes observed across the course of midlife. For example, for both men and women there is a struggle with the meaning of death, mortality, and life. A recognition of bodily changes also takes place, with the accompanying acknowledgement or rejection of changes in physical attractiveness. With these changes a restructuring of sexual identity and self-concept can occur, with women attempting to integrate more independent, aggressive, competitive parts of their personalities (Brim, 1977; Neugarten, 1968). For men there is the opportunity to integrate the more passive, dependent, intimacy-oriented parts of their personalities (Gutmann, 1977).

In a somewhat different perspective, Schlossberg (1984) viewed the midlife period as a time of transition. She defined transition as "any event or non-event, that is, the nonoccurrence of an anticipated event, that results in a change in relationships, routines, assumptions, and/or roles within the settings of self, work, family, health, and/or economics" (p.43). Given this definition, it is evident that although transitions are not restricted to the midlife period, individuals can still undergo major changes during their middle years. Schlossberg (1984) listed those issues that commonly emerge during midlife as (a) reevaluating one's life and dreams, (b) facing the gap between one's dreams and one's achievements, (c) facing mortality and aging, (d) fearing of stagnation, and (e) being caught in between one's children and parents. Those issues are not equally important for all individuals at midlife. Each person may be working on different concerns. For some it may be aging parents; for others it may be the job or relationships with children.

Most authors agree that midlife is a time of transition that includes changing attitudes toward self, family, and occupation. Biological aging alone does not cause midlife changes; but instead, multiple environmental, interpersonal, and intrapsychic factors are responsible (Brim, 1976; Lowenthal et al., 1975). Social and cultural expectations, as well as race, sex, and social class membership, can alter the way in which any change takes place in midlife.

Although there is documentation for the existence of various themes and issues that should be dealt with in midlife, this question still remains. Do people with a disability have, because of their condition, a more difficult time in negotiating the tasks of midlife?

PERSONS WITH DISABILITIES AT MIDLIFE

Obviously, the onset of disability during the adult years represents a transition, and individuals who are disabled in childhood undergo other transitions during adulthood. Thus, one might define four groups: (1) the nondisabled who confront midlife transitions, (2) those disabled early in life who have adjusted to their disabilities and confront midlife transitions, (3) those disabled earlier in life who have not adjusted to the disability and who must also confront midlife transition, and (4) those who become disabled during midlife and who must confront this transition along with others endemic to this period of life. For practical purposes, we can combine these four groups into two: the first two groups, for whom disability is not a special issue during midlife (either because it is not present or because it has already been dealt with); and the second two groups, for whom disability does represent a special midlife transition. We concentrate here on the latter.

We propose that those individuals who must confront the transition to disability in midlife, either because it occurs at that time or because it is brought into that period unresolved from earlier in life, are at special risk in dealing with the other transitions that typically accompany the middle years, such as changes in sexuality and in family and work roles. Hershenson (1981) suggested that disabilities typically affect competencies most directly and that the impact of the disability then spreads to the domains of personality and of goals. Most of the midlife transitions suggested by Cytrynbaum and Patrick (1979) and by Wortley and Amatea (1982) directly affect personality or goals. Thus, the person disabled in midlife is likely to be affected in all three domains simultaneously and therefore is left with fewer areas of strength on which he or she might draw in seeking to cope with any one transition.

Schlossberg (1984) suggested that a person's capacity to cope with any transition depends on the characteristics of (a) the transition, including its "trigger" (i.e., precipitating event), timing (i.e., on or off schedule in the person's expectations), source (internal or external to the person), amount of role change entailed, duration (temporary or permanent), the person's previous experience with similar transitions, and concurrent stress; (b) the person, including his or her socioeconomic status, sex role, age and stage of life, state of health, ego development, personality, outlook, commitments and values, and coping responses; (c) the environment, including social support (family and friends) and options available. For the person disabled in midlife, the trigger is the onset of disability (or its continuation as an unresolved impediment). The timing of this transition is almost never "on schedule," the source is always essentially external, and the duration will be lengthy. Role change, previous similar experience, and concurrent stress will vary from person to person. Obviously, the less the role change and concurrent stress and the greater the person's prior successful handling of similar transitions (illnesses or losses), the easier it is to cope with the transition to disabled status.

Conversely, the greater the number of other simultaneous transitions, the harder it will be for the person to cope with any one of them. A person who, in rapid sequence, gets divorced, loses a job, and suffers a stroke will have a harder time than will the person who becomes disabled but can maintain a marriage and return to a job. Likewise, the individual's personality and demographics are major factors in determining his or her ability to cope with the transition to disabled status. Can the person return to former employment, or does the person possess readily transferable skills? How does the person react to life changes in general and the impact of disability in particular? For some, becoming disabled may allow them to avoid other life changes, such as forestalling a divorce because of the spouse's guilt at the thought of abandoning a person with a disability. Thus, some adults may welcome the onset of disability, either for its situational effects in fending off other, more unpleasant transitions or because it allows them to gratify dependency needs. For most adults, however, disability represents an unwelcome transition. If family and friends are not supportive and the options seem limited, the transition is especially difficult. We propose a model that incorporates these considerations in such a way that implications for rehabilitation practice are suggested.

A MODEL OF THE MIDLIFE DISABLED

This model is an extension of Hershenson's (1981) model of career development of persons with disabilities. The model suggests that development can be conceptualized as involving three interactive domains: personality, competencies, and goals. The first domain to emerge, personality, involves the self-concept and motivational system. The second domain to emerge, competencies, involves habits, skills, and interpersonal relations. The final domain to emerge involves the formulation of appropriate, crystallized goals. Although these domains become focal in the posited sequence, each reciprocally influences the ongoing development of the other two; in an adult, the three domains exist in a dynamic balance so that changes in any one will affect the other two.

Applying the variables suggested by other authors, cited above, as the typical issues involved in midlife transitions, one can see that the domain of personality is directly involved in the changes of self-concept and the awareness of one's mortality that occurs at this time of life. The domain of competencies is directly affected by the physical changes of aging, the changes in sexuality, the family role changes (e.g., empty nest, responsibility for aged parents), and work-role restraints. The last of these factors involves the fact that, according to the federal Age Discrimination in Employment Act of 1967, one is considered an "older worker" at age 40, with significantly limited potential for advancement or job mobility compared with younger workers (U.S. Department of Labor, Bureau of Labor Statistics, personal communication, February 20, 1985). Finally, midlife personal and career goals change to conform to the changes in personality and in competencies. As a consequence of these intrapsychic changes, there are behavioral changes in interpersonal style, work behavior, and life interests and activities. This model is presented in Figure 10.1. In this figure, the direction of spread of direct affects is

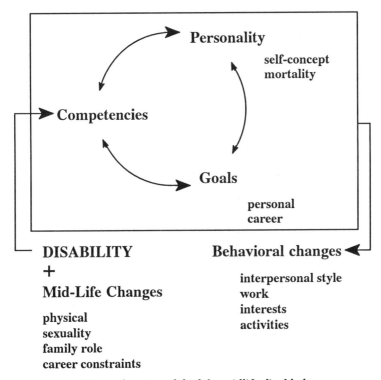

Figure 1. A model of the midlife disabled.

represented by large arrowheads and the reciprocal interactions between domains are represented by small arrowheads. Midlife issues relevant to each heading (inputs, domains, and resultant behavioral changes) are given in lower-case letters.

Thus, for anyone undergoing midlife transition, able-bodied or disabled, the result is a new dynamic balance among personality, competencies, and goals, with each of the three domains affecting the other two. These internal readjustments lead to changes in behavior patterns. For example, the awareness of one's mortality may lead to changes in personal or career goals, such that one may decide to "have a last fling" or to place less emphasis on achievement. Conversely, the same awareness of mortality may lead another individual to assume more serious and more demanding work or personal goals than in the past.

The dynamic balance among the domains can be even more complex. For example, physical changes (competencies) may affect self-concept (personality), which in turn may affect personal goals. This sequence of events may be reflected in changes in interpersonal style or life interests and activities. Also, the effects of midlife changes may be direct or paradoxical. For example, the awareness that one has limited time left to live may constrict one's attitudes and behaviors or may free one to try a wider range of alternatives.

To this model, which applies to both able-bodied persons and those with disabilities, must be added the impact of disability for the latter group. As indicated above, the disability may be either incurred at midlife or carried into the midlife period as an unresolved issue from earlier in life. In either case, the disability may be expected to have a special effect on midlife adjustment, both as a transition in its own right (from nondisabled to disabled status) and as an influence on other midlife transitions.

Typically, the onset of a disabling condition first directly affects competencies, and the effects then spread to personality and to goals (Hershenson, 1981). Thus, the transition from nondisabled to disabled status must be added to the transitions in physical changes of aging, sexuality, family role, and work role constraints that also have direct impact on competencies. Typically, the impact of disability is additive. For example, it is difficult enough to cope with the transitions of becoming an older worker, but is even more difficult to make the transition from being a younger, able-bodied worker to becoming an older, disabled worker. Similarly, with the spread of effect of the onset of disability, the realization that one can become, and indeed has become, disabled frequently intensifies concerns about one's mortality.

As noted above, however, on rare occasions the onset of a disability may facilitate or avoid another, more threatening midlife transitional issue. Thus, becoming disabled may save a person with strong dependency needs from having to assume the responsibility for care of an aged parent.

Thus, the onset of disability has a direct impact on the domain of competencies, which may simultaneously be affected by transitions involving physical aging, sexuality, family role changes, and work role constraints. The effect of the onset of disability has an impact on the domain of personality, which may simultaneously be undergoing changes in self-concept and awareness of one's mortality, and on the domain of goals, in which changes in personal or career goals may simultaneously be taking place, independent of the impact of the effects of the disability. Usually, the onset of disability involves an increased burden on the midlife transitional process, although in a limited number of cases it may present a preferable issue to some other issue that the person would otherwise have to face. Individual differences in prior life adjustment and current life situations, in the nature and impact of the disability, in coping style and resources, and in the specific midlife transitions the individual is simultaneously facing make it difficult to generalize further about the effects of midlife disability.

INTERVENTIONS WITH THE DISABLED PERSON AT MIDLIFE

The model proposed in this article suggests many guidelines for rehabilitation practice. Also, the rehabilitation counseling process offers some useful principles for assisting individuals to cope with a wider range of midlife transitions, including but not limited to the transition to disabled status. When the person disabled in midlife has been referred to, or is deciding to enter, the rehabilitation process, the counselor should encourage the client's adaptation both to the disability trauma and to perceived midlife issues. If the client cannot achieve adaptation to any of these concerns, then an overall rehabilitation goal of return to work or improvement in productivity will frequently not be reached. For most individuals their disabilities cause anxiety, anger, loss, confusion, and a strong uncertainty about the future. These factors, added to midlife concerns, could inhibit or actually prevent continued involvement in the rehabilitation process.

For this immediate goal of adjustment, we believe that a useful structure for rehabilitation counseling intervention is a modification of Cytrynbaum and Patrick's (1979) outline for the midlife transition, identified above. The intervention steps are presented below.

Reappraisal

This is a time of questioning and exploration. The initial or intake interview in the rehabilitation process provides an excellent opportunity for the counselor to assess the impact of the disability and midlife issues on the worker's personality, competencies, and work goals. It is also time to identify the client's residual strengths and work-related capacities, as well as to explore how the client coped with any previous transitions or trauma. Schlossberg (1984) stated that a successful transition during the midlife period depends on a balance between one's resources and deficits and also the degree of similarity or differences that one perceives about self and environment both before and after the trauma itself. The following case illustrates this point:

A 47-year-old lathe operator cannot return to his job because of an on-the-job injury, causing a right-hand amputation. The painful process of exploring new employment alternatives was eased because of a supportive family, an employer who encourages retraining, and the client's own confidence in his remaining capabilities.

During this reappraisal stage, the client should be encouraged to share any feelings of loss accruing from the disability and perceived midlife changes. We have observed in rehabilitation practice that most midlife concerns are not usually discussed by the client unless they are first identified by the counselor. The disability itself may be so emotionally overwhelming that any midlife changes are either denied or simply escape the client's awareness. The following case example illustrates this problem:

After experiencing many neurological symptoms, a 39-year-old, married woman and dance teacher was diagnosed as having multiple sclerosis. She was clearly saddened over her possible loss of earning power and over her loss of identity as a dancer. During the initial interview, she mentioned that her twin daughters were leaving next month for college in a distant state. Before the diagnosis, the impending absence of the girls was a source of considerable worry and loss, but the identification of her deteriorating health conditions overshadowed her already perceived losses.

The counselor's understanding of the possible influence of midlife issues on the disability could facilitate the client's attempts to tackle many associated adjustment problems.

Combined with the ventilation of losses and the exploration of the client's remaining competencies is the further necessity to identify the client's many needs. The following questions may be helpful in obtaining this identification:

- Does the client accept the need for change?
- Does the client recognize that the "old order" may not apply any longer?
- What does the client need to reevaluate work goals?
- What does the client need to change possible negative cognitions about self?
- What are the changes between the client's needs in the pretransition living and working environment from those in the now existing posttransition environment?
- What expectations does the client have for resuming family, social, and work relationships?
- What is the client's capacity for enjoying success?

Answers to these questions can offer information for the next step of intervention.

Remotivation

We believe that this is primarily a planning step, in which selected approaches are suggested, when necessary, to encourage the client to adapt to disability and midlife concerns and later to renew productive activity. Several of the barriers to occupational adjustment for the person with disability at midlife are self-imposed. Many clients believe there are very few job options available to them, or they have undergone a radical, unwarranted shift in thought regarding their time left to work. If the occurrence of the disability has also brought a personal confrontation with death or a drastic change in relationships to family (Jacques, 1955; Levinson et al., 1978), then a resulting, continued depression may inhibit any initiative to become a wage earner again. For these clients a number of strategies can be developed according to the following considerations.

Information

Information on the many options among work, career, educational, and community-related opportunities can be conveyed. These options are suggested with an emphasis on the client's residual competencies and the changing relationships and work goals that midlife and disability may introduce. The client's understanding of different choices, and even the possibility of career renewal, can bring hope and optimism. Encouraging the client to make a choice among selected options also generates for this client a sense of control over his or her future. The assessment phase of the rehabilitation process can emphasize the client's transferable skills and how work and living environments can be modified to accommodate new limitations.

Support Systems

It is necessary to identify those relationships among family, friends, and former work associates that can be used as sources of support in disability and midlife transition. The client needs to talk with someone about the changes that are occurring. Schlossberg (1984) explained that the opportunity to share confidences with family or with people in one's social network is an invaluable source of help in transition.

Coping Mechanisms

Those coping methods that have been called on in previous, important transitions should now be identified and realigned, when necessary, to this new transition. Because of the emotional impact of disability, clients may not be aware of what they did to deal successfully with an earlier, major change in their life. They may have sought more information, joined a self-help group for a short period, or become involved with distracting, self-satisfying activities. The usefulness of such coping strategies can be explored.

Setting of Realistic Goals

The formulation of rehabilitation goals and objectives should be based not only on sufficient evaluation information but also on the accuracy of the assessment of a client's needs in the context of disability and midlife issues. During the reappraisal stage of intervention, the client has the opportunity to identify personal needs. Now these needs can be reemphasized as the counselor helps the client to consider and to set vocational goals. Attention to these needs may demand, when writing the rehabilitation plan, intermediate rehabilitation objectives in personal problems, educational-vocational plans, and special areas of consideration (e.g., family, finances). This is illustrated in the following example:

> A 41-year-old waxing machine operator sustained severe burns when her machine exploded. After 16 months of medical treatment, she sought vocational rehabilitation services for possible reemployment. Assessment indicated that she had the mental capabilities for and interest in computer training. Evaluation also revealed a severe preoccupation with financial and self-esteem—related losses occurring from the disability, a radical change in the relationship to her husband because of facial disfigurement, and heightened feelings of uncertainty about whether she could undertake a formal training program with her physical limitations.
>
> Realizing that the client's life-threatening injury accelerated such midlife issues as the acceptance of her mortality, the recognition of biological limitation and health risks, and the possible restructuring of self-concept, the counselor, with the client's input, designed a rehabilitation plan that initially emphasized immediate, positive feedback from training and family and financial counseling. Before computer training was to commence, an educational program was arranged that had the possibility for bringing the client a sense of accomplishment. With family counseling, the client's sense of satisfaction became the foundation for a decision to recommit herself to relationships and to work goals.

Restructuring

This third intervention step implies that the client will actually begin to test the options suggested in the earlier phase of remotivation. Such testing involves letting go of past behaviors that are now detrimental to adjustment and taking a risk to explore new relationships and resources for growth. Again, the training stage of the rehabilitation process, when it is carefully structured for the client, can provide the opportunity for the client's later renewal and reintegration with work. During this step, clients also need the continued support of their counselor as well as further information.

SUMMARY

Midlife is one of the important and inevitable transitions during the life cycle. As do all transitions, it represents a process of change. The presence of a disability can contribute to the intensification of this experience. Attention and thoughtful intervention to midlife and disability concerns can set the stage for the client's participation in the rehabilitation process. The model and helping approaches suggested in this article put into a unified frame of reference the issues of midlife, the effects of disability at this time of life, and the interventions needed to deal with these factors.

REFERENCES

Age Discrimination in Employment Act of 1967, 29 U.S.C. § 621 (1984).

Baltes, P., & Danish, S. (1980). Intervention in life span development and aging: Issues and concepts. In R. R. Turner & H. W. Reese (Eds.), *Life span development psychology intervention* (pp. 49-78). New York: Academic Press.

Brim, O. (1976). Theories of the male mid-life crisis. *Counseling Psychologist, 6*(1), 2-9.

Brim, O. (1977). Theories of the mid-life crisis. In N. K. Schlossberg & A. E. Entine (Eds.), *Counseling adults* (pp. 1-18). Monterey, CA: Brooks/Cole.

Brim, O., & Ryff, C. (1980). On the properties of life events. In P. B. Baltes & O. G. Brim, (Eds.), *Life span development and behavior* (Vol. 3, pp. 368-388). New York: Academic Press.

Cytrynbaum, S., & Patrick, R. (1979, September). Mid-life development from a systems perspective. In S. Cytrynbaum (Chair), *Midlife development: Influence of gender, personality, and social systems*. Symposium presented at the meeting of the American Psychological Association, New York.

Erikson, E. (1975). *Life history and the historical moment*. New York: Norton.

Gilligan, C. (1982). *In a different voice*. Cambridge, MA: Harvard University Press.

Gould, R. (1978). *Transformations*. New York: Simon & Schuster.

Gutmann, D. C. (1977). The cross-cultural perspective: Notes toward a comparative psychology of aging. In J. E. Birren & K. W. Schaie (Eds.), *Handbook of the psychology of aging*. New York: Van Nostrand Reinhold.

Hershenson, D. (1981). Work adjustment, disability and the three R's of vocational rehabilitation. *Rehabilitation Counseling Bulletin, 2,* 91-97.

Jacques, E. (1955). Death and the mid-life crisis. *International Journal of Psychoanalysis, 46,* 502-514.

Levinson, D., Darrow, C., Klein, E., Levinson, M., & McKee, B. (1978). *The seasons of a man's life*. New York: Knopf.

Lowenthal, M., Thurnher, M., & Chiriboga, D. (1975). *Four stages of life: A comparative study of men and women facing transitions*. San Francisco: Jossey-Bass.

Neugarten, B. L. (Ed.). (1968). *Middle age and aging*. Chicago: Chicago University Press.

Norman, W., & Scaramella, T. (Ed.). (1980). *Mid-life: Developmental and clinical issues*. New York: Brunner/Mazel.

Schlossberg, N. (1984). *Counseling adults in transition*. New York: Springer Publishing Co.

Sheehy, G. (1974). *Passages*. New York: Dutton.

Sze, W. (Ed.). (1975). *Human life cycle*. New York: Jason Aronson.

Vaillant, G. (1977). *Adaptation to life*. Boston: Little, Brown.

Wortley, D., & Amatea, E. (1982). Mapping adult life changes: A conceptual framework for organizing adult development theory. *Personnel and Guidance Journal, 60,* 476-482.

11

Disability and Psychosocial Development in Old Age

Helen Q. Kivnick

During this century two important and far-reaching changes have affected our population of individuals aged 65 or older. First, this population has dramatically increased in number and in proportion of the total population. Second, the oldest segment of this population, those individuals over 75, has grown and will continue to grow far more rapidly than the aged population as a whole (Brody, 1985b). Members of this rapidly expanding group have consistently demonstrated significant levels of disability and dependency, using medical and health resources out of proportion to their numbers. They are likely to suffer from chronic conditions, and the normative physiological deterioration and debilitation of old age render them particularly vulnerable to long-term functional disability as a result of acute illness or trauma (Brody, 1981).

Researchers acknowledge the existence of a finite (or nearly finite) natural life span (Hayflick, 1977; Shock, 1960), and they recognize that the "older elders" of the present and foreseeable future are approaching this fixed, natural limit (Comfort, 1979; Fries, 1980). There remains, however, tremendous variability in the length of time before the onset of irreversible disability and dependence leading to death. Fries (1980) called for massive efforts to prolong this period of vigor and activity, compressing the inevitable disabilities of terminal, chronic disease into an increasingly brief senescence. Along these lines, Katz et al. (1983) developed a measure of *active life expectancy*, which predicts the number of years for which an individual of a specific age may expect to remain functionally healthy and independent.

In Fries's terms, within a finite overall life span both professionals and lay individuals must seek to prolong the period of active life expectancy, maximally postponing its termination and the concomitant onset of disability and dependence.

The author's research, discussed in this chapter, was primarily supported by Research Grant No. G008006801 from the National Institute for Handicapped Research.

This is precisely the task for which rehabilitation practitioners find themselves responsible in working with today's increasing numbers of aged individuals. Rehabilitation counselors and therapists strive to prevent or to minimize the functional handicaps and disabilities experienced by elderly persons as a result of impairments that may be either chronic or acute. That is, they work to improve and to maintain the optimal level of functioning of impaired older persons (Brody, 1985b).

But what is this optimal level? The tremendous variation among aged individuals in terms of habitual activities and accustomed roles suggests that evaluating functionality according to established norms or standards is grossly insufficient. These ambiguities often make it difficult for both therapist and patient to target appropriate disabilities for rehabilitation and to devise programs for effective rehabilitation. Although isolated psychosocial interventions often are employed to eliminate resistance to specific rehabilitation strategies (Greziak, 1979; Reagles, 1984), I believe that underlying psychosocial issues do, in fact, play a far more integral role in the rehabilitation of older persons. Consideration of life-cycle, psychosocial development can be useful, if not essential, in conceptualizing rehabilitation goals and objectives that are patient-specific, meaningful, and realistic.

LIFE-CYCLE THEORY

Life-cycle theory, as presented by Erikson and Erikson in 1950 and recently elaborated by Erikson, Erikson, and Kivnick (1986), regards a human life as comprising a series of eight successive stages, each of which is characterized by a focal psychosocial tension between two opposing tendencies. During each stage the individual ideally brings the focal tension into some kind of dynamic equilibrium to produce a particular developmental strength. These stages roughly correspond to chronological age and range from infancy, with its struggle to balance basic trust with mistrust to produce hope, through old age, balancing integrity with despair to produce wisdom.

At each stage the individual brings to bear on the focal tension the cumulative strengths that have been developed in earlier stages. In addition, however, at each stage the individual must continue to renew earlier strengths in an age-appropriate fashion and to preview or anticipate those psychosocial themes that have yet to become focal. The play-age child ideally balances the initiative and guilt in forging a rudimentary sense of purposefulness and creativity. These issues are not dealt with once and for all by the age of 5. It is a more mature purposefulness that enables an older woman, for example, to modify her long-time household and life-style to share her home with a young college student and to experience the security that such a living arrangement may provide. It is a renewed, age-appropriate creativity that prompts an older man to put his lifelong record collection on cassette tapes so that he can share them with his friends at the Senior Center without fear of breakage.

Throughout life the process of bringing a focal psychosocial tension into dynamic balance is largely unconscious and nonverbal. It is a product of the individual's vital involvement with the people, materials, ideas, and institutions that constitute the world in which the person exists. The process may be facilitated by discussion and thought. But the term *psychosocial* implies that at all stages in the life cycle, healthy development represents an interaction among the individual and his or her psychological dynamics, and the larger social world in which the individual is living.

According to life-cycle theory, the older individual seeks to develop a sense of personal integrity based on a core "self" that has somehow lived through all of earlier life, while also acknowledging the despair that is a realistic product of so many aspects of old age. Despair may result when the individual loses the capacities of earlier years and when he or she suffers impairment that seems to lead, inevitably, to disability and handicap. It may ensue as the individual begins to lose the friends and familiar routines of a lifetime. It may engulf those who confront unfortunate consequences of earlier decisions. It may be an understandable response to facing death as an event that can no longer be relegated to the distant future. The person who is able to reconcile this appropriate despair with a sense of integrity will begin to develop the wisdom that life-cycle theory describes, ideally, as emerging mature in the final stage of life.

DISABILITY AND DEVELOPMENT IN OLD AGE

In the terms discussed above, this final process of reconciling integrity with despair must involve the older person in integrating the psychosocial themes of earlier life in a new age-appropriate fashion. The reciprocal influence between this old-age psychosocial process and rehabilitation-related notions of impairment, disability, and handicap (Brody, 1985a) is the subject of the remainder of this chapter. Specific examples are drawn from the life experiences of 29 individuals (hereafter referred to as interviewees) whose current ages range from the early 70s through the middle 90s. These persons have been interviewed for the Guidance Study (Eichorn, Clausen, Haan, Honzik, & Mussen, 1981) since 1928, and from 1981 to 1983 they participated in two-session interviews with Erikson, Erikson, and Kivnick.

Trust and Mistrust

In its earliest form this tension involves the infant in a struggle between trust and mistrust in the stability and predictability of the world as perceived through the senses. Adequate, early integration results in the establishment of a rudimentary sense of hope, related to the individual's lifelong relationship with established religion. In later life, reconsidering this theme in terms of a lifetime of experience optimally leads the older person to a mature sense of faith.

Physical health and impairment constitute an arena in which the interviewees struggle to reestablish an appropriate balance between basic trust and mistrust. Senses whose acuity has become impaired no longer provide wholly trustworthy information about the world outside. Generalized debilitation or arthritis can make cleaning a cottage seem like cleaning a mansion even to a man who has lived in and cleaned the same cottage for the past 15 years. Such physiological impairments may contribute to an unfamiliar sense of mistrust in the world and the future. Many interviewees rely on a lifelong hopefulness to counter these dystonic feelings, optimistically asserting, "I've always muddled through whatever came along, and as long as I can do it my own way, why I guess I'll do like I've always done." Many also express religious faith that somehow everything will be all right—with themselves and with the world. In general, they draw on the hope and trustfulness of a lifetime as they struggle to live with maximum vitality despite chronic impairment and disability.

Instead of dwelling on current disabilities, which are a source of fear and sorrow, some interviewees recall earlier experiences of disabilities they have overcome. One octogenarian who, as an impoverished young mother, nearly died after months of being bedridden and unable to care for her children, speaks glowingly of the doctor who saved her without consideration of payment. Only in passing does she mention the ulcerous condition for which she has undergone surgery twice in the past few years or that after the most recent surgery she found herself dizzy and unable to walk unassisted for weeks.

Few, if any, of the interviewees directly verbalize fear or mistrust when discussing their own bodies. Particularly among those individuals for whom mistrust has been most prominent throughout life, such feelings seem to be expressed during old age in terms of blaming and mistrusting the physicians and other professionals (e.g., lawyers, clergy) on whom they must now rely. A 95-year-old who was not expected to survive any of several childhood diseases speaks with contempt and suspicion of the specialists who fitted her hearing aid, set her broken arm, and treated her recent bout with the flu.

Autonomy and Shame and Doubt

The tension between autonomy, on the one hand, and shame and doubt, on the other, has to do with very early issues of control over one's own body, one's own behavior, and, in a larger sense, one's own life. Once, as a toddler, the individual has established basic control over sphincter and skeletal muscles, he or she spends a lifetime struggling to maximize willfulness while expressing discriminating self-restraint. Issues of independence and helplessness remain connected with the body, and they resurface throughout life in times of bodily damage (e.g., illness or injury) and other forms of bodily change (e.g., pregnancy).

Old age, with its decreasing physical prowess and increasing likelihood of physical impairment, is such a time of bodily change. Psychosocial health demands that the old person somehow acknowledge and adapt to changing capacities, requirements, and strengths. The interviewees find themselves having to alter body images to accommodate arthritis, canes, walkers, wheelchairs, amputations, prosthetics, and visual and hearing aids. They must tolerate the shame they inevitably experience at being incontinent, at responding to a misheard remark in a conversation, or at forgetting the topic of a discussion. In the face of disabilities that realistically threaten independent living, which they prize highly, most of them seek to encapsulate their impairments. They strive to substitute available behaviors for those they can no longer manage. They struggle to rely on themselves to the maximum extent possible.

The interviewees rather proudly describe themselves today as stubborn, self-reliant, defiant, and uncompromising. For most of them this is an accurate description of current behavior and a reflection of a lifelong sense of autonomy. For some, however, these proud assertions seem to represent a desperate attempt to retain a sense of autonomous self-directedness after having behaviorally almost surrendered to helplessness. One woman insists that constant pain and chronic anemia do not prevent her from entertaining when she chooses to see friends. Subsequent conversation, however, indicates that she has not felt able to prepare even a simple meal for herself and her husband for over 1 year.

To the extent that the older person is able to retain some control and to compensate for various losses of control, a dynamic balance between shame and autonomy can be maintained. He or she must learn to accept appropriate assistance as a supplement to and a facilitator of personal will, rather than as a threat to or substitute for independence. The essence of integrity is not to deny the shame and diminished self-reliance that result from disability but it is to reconcile shame and autonomy anew as a basis for minimizing disability and maintaining a realistic sense of individual willfulness.

Initiative and Guilt

The play-age child struggles to balance a sense of boundless, energetic activity with an opposing sense of anxious guilt over the consequences of such activity. Driven by curiosity and by a sense of personal expansiveness, the playing child engages in exploration and experimentation and, ideally, develops a robust sense of purposefulness. In old age the individual seeks to maintain this sense of playfulness and assertive involvement with the world in the face of muscular, skeletal, and sensory impairment and despite social circumstances that often mitigate against such involvement. The older person strives to pursue the curiosity and imagination that are now tempered by a lifetime of experience and learned moderation. This theme is the basis for activities having to do with creativity and recreation.

Reworking initiative and guilt in old age requires ongoing participation in a diversity of activities. Adequate old-age reintegration of this tension is therefore especially closely related to the impairments that may interfere with various forms of activity. The older person finds himself or herself challenged to let go of some accustomed activities and forms of direct, assertive exploration without experiencing the intolerable guilt and frustration that prevented voluntary inactivity earlier in life. The older person is simultaneously challenged not to let go of too many activities without substituting new involvements.

Some interviewees seem to draw, quite naturally, on lifelong purposefulness. One woman, for example, relinquished the family farm after her husband's death, recognizing that she could not adequately care for its acreage on her own. She maintains a backyard garden, however, and takes a long walk every morning and evening "... to stay in touch with the sun and the stars." A man uses his now-diminished energy as an excuse to concentrate on those activities that are of most personal importance, explaining, "If I tried to keep this place tidy like my wife did I wouldn't have the energy to prepare for my classes at the Center."

For older people whose lifelong sense of initiative has been less robust, relatively minor disabilities may trigger massive disinvolvement. One woman has abandoned golf, lawn bowling, and gardening because of an ankle sprained over 1 year ago. Another gave up her lifelong avocations of piano playing and oil painting at the first sign of intermittent back pain 20 years ago. Neither of these women has taken up substitute activities; neither is involved in an ongoing program of rehabilitation. Both complain of boredom and frustration. Both of these women have allowed impairments to become major handicaps. For both of them, a lifelong psychosocial weakness or fragility seems to have been exacerbated by physiological impairment in later life.

Industry and Inferiority

The school-age child develops the capacity for mastering skills and procedures, tools and materials, facts and laws. The sense of diligent industriousness must be balanced, however, with that of realistic inferiority if the individual is to be capable of the genuine competence that is essential to healthy participation in the world at large. In old age, challenges to mastery and competence abound, threatening the older person with incapacitating feelings of inferiority. Skeletal, muscular, and sensory deterioration are likely to contribute to the realistic diminution of longtime skills that rely on physical strength, sensory acuity, and fine motor coordination. In addition, as older persons face the certainty of death and the terror of serious, permanent disability for themselves and their age mates, they must confront humankind's ultimate incompetence to conquer or master this final inevitability.

Somehow, in the face of these and other sources of inferiority, the older individual must renew an appropriate sense of competence. Such competence is likely to rest on finding arenas in which to demonstrate the skills, knowledge, and experience developed over a lifetime. It is also likely to be associated with the capacity for new learning and mastery and for vicarious satisfaction in the achievements of the next generations.

Many interviewees achieve maximum feelings of competence by narrowing their spheres of involvement and concentrating on remaining proficient (or developing new proficiency) in one or two specific arenas. A woman who has difficulty walking spends most of the time writing short stories and autobiographical vignettes. Another who can no longer lift her arms above her head passes the hours crocheting shawls and blankets for her institutionalized age mates. A third comments, "I used to be a very good cook. But now I just can't be bothered. All that bending and stretching, and that tiny type in those recipe books. If I were bored I might feel bad about letting it go. But I'm always leading this group or that group. I'm a docent at the museum. And I'm studying art history. That's enough for a little old lady."

Several of the interviewees control inferiority by revising their criteria for adequate accomplishment. For one man serviceability has assumed priority over perfection: "I couldn't make a living building tables like this, but it serves my purposes just fine." Others focus on the simple completion of tasks, one by one. A woman explains, "Today my job was to do the laundry, and I accomplished that so I feel satisfied."

Many older people take pleasure in directing others in activities of which they themselves are not capable. A woman is quite proud of the beautiful home she has just remodeled. "Of course I didn't do the actual work myself. But I made all the decisions and I instructed them every step of the way." Others are able to experience vicarious achievement in the proficiencies of children and grandchildren.

Identity and Identity Confusion

As a period of transition from childhood into adulthood, adolescence represents a time when the young person consolidates the developmental gains of childhood, clarifying the strengths and weaknesses developed so far and the goals toward which he or she will move in the future. In addition, the young person seeks to develop a sense of self comprising appropriate measures of consistency, conflict, and confusion. The older individual seeks to make sense of the self that has lived through many decades to understand how to continue to live in the present and also to prepare, as effectively as possible, for the as yet unknowable future. In comparing early hopes and dreams with life actually lived, the older person seeks to come to terms with the realities of his or her capacities in a unique context of uncontrollable life circumstances.

The interviewees take great pride in characterizing themselves as independent, self-confident, and self-reliant. Massive old-age disability, however, seriously challenges this aspect of lifelong identity. Many struggle, despite a wide variety of chronic, disabling conditions, to continue to demonstrate the qualities that are essential to maintaining lifelong identity. They may integrate realistic disability by modifying current descriptions of themselves as follows: "I'm as independent as I can be"; "I'm pretty darned self-reliant for a helpless old lady."

Disability seems to have fewer kinds of impact on interviewees' reinvolvement with issues of identity and identity confusion than with several other psychosocial themes. Their sense of lifelong identity, however, is extremely important in the ways they accept, master, and succumb to various forms of disability. Those who have thought of themselves all along as "feisty" and resilient, like the individuals quoted above, seem to be able to accept a measure of disability with integrity. In contrast, those who view themselves as lifelong victims seem to regard old-age disability as final confirmation of their victimization. Those who view themselves as perpetual failures seem to use current disability to explain this failure.

Qualities such as fragility, weariness, and helplessness were regarded as major liabilities when they emerged in earlier life, setting some individuals uncomfortably apart from their peers. The interviewees, however, seem to take for granted that older persons, themselves included, may be weak, tired, and unproductive. Because disability is so much a part of the stereotyped conceptualization of aging, many interviewees seem to be able to accept it in themselves without experiencing the despair that results from being identified as unpleasantly unusual.

Intimacy and Isolation

The intimacy of young adulthood rests on a maturing capacity for mutuality and reciprocity, that is, for commitment that involves sacrifice and compromise in sexuality, in play, and in work. An appropriately discriminating willingness (and also refusal) to compromise represents the essence of a dynamic balance between intimacy and isolation. In old age the individual must reconcile the sense of intimacy with that of appropriate isolation, in the context of relationships that have endured for many decades, along with those that are most recent. In closeness with people of all ages, long-established contact patterns and comfortable balances must give way to new ones—balances between caring and being cared for, between compromising and insisting, between collaborating and going it alone. Issues of genital potency arise here, as the sexual quality of long-intimate relationships undergoes age-related changes.

Friends whose intimacy has been based on sharing activities may suddenly find themselves needing to provide certain kinds of care, to make certain accommodations, simply to be able to have contact at all. A woman in her 80s who has had a leg amputated recalls,

> when I first moved up here I used to drive back to Vallejo all the time to see my friends. We'd play bridge or shop, or just have coffee like we always did. When I had to stop driving they would come here to see me. I'd make lunch or bake a nice cake. We'd go for a ride. But now I'm stuck in this chair. I never know a day ahead if I'll have the

energy to make a guest even a cup of coffee. And my friends are getting up in years, too. They can't just hop in the car and drive 2 hours all that easily. And how could we go out? It takes two strong young ones to get me into the car. I miss them all the time, but I don't blame them for not coming.

Some older persons in this kind of position have been fortunate in making new, often young friends who live nearby. Some have not, and they accommodate to new loneliness by relying on old friendships, nourished through letters and telephone calls or treasured in memories and photograph albums.

Generativity and Stagnation

The central challenge of the prolonged period of middle adulthood is to balance the capacities to care for and to be responsible for others with the opposing capacities to relax appropriately and to become absorbed in the self. The Hindus refer to the essence of adulthood as responsibility for "the maintenance of the world" (Erikson, 1982). The reconciling of generativity and stagnation in old age involves forms of caring and nurturing that exist largely beyond middle age's direct responsibility for the maintenance of the world. The social roles of aging parent, grandparent, consultant, adviser, and mentor all serve an important psychosocial function in this stage because they represent involvements in which the older person can express "postmaintenance" generativity.

In many ways, these are roles whose performance is not inhibited by the variety of impairments and disabilities that afflict older persons. With a few notable exceptions, although physiological disabilities have influenced the kinds of grandparenting behaviors, for example, in which interviewees can participate, these disabilities have not detrimentally influenced the quality of these people's grandparenting. The exceptions to this generalization are those individuals with serious cognitive and emotional disabilities and those who suffer from pervasive, chronic pain to such an extent that they do not seem to be able to attend to anything but their own suffering.

As a complement to active, age-appropriate caring for, the older person must also participate in being cared for age-appropriately. He or she must learn to accept the care that is required and that which is offered, in a way that is, itself, caring and that enhances the carer's own feelings of generativity. Particularly for the interviewees who have always insisted on being in charge, disability seems to enable them to engage in this "caring by receiving" in ways that would have been impossible in their younger, more able-bodied years.

Integrity and Despair

At the end of the life cycle, the individual participates in a final integration of the multifarious aspects of the self and life's choices and experiences. This integration must be reconciled with the despair that may emerge as a function of lifelong guilts and contradictions, inability to make amends, insufficient time to start over, powerlessness to alter the past, and inexorable deterioration as a prelude to inescapable death. A major part of this final integration involves reviewing all of the thematic tensions that were focal earlier in the life cycle and bringing these tensions into a dynamic balance that is appropriate to old age, as discussed above.

Many interviewees insist, "I don't feel old physically or mentally" or "I sometimes forget I'm old." They acknowledge that they have lived a long time. They recognize that they are at a chronological age at which their own parents or grandparents died. They complain of physiological impairments and disabilities. But they seem to engage in a kind of compartmentalization, in which admitting to feeling "old" would represent giving in to overwhelming despair.

CONCLUSION

In the process of reconciling each psychosocial theme for the last time, the older person is influenced by the disability that may prove to be a source of mistrust, shame, or guilt. For each theme, healthy psychosocial process requires that the individual accept these dystonic feelings and bring them into a new, somehow livable equilibrium with strengths. Thus, disability is an integral part of psychosocial development in old age. Disability plays a more complicated role, however, as a catalyst for psychosocial process and as the object of that process. Many old people are able to draw on lifelong strengths to prevent impairments from becoming disabilities and disabilities from becoming handicaps. Others succeed in encapsulating inevitable disabilities, in keeping them specific, and in compensating with other behaviors. Such resilient responses build on a lifetime of psychosocial strength, and they enhance essential syntonic tendencies in old age. For individuals whose lifelong psychosocial equilibriums are more fragile or brittle, however, disability in old age may prove to be a source of despair that, on a temporary or more permanent basis, may prove to be impossible to integrate.

I suggest that psychosocial intervention be viewed as more than a means of eliminating obstacles to rehabilitation (i.e., to the prevention and diminution of the disability and handicap that often result from old-age impairment). In addition to this legitimate role, it is suggested that practitioners consider psychosocial intervention explicitly as it promotes healthy psychosocial development in old age—and at all stages of the life cycle. Although such intervention may seem, at best, to be tangentially related to rehabilitation, my research strongly suggests that ongoing psychosocial resilience and vitality are essential strengths on which the older person must draw to limit the deleterious ramifications of impairments that are the inevitable result of acute trauma and chronic disease.

REFERENCES

Brody, E. M. (1981). "Women in the middle" and family help to older people. *Gerontologist, 21,* 471-479.

Brody, S. J. (1985a). Is rehabilitation a legitimate intervention for the elderly? Goals and expectations. In C. Gaitz (Ed.), *Aging 2000: Our health care destiny* (Vol. 1). New York: Springer Publishing Co.

Brody, S. J. (1985b). Merging rehabilitation and aging policies and programs: Past, present, and future. In D. Olson, C. Granger, & T. Byerts (Eds.), *Rehabilitation of the aged disabled.* Boston: Butterworth.

Comfort, A. (1979). *The biology of senescence.* New York: Elsevier Press.

Eichorn, D. H., Clausen, J. A., Haan, N., Honzik, M. P., & Mussen, P. H. (1981). *Present and past in middle life.* New York: Academic Press.

Erikson, E. H. (1982). *The life cycle completed.* New York: Norton.

Erikson, E. H., & Erikson, J. M. (1950). Growth and crises of the "healthy personality." In J. Milton (Ed.), *Symposium on the healthy personality.* New York: Josiah Macy Jr. Foundation.

Erikson, E. H., Erikson, J. M., & Kivnick, H. Q. (1986). *Vital involvement in old age.* New York: Norton.

Fries, J. F. (1980). Aging, natural death, and the compression of morbidity. *New England Journal of Medicine, 303,* 130-135.

Greziak, R. C. (1979). Aspects of rehabilitation psychology. *Professional Psychology, 10,* 511-520.

Hayflick, L. (1977). The cellular basis for biological aging. In L. E. Finch & L. Hayflick (Eds.), *Handbook of the biology of aging.* New York: Van Nostrand Reinhold.

Katz, S., Branch, L. G., Branson, M. H., Papsidero, J. A., Bech, J. C., & Greer, D. S. (1983). Active life expectancy. *New England Journal of Medicine, 309,* 1218-1224.

Reagles, S. (1984). Chronic pain: Principles for rehabilitation counselors. *Rehabilitation Counseling Bulletin, 28,* 15-27.

Shock, N. W. (1960). Mortality and measurement of aging. In B. L. Stehler, J. D. Ebert, H. B. Glass, & N. W. Shock (Eds.), *The biology of aging.* Washington, DC: American Institute of Biological Sciences.

Part II: *Developmental and Family Issues in Disability—Study Questions and Disability Awareness Exercise*

1. What are the similarities and differences between the loss associated with the birth of a child with a handicap as compared to the loss associated with the onset of a disability during the teenage years?
2. Discuss how the initial loss experience at birth may change over time.
3. Is the loss experienced by the mother and father of a child with a disability the same? Different? How?
4. In what way are the challenges faced by adolescents with chronic illness and disabilities different from those experienced by adults?
5. What are the major changes a person experiences during midlife and how are they affected when a person must cope with a disability?
6. What are the unique challenges faced by the older person experiencing a disability?
7. Is there a difference between the problems encountered by a person with a disability who becomes elderly as compared to an elderly person who becomes disabled?

RETURN UNOPENED

The parents of children with disabilities face difficult situations for which they are often not prepared and which they must frequently resolve alone. The process of problem resolution can be stressful, painful, and demanding on the family system as well as on the marital relationship. A child might become a source of conflict between the parents regarding the best approach to the child's future care.

Goals

1. To prevent the potential impact of a child with a disability on selected aspects of the marital relationship.
2. To involve participants in the exploration of their personal reaction to a specific situation.

Procedure

1. Participants read the following role description: "You are the parent of a two-week-old hospitalized child who is severely handicapped. You have not had the child home from the hospital. One spouse wants to put the child in an institution,while the other wants to bring her home."
2. When this is read, all members will write their responses concerning which position they would take and what they would do.
3. Having written the response, group members explore their reactions to this situation.

Part III

The Personal Impact of Disability

The personal response to disability, at any given time, can vary on a continuum from denial of its existence to exaggeration of its consequences. This response is dependent upon a number of variables, including environmental, social, and psychological characteristics of the respondent.

The relationship between disability and psychological adjustment is the theme of the twelfth chapter by Shontz. Six important principles that refute many commonly held beliefs about persons who are physically challenged are provided. Shontz concludes that "the understanding of psychological reactions to physical disability requires the understanding of individual human beings in all their complexity."

Several theoretical models have been proposed to describe the psychosocial phases of adjustment to disability. These models differ significantly regarding their origins, theoretical orientation, number of phases, and specificity. In spite of the wide divergence, Livneh, in Chapter thirteen, provides a unified model based on an extensive literature review of over 40 explicit and implicit stage models. His synthesis provides the rehabilitation theoretician and practitioner with a useful tool for understanding the reaction of persons to disability, and thereby assisting them with the emotional acceptance of and adjustment to life with a disability. In Part VI, Interventions, Livneh presents intervention strategies based on this unified adaptation model.

Denial plays a paradoxical role in a person's rehabilitation. On one hand, it impedes rehabilitation by impairing an individual from fully recognizing disability and its limitations. On the other hand, it motivates an individual to work on rather than give in to unacceptable limits. Naugle, in the final chapter of Part III, discusses both the motivating and inhibiting role of denial in a person's rehabilitation. The importance of the family in the adjustment process and the essential prerequisites of a therapeutic approach to counter the negative effects of denial are thoughtfully presented.

12

Six Principles Relating Disability and Psychological Adjustment

Franklin C. Shontz

Recently, I agreed to write a brief article summarizing the principles that describe the psychological aspects of physical disability and handicap. The article is to appear in a forthcoming professionally oriented encyclopedia, the readership of which will probably consist of physicians and psychologists who know little or nothing about the topic. My problem was to select the most important things that such a group should know. Although that task seemed impossible at first, I ultimately found that the mass of things that should be said were reducible to six general propositions.

The thought then occurred to me that the propositions might be interesting to people who are professionally identified with rehabilitation psychology, either for their own information or for presentation to others. At the very least, a public statement of the propositions should provoke discussion and stimulate their revision and improvement.

The first two propositions are confutative; they assert that some commonly held beliefs are false. These propositions describe stereotyped ideas that are not confirmed by systematically collected data; in fact, careful observation provides an ample supply of cases that clearly contradict the stereotypes. The other four propositions are affirmative. They assert relationships that are probably true, according to the best information and most authoritative opinion currently available.

To people who are familiar with the field of rehabilitation psychology, the propositions may seem to state the obvious. I hope so, for that will mean we agree on several most important points.

CONFUTATIVE PROPOSITIONS

1. *Psychological reactions to the onset or imposition of physical disability*

From *Rehabilitation Psychology,* 24(4) (1977), 207–210. Reprinted by permission.

are not uniformly disturbing or distressing and do not necessarily result in maladjustment.

A corollary to this is that *psychological reactions to the removal of physical disabilities are not uniformly or necessarily pleasant and do not necessarily lead to improved adjustment.*

Some consequences of physical illnesses and disabilities on behavior are direct and consistent; for example, completely severing the optic nerves blocks behavioral responses to visual stimuli. Properly speaking, however, direct consequences such as these are *effects of* rather than *reactions to* disabilities, and reactions are the only concern of this proposition. Though many efforts have been made to correlate disability with overall personality maladjustment, no systematic evidence has yet been published to show that reactions involving psychiatric disturbance occur any more frequently within a truly representative sample of people with disabilities than within the general population. In fact, overall personal adjustment improves when disability, or a handicap, solves life problems. The personality resources of an individual may be strengthened, not weakened, when the stresses that disability imposes are successfully managed.

The corollary to the first proposition is supported by reports that removal of physically disabling conditions sometimes increases guilt, anxiety, or maladjustment. Guilt may stem from the belief that one is unworthy, particularly in cases in which the beneficiary believes that personal benefit has been gained at the expense of the health or welfare of others. Anxiety arises when a recovered person is forced to face problems that never arose before or that could be successfully avoided during the period of disablement.

2. *Reactions (favorable or unfavorable) to disabilities are not related in a simple way to the physical properties of the disabilities.*

In massed data, studies of persons with physical illnesses suggest that, as a group, such persons show a tendency to experience heightened body anxiety and depression. However, these studies provide no reason to believe that such responses differ from what would occur under equally strong stress of psychological origin. Well-designed research, testing the relationship between degree or type of disability and strengths of personality traits or types of personality organizations, is practically nonexistent. What studies there are have produced no correlations of any appreciable magnitude or dependability. Knowledge of the type or degree of a person's physical disability provides virtually no information about that person's personality.

AFFIRMATIVE PROPOSITIONS

1. *The shorter and less complex the causal linkage between the body structure affected by disability and the behavior in question, the more predictable the latter is from the former.*

When a cause-effect network consists of physiochemical processes alone, the linkage is *direct* and predictability is high. For example, neurological damage usually has fairly consistent and predictable effects on reflexive responses.

When a cause-effect network concerns instrumental skills, such as dressing and ambulation, that involve learned components, linkage is less direct and predictability diminishes accordingly.

Cause-effect networks that affect emotional states are even less direct than those involving instrumental acts, so predictability is correspondingly lower. At this level, the analysis of the psychological aspects of disability crosses the line from being mainly concerned with the effects of disability to being mainly concerned with the person's reactions or adjustment to disability.

Finally, when the cause-effect network involves such complex matters as the meaning of disability in the total life situation of the person or the place of disability in the self-concept, predictability virtually disappears. At this level of analysis, with so many factors other than the body state are operative that correlation between disability is not only minimal but would be truly amazing if it occurred.

2. *The less direct the linkage between the body structure affected by disability and the behavior in question, the more appropriate it is to describe the influence of disability as facilitative, rather than as causal or coercive.*

The term facilitative implies that, while a disability may make one particular trait or type of psychological adjustment easier to adopt or more attractive than others, no disability requires any specific type of molar reaction. Suppose, for example, that a person with a spinal cord injury who can no longer engage in conventional sexual activities reacts by becoming bitter or despondent. Reactions like these are made more probable (i.e., facilitated) by the occurrence of spinal cord injury in a person of a certain age and sex who has certain ideas about the importance of sexual identity in the self-concept. But the reactions are not forced upon the person, they do not arise automatically, and they are not a direct product of the spinal cord injury. Teaching persons with spinal cord injuries to find new means to gain sexual satisfaction or intimacy often restores emotional balance, even though it does not remove or alter the physical disability.

3. *Environmental factors are at least as important in determining psychological reactions to disabilities as are the internal states of the persons who have the disabilities.*

Obvious illustrations of the meaning of this proposition are to be found everywhere in the adversities that architectural barriers impose on the mobility and the educational, vocational, and interpersonal adjustment of persons with disabilities. Barriers such as these contribute to the overall message often communicated to persons with disabilities that they are judged as inferior and will be kept that way. Maladjustment surely follows when someone accepts that judgment as accurate and fair. The effects of attitudes of devaluing pity or of stigmatization are more subtle but are equally important. These lead to the portrayal of persons with disabilities in the media either as miserable, suffering, helpless creatures whose greatest need is for charity or as supercourageous beings who deserve medals merely for traveling from one place to another or attending college. Anyone who is constantly exposed to such ideas about himself will find it extremely difficult to accept himself as a competent, worthwhile, normal person.

4. *Of all the factors that affect the total life situation of a person with a disability, the disability itself is only one, and often its influence is relatively minor.*

This proposition is stated affirmatively. However, it also confutes the commonly held belief that a physical disability is of necessity the most important thing in a person's life. When a disability interferes with, stops, or actually reverses psychological growth, it is a source of worry and concern. It may even lead to maladjustment; however, the forms that maladjustment takes among persons with disabilities do not differ from the forms it takes in others. By contrast, when a disability opens up opportunities for learning, challenges the persons to achieve successfully, in short, promotes ego growth, it is a source of growth and ultimate maturity.

This is the most important of the six propositions. It implies that, in the final analysis, the understanding of psychological reactions to physical disability requires the understanding of individual human beings in all their complexity.

A Unified Approach to Existing Models of Adaptation to Disability: A Model of Adaptation

Hanoch Livneh

The impact of a sudden physical trauma on an individual's life creates overwhelming physical, psychological, social, vocational, and economic effects. In the past, several theoretical models have been proposed to account for what is believed to be a series of psychosocial phases of adjustment to an adventitious physical disability. Foremost among the advocated models, often referred to as "stage theories" or "crisis theories" are those suggested by Blank (1957, 1961), Bray (1978), Cholden (1954), Cohn-Kerr (1961), Crate (1965), Dunn (1975), Falek and Britton (1974), Fink (1967), Gray, Reinhardt, and Ward (1969), Gunther (1969, 1971), Hohmann (1975), Kerr and Thompson (1972), Krueger (1981–1982), Krystal and Petty (1961), Lawrence and Lawrence (1979), Matson and Brooks (1977), Meyer (1971), Peter (1975), Roessler and Bolton (1978), Russell (1981), Shands (1955), Shontz (1965, 1975), Vargo (1978), Walters (1981), Weller and Miller (1977), and Whitehouse (1962).

Several of these authors have developed their theories based on their clinical impressions in dealing with a wide variety of disabling conditions. Others have attempted to suggest broader stage theories encompassing physical impairments in general.

A review of the above-cited and additional models (see References section) suggests that these models tend to differ in three major dimensions: (1) clinical-theoretical orientation, (2) nature of disability (e.g., suddenness of onset, degree of severity, degree of visibility, body part or function affected), and (3) number of stages suggested to account for the variability in human adaptation to disability process. Briefly, several of the models appear to be more concrete and specific in nature than others. They follow a clinical approach and place emphasis solely on stages observed in patients from actual hospital or rehabilitation setting. Behavioral indicators and client verbal statements often accompany each stage description (e.g., Blank, 1957; Bray, 1978; Dunn, 1975; Gunther, 1971; Matson & Brooks, 1977). In contrast, the other end of the continuum is represented by models that focus on more theoretical and abstract delineation of the stages. They utilize conceptual terminology and often refer to inferred psychodynamic processes and structures in their discussion of the different stages of adjustment. Generally, they do not base their stages on actual clinical or field-based data (e.g., Krueger, 1981-1982; Russell, 1981; Shontz, 1965, 1975).

The different models also address a wide variety of disability-related factors. A number of models depict crisis-type situations, in which the sudden, traumatic nature of the impairment is foremost (e.g., amputations, myocardial infarction, spinal cord injury). Other models describe stages of adjustment of disabling conditions of a more gradual nature (e.g., cancer, Huntington's disease, multiple sclerosis). Models also differ regarding the life-threatening nature of the disability (e.g., cancer or myocardial infarction versus blindness or deafness), the emphasis on the visibility or cosmetic effect involved (e.g., amputations, spinal cord injury versus deafness, cardiovascular diseases) and the specific body part(s) or function(s) lost or affected.

Finally, the models also reflect differential observations or inferences regarding the number of stages necessary to explain the process of adaptation. Several of the authors are content with the use of only a small number of stages—usually two or three—to explain the adjustment process (e.g., Blank, 1957; Cholden, 1954; Vargo, 1978). Others, comprising the majority of models, suggest from four to six stages (e.g., Cohn-Kerr, 1961; Dunn, 1975; Falek & Britton, 1974; Fink, 1967; Shontz, 1965). Bray's (1978) model includes a discussion of ten distinct stages presented under three broad phases of adjustment.

As can readily be seen from the previous discussion, no clear consensus has been reached among researchers and theoreticians concerning the nature of the adjustment process to physical disability. The major purposes of this chapter are: (a) to outline the implicit assumptions underlying the different models of adjustment to disability; (b) to suggest a unified model of adjustment to physical disability based on an extensive literature review of over 40 explicit and implicit stage models; (c) to analyze each of the stages of the proposed unified model as to its: (i) underlying defense mechanisms, (ii) affective correlates, (iii) cognitive correlates, (iv) behavioral correlates, and (v) direction of energy expanded; and (d) to compare the unified model to several existing models of adjustment to threat, loss and disability.

BASIC ASSUMPTIONS SHARED BY "STAGE MODELS"

1. The onset of a traumatic event has a sudden, unexpected, and massively extensive effect on the person's life (Gunther, 1971).

2. In order for an adjustment process to be implemented, the trauma should result in permanent, significant, overt, and perceptually undeniable changes in the body or its functions (Gunther, 1971).

3. In order for the individual to adapt to an altered body, including imposed physical limitations, certain changes are expected in his or her body image, self-concept, and personal identity (Gunther, 1971).

4. The adjustment process, as the term implies, is not a static but a dynamic and ongoing process. Adjustment, or adaptation as it is often referred to, is also considered to be the final positive outcome of this process (Kahana, Fairchild, & Kahana, 1982).

5. The impact of a sudden physical disability creates alterations in the individual's psychological equilibrium. A state of disequilibrium results with gradual attempts at achieving a renewed equilibrium. The attainment of a new psychological equilibrium is equivalent to the so-called final adjustment, adaptation, reorganization, or reintegration.

6. Normal adaptation to misfortune involves a temporal sequence of psychosocial development stages.

7. The initiation and progression of the stages of adjustment to disability occur rather automatically. The sequencing of these stages and the transition from one stage to the next seem to be internally triggered.

8. Most, if not all, stages in the process of adjustment to disability are transitional and temporary in nature.

9. Success in transitioning through the different psychosocial stages of adaptation produces increased psychosocial growth and maturity (Shontz, 1980).

10. The universality of the stages of adaptation is underscored by human variability and uniqueness. Although *most* people experience *most* of the stages, not *all* people will exhibit *all* of these stages.

11. The process of adaptation to disability is not irreversible. Although there exists a theoretically ordered sequence of stages, individuals experiencing these stages, under certain and not always understood circumstances, may regress to presumably earlier stages, "get stuck" in a certain stage for long periods of time, or pass through a particular stage with only a transient experience (Gunther, 1969).

12. The process of adaptation does not necessarily consist of discrete and categorically exclusive stages. The stages may fluctuate, blend, or overlap with one another (Gunther, 1969). A person may be, at one specific point of time, at more than one stage, and may even experience several reactions daily (Dunn, 1975).

13. Any attempt to capture the stages or the entire adaptation process in specific time references is futile at best. Most stages may and do fluctuate in their length as a result of individual differences. These fluctuations may

extend from short-time (hours, days) to long-time (months, years) periods.

14. Not all individuals who become disabled reach the theoretical end point of the adaptation process, the so-called "final adjustment." Many will be "stuck" at a certain phase along the adaptation continuum.

15. Each stage of adaptation includes certain potentially observable or inferred correlates. These correlates may be classified into three major domains: affective—the specific feelings and their level of intensity reflective of each stage; cognitive—the mental operations and thought processes inherent in each stage; and behavioral—the observable, bodily or verbal, activities in which the person engages at the time.

16. The content (feelings, thoughts, behaviors) manifested in these stages of adaptation is only descriptive in nature. It is not meant to reflect value-laden perceptions. The correlates used to better portray these stages are not "good" or "bad"; they are offered only in a descriptive, clarifying context.

17. Defense mechanisms and coping strategies are not one and the same (Krueger, 1981-1982; Verwoerdt, 1972); defense mechanisms operate to avoid anxiety or psychic pain and are usually overutilized early in the adaptation process in relation to internal wishes and needs. Coping strategies, on the other hand, involve methods of adaptation to the physical and social environments and are utilized, in general, relatively late in the adaptation process.

18. Although the ensuing series of adaptation phases is self-triggered (see assumption #7), appropriate external interventions at different points in time, in the form of psychosocial, behavioral, or environmental interventions, may positively affect the nature, ordering or coping mechanisms adopted to negotiate these stages. As such, they are important in helping the disabled individual to better master the physical, psychosocial, and behavioral limitations imposed by the impairment.

STAGES OF ADJUSTMENT TO PHYSICAL DISABILITY

The present section suggests a unified model for conceptualizing the process of adjustment to physical disability (see Figure 13.1). The stages included and discussed are as follows:

I. Initial impact. This stage includes two substages: (1) shock and (2) anxiety.

II. Defense mobilization. This stage includes two somewhat similar components: (i) bargaining and (ii) denial.

III. Initial realization or recognition. The third stage is also subdivided into two parts: (i) mourning and/or depression and (ii) internalizing anger.

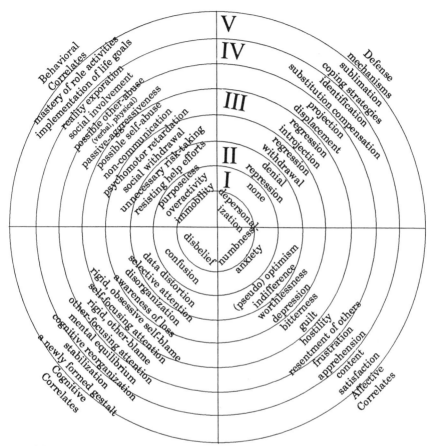

I. Initial impact: (1) shock, (2) anxiety
II. Defense Mobilization: (1) bargaining/denial
III. Initial realization: (1) mourning/depression, (2) internalized anger
IV. Retaliation: (1) externalized anger
V. Reintegration: (1) acknowledgment, (2) acceptance and final adjustment

Figure 13.1   Unified Model of Adjustment to Disability

IV. Retaliation or rebellion. The present stage is comprised of one major category including both direct and indirect methods of externalizing anger and aggressiveness.

V. Reintegration or reorganization. This final stage is composed, in essence, of three separate substages: (i) a cognitive substage (acknowledgement or reconciliation), (ii) an affective substage (acceptance or assimilation), and (iii) a behavioral substage (final adjustment, adaptation, or reconstruction).

The stages included in the above model are addressed by most, but not all, models reviewed. Also, their temporal ordering seems to reflect a general consensus among the majority of stage models considered. On the other hand, the defense mechanisms associated with these stages appear to be referred to in only a small number of the models. As expected, these references are strongly psychoanalytic in their approach (see for example, Castelnuovo-Tedesco, 1981; Krueger, 1981-1982; Siller, 1960; Verwoerdt, 1972; Yorke, 1980).

INITIAL IMPACT

The first stage in the process of adaptation to a physical disability depicts the individual's first reaction to encountering: (a) a sudden, severe, and unexpected physical (bodily) trauma (e.g., spinal cord injury, limb amputation, myocardial infarction) or (b) a sudden and seemingly unexpected onset of life-threatening disease (cancer, multiple sclerosis, Huntington's disease). Initial impact encompasses two separate substages—shock and anxiety.

Shock

Immediately following the onset of a sudden and overwhelming physical insult or the notification of contracting (becoming aware of) a life-endangering disease, the individual lapses into a psychic shock (Cholden, 1954; Krystal & Petty, 1961; Shands, 1955).

Defense mechanisms utilized

None. Theoretically, the psychic shock is a predefense mobilization stage. The individual has not experienced the surging panicky affect that later results in the adoption of defense measures, nor has he or she cognitively grasped the seriousness of his or her present condition. In reality, however, depersonalization—a seldom-used defense mechanism—is being called on to stave off a vaguely sensed, but overwhelmingly burdening reality (Blank, 1957; Cholden, 1954). The main function of depersonalization, operating as an emergency and generalized protective anesthesia, is to defend the self against anxiety and dissolution (Blank, 1957, 1961; Krystal, 1961; Krystal & Petty, 1961).

Affective correlates

The following emotions (in essence lack of emotive responsiveness!) are associated with this stage: numbness, bluntness, detachment, and emptiness. Blank (1961) comments that the patient feels unreal and that the world, too, seems unreal. The recently injured person is dazed, confused, and stunned. All of these reactions signify a shallow, vague, and emptied-out affect (Gunther, 1969, 1971).

Cognitive correlates

The thought processes during this stage are slowed down and characterized by disbelief, frozen psychological functioning, disorganization (Fink, 1967; Gunther, 1969), confusion, disorientation, thought disintegration and chaotic disruption, impaired concentration, a sense of loss of reality, alienation from one's self, or even loss of consciousness, all of which suggest an attempt at preoccupation with inner processes (Gunther, 1971; Shands, 1955).

Behavioral correlates

The experience of shock results in an activity standstill. The affected person appears immobile, stuporous, unresponsive, and apathetic. Blank facial expression, meager speech, or even mutism are often accompanying occurrences (Blank, 1961). A resemblance to catatonic type behavior is often noticeable (Blank, 1957). It is as if the self's executive functions broke down (Weller & Miller, 1977). This loss of self-control and ego-constriction are manifested in an almost reflexive withdrawal of interest in the environment (Cholden, 1954).

Energy direction

While in the shock stage, the individual's energies are summoned to preserve the self from dissolving under the bombardment of overwhelming and painful stimuli. The self is called up to react under extreme emergency conditions, and the energy is, therefore, directed inward to salvage the self from disintegration.

Anxiety

Following the protective psychic shock, the individual is gradually exposed, at least partially, to converging and painful sensations associated with the traumatic event. The self reacts in a panic-stricken fashion. The individual is unexpectedly confronted with his or her own mortality (Bray, 1978).

Defense mechanisms utilized

None. The anxiety stage is the precursor to mobilization of defense mechanisms. In other words, when the individual is still in this stage, no defense mechanisms are yet marshalled to reduce anxiety. The psychological defenses operate at the self's command to ward off unmanageable levels of anxiety.

Affective correlates

The major emotion triggered in this stage is, as expected, anxiety or panic. Hysteria-like symptoms are characteristic of such a response (Weller & Miller, 1977).

Cognitive correlates
Similar and continued manifestations of the confused thinking of the shock stage
are evident. Normal coordinated thinking is disrupted (Fink, 1967), and the person
lacks the ability to plan, reason, or understand. Cognitive flooding and disorganization are typical reactions (Shontz, 1965, 1975).

Behavioral correlates

Behaviorally, the panic-stricken individual appears purposelessly overactive, irri-
table and distraught (Falek & Britton, 1974). Various somatic complaints, including breathlessness, choking sensations, and rapid speech and pulse rate, are
observed. The person presents a helpless picture of himself or herself.

Energy direction

Because the anxiety stage is reflective of the person's reaction to threat of self-
preservation, energies, as in the previous stage, are internally directed to protect
the wounded self. At this time, also, the first intellectual activities are being initiated towards relieving anxiety and reestablishing the lost equilibrium (Falek &
Britton, 1974).

DEFENSE MOBILIZATION

The next stage in the adaptation process is that of regrouping defenses to combat
the trauma's devastating initial impact. This stage is composed of two somewhat
overlapping substages, which nevertheless maintain their own unique characteristics under most conditions. The substages are: bargaining, often termed "expectancy of recovery," and denial. Due to their overriding similarities, the two will be
discussed jointly, after a brief description and comparison of their main features.

Bargaining signifies a reaction through which an individual attempts: (a) to
negotiate a deal with God or someone more tangible (e.g., dead parent) regarding
the obliteration of his or her physical impairment in the case of a chronic, irreversible disability. The content of this negotiation resembles a contract between the
individual and the all-powered entity to reverse the present stage of affairs in response to a promise to atone and correct one's own by seeking second or multiple
opinions, or by visiting numerous medical experts. The main feature of bargaining
is, therefore, the person's expectancy of ultimate recovery through restitution
agreement (Bray, 1978) or protest (Fitzgerald, 1970). Denial, similarly, also includes the element of expecting to recuperate. Here, however, the individual seems
to have abandoned the deal-making and protesting overtures and instead retreats
from the painful realization of the disability and its ensuing concomitants.

Two additional points may further help to differentiate between the bargaining and denying reactions. Whereas bargaining is usually short-term in nature, denial may extend over a long period of time. Secondly, the two also differ with

regard to the extent of the defensive retreat employed. Bargaining involves a relatively moderate level of suppression of the impaired physical condition and its consequences. Denial, on the other hand, implies a more extensive level of suppression or negation of the disability and its ramifications in order to maintain self-integrity.

Defense mechanisms utilized

Underlying bargaining and denial are obviously the defense of denial and also repression, suppression, isolation (of affect), undoing, and to a lesser extent rationalization and intellectualization. The purpose of these defenses is to refuse, reverse, or cancel out the negative affect associated with the traumatic event by removing it from awareness or putting it "out of existence" (Niederland, 1965), or to control, depreciate and redefine its implications (Kiely, 1972; Krueger, 1981–1982; Weisman, 1974).

Affective correlates

During the defense mobilization stage, the person usually appears to be hopeful and (pseudo) optimistic (bargaining). Similar reactions are also manifested while resorting to denial. Examples of feelings pointing to denial, recited in the literature are: carefree, cheerfulness, placidity, aloofness, indifference, and nonchalance (Hackett & Cassem, 1974; Weller & Miller, 1977). Others have reported a sense of emotional relief and unrealistic euphoria (Fitzgerald, 1970; Shontz, 1965), happiness and joy (Parker, 1979) in addition to feeling content, pleased, and satisfied. These reactive measures, which act as a protective mechanism against the individual's real but submerged feelings of anxiety, are not always successful in their defensive mission. Periodically, when the adopted defensive measures fail or temporarily allow penetration of painful reminders from reality, the person may suddenly flare up in anger, collapse into despair (Weller & Miller, 1977), or become negativistic and suspicious (Whitehouse, 1962).

Cognitive correlates

As a rule, denial involves attempts at escaping any information or data that may act as reminders of reality. These efforts take the form of harboring hopes for recovery, insisting that the recovery will be complete and awaiting miraculous medical cures or divine interventions (Gunther, 1969, 1971). Common to all these beliefs are active, rigid, and deliberate cognitive processes that strive to protect the self from the flood of neighboring painful emotions (Weller & Miller, 1977). It is a selective attention–inattention deployment process that distorts factual events through minimizing, ignoring, forgetting, avoiding, denying, suppressing, and repressing unacceptable realities (Kiely, 1972).

Behavioral correlates

Numerous examples of behaviors and activities suggestive of bargaining and denial have been observed. Briefly, some of the more prominent ones are: seeking constant information, continuously consulting medical experts, contracting with God (as indicative of bargaining), taking unnecessary risks, setting unrealistic goals, refusing to accept information regarding the nature of the disabling condition or its implications, not comprehending what has been said (Falek & Britton, 1974), having unrealistic expectations for drugs or surgical techniques (Dunn, 1975), resisting and rejecting staff efforts (Hohmann, 1975), resisting home remodeling, removal of architectural barriers, or insisting on recovery of lost mobility functions in spinal cord injured persons (Krueger, 1981–1982), refusing to meet other patients, attempting to continue previous activities, holding to past life routines and values, and refusing offers made by others to help (Matson & Brooks, 1977), unwillingness to participate in rehabilitation activities, depreciating immediate tasks and problems as unimportant (Gunther, 1971), and resisting or evading future planning (Mueller, 1962). The persistence of denial is also evident in dreams, phantom pain, and daydreaming (Krueger, 1981–1982). When defensive shielding is threatened or temporarily collapses, behaviors may take the form of overcompensating for deficiencies, lashing angrily at staff and family members, or acting resentful when attempts at help are made.*

Energy direction

When the individual with disability enters the bargaining/denial stage, energy shifts its course and is directed toward the outside world. This process is quite evident in the countless efforts made to act "as if" nothing has happened and no physical limitations have marred the individual's functioning level (Wright, 1960). The person's energy is directed externally toward preventing the outside reality from penetrating through the self's defensive shield.

INITIAL REALIZATION

The period of initial or partial recognition of one's disability is one of great emotional turmoil and ambivalence. The reality of the traumatic events and their future

---

*A point should briefly be made regarding the nature of the denial mechanism. Denial, in essence, encompasses a variety of processes. Gunther (1971) and Krueger (1981–1982), for example, distinguish among three forms of denial: (a) denial of the continuing existence of the impairment; in other words, not acknowledging the permanence or irreversibility of the physical condition; (b) denial of the extent or the severity of the impairment of loss; and (c) denial of the consequences and implications of certain obligatory life adjustments. Discussion of several forms of denial is also offered by Crate (1965). For the interested reader, further discussion of the concept of denial is provided by Beisser (1979), Cassem and Hacket (1971), Hughes (1980), Krystal & Petty (1961), Levine and Zigler (1975), Lipp, Kolstoe, James, and Randall (1968), Nemiah (1964), and Weinstein and Kahn (1955).

effects on the person's life are now being processed and realized for the first time. Three reactions are evident: mourning (grief), reactive depression, and internalized anger.

Mourning and Depression

Mourning and depression are highly similar reactions, differing mainly in the positions they occupy on a temporal continuum. Whereas mourning, or grief as it is often called, is of short duration, depression is mourning of a lost body part or function extended over a longer period of time. A second feature that may help to differentiate the two, relates to their level of focusing. In mourning the focus is on the specific loss. In a sense, it is grieving of "what one once was, or had, that is no longer present." Depression, on the other hand, is of a more general and diffuse nature. The individual maintains bereavement not only of the loss of a body part or function, but also of its implications and consequences for the future. In other words, "what one once was, or had, that will never be" (see also Stewart & Rossier, 1978; Tucker, 1980). Psychodynamically, expressions of grief and depression are judged to be necessary prerequisites to future acceptance of loss and readaptation (Blank, 1961; Peter, 1975). This is accomplished through abandonment of the "old self" or of old adaptive mechanisms and the rebirth, reformation of a new self-image or the adoption of new, appropriate adaptive mechanisms (Blank, 1961; Shands, 1955; Wright, 1960).

Defense mechanisms utilized

The major defenses operating during this stage are withdrawal, avoidance, regression, and fantasy. Realizing, for the first time, the fate that has befallen him or her and experiencing a changed body, the grieving person withdraws or retreats into himself or herself, avoiding interpersonal contacts. This distancing tendency creates a certain protective buffer zone that helps the individual tune into his or her sense of loss without being unduly interrupted by physical or social environmental stimuli. As a natural consequence of the absence of outside stimulation, the individual tends to internally compensate for it by engaging in fantasy-like activities. These fantasies often evolve around the lost object or body part. Regression, which under these circumstances often operates as a protective mechanism, leads to the adoption of earlier and more childish forms of behavior, such as observed in dependent-like mannerisms.

Affective correlates

As the term implies, depression is an affective reaction whose main features include feelings of: sadness, worthlessness, helplessness, hopelessness, futility, despair, self-depreciation or aversion, inadequacy, insecurity, dejection, desolation, devastation, despondency, distress, discouragement, and self-pity. Clearly all of which reflect internal turmoil and turbulent awareness of a loss of a highly valued function.

Cognitive correlates

The salient feature characterizing the depressed individual is his or her awareness of the loss and resulting disability. The person has arrived at the point of recognizing the permanence, severity, extent, and consequence of the disability (Crate, 1965; Krueger, 1981–1982). At the same time, the burden of the depressive mood results in disorganized cognitive structure (Shontz, 1965) and concentration difficulties (Roessler & Bolton, 1978). The awareness of the loss of a sense of wholeness may be generalized and, therefore, threaten other symbolic losses in social positions (i.e., work, home, school) (Cohn-Kerr, 1961; Weller & Miller, 1977).

Behavioral correlates

The major observable features of a person who is in a state of mourning or depression are low energy level, psychomotor retardation, minimal and aimless activity, and somatic preoccupation (Cholden, 1954; Gunther, 1971). The depressed person is characterized by social withdrawal, turning away from others, resignation (to fate), passivity, and dependency (Bray, 1978). Introversion of interests or lack of interests in usual activities are noticeable (Falek & Britton, 1974). Episodes of weeping occur with regular frequency (Hohmann, 1975), sighing is frequently observed coupled with slouched sitting postures and head being covered. Suicidal ideation is often evident. Changes in daily activities, such as: sleep disturbances—both excessive sleeping and insomnia, eating disorders—loss of appetite often leading to weight loss, and speech difficulties—slowed and monotonous tone of voice, occur as well. When depression extends over long periods of time (several months or years), the individual's personal habits begin to deteriorate, as evidenced in unkempt personal appearance.

Internalized Anger

A related phenomenon observed in the stage of initial realization is that of inwardly directed anger. A disagreement seems to exist as to the temporal placement of depression, internalized anger, and externalized aggression. Several authors (i.e., Bray, 1978; Falek & Britton, 1974; Lawrence & Lawrence, 1979) view hostility directed inwardly as leading to internalized anger which, in turn, creates guilt and depression. Others, in contrast (Hohmann, 1975; Kerr & Thompson, 1972; Parkes, 1972), suggested that depression and internalized anger appear first to be projected outwardly; at a later time, in the form of hostility and aggressive behavior. To try and address the psychodynamics behind both approaches is beyond the scope of this chapter. It should be stated, however, that most models reviewed appeared to place mourning, depression, withdrawal, and internalized anger (a clear differentiation among these reactions is not always made) as antecedents to externalized anger or other-blame. Further discussion of the concept of self-blame and its anchoring within the adjustment to disability paradigm may be found in Atkins, Lynch, and Pullo (1982), and Wright (1960).

Internalized anger refers to a self-directed reaction associated with blaming self, and its ensuing guilt feelings regarding the onset of the disability or the resulting loss.

Defense mechanisms utilized

Operating behind this stage are the defense mechanisms of introjection (internalization) and regression. The introjection mechanism functions in such a manner as to find a reason behind the traumatic loss. Seeking self-blame can, then, turn into atonement and feelings of self-sacrifice (real or imagined). Regressive behavior may be viewed in this context as an attempt to control, manipulate, or depend on others (Herman, Manning & Teitelman, 1971).

Affective correlates

When hostility is directed inwardly, it ordinarily leads to feelings of self-blame, self-recrimination, guilt, and shame. The individual is described as being bitter, resentful, and easily embarrassed. In certain cases when the disability or loss, viewed as a punishment for sin or transgression (real or imagined), is perceived as being less than deserved, the person may still feel remorse and in need of further atonement.

Cognitive correlates

The theme of the disability or illness as a punishment or retribution for transgressions, usually against God, is most often encountered at this stage (Hohmann, 1975; Lawrence & Lawrence, 1979; Siller, 1976; Verwoerdt, 1972). This belief of committed wrongdoing is often followed by further vague suicidal thoughts (Krueger, 1981–1982). The individual's cognitive style is, therefore, characterized by focusing attention on self with concomitantly observed obsessive, narrow, and rigid thought processes (Kiely, 1972).

Behavioral correlates

The individual who perceives himself or herself as the cause of the misery is subject to self-abuse and self-injurious episodes. As was already noted, suicidal ideation and verbalization are also often present. Behavior may, in addition, be described as passive-aggressive (Bray, 1978), uncommunicative and withdrawn (Hohmann, 1975). When drawn out of his or her self-imposed silence, the person often appears argumentative. Lipbiting, facial twitching, and wriggly body movements are visible as well.

Energy direction

As the term implies, internalized anger refers to the process in which psychic energy is directed inwardly. The energy is utilized toward fueling the affective reservoir of self-recrimination, guilt, and shame. No conscious attempt is made to protect the self from the harsh realities of the external world.

RETALIATION

The stage of retaliation or rebellion against fate and perceived dependency and weakness is synonymous with externalized anger or overt hostility. The individual's anger is now projected onto the external world in the form of hostility (direct and indirect) toward other people, objects, or environmental conditions.

Defense mechanisms utilized

The defensive (actually offensive) reaction operating to foster most aggressive behavior is that of projection, often referred to as externalization, or acting out (Shontz, 1980; Verwoerdt, 1972; Weisman, 1974). The individual ascribes his or her undesirable feelings, thoughts, or actions to others, often blaming them for one's personal problems. A related defense mechanism often assumed to be operating at this stage is displacement. When adopting displacement, the individual is said to be transferring a negative affect from its originally targeted object (i.e., family member) to a less threatening or emotionally invested substitute (i.e., medical staff member). Finally, regression may be used as an added defensive reaction at this stage. When coupled with projection or displacement, it may trigger more passive ways of resistance, such as dependency, obstinacy or uncooperativeness.

Affective correlates

The externalizing individual is described as being hostile, aggressive, overtly bitter, resentful of others, and occasionally filled with rage (Bray, 1978; Falek & Britton, 1974; Vargo, 1978). These emotional reactions are indicative of the person's acting out of his or her frustrations onto the external world.

Cognitive correlates

The cognitive style manifested in this stage has been termed as vigilante focusing by Kiely (1972). Mental focusing, as discussed by Kiely, reveals rigidity of opinion, inflexibility in adaptation, doubtfulness, and skepticism regarding medical staff competence or concern (1972). Psychic energy is mobilized to fight off the threat that the disability or loss imposes (Lawrence & Lawrence, 1979). The themes of blaming others and retaliating against outside agents who are conceived to be either responsible for, or reminders of, the personal misfortune are notably evident. The person is protesting the blows and unfairness of a cruel fate or God (Verwoerdt, 1972; Weller & Miller, 1977) and the perception of being unjustifiably punished (Parkes, 1972, 1975). A major difference between reactions in this stage and those in the bargaining stage is the rebellious attitude that permeates the person's thought processes and behavior during the retaliatory phase.

Behavioral correlates

The behavioral manifestations of externalized anger are extensions of the person's affective and cognitive reactions. Two types of reactions may be observed: (a) a more direct and active way of expressing anger, and (b) a more indirect and passive one. Overt modes of hostility take the form of projecting anger directly onto the environment, blaming and accusing others (doctors, nursing staff, family members, friends, employers, etc.) for the loss, the resulting limitations, misdiagnosis, or prolongation of the disability through erroneous treatment (Crate, 1965; Gunther, 1969; Hohmann, 1975; Krueger, 1981–1982). The individual uses profane and abusive language and is quick to criticize (Mueller, 1962). He or she may even engage in directly assaulting or striking out at someone physically (Hohmann, 1975; Siller, 1969). When regressive tendencies are incorporated into such a reaction, temper tantrums and resistive and rebellious behaviors are observed (Mueller, 1962).

More covert and passive forms of externalized anger are portrayed by individuals who seem to be displacing their hostility. Their passive-aggressive methods include different modes of obstruction of the rehabilitation treatment programs (Weller & Miller, 1977). Other forms of rebellious behavior observed are manipulativeness, uncooperativeness, not taking medication, misinterpreting instructions (Siller, 1969), being provocative, demanding special privileges, acting impatiently, and testing staff patience and tolerance (Gunther, 1971).

Energy direction

As was observed, the defense mechanism or projection operates to act out unacceptable feelings and thoughts and focuses them on the external environment. Mobilized psychic energy is, therefore, utilized as a "fight" reaction (Verwoerdt, 1972) to any perceived threatening obstacle in one's path, be it a person (e.g., physician, spouse), an object (e.g., narrow door, stairs), or an intangible being (e.g., God, fate). The energy direction has shifted, once again, from the previous stage of internalized anger and the individual seems, at the present, to be approaching the readiness level necessary for tackling the multitude of obstacles created and posed by the external environment.

REINTEGRATION

The final stage in the adjustment process, that of reintegration or reorganization, may be conceived to include three separate substages. They are: Acknowledgement or Reconciliation, Acceptance or Assimilation, and Final Adjustment or Adaptation. Each of the three substages will be further defined and discussed.

Acknowledgement

The first substage of reintegration is characterized by the individual's intellectual recognition (reconciliation) of not merely the permanency of the impairment, but also of its future implications. These implications include: the physical, personal, social, familial, vocational, and economic ramifications of the disability (Gunther, 1969). The person begins to acknowledge changes in how he or she perceives himself or herself (Crate, 1965), seems to be gaining a new sense of self-concept (Weller & Miller, 1977), and approaches a stage of initial stabilization (Cogswell, 1976; Gunther, 1969).

Defense mechanisms utilized

The defenses that play a major role at this stage are identification, compensation, substitution, and, to a lesser degree, reaction formation and intellectualization. Intellectualization operates so as to render the individual more capable of cognitive mastering the threat of, what is perceived to be, a new identity. Its role here is, therefore, somewhat different than when operating at the denial stage, although the ultimate goal may be quite similar—to assist in mentally controlling a threatening or anxiety-provoking situation.

The defense mechanisms of substitution, compensation and sublimation (see following discussion) function similarly as a way to constructively master the threat (Verwoerdt, 1972). Reaction formation also serves as a compensatory device to substitute positive actions for lost skills (Shontz, 1980). All of these defenses are viewed as restitutive reactions by Siller (1960, 1969). Finally, the disabled person begins to identify with others who have similar problems (Crate, 1965). This identification serves the purpose of helping the individual toward acceptance of self as an individual with a physical impairment. It extends the person's acceptance of and feeling of pride in group achievements (Wright, 1960).

Affective correlates

Some of the emotions that surface during this stage are frustration (temporary in nature; Falek & Britton, 1974) and accompanying nervousness and apprehension associated with the planning of new life goals and the adoption of new values.

Cognitive correlates

The acknowledgement stage signifies the beginning of a new cognitive reorganization and equilibrium (Falek & Britton, 1974; Fink, 1967). The individual appears to be reaching a state of inner realignment and reorientation toward both self and the world (Resolution of loss [Lawrence & Lawrence, 1979; Verwoerdt, 1972]). In addition, following a process of self-confrontation (Matson & Brooks, 1977), previously held values are reappraised, life priorities begin to be reordered and rearranged, and new meanings are sought after and constructed.

Behavioral correlates

The acknowledging person shows a renewed encounter with and exploration of reality. This encounter is characterized by willingness to form new relationships and get socially involved with others—in both rehabilitation programs and outside of rehabilitation settings (Bray, 1978; Matson & Brooks, 1977; Walters, 1981; Yano, Alexander, & Kuwanoe, 1976). The involvement is portrayed by behaviors often described as compromising, yet active and assertive in nature (Bray, 1978). The initiation of the coping process is evident in such activities as goal setting, attempting to master new situations, and to obtain solutions to problems (Cohn-Kerr, 1961; Shontz, 1975; Yano, Alexander, & Kuwanoe, 1976). In other words, active steps to adjust to the person's new lifestyle and to cope successfully with the loss and resulting disability are tried out for the first time (Lawrence & Lawrence, 1979).

Energy direction

During the acknowledgement stage, the person seems to find, for the first time, a certain balance or reconciliation between his or her inner needs and the environmental demands. This stage, which reflects the beginning of approaching a renewed equilibrium, is, therefore, characterized by a balanced energy investment. Both internal (i.e., physical, psychological) and external processes (i.e., social, vocational) are invested with energy.

Acceptance and Final Adjustment

The final two substages in the adaptation process are emotional acceptance (assimilation) of the disability and adjustment (successful reconstruction) to life with a disability. Following the cognitive reconciliation (acknowledgement) with the permanency of the disability and its implications for future plans and goals, the individual is further prepared to assimilate, affectively, the ramifications of the disability as pertaining to his or her new and evolving self-concept (acceptance). When this task is completed, the person with a disability has reached the final phase of the coping process. This final phase is characterized by behavioral adaptation and social and vocational integration into the outside world (successful adjustment). Although in theory these two substages—acceptance and adjustment—may be differentiated from each other, in actuality, their similarities outweigh their differences. The discussion that follows pertains, therefore, to both substages equally.

Defense mechanisms utilized

None. It is the premise of the present chapter that the final phase of the adaptation process (the substages of acceptance and adjustment of the reintegration stage) is free of defense mechanism utilization with the possible exclusion of sublimation (see discussion by Haan, 1963; Kroeber, 1963). Although compensation and substitution in addition to sublimation may still be recognized to operate at this time, their use is only rudimentary in nature. For all practical purposes the person with disability who has reached this level of coping does not resort, or need to resort, to the use of defense mechanisms beyond the possible and occasional need to handle normal daily life stresses. The distinction between defense mechanisms and coping strategies, alluded to in the present context, is discussed by Haan (1963) and Kroeber (1963).

Affective correlates

The individual with disability, at this level, feels positive, satisfied, content, and confident in himself or herself. The emotional reactions may be viewed as reflective of a restored and positive self-worth (Fink, 1967; Parker, 1979; Shontz, 1965; Verwoerdt, 1972). Self-approval and self-acceptance are evidence in daily activities (Siller, 1969; Vargo, 1978). The person is, therefore, more able to live with his or her disability, viewing it as a not-to-be-denied but containable obstacle to overcome.

Cognitive correlates

The thought processes, at this junction, mirror the emergence of a new personal identity of a newly formed gestalt (Bray, 1978; Shontz, 1965). The individual has explored and assimilated new meanings in life, identified and reviewed new goals and tasks, and reordered old ones (Roessler & Bolton, 1978). The cognitive structure (e.g., thinking, planning, coordinating) is already stabilized and reorganized at this point (Fink, 1967; Shontz, 1965), a fact that renders the task of concentrating on emotional assimilation easier. The person recognizes his or her imposed physical restrictions, but also realizes the remaining or newly discovered potentialities (Krueger, 1981–1982; Verwoerdt, 1972) as well as the need for a mutual accommodation of both personal and environmental experiences (Shontz, 1975).

Behavioral correlates

The attention of the adapting individual is directed toward a variety of domains. Blank (1957) suggests a need for problem solution in the social, mobility, and vocational areas. Gunther (1971) recommends the mastery of social, familial, and work-role activities as the most crucial ones. Dunn (1975) sees the person as adapting physically, socially, and psychologically. Finally, Hohmann (1975) views home, work, and education as the major domains of activity at this phase. It is, therefore, evident that the final stage of adaptation is characterized by testing out different living environments (e.g., home, work, community). This period is seen as an attempt to implement specific goals and objectives, satisfying one's needs, overcoming obstacles, assuming responsibility for one's own care, and mastering new behaviors and social roles. The person is judged to be motivated, autonomous, energetic, problem-solving, spontaneous, purposeful, future-oriented, effective, determined and actively coping (Gunther, 1971; Lawrence & Lawrence, 1979). He or she directly engages in life planning and is moving on to a more mature level of functioning (Peter, 1975). The individual is both self-independent, but also other-dependent when deemed necessary.

Energy direction

In line with the balanced energy state that has been achieved in the previous stage (acknowledgement), a continuation of a similar harmonious state is maintained throughout the final phase of adjustment. There seems to be, however, a certain shift in energy direction toward the external environment. This moderate shift possibly reflects the need for active interaction with the outside world during this phase. People with disabilities invest energy in both personal (e.g., reorganization of one's values and goals) and other socially-oriented matters (Matson & Brooks, 1977). Energies are directed towards achieving personal independence and learning productive strategies for dealing with obstacles created by the external world (Vargo, 1978).

FURTHER COMMENTS

Related Models

The foregoing discussion evolved around the adaptation process observed in or inferred from personal adjustment to physical disability. Similar models have been suggested for at least three other related adaptation processes. They are: (a) Grief associated with the dying process, (b) Grief associated with family tragedies, and (c) Adaptation to catastrophic events. It is beyond the scope of the present chapter to address these areas. However, it should be recognized, that most of the models that offer to describe and elucidate the phases associated with the above tragic events, bear a strong similarity to models reviewed in the present chapter.

The adaptation to the dying process is usually discussed from two vantage points. First, reconciling oneself to one's own death resulting from chronic and deteriorating physical disease and second, grieving the death, or impending death, of a close relative, friend, or a loved one. Excellent discussion of the phases associated with these processes can be found in Engel (1964), Hughes (1980), Kübler-Ross (1969), Parkes (1965, 1972, 1975), Schoenberg, Carr, Kutscher, Peretz, & Goldberg (1974), Schoenberg, Carr, Kutscher, & Peretz (1970), and Weisman (1972, 1974).

The models suggested for perceiving the impact of a disability in the family network may generally be classified into two groups. First, models that describe the emotional reactions to a severe illness or disability sustained by one of the family members within the family context and second, the adaptation of parents to the birth of a severely malformed infant. Reviews of these models are included in Coelho, Hamburg and Adams (1974), Drotar, Baskiewicz, Irvin, Kennell, and Klaus (1975), Hamburg and Adams (1967), Livsey (1972), Mailick (1979), Moos (1977), Opirhory and Peters (1982), Power and Dell Orto (1980), Reagles (1982), Schoenberg, Carr, Kutscher, Peretz and Goldberg (1974), and Weller and Miller (1977).

Finally, attention, albeit limited, has been paid to the topic of individual and familial adjustment to catastrophic or natural disasters (e.g., floods, earthquakes, wars, imprisonment). Relevant discussion may be found in Moos (1976), Parad, Resnick and Parad (1976), and Wolfenstein (1957).

Theoretical Perspectives

The model for the process of adaptation to physical disability delineated in the present and other publications may be couched within several psychodynamic theories. Although the model itself is atheoretical in its structure, reflecting a rather descriptive set of observations and clinical inferences, it is possible to review its stages from several existing theoretical perspectives.

Maslow's Hierarchy of Needs Theory (1954, 1968)

Maslow postulates five major classes of human needs arranged in a progressive universal order from basic physiological needs, which must be met first, through safety, love, belongingness, esteem, and finally, self-actualization needs. The similarity between Maslow's need theory and the present model lies in the following domains. First, both views espouse a sequential development of human functioning. Certain needs or adaptation stages are seen, usually although not necessarily, as prerequisites to successful progression to higher, more complex, or more adaptive phases. Satisfying lower (i.e., physiological, safety) needs, or successfully negotiating initial stages of adjustment (i.e., resolving anxiety, denial, or mourning), are generally believed to be preconditions for meeting higher (i.e., self-esteem, self-actualization) needs or achieving final adjustment. Second, both models postulate that in order to survive or adapt, physically and psychologically, it is necessary for the lower hierarchical needs and initially faced adjustment stage to be met and resolved first. Gratifying basic physiological needs (thirst, hunger, sleep, etc.), and successfully overcoming the stages of shock and anxiety associated with sudden traumatic experiences, are mandatory for the person's survival. Finally, both models suggest a certain sequelae from an initial preoccupation with internal conditions for need satisfaction and adaptation to emphasis on external conditions (e.g., familial, social, vocational, economic) for gratifying higher needs and adapting to disability.

Support for this argument may be found indirectly in the writing of Fink (1967), Shontz (1965), and Tucker (1980), who suggested an association between the first emergency reactions of psychic shock, anxiety, and denial (defensive retreat) and the stages of safety and security included in Maslow's paradigm. During these stages, Maslow's theory emphasizes the need for protection and freedom from pain and anxiety paralleling the concerns that often surface during the initial stages of psychosocial adjustment to disability. During the reintegration stage of adjustment to disability, esteem and self-actualization needs to appear to be of the utmost importance. The individual shows readiness for reestablishing and satisfying his or her self-worth, self-regard, self-acceptance, and self-valuation needs that were previously damaged (see depressive reactions during initial realization phase). In addition, the person with a disability also seeks to fulfill related needs, such as receiving respect from others and gaining renewed status and social success (Maslow, 1968). Mastery and competence needs, viewed as an integral component of the acceptance-adjustment phase, also seek gratification. The adjusted individual, disabled or nondisabled, can then satisfy his or her highest level needs, these involving self-fulfillment of one's personal capacities and potentialities, and further grow to incorporate the transcendent meta-needs of seeking truth, justice and beauty (Maslow, 1968). The resemblance to transcending one's physical limitations by aspiring to higher, physique-free goals and hopes is clearly alluded to here.

Horney's Neopsychoanalytically Oriented Interpersonal Theory (1945)

Karen Horney postulated a three-mode theory of movement in relation to other people. The three movement modes are: (a) moving toward people—the self-effacing solution in which the individual is compliant, represses wishes for assertiveness, shoulders blame, feels helpless, inferior, dependent, lost, and anxious. A certain resemblance may be detected between this personality type and behavior characterizing the first phase of adjustment to disability, that of initial impact. The disabled individual, at this level, manifests anxious and dependent behavior and seeks the closeness and support of family and medical staff members. (b) Moving away from people—the resignation solution. The person seems to demonstrate two types of behavior: first, detachment and shallowness coupled with suppression, denial, or rejection of all feelings, and second, persisting resignation, passive resentment of dependency and the formation of imaginary relationships. Again, a certain degree of parallelism can be spawned between the preceding behavioral descriptions and those evident in the phases of defense mobilization, characterized by denial and suppression of painful affect, and initial realization, noted by its ambivalent recognition of loss and ensuing depressive mood, withdrawal, resignation, proceeding by internalized resentment and anger. (c) Moving against people—the expansive solution, described as an attempt at aggressive mastery. The person is driven to assert him or herself and is competitive, arrogant, and vindictive. A parallelism between this behavioral style and that of the person in the retaliatory stage (rebellious and externally aggressive) cannot be dismissed.

A word of caution should be inserted. Whereas Horney's theory attempts to describe the behavior of relatively static, consistent, and distinct personality types, the present model refers to the continuous, ever-changing and overlapping developmental process of adjustment to physical disability. Also, Horney terms these three modes of behavior as neurotic styles of behavior. The adjustment to disability phases, on the other hand, refrain from adopting psychiatric jargon, excluding maybe the brief discussion of the inferred defense mechanisms underlying these stages. The individual is viewed, rather, as coping with a major life crisis and the description of this coping process is restricted to the discussion of observed and inferred clinical phases.

Verwoerdt's Model of Psychopathological Responses to Physical Illness (1972)

Verwoerdt's discussion bears resemblance to Horney's theory. He also suggests a three-mode movement model. The three modes are: (1) retreating from the threatening situation or moving away from people. These defensive modes are represented by two types of reactions—regression and withdrawal. These reactions result in helplessness, dependency, isolation and self-preoccupation. They are similar to the reactions observed in the initial realization stage of adaptation. (2) excluding the threatening situation or its significance from awareness. The person suppresses and denies certain thoughts or feelings from his or her awareness. Other defenses included in this category are, according to Verwoerdt, rationalization and depersonalization, again, yielding the same protective results of dissociating the self from painful external stimuli. Exclusion of threat, therefore, resembles reactions of the defense mobilization stage of adaptation. Verwoerdt views this type of reaction as moving against self, when it occurs within the context of family interrelationships. This movement may also result in self-accusation and covert hostility toward family members (when internalization is adopted) and reminds one of behavior exhibited in the latter part of the initial realization stage, that of internalized anger. Also, moving against other family members is possible and is characterized by projection and holding others responsible for one's plight (when externalization is used). Feelings of hostility and angry accusations mirror this reaction which resembles responses observed during the stage of retaliation. (3) Finally, mastery and control of the threatening situation are characterized by counterphobic reactions with acceptance and sublimation being the most drawn upon defenses. These reactions are considered, by Verwoerdt, to represent the ideal resolution of loss or coming to terms with the disability. Mastery and control are regarded as invaluable behavioral components of the final stage of adaptation, hence the substantial correspondence between the two models is further enhanced.

Siller's Childhood Reactions to Disability Model (1960)

This model includes discussion of both modes of reaction and associated defense mechanisms. Siller classifies reactions to disability as follows: (a) avoidance reactions (negative orientation) which include: denial, repression, withdrawal, depression, and aggression. This general category, therefore, does not distinguish among the present model's stages of defense mobilization (denial and repression), initial realization (depression and withdrawal) and retaliation (aggression). (b) restitutive reactions (positive orientation) constituted of: compensation, independence, sublimation, assertion, substitution and determination. Again, the reactions to disability and their associated defense mechanisms are coalesced into a joint category. All these reactions, however, correspond to reactions in the reintegration stage suggested by the present model. In addition to the above dichotomous categorization, Siller alludes to a third, albeit less significant, group of reactions labeled insecurity reactions. These include reactions or feelings of inferiority, shame, fear, and dependency. These expressions are not considered to be reactions independent of the other two categories of reactions and may be submerged into either of them.

Lipowski (1969, 1970) and Kiely (1972) Coping Models

These models evolve around the coping strategies triggered by threat and loss due to severe physical illness. Lipowski and Kiely view these strategies as reflecting relatively enduring modes of coping style. These coping styles are considered in terms of their cognitive, affective, and behavioral aspects. (a) cognitive coping styles—two general modes or opposing poles occupying a single dimension of dealing with illness or injury are delineated. The first is termed minimization, and it operates through the mechanisms of denial, repression, rationalization, or ignoring of the illness, its existence, significance, or consequences. The second mode, vigilant focusing, is characterized by hyper vigilance, focused attention, self-obsession, rigid thinking, and inflexibility of behavior. The failure of these measures results in anxiety and hostility. (b) affective coping responses—two underlying dimensions are inherent in the operation of the affective response style. The first seems to relate to the unpleasantness–pleasantness of the affect. It appears that most responses to the onset of severe illness or injury reside on the negative end (i.e., anxiety, depression, anger). Although the surfacing of certain emotions, which are positive or even euphoric and manic in nature, is well recognized. The second dimension appears to measure the intensity of the feelings—from high intensity of emotionality (e.g., anxiety, anger) to low level of intensity (e.g., depression, helplessness). (c) behavioral coping patterns—three principal styles are noted: tackling, capitulating, and avoiding. Tackling refers to adaptive, active and energetic engagement in tasks carried on as a result of the illness or injury and the attempt to minimize its effects. It is similar to the mastery and control of threat responses outlined by Verwoerdt (1972) and to the restitutive reactions discussed by Siller (1960). Capitulating behavior is characterized by maladaptive, passive, inactive withdrawal, and dependent responses. It resembles moving toward people (Horney, 1945) and retreating from threat (Verwoerdt, 1972) behaviors. Finally, the avoidance style manifests an active effort to disengage oneself from the constraints of accepting the illness and its implications. This behavior is associated with Horney's moving away from people, Verwoerdt's excluding the threat, and Siller's avoidance reactions. Lipowski's (1969, 1970) and Kiely's (1972) models appear to treat the process of adjustment to illness, injury, or disability from a more static vantage point, considering the three response modes as somewhat finalized reactions or coping styles. On the other hand, they also expand on the present model by adopting a dimensional approach, suggesting not only three types of coping styles (cognitive, affective, and behavioral), but also proceed to further explore each style according to continua such as focusing-defocusing (cognition), pleasantness-unpleasantness and level of intensity (affect) and direction of movement (behavior).

SUMMARY

The intent of the present chapter was to propose a synthesis of various models dealing with process of psychosocial adaptation to physical disability. A literature review of over 40 stage or reaction to disability models has led to a conclusion that these models may be described in terms of five broad categories that can be delineated as follows: I. Initial impact, consisting of shock and anxiety substages; II. Defense mobilization which encompasses the substages of bargaining and denial; III. Initial realization or recognition, which includes the subcategory of mourning or depression in addition to that of internalized anger; IV. Retaliation or rebellion stage, often referred to as externalized anger or aggression; and V. Reintegration or reorganization, which is further subcategorized according to its cognitive (acknowledgement), affective (acceptance), and behavioral (final adjustment) components.

Each of the above stages of adaptation was discussed according to the following five indicators: (1) typical defense mechanisms used; (2) affective correlates—the types of associated emotions; (3) cognitive correlates—the nature of operating thought processes; (4) behavioral correlates—the variety of observed activities; and (5) the direction (internal, external) assumed by the energies summoned.

Finally, the model outlined here was compared to several other existing models. Furthermore, it was suggested that although the present model is atheoretical in how its process, structure and content are being perceived, it is possible to embed it within a number of existing psychodynamic conceptualizations (i.e., those of Maslow, Horney, Verwoerdt, Siller, Lipowski, & Kiely).

REFERENCES

Adams, J. E., & Lindemann, E. (1974). Coping with long-term disability. In: G. V. Coelho, D. A. Hamburg & J. E. Adams (Eds.), *Coping and adaptation*. New York: Basic Books (Chap. 7, pp. 127–138).

Atkins, B. J., Lynch, R. K., & Pullo, R. E. (1982). A definition of psychosocial aspects of disability: A synthesis of the literature. *Vocational Evaluation and Work Adjustment Bulletin, 15*(2), 55–62.

Beisser, A. R. (1979). Denial and affirmation in illness and health. *American Journal of Psychiatry, 136*(8), 1026–1030.

Blank, H. R. (1957). Psychoanalysis and blindness. *Psychoanalytic Quarterly, 26*, 1–24.

Blank, H. R. (1961). The challenge of rehabilitation. *Israel Medical Journal, 20*(5–6), 127–142.

Bray, G. P. (1978). Rehabilitation of spinal cord injured: A family approach. *Journal of Applied Rehabilitation Counseling, 9*(3), 70–78.

Cassem, N. H., & Hackett, T. P. (1971). Psychiatric consultation in a coronary care unit. *Annals of Internal Medicine, 75*, 9–14.

Castelnuovo-Tedesco, P. (1981). Psychological consequences of physical defects: A psychoanalytic perspective. *International Review of Psycho-Analysis, 8*, 145–154.

Cholden, L. (1954). Some psychiatric problems in the rehabilitation of the blind. *Bulletin of the Menninger Clinic, 18*, 107–112.

Coelho, G. V., Hamburg, D. A., & Adams, J. E. (Eds.) (1974). *Coping and adaptation*. New York: Basic Books.

Cogswell, B. E. (1976). Conceptual model of family as a group: Family response to disability. In: G. L. Albrecht (Ed.), *The sociology of physical disability and rehabilitation*. Pittsburgh, PA: University of Pittsburgh Press (Chap. 6, pp. 139–168).

Cohn-Kerr, N. (1961). Understanding the process of adjustment to disability. *Journal of Rehabilitation, 27*, 16–18.

Crate, M. A. (1965). Nursing functions in adaptation to chronic illness. *American Journal of Nursing, 65*(10), 72–76.

Drotar, D., Baskiewicz, A., Irvin, N., Kennell, J., & Klaus, M. (1975). The adaptation of parents to the birth of an infant with a congenital malformation: A hypothetical model. *Pediatrics, 56*(5), 710–717.

Dunn, M. E. (1975). Psychological intervention in a spinal cord injury center: An introduction. *Rehabilitation Psychology, 22*(4), 165–178.

Engel, G. L. (1964). Grief and grieving. *American Journal of Nursing, 64*(9), 93–98.

Falek, A., & Britton, S. (1974). Phases in coping: The hypothesis and its implications. *Social Biology, 21*(1), 1–7.

Fink, S. (1967). Crisis and motivation: A theoretical model. *Archives of Physical Medicine and Rehabilitation, 48*, 592–597.

Fitzgerald, R. G. (1970). Reactions to blindness: An exploratory study of adults with recent loss of sight. *Archives of General Psychiatry, 22*, 370–379.

Gray, R. M., Reinhardt, A. M., & Ward, J. R. (1969). Psychosocial factors involved in the rehabilitation of persons with cardiovascular diseases. *Rehabilitation Literature, 30*(12), 354–359, 362.

Gunther, M. S. (1969). Emotional aspects. In: D. Ruge (Ed.), *Spinal cord injuries*. Springfield, IL: Charles C. Thomas (Chap. 12, pp. 93–108).

Gunther, M. S. (1971). Psychiatric consultation in a rehabilitation hospital: A regression hypothesis. *Comprehensive Psychiatry, 12*(6), 572-585.

Haan, N. (1963). Proposed model of ego functioning: coping and defense mechanisms in relationship to IQ change. *Psychological Monographs, 77*(8) (whole No. 571).

Hackett, T. P., & Cassem, N. H. (1974). Development of a quantitative rating scale to assess denial. *Journal of Psychosomatic Research, 18*, 93-100.

Hamburg, D. A., & Adams, J. E. (1967). A perspective on coping behavior. *Archives of General Psychiatry, 17*, 277-284.

Herman, C. D., Manning, R. A., & Teitelman, E. (1971). Psychiatric rehabilitation of the physically disabled, the mentally retarded and the psychiatrically impaired. In: F. H. Krusen, F. J. Kottke, & P. M. Ellwood (Eds.), *Handbook of physical medicine and rehabilitation*. Philadelphia, PA: W. B. Saunders (Chap. 38, pp. 761-768).

Hohmann, G. W. (1975). Psychological aspects of treatment and rehabilitation of the spinal cord injured person. *Clinical Orthopaedics, 112*, 81-88.

Horney, K. (1945). *Our inner conflicts*. New York: Norton.

Hughes, F. (1980). Reactions to loss: Coping with disability and death. *Rehabilitation Counseling Bulletin, 23*(4), 251-257.

Kahana, E., Fairchild, T., & Kahana, B. (1982). Adaptation. In: Mangen, D. J., & Peterson, W. A. (Eds.), *Research instruments in clinical gerontology: Vol. 1. Clinical and Social Psychology*. Minneapolis, MN: University of Minnesota Press (Chap. 4, pp. 145-193).

Kerr, W. G., & Thompson, M. A. (1972). Acceptance of disability of sudden onset in paraplegia. *Paraplegia, 10*, 94-102.

Kiely, W. F. (1972). Coping with severe illness. *Advances in Psychosomatic Medicine, 8*, 105-118.

Kroeber, T. C. (1963). The coping functions of the ego mechanisms. In: R. White (Ed.), *The study of lives*. New York: Atherton Press (Chap. 8, pp. 178-198).

Krueger, D. W. (1981-1982). Emotional rehabilitation of the physical rehabilitation patient. *International Journal of Psychiatry in Medicine, 11*(2), 183-191.

Krystal, H., & Petty, T. A. (1961). The psychological processes of normal convalescence. *Psychosomatics, 2*, 366-372.

Kübler-Ross, E. (1969). *On death and dying*. New York: Macmillan.

Lawrence, S. A., & Lawrence, R. M. (1979). A model of adaptation to the stress of chronic illness. *Nursing Forum, 18*(1), 33-42.

Levine, J., & Zigler, E. (1975). Denial and self image in stroke, lung cancer, and heart disease patients. *Journal of Consulting and Clinical Psychology, 43*(6), 751-757.

Lipowski, Z. J. (1969). Psychosocial aspects of disease. *Annals of Internal Medicine, 71*(6), 1197-1206.

Lipowski, Z. J. (1970). Physical illness, the individual and the coping processes. *International Journal of Psychiatry in Medicine, 1*, 91-102.

Lipp, L., Kolstoe, R., James, W., & Randall, H. (1968). Denial of disability and internal control of reinforcement: A study using a perceptual defense paradigm. *Journal of Consulting and Clinical Psychology, 32*(1), 72-75.

Livsey, C. G. (1972). Physical illness and family dynamics. *Advances in Psychosomatic Medicine, 8*, 237-251.

Mailick, M. (1979). The impact of severe illness on the individual and the family: An overview. *Social Work in Health Care, 5*(2), 117-128.

Maslow, A. H. (1954). *Motivation and Personality*. New York: Harper.

Maslow, A. H. (1968). *Toward a psychology of being*. New York: Van Nostrand Reinhold.

Matson, R. R., & Brooks, N. A. (1977). Adjusting to multiple sclerosis: An exploratory study. *Social Science and Medicine, 11*, 245-250.

Meyer, G. G. (1971). The psychodynamics of acute blindness. *Ophthalmology Digest, October*, 31-37.

Moos, R. H. (Ed.) (1976). *Human adaptation: Coping with life crises*. Lexington, MA: D. C. Heath.

Moos, R. H. (Ed.) (1977). *Coping with physical illness.* New York: Plenum Press.

Mueller, A. D. (1962). Psychological factors in rehabilitation of paraplegic patients. *Archives of Physical Medicine and Rehabilitation, 43*(4), 151-159.

Nemiah, J. C. (1964). Common emotional reactions of patients to injury. *Archives of Physical Medicine and Rehabilitation, 45,* 621-623.

Niederland, W. G. (1965). Narcissistic ego impairment in patients with early physical malformation. *The Psychoanalytic Study of the Child, 20,* 518-534.

Opirhory, G., & Peters, G. A. (1982). Counseling intervention strategies for families with the less than perfect newborn. *Personnel and Guidance Journal, 60*(8), 451-455.

Parad, H., Resnick, H., & Parad, L. (Eds.) (1976). *Emergency and disaster management: A mental health sourcebook.* Bowie, MD: Charles Press.

Parker, R. M. (1979). Assessing adjustment to disability through determining predominant feeling states. Paper presented at the American Rehabilitation Counseling Association Meeting, Las Vegas, Nevada.

Parkes, C. M. (1965). Bereavement and mental illness. Part 1. A clinical study of the grief of bereaved psychiatric patients. *British Journal of Medical Psychology, 38,* 1-12.

Parkes, C. M. (1972). *Bereavement: Studies of grief in adult life.* New York: International Universities Press.

Parkes, C. M. (1975). Psycho-social transitions: Comparison between the reactions to loss of a limb and loss of a spouse. *British Journal of Psychiatry, 127,* 204-210.

Pearlin, L. I., & Schooler, C. (1978). The structure of coping. *Journal of Health and Social Behavior, 19,* 2-21.

Peter, A. R. (1975). Psychosocial aspects of spinal cord injury. *Maryland State Medical Journal, 24*(2), 65-69.

Power, P. W., & Dell Orto, A. R. (Eds.) (1980). *Role of the family in the rehabilitation of the physically disabled.* Baltimore, MD: University Park Press.

Reagles, S. (1982). The impact of disability: A family crisis. *Journal of Applied Rehabilitation Counseling, 13*(3), 25-29.

Roessler, R., & Bolton, B. (1978). *Psychosocial adjustment to disability.* Baltimore, MD: University Park Press.

Russell, R. A. (1981). Concepts of adjustment to disability: An overview. *Rehabilitation Literature, 42*(11-12), 330-338.

Schoenberg, B., Carr, A. C., Kutscher, A. H., & Peretz, D. (Eds.) (1970). *Loss and grief: Psychological management in medical practice.* New York: Columbia University Press.

Schoenberg, B., Carr, A. C., Kutscher, A. H., Peretz, D., & Goldberg, I. (Eds.) (1974). *Anticipatory grief.* New York: Columbia University Press.

Shands, H. C. (1955). An outline of the process of recovery from severe trauma. *Archives of Neurology and Psychiatry, 73,* 403-409.

Shontz, F. C. (1965). Reactions to crisis. *The Volta Review, 67*(5), 364-370.

Shontz, F. C. (1975). *The psychological aspects of physical illness and disability.* New York: Macmillan.

Shontz, F. C. (1980). Theories about the adjustment to having a disability. In: W. M. Cruickshank (Ed.), *Psychology of exceptional children and youth* (4th Ed.). Englewood Cliffs, NJ: Prentice-Hall (Chap. 1, pp. 3-44).

Siller, J. (1960). Psychological concomitants of amputation in children. *Child Development, 31,* 109-120.

Siller, J. (1969). Psychological situation of the disabled with spinal cord injuries. *Rehabilitation Literature, 30*(10), 290-296.

Siller, J. (1976). Psychological aspects of physical disability. In: J. Meislin (Ed.), *Rehabilitation Medicine and Psychiatry.* Springfield, IL: C. C. Thomas (Chap. 28, pp. 455-484).

Stewart, T. D., & Rossier, A. B. (1978). Psychological consideration in the adjustment to spinal cord injury. *Rehabilitation Literature, 39*(3), 75-80.

Tucker, S. J. (1980). The psychology of spinal cord injury: Patient–staff interaction. *Rehabilitation Literature, 41*(5-6), 114-121.

Vargo, J. W. (1978). Some psychological effects of physical disability. *The American Journal of Occupational Therapy, 32*(1), 31-34.

Verwoerdt, A. (1972). Psychopathological responses to the stress of physical illness. *Advances in Psychosomatic Medicine, 8,* 119-141.

Walters, J. (1981). Coping with a leg amputation. *American Journal of Nursing, 81*(7), 1349-1352.

Weinstein, E. A., & Kahn, R. L. (1955). *Denial of illness: Symbolic and physiological aspects.* Springfield, IL: C. C. Thomas.

Weisman, A. E. (1972). *On dying and denying: A psychiatric study of terminality.* New York: Behavioral Publications.

Weisman, A. E. (1974). *The realization of death: A guide for the psychological autopsy.* New York: Aronson.

Weller, D. J., & Miller, P. M. (1977). Emotional reactions of patient, family, and staff in acute-care period of spinal cord injury: Part I. *Social Work in Health Care, 2*(4), 369-377.

Whitehouse, F. A. (1962). Cardiovascular disability. In: J. F. Garrett & E. S. Levin (Eds.), *Psychological practices with the physically disabled.* New York: Columbia University Press (Chap. 3. pp. 85-124).

Wolfenstein, M. (1957). *Disaster.* Glencoe, IL: The Free Press.

Wright, B. A. (1960). *Physical disability—A psychological approach.* New York: Harper & Row.

Yano, B., Alexander, L., & Kuwanoe, C. (1976). Crisis intervention: A guide for nurses. *Journal of Rehabilitation, 42*(5), 23-26.

Yorke, C. (1980). Some comments on the psychoanalytic treatment of patients with physical disabilities. *International Journal of Psycho-Analysis, 61,* 187-193.

14

Denial in Rehabilitation: Its Genesis, Consequences, and Clinical Management

Richard I. Naugle

Approximately 1 million people sustain central nervous system injuries annually; of that number, approximately 300,000 sustain some sort of permanent disability (Jennett & Teasdale, 1981). To meet the needs of this growing population, medical–surgical methods have become sophisticated to the extent that individuals with greater degrees of impairment are surviving their accidents. Rehabilitation regimens routinely include the requisite therapies (e.g., cognitive, physical, occupational, speech, and language) to retrain or educate individuals regarding compensatory strategies to help them adjust in areas of deficit resulting from their injuries.

The understanding and treatment of psychological problems resulting from these injuries lags behind medical advances (Weller & Miller, 1977a). This is not to say that the psychological issues have been completely overlooked; some authors have described a constellation of psychological factors that are common among neurologically impaired persons (e.g., Dikmen & Reitan, 1977; Feibel, Berk, & Joynt, 1979; Stewart & Rossier, 1978; Tucker, 1980), including identity and self-esteem issues, the reenactment of emotionally charged developmental concerns related to mastery and competence, and feelings of anxiety, guilt, and depression.

Many writers have theorized that, because of these affectively laden sequelae, a period of denial is typical in the rehabilitation process (Fink, 1967; Gunther, 1971; Hamburg, Hamburg & Goza, 1953; Krystal & Petty, 1961; Shands, 1965; Shontz, 1965; Weller & Miller, 1977a). Used in this context, "denial" refers to the tendency to negate or downplay the long-term consequences of an injury because of their psychological implications. This is in contrast to the denial of deficit, or "anosognosia" associated with and directly attributed to a focal cortical lesion. That is, individuals frequently deny the severity of their injuries and the disability that occurs as a consequence of those injuries. As a result of this denial, individuals may be reluctant to involve themselves in the rehabilitation program or to undertake the changes that must be made to compensate for abilities that are lost or impaired.

Rehabilitation staff are often perceived as negative or antagonistic because of their attempts to address deficits that are not fully recognized by the individual as a consequence of his or her denial. In part through his or her interactions with friends and family members over time, the individual's denial diminishes and he or she gradually acknowledges those deficits and is able to undertake the tasks of rehabilitation. Families often unintentionally contribute to that denial, however, and are less able to help the individual through this adjustment process.

Many writers in the area of family stress theory regard the effect of family members' perceptions as crucial in the adjustment to a stressful event such as a traumatic brain injury or spinal cord injury (e.g., Boss, 1977; Hill, 1949; McCubbin, Joy, Cauble, Patterson, & Needle, 1980). To date, however, there has been no attempt to apply these theoretical models to the rehabilitation process. Little has been offered in the way of a therapeutic approach for such persons and their families. The treatment approach outlined herein has been designed in accordance with the recommendations derived from family stress theory and incorporates some basic tenets of psychotherapy—those of "timing" and "dosage." As a result of this treatment approach, family members will more readily become less "ability-centered" and more "individual-centered." Consequently, denial and its deleterious effects would be minimized, thereby enabling individuals and their family members to more readily arrive at an accurate understanding of the disability and enabling them to more effectively contribute to the adjustment process.

PSYCHOLOGICAL SEQUELAE OF NEUROLOGICAL IMPAIRMENT

Behavioral aftereffects of severe neurologic injuries have profound, far-reaching implications for one's self-perception. It is precisely for this reason that the severity or chronic nature of those deficits is often downplayed or minimized. Stewart and Rossier (1978) suggested a number of psychological sequelae to be considered in understanding an individual's adjustment to one such deficit—paralysis. The loss of bowel and bladder control, sexual impotence, and physical dependence have dramatic ramifications with regard to one's self-perception or identity.

Identity Issues

Major problems such as those resulting from spinal cord injury or traumatic brain injury create a "state of flux" during which one's character structure might progress or regress (Green, Pratt, & Grigsby, 1985; Stewart & Rossier, 1978). The development of the ability to use a wheelchair, communication devices, or other adaptive equipment to accomplish even the most routine tasks of daily living is one facet of this process. Regarded in this context, paralysis is a life crisis that must be integrated with the existing personality. The resulting modified identity may reflect new strengths developed in an effort to compensate for those losses that have occurred (Green et al., 1985). Conversely, there may be a regression to a more dependent existence with the paralysis used as a justification for that regression (Stewart & Rossier, 1978).

The stage in the individual's life cycle at which paralysis occurs in part determines the nature of the identity issues that result. For example, an infant with birth defects may later grieve for what he or she might have become and may be envious of others' abilities. The difficulty the child's parents may have in expressing their guilt and anger, and the tendency they may have to overprotect a child with disabilities both affect the phenomenological world in which the child develops. Impairment occurring during adolescence is likely to affect the major life choices regarding identity, sexuality, and career that take place at that time. Acceptance by others and peer group membership may be profoundly affected. The adolescent and his or her family are forced to face the issues of loss and deterioration usually associated with advanced age. Paralysis occurring during one's "twilight years" fits into the context of the decline and loss of abilities already established (Stewart & Rossier, 1978).

The need to readdress issues that had been resolved in the course of one's development contributes to this identity confusion. For example, sacral malfunctioning with consequent impairment of sexual, bowel, and bladder control often initially elicits shame and humiliation. Stewart and Rossier (1978) point out that both the physiological and developmental issues raised by Erikson (1964), for example, regarding bowel and bladder control, are reactivated; the inconvenience of this loss of ability is often secondary in relative importance to the psychological issues. In the case of paralysis of the upper extremities, the additional helplessness with regard to self-care (feeding and hygiene) adds to the humiliation that is usually a result of the physical handicap. Loss of the use of one's hands as expressive instruments is yet another aspect of such paralysis (Stewart & Rossier, 1978). It is not surprising that these dramatic behavioral changes entail acute affective responses.

Affective Sequelae

Depression has been recognized frequently as a common consequence of spinal cord injury (Bleuer, 1951; Engel, 1961; Folstein, Maiberger, & McHugh, 1977; Oradel & Waite, 1974; Schwab, 1972; Stewart & Shields, 1985). Anxiety, along with either its mobilizing or immobilizing quality, is also common. Feibel, Berk, and Joynt (1979), in their study of persons with stroke, found that 37% were moderately to severely depressed six months following their discharges from the hospital; anxiety and anger were reported in 32% at that same time. Almost 50% of aphasic individuals with chronic impairments showed significant depression (Robinson & Benson, 1981). Perceived helplessness and hopelessness, loss of self-esteem, and the feeling that one is no longer "strong, loving, and lovable" (Stewart

& Rossier, 1978) all contribute to the development of these feelings of depression. Divorce and unemployment following injury frequently contribute to a longstanding sense of despair in neurologically impaired persons.

THE NATURE OF A SUCCESSFUL ADJUSTMENT

This review of some psychological concomitants of neurological impairment suggests the nature of a "successful" or optimal adjustment. Such an adjustment would include a resolution of some psychological and developmental issues, identity concerns, and affective sequelae:

> The paralyzed must be able to accept and live with and make the best use of a body that does not live up to former standards or to the standards enjoyed by the non-paralyzed. If he cannot give up this quest for what he can no longer have—normal functions—he will be doomed . . . to constant frustration and depression. (Stewart & Rossier, 1978, p. 80)

Shontz (1965), in what is perhaps the most detailed characterization of a successful resolution, described this optimal result in terms of self-experience and emotional adjustment. Stated briefly, his conception of adaptation entails a reordering of priorities and a "reintegration of the self" with a renewed sense of worth. A decrease in levels of anxiety and depression is concomitant with an increase in the feeling of satisfaction as one begins to adjust to one's disability. The individual begins to gradually master the array of somatic and prosthetic resources available and eventually incorporates these devices into the self-perception. In short, the rehabilitation process culminates with the development of a new cohesive self: the "progressive mastery of new ego skills" leads to the reestablishment of self-esteem (Bray, 1978; George, 1980; Green, Pratt, & Grigsby, 1985; Gunther, 1971; Pearlin & Schooler, 1978).

Denial as an Impediment to Optimal Adaptation

In the process of arriving at this optimal level of adjustment, the individual is likely to progress through a number of stages. Many writers have speculated as to the continuum of stages of adjustment to loss in general (e.g., Freud, 1957; Kübler-Ross, 1969) and loss related to neurological impairment in particular (e.g., Fink, 1967; Gunther, 1971; Hamburg, Hamburg, & Goza, 1953; Krystal & Petty, 1961; Shands, 1965; Weller & Miller, 1977a). It is not the goal of this chapter to establish the validity of any of these typologies or even to review them in detail. Rather, it will suffice to look at their common recognition of a stage of denial.

Neurologic injury is often a sudden and unexpected trauma that threatens one's self-esteem by leading to "permanent, significant, overtly obvious and hence perceptually undeniable changes in the body or its functions" (Gunther, 1971). One defends one's self-perception by negating or downplaying the seriousness of the injury, the chronicity of its effects, or the changes that are necessary in order to compensate for lost or impaired abilities. This denial allows the individual to maintain a sense of competence in the face of actual incompetence. Yet this early period of denial postpones the inevitable confrontation and subsequent acceptance of the existence, severity, or implications of the impairment. Only after that denial diminishes is an optimal recovery from the injury possible:

> As the denial slips away . . . a new, more realistic basis for hope may be opened to the individual: relationships and activities with the staff in which he can be valued, despite persistence of many of his physical and functional changes. Hope for recovery, then, becomes shifted to the realm of current reality experienced with staff and related to healthy self-esteem restoration . . . rather than remaining totally fixated to a fantasy of future undoing of body damage. (Gunther, 1971, p. 582)

This adjustment has been termed by Bray (1978) as "assimilation." To reach this end, the individual must begin a self-analysis and a restructuring of the meaning of his or her life; later, goals are identified and sought (Bray, 1978; Green et al., 1985). The individual must eventually recognize that he or she remains capable of worthwhile, valued activity and that he or she can still be accepted and perceived by others as competent (Siller, 1969). The sense of competence based on premorbid abilities and now sustained by denial is recognized as dysfunctional and is replaced by a more functional competence. Recognition of this is achieved with the passage of time, as denial wanes. The frank impairment of abstract thinking so common among traumatically brain injured individuals and noted to a lesser degree in persons with spinal cord injury (Davidoff, Morris, Roth, & Bleiberg, 1985; Wilmot, Cope, Hall, & Acker, 1985) renders this transitional period a slow, difficult process. The involvement of significant others throughout this adjustment is critical.

THE ROLE OF THE FAMILY IN THE ADJUSTMENT PROCESS

Thus far, the nature of the disability has been viewed in terms of some intrapsychic issues that are likely to arise. Some writers, however, have contended that disability is a social fact that is imposed through one's relationships with others (Kutner, 1971; McDaniel, 1976; Stewart, 1977). Consistent with this notion, Tucker (1980) claimed that persons treated within a milieu that stresses psychosocial issues exhibit more physical gains than do those who undergo more conventional treatment regimens.

In his review of the factors that have an impact on the adjustment process, Gunther (1971) emphasized the importance of the reactions of both rehabilitation staff and family members to disability. Although these relationships and interactions with significant others can have profound and far-reaching effects on the person's reactions to acquired disabilities, the interpersonal dynamics that might account for this effect are yet to be explored. That influence can be of a negative nature if family members exacerbate the depression and anxiety already present in the aftermath of the injury; their influence could be of a positive nature if they focus on more growth-oriented aspects of the recuperative process. This latter approach would be more likely to encourage the individual to adopt a "realistic optimism" with which to approach the tasks of rehabilitation. That is, as denial subsides and the individual becomes increasingly aware of the longstanding consequences of the injury, family members who continue to lament the person's disability and insist that he or she return to premorbid levels of ability will be likely to increase the individual's depression and anxiety. Conversely, family members who accept the limits imposed by the injury but encourage the development of other abilities unaffected by the injury and the adoption of compensatory strategies to offset deficits will more likely decrease depression and anxiety.

To encourage an acceptance and eventual adaptation to disability, it follows that a comprehensive rehabilitation approach must necessarily include the person's family members and address the sources of stress experienced by the family unit. Weller & Miller (1977a) concluded that:

> . . . , it is during this [acute, immediate posttrauma] period of . . . , emotional stress upon all concerned that evaluation and treatment of psychosocial aspects are especially useful, both for withstanding the crisis and for entering the subsequent long, chronic period of adjustment. (p. 369)

This adjustment can be seriously compromised if family members detract from or fail to contribute to the recovery process. To be maximally effective, the treatment regimen should include family members and encourage them to adopt an attitude that is less likely to impede the individual's adjustment (McCubbin, Joy, Cauble, Patterson, & Needle, 1980; Roskins & Lazarus, 1980). In the case of neurological deficits, the role of the rehabilitation staff is to help family members straddle the fine line between helping the individual to accept a realistic appraisal of his or her level of disability without endorsing a resignation to that impairment.

Regrettably, communication between treating professionals and families is an often-cited problem (Brooks, 1986; Oddy, Humphrey, & Uttley, 1978; Romano, 1974; Thomsen, 1974). Nearly one-half of the relatives of persons being treated for closed head injuries complain that their relationships with clinicians are inadequate (Brooks, 1986). They frequently contend that they are unable to comprehend staff, speculate that therapists are misrepresenting their findings or opinions, or find the staff to be inaccessible (Thomsen, 1974).

This breakdown is a serious breach of the responsibilities of the health care professional. Hill's Family Stress Model provides a theoretical framework for further understanding the importance of the family unit and underscores the absolute need for a strong, constructive relationship between family members and staff.

Hill's Family Stress Model

Hill (1949) formulated a model of family adjustment to crises and other stress-inducing events that, to date, remains essentially unchanged. According to that model, a crisis (X) is the result of the interaction of three factors: (1) the trauma and related hardships; (2) the family's resources to meet that crisis; and (3) the family's perception of the event. For example, consider the following: a husband and father of two children is injured in an automobile accident and as a result of his injury loses the use of his legs. The loss of the use of his legs, the inability to continue in his present job, the resulting lack of income, and the responsibilities placed on others (his wife, friends, and relatives) to transport him are included in Hill's factor 1. The cohesiveness of the family, the flexibility of its members to accommodate to the changes that must be made and their financial resources are included in Hill's factor 2. These factors interact with the realistic or unrealistic perception of the event and its aftermath as well as the perception of the consequent changes as either catastrophic or merely inconvenient (factor 3) to result in "X": the experience of the crisis.

The Effect of Perception

Factors 1 and 2 of Hill's model have received considerable attention since their conceptualization (Boss, 1977; Burr, 1973; George, 1980; Hansen, 1965; Hansen & Johnson, 1979), but "in the study of family stress . . . the variable of perception remains somewhat of an enigma" (McCubbin et al., 1980, p. 861). George (1980) concurred that the cognitive ability to perceive the stressor realistically is crucial if family members are to cope with a stressful situation. The perception of a given stressful event may serve as a mediating role; that is, the impact of that event can be significantly reduced if that perception leads to a better understanding of what happened and why (Boss, 1977; Gerhardt, 1979; McCubbin et al., 1980):

> The difference between events which eventually lead to breakdown or dysfunction [and those which do not] may depend upon the presence or absence of explanations which help the family to make sense of what happened, why the event happened, and how one's social environment can be rearranged in order to overcome the undesirable situation . . . meaning also renders stressful situations less irrational, less unacceptable and more understandable. (McCubbin et al., 1980, pp. 865–866)

Clearly, a comprehensive understanding of the disability and its consequences constitutes an important component of the coping process. Yet, just as the individual resists acknowledging the severity and nature of his or her disability, so does the family. Families frequently support denial by insisting on the eventual return to a premorbid level of ability (Weller & Miller, 1977b). The implications of the family's denial can be subtle but they are nevertheless apparent; insistence on complete recuperation communicates to the individual that he or she will be less than whole and, consequently, will not be valued or considered worthy until all effects of the disability have been overcome. Yet in the majority of cases of spinal cord injury and head trauma, such total rehabilitation is not possible; the denial of the family members merely impedes the resolution of denial and the consequent reestablishment of identity and self-esteem (Feibel, Berk, & Joynt, 1979).

Families must be willing and able to assess both the severity of the impairment and the likelihood that improvement will occur. They must eventually be able to shift their focus from the recovery of abilities to the reestablishment of the individual's sense of self-worth. Stated simply, they must become "individual-centered" rather than "ability-centered." It falls to the rehabilitation staff to assist family members in the acquisition of information and their understanding of the nature of the recuperative process. Attempts to merely educate the family regarding prognosis may be poorly received; often such information is not effectively communicated, and staff are frequently perceived in a negative, adversarial light for attempting to inform families of a poor prognosis. Consider the remarks of a 27-year-old man with quadriplegia:

> It makes me wonder . . . where is the psychology on the doctor's part that's preaching no hope with someone that's already being down so bad from having such a drastic . . . thing happen to them. Their life has been changed . . . in a split second. And when you're already down and they're telling you there's no hope, no hope. Well, how do they expect you to recoup? I think there's a lot of . . . positive thought that's got to go into getting you back on your feet and getting a positive mental outlook again that's being overlooked. (Wershba, 1982, p. 14)

To avoid an antagonistic relationship between treatment staff and the individual and his or her family, the rehabilitation team is advised to avoid forcing the acceptance of a frank, poor prognosis or attempting to confront denial. Instead, it is recommended that the team recognize that denial is both a common and likely reaction, understand its positive and negative effects, and adopt a more constructive approach that emphasizes the individual's strengths. In doing so, the individual will be more likely to adopt a "realistic optimism," will join a more constructive relationship with staff, and will more readily invest him or herself in the tasks of rehabilitation. A more accurate, more comprehensive understanding of the disability (in terms of both its irreversible consequences as well as aspects that can be improved) would be achieved more effectively and would allow the individual and family members to adopt more realistic expectations for recuperation. Encouraging the individual to improve those abilities that can be improved and to accept the fact that some abilities are irreversibly impaired will likely result in fewer failure experiences for the individual, which in turn will lead to more positive self-regard.

The Prerequisites of a Therapeutic Approach

The extensive use of denial as a defense mechanism (Fink, 1967; Freud, 1957; Gunther, 1971; Hamburg, Hamburg, & Goza, 1953; Krystal & Petty, 1961;

Kübler-Ross, 1969; Shands, 1965; Shontz, 1965; Weller & Miller, 1977b) suggests that a therapeutic approach that ignores family members' denial would be futile. In traditional psychotherapy, denial is routinely encountered and, to the extent that psychotherapy is successful, that denial is effectively managed to allow for "threatening" insights and self-perceptions to occur.

Weiner (1975) emphasized the importance of timing and dosage of information in attempting to bypass defensiveness in the course of psychotherapy. An individual (and, in this case, family members) is likely to be more open to otherwise threatening material when the presentation of that material is carefully regulated. Timing must take into consideration the person's "frame of mind;" if resistance to the ego-threatening information is high, no amount of convincing or documentation is likely to "legitimize" that material. In fact, a resistant individual may even become more anxious and defensive in the face of a barrage of distressing and unwanted information.

Equally important is the concept of dosage. If the individual is overwhelmed with information, that material is less likely to be accepted. Failure to recognize and accommodate an individual's tolerance level for distressing information may have the effect of interfering with participation in any treatment regimen. Smaller "doses" of information allow the individual to assimilate that information at a more controlled, self-determined rate.

The content and amount of information to be included in a given dose vary from individual to individual and over time for the same individual (Weiner, 1975). In the case of individuals with neurological impairments and their family members, the counselor might be advised to instruct family members about prognostic indicators. The would allow them to arrive at a realistic appraisal of the individual's disability at a self-determined rate and, consequently, they will more readily realize the changes that will have to be made to accommodate the disability. That is, traditional psychotherapeutic theory suggests that patients and their family members, if provided with a comprehensive explanation of the details regarding the nature of the injury or trauma and the signs that suggest both good and poor prognoses for the abilities affected by that injury or trauma, will more readily arrive at a realistic appraisal of the long-term consequences of the disability.

Content of the Didactic Approach

The roles of many premorbid variables are becoming increasingly understood. The work of Brooks (1986) has shown repeatedly that educational level (i.e., years of formal schooling) is a much better predictor of cognitive outcome than medical factors such as the presence or absence of a hematoma or a skull fracture. In Brooks's words, "What the patient has not achieved before the injury sets real limits on what the patient will be able to achieve after the injury" (1986, p. 2). It is my position that to inform family members of this general rule would less likely elicit the same degree of denial than would the statement that the person's limited intellect imposes constraints on the extent of his or her cognitive recovery.

Similarly, it is known that typical periods of recovery can be predicted on the basis of age; children younger than 5 years old can expect to recover for decades whereas a 20–40 year old can realistically anticipate recovery over approximately 5 to 6 years. Persons 40–60 years of age typically improve over the 2 years post injury, and those over 60 years of age rarely improve beyond 9 months following the injury (LeMay & Geschwind, 1978). These estimates are meant to provide a rough estimate of the recovery period but cannot and should not be assumed to be definite; variation across individuals is considerable and, for example, an individual who is 60 years of age may continue to improve over the course of several years. In virtually all cases, rehabilitation efforts produce their greatest effects early in the recovery phase; improvement gradually wanes until further recovery is unlikely. Family members should be informed of these general "rules of thumb" and should be permitted—even encouraged—to reach their own conclusions regarding the individual. Length of coma, the duration of posttraumatic amnesia, the location of the insult, the extent and severity of cerebral damage, the presence of seizures, and medical complications have all been linked to prognosis (Adamovich, Henderson, & Auerbach, 1985). Although they are less profound than the correlates of certain premorbid factors, the presence or absence of hematoma has been reported to have clear ramifications for the recovery potential of persons with closed head injuries (Cullum & Bigler, 1985).

Studies regarding the clinical outcome of specific diagnostic groups are becoming more prevalent in the literature and are providing much needed information for both clinicians and families. The work of Levy, Caronna, Singer, Lapinski, Frydman, and Plum (1985) is a case in point. Their work identified the most salient predictors of a "positive outcome"—pupillary light reflexes, the development of spontaneous eye movements that were roving conjugate or better, and the findings of extensor, flexor, or withdrawal responses—at various times in the course of recovery from hypoxic-ishemic coma. Informing individuals and their families of these factors and their relationship to recovery rather than informing them of the extent of recovery that can be expected is also less likely to elicit denial.

Education regarding the general course of recovery (to the extent that it is understood) would also be constructive rather than "threatening." In the case of paralysis, family members could be instructed to look for proximal strength to return before distal strength, or for flexors to recover before extendors (Brunstrom, 1977). Because gains are slow in the early stages of recovery, expectations should be that further recuperation will be slow. In contrast, the individual who progresses rapidly initially following the injury should be expected to continue to make significant gains (Miller, 1984). Much has been learned in recent years regarding the course of recovery from aphasia resulting from focal, discrete lesions (Adamovich et al., 1985). Other research that would provide similar clues about the "hierarchy" of recovery with regard to other deficits is needed, and the results of that research should be included in didactic family sessions. By informing family members of these general rules, they will be more likely to arrive at and accept more accurate estimates of the person's level of deficit. Furthermore, whenever possible, the individual and family members should be instructed as to the neuropathy responsible for the observed behavioral sequelae. Review of Computerized Axial Tomography (CAT) or Magnetic Resonance Imaging (MRI) scans, or electroencephalographic recordings is recommended.

The process of providing such information to family members would presumably help them to arrive at realistic conclusions at self-determined rates and would be less likely to elicit the denial and the other deleterious effects so prevalent in the literature and noted in practice when the typical, more direct approach is adopted and families are informed of a "definitive" prognosis. Moreover, the negative light in which clinical staff are viewed for having delivered a pessimistic prognosis would be avoided.

It is concluded that, as a result of a more realistic appraisal of the disability, the family's expectations for recovery will shift from "ability-centered" (i.e., focused on the total recovery of permanently lost or impaired abilities) to "individual-centered" (i.e., focused on the development of necessary compensatory strategies and the constructive restructuring of self-perception). As a result of this shift to an individual-centered approach, self-esteem will be improved and level of depression as a result of the injury will be diminished. With this improved affective state and restored self-esteem, the individual will be more likely to have the necessary motivation and endurance to pursue the work of rehabilitation.

REFERENCES

Adamovich, B. B., Henderson, J. A., & Auerbach, S. (1985). *Cognitive rehabilitation of closed head injured patients: A dynamic approach.* San Diego: College Hill Press.

Bleuer, E. P. (1951). *Textbook of psychiatry.* New York: Dover.

Boss, P. (1977). A clarification of the concept of psychological father presence in families experiencing ambiguity of boundary. *Journal of Marriage and the Family, 39,* 141–151.

Bray, G. P. (1978). Rehabilitation of spinal cord injured: Family approach. *Journal of Applied Rehabilitation Counseling, 8,* 70–78.

Brooks, N. (1986). Recovery and prediction of cognitive outcome. *Research Forum: New Medico Head Injury System, Office of Research, 2,* 1–3.

Brunstrom, S. (1977). *Movement therapy in hemiplegia.* New York: Harper & Row.

Burr, W. (1973). *Theory construction and the sociology of the family.* New York: John Wiley & Sons.

Cullum, M. C., & Bigler, E. D. (1985). Late effects of hematoma on brain morphology and memory in closed head injury. *International Journal of Neuroscience, 28,* 279–283.

Davidoff, G., Morris, J., Roth, E., & Bleiberg, J. (1985). Cognitive dysfunction and mild closed head injury in traumatic spinal cord injury. *Archives of Physical and Medical Rehabilitation, 66,* 489–491.

Dikmen, S. & Reitan, R. M. (1977). Emotional sequelae of head injury. *Annals of Neurology, 2,* 492–494.

Engel, G. L. (1961). Is grief a disease? Challenge for medical research. *Psychosomatic Medicine, 23,* 18–22.

Erikson, E. H. (1964). *Childhood and society.* New York: W. W. Norton.

Feibel, J. H., Berk, S., & Joynt, R. J. (1979). The unmet needs of stroke survivors. *Neurology, 29,* 592.

Fink, S. L. (1967). Crisis and motivation: A theoretical model. *Archives of Physical Medicine and Rehabilitation, 48,* 592-597.

Folstein, M. F., Maiberger, R., & McHugh, P. R. (1977). Mood disorder as a specific complication of stroke. *Journal of Neurology, Neurosurgery, and Psychiatry, 40,* 1018-1020.

Freud, S. (1957). *The standard edition of the complete psychological works of Sigmund Freud.* London: Hogarth Press, XIV.

George, L. (1980). *Role transitions in later life.* Belmont, CA: Brooks/Cole.

Gerhardt, V. (1979). Coping and social action: Theoretical reconstruction of the life event approach. *Sociology of Health and Illness, 20,* 195-225.

Green, B. C., Pratt, C. C., & Grigsby, T. E. (1985). Self concept among persons with long-term spinal cord injury. *Archives of Physical Medicine and Rehabilitation, 65,* 751-754.

Gunther, M. S. (1971). Psychiatric consultation in a rehabilitation hospital: A regression hypothesis. *Comparative Psychiatry, 12,* 572-585.

Hamburg, D., Hamburg, G., & Goza, S. G. (1953). Adaptive problems and mechanisms in severely burned patients. *Psychiatry, 16,* 284-291.

Hansen, D. (1965). Personal and positional influence in formal groups: Compositions and theory for research on family vulnerability to stress. *Social Forces, 44,* 202-210.

Hansen, D., & Johnson, V. (1979). Rethinking family stress theory: Definition aspects. In: W. Burr, R. Hill, F. Nye, & I. Reiss (Eds.), *Contemporary stories about the family* (Volume 1) (pp. 582-603). New York: Free Press.

Hill, R. (1949). *Families under stress.* New York: Harper & Row.

Jennett, B., & Teasdale, G. (1981). *Management of head injuries.* Philadelphia: F. A. Davis.

Krystal, H., & Petty, T. A. (1961). Psychological processes of normal convalescence. *Psychosomatics, 2,* 366.

Kübler-Ross, E. (1969). *On death and dying.* New York: MacMillan.

Kutner, B. B. (1971). The social psychology of disability. In W. Neff (Ed.), *Rehabilitation psychology.* Washington, DC: American Psychological Association.

LeMay, M., & Geschwind, N. (1978). Asymmetries of the human cerebral hemispheres. In A. Carmazza and E. Zurif (Eds.), *Language acquisition and language breakdown* (pp. 102-116). Baltimore: Johns Hopkins University Press.

Levy, D. E., Caronna, J. J., Singer, B. H., Lapinski, R. H., Frydman, H., & Plum, F. (1985). Predicting outcome from hypoxic-ischemic coma. *Journal of the American Medical Association, 253,* 1420-1426.

McCubbin, H. I., Joy, C. B., Cauble, A. E., Patterson, J. M., & Needle, R. H. (1980). Family stress and coping. *Journal of Marriage and the Family, 4,* 855-871.

McDaniel, J. W. (1976). *Physical disability and human behavior.* New York: Pergamon Press.

Miller, E. (1984). *Recovery and management of neuropsychological impairments.* New York: Wiley & Sons.

Oddy, M., Humphrey, M., & Uttley, D. (1978). Stresses upon the relatives of head-injured patients. *British Journal of Psychiatry, 133,* 507-513.

Oradel, D. M., & Waite, N. S. (1974). Group psychotherapy with stoke patients during the immediate recovery phase. *American Journal of Orthopsychiatry, 44,* 386-395.

Pearlin, L., & Schooler, C. (1978). The structure of coping. *Journal of Health and Social Behavior, 19,* 2-21.

Robinson, R. G., & Benson, D. F. (1981). Depression in aphasic patients: Frequency, severity, and clinical-pathological correlations. *Brain and language, 14,* 282-291.

Romano, M. D. (1974). Family response to traumatic head injury. *Scandinavian Journal of Rehabilitation Medicine, 6,* 1-4.

Roskins, E., & Lazarus, R. (1980). Coping theory and the teaching of coping skills. In D. Davidson & S. Davidson (Eds.), *Behavioral medicine: Changing health lifestyles* (pp. 38–69). New York: Brunner Mazel.

Schwab, J. J. (1972).Emotional considerations in cancer and stroke: In stroke. *New York State Journal of Medicine, 72,* 2877–2880.

Shands, H. C. (1965). An outline of the process of recovery from severe trauma. *Archives of Neurology, 73,* 403.

Shontz, F. C. (1965). Reactions to crisis. *Volta Review, 67,* 364–370.

Siller, J. (1969). Psychological situation of disabled with spinal cord injuries. *Rehabilitation Literature, 30,* 290–296.

Stewart, T. D. (1977). Spinal cord injury: A role for the psychiatrist. *American Journal of Psychiatry, 234,* 538–541.

Stewart, T. D., & Rossier, A. B. (1978). Psychological considerations in the adjustment to spinal cord injury. *Rehabilitation Literature, 39,* 75–81.

Stewart, T., & Shields, C. R. (1985). Grief in chronic illness. *Archives of Physical Medicine Rehabilitation, 66,* 447–450.

Thomsen, I. V. (1974). The patient with severe head injury and his family. *Scandanavian Journal of Rehabilitation Medicine, 6,* 180–183.

Tucker, S. J. (1980). The psychology of spinal cord injury: Patient-staff interaction. *Rehabilitation Literature, 41,* 5–6.

Weiner, I. B. (1975). *Principles of psychotherapy.* New York: Wiley.

Weller, D. J., & Miller, P. M. (1977a). Emotional reactions of individual, family, and staff in the acute-care period of spinal cord injury (Part 1). *Social Work in Health Care, 2,* 369–377.

Weller, D. J., & Miller, P. M. (1977b). Emotional reactions of patient, family, and staff in the acute-care period of spinal cord injury (Part 2). *Social Work in Health Care, 3,* 7–17.

Wershba, J. (1982). Step by step. *60 Minutes,* XV, 8, November 7, 1982, 11–16.

Wilmot, C. B., Cope, N., Hall, K. M., & Acker, M. (1985). Occult head injury: Its incidence in spinal cord injury. *Archives of Physical and Medical Rehabilitation, 66,* 227–231.

Part III: *The Personal Impact of Disability—Study Questions and Disability Awareness Exercise*

1. Are there any situations you can think of in which the removal of a disabling condition may not result in the happiness of a person?
2. Explain why a person who loses one arm may have a more difficult time adjusting than a person who loses two arms and one leg?
3. What are the differences between adaptation to a sudden onset of a disability (spinal cord injury) as compared to a gradual onset (multiple sclerosis)?
4. Are the stages of adjustment to a physical disability similar to the adjustment to an emotional disability?
5. Are the principles and assumptions related to the adaptation to disability applicable to AIDS?
6. Can denial ever be helpful in the adjustment to a disability? Give an example.
7. What do you think is the most commonly held "myth" regarding persons with disabilities? What suggestions do you have regarding the reduction of that myth in our society?
8. You've just been told you have only one month to live. How would this information affect you? Would you benefit from a group experience with other people with terminal illness?
9. Imagine that one week from now a severe myocardial infarction will result in your living under major limitations, e.g., no sexual activity for one year, no working, and the knowledge that your next attack could be your last. Discuss your activities for this week.
10. You have been told that chances are very good that you will have a heart attack in six months unless you drastically change your lifestyle. Develop a program designed to help you delay or avoid having a heart attack. Can you follow through with this program? What would be most difficult for you to change?

11. You have just been informed by your physician that due to your heart condition you must change your occupation. What would you do?

HERE TODAY, GONE TOMORROW

Personal health is frequently taken for granted. In order to provide the reader with a perspective on his or her personal values related to physical well-being, this experience focuses on the impact of disability from a personal frame of reference.

Goals

1. To heighten awareness of the role good health plays in a person's life.
2. To stress the importance and temporality of a person being "able-bodied."
3. To put into perspective the values of people faced with limited time frames regarding loss of physical and emotional functioning.

Procedure

1. The leader begins by asking "Have you ever considered what a loss of health would mean to you?"
2. Cards are distributed to each member. They contain one of the following statements: "You have just been informed that you have a degenerative disease and you will be very disabled in: (a) five years, (b) one year, (c) 6 months, (d) 3 months, (e) 1 month, (f) 1 week, (g) 1 day, (h) 1 hour, (i) 1 minute.
3. Participants are instructed to write what they would do for each of these time frames (Time: 10 minutes).
4. When completed, one person is asked to read his response for a specific time frame. This is done until each time frame is covered.
5. Discussion may focus on the quantitative and qualitative aspects of the responses, that is, does a respondent stress doing for self or for another?
6. Explore the differentiating effect of time and relate this to the reality that some people do not have the opportunity to be aware of a degenerative condition and must deal with a traumatic event, such as immediate loss due to trauma.

Part IV

The Interpersonal and Attitudinal Impact of Disability

The societal response to disability is, in part, a reflection of the attitudes of others toward disability and toward persons with disabilities. This attitude is often negative and it affects the interpersonal relationships between persons with disabilities and those who are able-bodied, as well as society's attempts to rehabilitate persons with handicaps.

Interactions that are not constructive are typically described as strained or anxiety provoking for both participants. In some cases this strain, in combination with negative attitudes, contributes to persons who have disabilities being socially excluded from others. In other cases, they may be intruded on through stares or questioned out of curiosity.

In Chapter 15, "Communication Barriers Between the 'Able-Bodied' and 'the Handicapped,' " Zola emphasizes the difficulties of both telling and hearing the story of having a disability. He presents a thoughtful analysis of this problem and its deep roots in Western culture. He notes that these communication problems result in everyone being deprived of the knowledge, skills, resources, and motivation to promote change.

Based on qualitative research on community programs for people with severe disabilities, Taylor and Bogdan, in Chapter 16, present an intriguing view of accepting relationships between people with disabilities and persons without disabilities. In contrast to a "sociology of deviance" the authors outline the theoretical framework for a "sociology of acceptance" and discuss the implications that this framework can have for rehabilitation.

Livneh, in Chapter 17, traces the origins of negative attitudes toward persons with disabilities and examines numerous variables as possible correlates of negative attitudes. His classification system provides a useful means for categorizing and discussing sources of negative attitudes.

The chapters in Part IV enable the reader to more clearly understand the interpersonal and attitudinal impact of disability, how the lives of persons with disability are affected, and how they may be changed.

15

Communication Barriers Between "the Able-Bodied" and "the Handicapped"

Irving Kenneth Zola

"Why doesn't anyone understand what it's like?" is a lament of many who try to convey to others the nature of being physically handicapped or chronically ill. It is a story difficult to hear as well as to tell—a difficulty rooted deep in Western culture. Slater put it well:

> Our ideas about institutionalizing the aged, psychotic, retarded, and infirm are based on a pattern of thought that we might call The Toilet Assumption—the notion that unwanted matter, unwanted difficulties, unwanted complexities and obstacles will disappear if they are removed from our immediate field of vision... Our approach to social problems is to decrease their visibility: out of sight, out of mind ... The result of our social efforts has been to remove the underlying problems of our society farther and farther from daily experience and daily consciousness, and hence to decrease in the mass of the population, the knowledge, skill, resources, and motivation necessary to deal with them. (Slater, 1970, p. 15)

It is, however, increasingly less acceptable to exile "problem" bearers in far-away colonies, asylums, and sanitaria. A recent compromise has been to locate them in places which, if not geographically distant, are socially distant—places with unfree access, like ghettos, special housing projects, nursing homes, or hospitals. This, too, is imperfect. So a final strategy makes them socially indistinct. They are stereotyped. But I never fully appreciated the resultant distancing and isolation

From *Archives of Physical Medicine and Rehabilitation,* 62(1981), 355–359. Reprinted with permission.

Presented as part of the Interdisciplinary Forum on "Quality of Life: The Costs of Being Disabled—Financial and Psychological" at the 56th Annual Session of the American Congress of Rehabilitation Medicine, Honolulu, November 12, 1979. Excerpted from Dr. Zola's book "The Missing Piece" (Temple University Press, 1981).

until it happened to me! I use a cane, wear a long leg brace, and a back support, walk stifflegged with a pronounced limp. All in all, I think of myself as fairly unusual in appearance and thus easily recognizable. And yet for years I have had the experience of being "mistaken" for someone else. Usually I was in a new place and a stranger would greet me as Tom, Dick, or Harry. After I explained that I was not he, they would usually apologize saying, "You look just like him." Inevitably I would meet this Tom, Dick, or Harry and he would be several inches shorter or taller, 40 pounds heavier or lighter, a double amputee on crutches, or a paraplegic in a wheelchair. I was continually annoyed and even puzzled how anyone could mistake "him" for the "unique me." What eventually dawned on me was that to many I was handicapped first and foremost. So much so that in the eyes of the "able-bodied," I and all the other "looked alike."

But more is going on here than the traditional stereotyping of a stigmatized ethnic group. The social invisibility of the physically handicapped has a more insidious development. Young children care little about skin color, or Semitic or Oriental features. Only as they grow older are they eventually taught to attend to these. Quite the opposite is true with regard to physical handicap. When small children meet a person using a wheelchair or wearing a brace, they are curious and pour forth questions like, "Why are you wearing this? What is it? Do you take it off at night? How high up does it go? Can I touch it?" If, however, there are any adults or parents within hearing, they immediately become fidgety and admonish the children, "It's not nice to ask such things" or "It's not nice to stare at people who are ... " The feature in question—the limp, the cane, the wheelchair, the brace—is quite visible and of great interest to children, but they are taught to ignore it. They are not, of course, taught that it is an inconsequential characteristic, but with the effect, if not in words, that it is an uncomfortable and all-encompassing one. They are taught to respond globally and not particularistically—to recognize a handicapped person when they see one but to ignore the specific characteristics of the handicap. Is it any wonder that a near-universal complaint is, "Why can't people see me as someone who *has* a handicap rather than someone who *is* handicapped?" Young children first perceive it that way but are quickly socialized out of it.

But why all this effort? Why this distancing of the chronically ill and handicapped? Why are we, the chronically ill and physically handicapped, so threatening that we must be made socially invisible? The answer is found both in the nature of society and the nature of people.

The United States is a nation built on the premise that there is no mountain that cannot be levelled, no river untamed, no force of nature unharnessed. It should thus be no great surprise that we similarly claim that there is no disease that cannot be cured. And so there is a continual series of wars—against heart disease, cancer, stroke, birth defects. They are wars worthy enough in themselves but ones that promise nirvana over the next hill, a society without disease. It is, however, as Dubos has claimed, but a mirage:

Organized species such as ants have established a satisfactory equilibrium with their environment and suffer no great waves of disease or changes in their social structure. But man is essentially dynamic, his way of life is constantly in flux from century to century. He experiments with synthetic products and changes his diet; he builds cities that breed rats and infection; he builds automobiles and factories which pollute the air, and he constructs radioactive bombs. As life becomes more comfortable and technology more complicated, new factors introduce new dangers. The ingredients for Utopia are agents for new disease. (Dubos, 1961)

I am not arguing for any cessation in these campaigns to alleviate suffering. Rather, I am concerned with their side effects. People no longer die. Doctors simply lost the battle to save them. With society so raging against the anthropomorphic killer "diseases," should it be a surprise that some of the anger at the diseases spills on its bearers? In this context, the physically handicapped become objects, the permanent reminders of a lost and losing struggle, the symbol of a past and continuing failure.

Finally, the discomfiting confrontation of the "able-bodied" with the "disabled" is not just a symbolic one. For there is a hidden truth to the statement often heard when such a meeting occurs, the shudder and occasional sigh, "I'm glad it's not me." But the relief is often followed by guilt for ever thinking such a thought—a guilt one would just as soon also not deal with. Thus, the threat to be removed lies not merely in society's failure but in the inevitability of one's own. The discomfort that many feel in the presence of the aged, the suffering, the dying *is* the reality that it *could* just as well be they. For, like it or not, we will all one day get to grow old, and to die. And in high-technology America, this means dying *not* of natural causes and old age but of some chronic disease. But in the United States this is a reality we never tire of denying.

All this, then, is the burden that we, the chronically ill in general and the physically handicapped in particular, carry. In every interaction, our baggage includes not only our own physical infirmity but the evocation of and sense of infirmity in others and the consequent incapacity to deal with both this empirical and symbolic reality.

ON THE DIFFICULTY IN TELLING

The story of having a disability or illness is difficult to tell as well as to hear. There is thus a complementary question to the one with which I opened this chapter: "Why can't I make anyone understand what it's like to be handicapped?" To me, the different emphasis implies that the spokesperson may be at a loss "to tell it like it is." Part of the problem may lie in the vantage point of these speakers. Erving Goffman once noted that "minority" group spokesmen may occupy that position precisely because they are successful adapters and, thus, in many ways closer to the "normals" (Goffman, 1963). Yet to that extent, they are ironically less representative of the group they are supposed to represent. For instance, I and many other "successful mainstream adapters" have not numbered among our close friends and acquaintances *any* handicapped people—an "alienation" from our disability, which has escalated almost to the level of an unconscious principle. Moreover, almost every written account about a "successful" handicapped person, as well as every "success" I have met (including myself), usually regards, as a key element, the self-conception: "I never think of myself as handicapped." Yet the degree to which this is true may have made it virtually impossible to tell anyone what it is like to be disabled in a world of normals. In a real sense, we don't know. Thus, what the public learns from our example is decidedly limited.

Franklin Delano Roosevelt is a case in point. To normals as well as the handicapped, he is the ultimate example of successful adaptation. For after being afflicted with polio and left a virtual paraplegic he went on to become President of the United States. What better evidence of success? And yet the newer biographies reveal a man not so pleasant as an individual, not so happy with his lot, and possessed of certain drives and needs that for another person less famous might have been labelled clinically pathologic. Moreover, whatever his political achievements, his social success was a more limited one. The public knew that he had suffered polio, was confined to a wheelchair, and used crutches rarely, but he was careful never to "confront" the public. He never allowed himself to be photographed in a wheelchair or on crutches. He photogenically passed. But few of us can so control, manipulate, and overcome our environment. So too with the other folk heroes of disease. They are not the little people, not the millions, but the few who are so successful that they also "passed"—the polio victim who later broke track records, the one-legged pitcher who made it to the major leagues, the pianist who was blind, the singer who had a colostomy. They were all so good that no one knew or had to be aware of their "handicap" and therein lay part of their glory.

I do not wish, however, to leave the impression that the only impact of the media, particularly television, on the public's view of the handicapped is in the distorted picture of success. The general problem is perhaps more depressing. For the handicapped are rarely portrayed in successful terms. In the most systematic and incisive analysis I have yet seen, Dr. Bonnie D. Leonard claims that the overall TV portrayal of people with a handicap is quite dismal (unpublished data). In a study focused on prime-time shows, she notes that not only are they numerically underrepresented but whether the dimension be demographic, economic, social, personal, or interactional, the handicapped are continually depicted as almost irredeemably inferior to or dependent on the able-bodied. They are retrieved from this status only by a miracle—the unflagging persistence of a skilled physician or the undaunted love of a good person. So "one-down" are they that she characterizes their position as "less than human and beyond servility."

But it is the "success" stories that are more familiar to the public and which in some ways are equally destructive. A specific example sticks painfully in my mind. I am a sports fan and, as such, an avid watcher of major events. The 1976 Olympics found me glued to my TV set and I was pleasantly surprised by a documentary that related to me quite personally. I think it was called "Six Who Overcame" and told how six athletes had overcome some problem (five were directly physical) and gone on to win Olympic gold medals. One story really grabbed me. It was about Wilma Rudolph, a woman who had polio as a child. Through pictures and words, her struggle was recreated. Love, caring, exercise, and hard work repeated endlessly, until she started to walk slowly with crutches and then, abandoning them, began to run. And there in the final frames she was sprinting down the track straining every muscle. With tears streaming down my face, I shouted, "Go on, Wilma! Do it! Do it!" And when she did I too collapsed, exhausted and exhilarated. But scarcely 90 minutes later, I was furious. For a basic message of the film sank in. In each case the person overcame. But overcame what? Wilma's polio was not my polio! And all the love, caring, exercise, and hard work could NEVER have allowed me to win a running race, let alone compete in one.

My point is that in almost all the success stories that get to the public, there is a dual message. The first one is very important—that just because we have polio, cancer, or multiple sclerosis or have limited use of our eyes, ears, mouth, and limbs, our lives are *not* over. We can still learn, be happy, be lovers, spouses, parents, and even achieve great deeds. It is the second message that I have recently begun to abhor. It states that if a Franklin Delano Roosevelt or a Wilma Rudolph could OVERCOME their handicap, so could and should all the disabled. And if we fail, it's *our* problem, *our* personality, *our* weakness. And all this further masks what chronic illness is all about. For our lives or even our adaptations do not center around one single activity or physical achievement but around many individual and complex ones. Our daily living is not filled with dramatic accomplishments but with mundane ones. And most of all, our physical difficulties are not temporary ones to be overcome once-and-for-all but ones we must face again and again for the rest of our lives. That's what chronic means!

ON THE STORY TO BE TOLD

Now, this great achievement syndrome blinds not only the general public but also the achievers. We are paid the greatest of compliments when someone tells us, "You know, I never think of you as handicapped." And we gladly accept it. We are asked, "How did you make it against such great odds?" And we answer the question. And yet in both the accepting and the answering we further distance ourselves from the problems of having a handicap. In a sense they become both emotionally and cognitively inaccessible. I am not using these words lightly. I do indeed mean emotionally and cognitively inaccessible.

Let me illustrate with a personal example. I do a great deal of long-distance traveling and, as such, often find my jet flight located on the furthest runway from the entrance. Adjusting to this, I ordinarily allow myself an extra 20 to 30 minutes to get there. I regarded this for most of my life as a minor inconvenience. And if perchance you had asked me then if I experienced any undue tiredness or avoidable soreness, I would have firmly and honestly answered, "No." But in 1977, a new "consciousness" altered all this. Piqued at why I should continue to inconvenience myself, I began to regularly use a wheelchair for all such excursions. I thought that the only surprise I would encounter would be the dubious glances of other passengers, when, after reaching my destination, I would rise unassisted and walk briskly away. In fact I was occasionally regarded as if I had in some way "cheated." Much more disconcerting, however, was that I now arrived significantly more energetic, more comfortable, freer from cramps and leg sores than in my previous decades of travelling. The conclusion I drew was inevitable. I had *always* been tired, uncomfortable, cramped, and sore after a long journey. But with no standard of comparison, these feelings were incorporated into the cognitive reality of what travelling was for me. I did not "experience" the tiredness and discomfort. They were cognitively inaccessible.

What I am contending is shockingly simple. The very process of successful adaptation not only involves divesting ourselves of any identification with being handicapped, but also denying the uncomfortable features of that life. To not do so might have made our success impossible! But this process has a cost. One may accept and forget too much.

I remember, however, but fragments of a story. For there is no special world of the handicapped, and herein lies another major problem in telling the story. There are several reasons for this lack. First, while most minority groups grow up in some special subculture and, thus, form a series of norms and expectations, the physically handicapped are not similarly prepared. Born for the most part into normal families, we are socialized into that world. The world of sickness is one we enter only later—poorly prepared, and with all the prejudices of the normal. We think of ourselves in the shadows of the external world. The very vocabulary we use to describe ourselves is borrowed from that society. We are *de*-formed, *dis*-eased, *dis*-abled, *dis*-ordered, *ab*-normal, and most telling of all, an *in*-valid. And most all share, deep within ourselves, the hoped-for miracle to reverse the process—a new drug or operation that will return us to a life of validity.

A dramatic but mundane way of characterizing an aspect of our dilemma is seen by looking at the rallying cries of current "liberation" movements. As the "melting pot" theory of America was finally buried, people could once again say, even though they be three generations removed, "I'm proud to be Greek, Italian, Hungarian, Polish." With the rise of Black Power, a derogatory label became a rallying cry, "Black is beautiful!" And when Female Liberationists saw their strength in numbers, they shouted, "Sisterhood is powerful!" But what about the chronically ill and disabled? Can we yell, "Long live Cancer!" "Up with Multiple Sclerosis!" "I'm glad I had Polio!" Clearly, a basis of a common positive identity based on our disability is not readily available.

For all these reasons, whatever world the physically handicapped and chronically ill inhabit, it is fragmentary in structure and content. It is, thus, difficult enough to integrate into one's own experience, let alone communicate to others.

There is a certain inevitable restraint, for what comes out seems like a litany of complaints. And no one—at least in my society—likes a complainer! But it is a reality, my reality, and as such I record it.

Chairs without arms to push myself up from; unpadded seats that all too quickly produce sores; showers and toilets without handrails to maintain my balance; surfaces too slippery to walk on; staircases without banisters to help hoist myself; buildings without ramps, making ascent exhausting, if not dangerous; every curbstone a precipice; car, plane, and theater seats too cramped for my braced leg; and trousers too narrow for my leg brace to pass through. With such trivia is my life plagued. Even for me, who is relatively well off, mobility provides its daily challenges. If I am walking with a companion, he or she must always be on my right, else will inadvertently kick my cane and throw me off balance. My moment-by-moment concerns are even more mundane. For I must be extraordinarily watchful as to where I place both my cane and my leg. If not, inevitably my cane tip will slide on an oil slick or I will stub my toe on an uneven piece of sidewalk, thus lose my balance and fall. In short, I should walk as if looking for pennies.

But I resist impositions that impede social interaction. For if I am constantly looking down to where my foot or cane must be placed, then I cannot look directly at a person with whom I am conversing. And so I pay the price and run the risk, which means I stumble and fall all too often.

The problems of long-distance travel go even deeper. Every departure from home base is fraught with difficulties, from how long one can go without toilet facilities to how long one must sit in a cramped position; from the lack of a special diet to the lack of a special bed; from the absence of familiar and reliable surroundings to the absence of familiar and reliable help. Each slams home our dependency—our sense of "living on a leash." The leash may be a long one but it nevertheless exists.

This was especially hard for me, who had quite successfully repressed "my leashes." Whenever on long-term travel, I automatically packed my spare leg brace and back support, but never on any short-term trip. And then one day the impossible happened. On a trip to New Delhi, India, my brace snapped. And there I was with a piece of steel protruding through my trousers, unable to put my full weight any longer on my right leg, thousands of miles from home and, I thought, from help. Never had I felt so absolutely helpless. Worse, I felt foolish, embarrassed, even guilty, as if I had some role in my brace snapping. I have never experienced such a sense of total panic. It was as if I suddenly felt that I would never be able to move again—that I would forever remain in this spot with my leg dangling.

But I am "blessed" with a certain amount of income and position. Even in New Delhi, India, I can "command," and that is the appropriate word, resources to deal with my problem. What happens to all those without sufficient money or power to alter their environment—those without resources to have railings built or clothes custom-made or sufficient influence to have meetings take place in more physically accessible locations—those without power to command *immediate* repair of their brace or wheelchair? I suspect that they ultimately give up, unable to change or manipulate the world; they simply cut out that part of their life which requires such encounters, all of which contributes to a real as well as social invisibility and isolation.

Most germane to my point about telling it like it is: What happens when none of these unpleasant events occur? What happens when it all goes off without a hitch? With whom can I share the satisfaction that I did not trip, that my brace did not break, that I did not have difficulty with toilet facilities, that I made it by myself? When hospitalized with polio, I was tearful when I first defecated without the aid of laxative. Even more exciting, after months of impotence, was my first erection. My first steps at walking I could share, but not excessively, with my parents and my friends. My bowel movements were at least acknowledged by the medical and nursing staff. But my sexual issues were kept achingly to myself. Even amongst my fellow residents, socialized as they were into the world of the normal, there was only limited access to any sharing. There was an implicit limit on how much "the others" want to hear about your "minor" successes and failings. Too much time and too much affect and one ran the risk of being thought "too preoccupied" or even "hypochondriacal." Thus gradually the lesson was learned that no one, including myself, really wanted to hear the mundane details of being sick or handicapped, neither the triumphs nor the hardships.

I am sure the specific details and hardships of having a handicap or chronic disease vary from person to person. But not the core problem. The story is inevitably difficult to both hear and tell. To the teller, it is especially hard to acknowledge. Indeed, to even think of the world in such a realistic, paranoid way might make it too depressing a reality to tolerate. As such, the only defense, the only way to live, is to deny it. But then it becomes socially invisible to *all*. We are sadly left as Slater (1970) has articulated—both those with physical handicaps and those without, *all* are deprived of the very knowledge, skill, resources, and motivation necessary to promote change.

REFERENCES

Dubos, R. J. (1961). *Mirage of health: Utopias, progress and biological change.* New York: Doubleday, quote is from flyleaf.

Goffman, E. (1963). *Stigma: Notes on management of spoiled identity* (pp. 105–125). Englewood Cliffs, NJ: Prentice-Hall.

Slater, P. E. (1970). *Pursuit of loneliness: American culture at breaking point* (p. 15). Boston: Beacon Press.

16

On Accepting Relationships Between People With Mental Retardation and Nondisabled People: Towards an Understanding of Acceptance

Steven J. Taylor
Robert Bogdan

Mrs. Parker is an older woman who lives in a middle-class neighborhood in a Midwestern city in the United States. For the past eight years, she and her husband have been foster parents for a young girl named Amy. Amy has severe hydrocephaly and a multitude of associated problems, including blindness, frequent seizures, and hypothermia. She is fed through a tube and is susceptible to choking, infections, bed sores, and sudden drops in body temperature. Mrs. Parker speaks lovingly of Amy and keeps a scrapbook filled with pictures of her, locks of hair, and other mementos. According to Mrs. Parker, she hates to be away from Amy and would be lost if anything ever happened to her. She says that Amy has done as much for her life as she has done for Amy's.

Al and Gertrude are a middle-aged couple who live in a modest house in a working-class neighborhood in the state capitol of an American upper Midwestern state. Living with them is David, a four-year-old diagnosed as mentally retarded, blind, and physically handicapped. Al and Gertrude are David's foster parents, but

This chapter was prepared as part of the Research and Training Center on Community Integration, funded by the National Institute on Disability and Rehabilitation Research, US Department of Education (Co-operative Agreement No. G0085C03503). The opinions expressed herein are solely those of the authors and no official endorsement by the US Department of Education should be inferred. We owe a debt of gratitude to Pam Walker, Zana Lutfiyya, Julie Racino, Nancy Zollers, Rannveig Traustadottir, Beth Teelucksingh and Dora Bjarnason, who provided many of the examples and contributed many of the ideas contained in this article. We would also like to thank Gunnar Dybwad, Dianne Ferguson, Douglas Biklen, Betsy Edinger and Janet Bogdan for their contribution to this article.

they also happen to be his great aunt and uncle. When asked how they came to be David's foster parents, they explained that his father could not accept his disabilities and his parents had placed him in an institution: "We just couldn't stand to see David there. He's family."

Mary is on the board of directors of an agency that operates group homes and other community living arrangements in a Western American state. She became involved with the agency when it established a group home in her neighborhood. Bothered by the negative reactions of her fellow neighbors, she decided to become involved with the home and agency. As she explained, "I see the group home as a public responsibility of this community." Through her involvement with the home, she has developed a close friendship with Tony, a resident who is labeled moderately retarded. She visits Tony often and takes him to her own home: "I and my husband, we really love Tony."

Since the 1960s, the social sciences—specifically sociology, and anthropology—have had a profound impact on the fields of mental health and mental retardation. From a sociological or anthropological perspective, mental illness and mental retardation are social and cultural phenomena (Scheff, 1966; Dexter, 1967; Edgerton, 1967; Vail, 1967; Braginsky & Braginsky, 1971; Mercer, 1973; Hobbs, 1975; Jacobs, 1980; Bogdan & Taylor, 1982; Bercovici, 1983; Evans, 1983; Langness & Levine, 1986). According to this perspective, people labeled mentally retarded and mentally ill are placed in a deviant social role, subjected to stigma and rejected by the community at large. Many of the concepts and ideas that have dominated the fields of mental health and mental retardation over the past two decades are rooted in this social science perspective (Taylor & Bogdan, 1980). For example, the concept of normalization is based on an understanding of mental retardation and mental illness as forms of deviant behavior (Wolfensberger, 1972; see also, Wolfensberger, 1975).

If sociocultural theories of deviance are true, then how are we to understand people like Mrs. Parker, Al and Gertrude, and Mary? In other words, if society rejects and excludes people with demonstrable differences, including mental retardation, how can we explain individuals and social groups who come to accept, like, and love others with the most severe and profound disabilities?

This chapter represents one of the beginning steps toward the development of what we have referred to as the "sociology of acceptance" (Bogdan & Taylor, 1987), as applied to people with mental retardation, and especially those with severe disabilities. As a theoretical perspective, the sociology of acceptance is directed toward understanding how those who are different, who might be termed deviant, come to be accepted by other people.

Though we propose a sociology of acceptance, this is not to reject the contribution of social science perspectives on deviance. Like all theories, sociological and anthropological notions of deviance illuminate some phenomena and obscure others. These perspectives are not wrong or misguided. They are, however, one-sided and cannot account for much of what we have observed in the empirical world.

Because social science perspectives on deviance have come to be so widely accepted and taken for granted in the fields of mental health and mental retardation and because our analysis builds on the sociology of deviance, we discuss these perspectives as a point of departure for our discussion of acceptance. We will not attempt to critique these perspectives but simply to present them in terms of their general purposes.

SOCIAL SCIENCE PERSPECTIVES ON DEVIANCE

Beginning in the 1930s, if not earlier, sociologists started to develop what has come to be known variously as "labeling theory," the "societal reaction perspective," or the "interactionist perspective" on deviance (Tannenbaum, 1938; Lemert, 1951; Kitsuse, 1962). According to this perspective, deviance is created by society through the establishment and application of social rules. Becker's (1963) seminal study, *Outsiders*, provides the clearest formulation of this perspective:

> . . . *social groups create deviance by making rules whose infraction constitutes deviance,* and by applying those rules to particular people and labeling them as outsiders. From this point of view, deviance is *not* a quality of the act the person commits, but rather a consequence of the application of others of rules and sanctions to an "offender." The deviant is one to whom that label has successfully been applied; deviant behavior is behavior that people so label. (emphasis in original) (p. 9).

As applied to the study of mental retardation, this perspective has yielded four general insights. First, *mental retardation is a social and cultural construct.* Like other forms of deviance, mental retardation can be viewed not as an objective condition, but as a concept that exists in the minds of people who attach that label to others (Bogdan & Taylor, 1982; Langness & Levine, 1986). As Mercer (1973) writes:

> Persons have no means and belong to no class until we put them in one. Whom we call mentally retarded, and where we draw the line between the mentally retarded and the normal, depend upon our interest and the purpose of our classification. The intellectual problem of mental retardation in the community is, ultimately, a problem of classification and nomenclature. (p. 1)

While this perspective does not deny that intellectual or organic differences may exist between people, it suggests that the meaning of the label "mental retardation" depends on the society and culture and that the labeling of someone as mentally retarded is a social accomplishment rather than an exercise in the application of objective scientific procedures.

Second, *the label of mental retardation carries with it a stigma.* In sociological and anthropological terms, a stigma is not merely a difference, but a character-istic that deeply discredits a person's moral character (Goffman, 1963; Langness & Levine, 1986). Edgerton's (1967) classic study, *The Cloak of Competence*, pro-vides the clearest analysis of stigma in the lives of people with mental retardation. As Edgerton (1967) writes,

> The label of mental retardation not only serves as a humiliating, frustrating, and dis-crediting stigma in the conduct of one's life in the community, but it also serves to lower one's self-esteem to such a nadir of worthlessness that the life of a person is scarcely worth living. (p. 145)

Third, *labeling someone as mentally retarded creates a self-fulfilling proph-ecy* (Merton, 1948). According to W. I. Thomas & D. S. Thomas's (1928) famous sociological dictum, "If men define situations as real, they are real in their conse-quences" (p. 572). People with mental retardation play a social role in which they are rewarded for behavior that conforms to societal expectations and punished for behavior that departs from those expectations (Bogdan & Taylor, 1982; Mercer, 1973). Wolfensberger (1972) writes:

> When a person is perceived as deviant, he is cast into a role that carries with it powerful expectancies. Strangely enough, these expectancies not only take hold of the mind of the perceiver, but of the perceived person as well . . . Generally, people will play the roles they have been assigned. This permits those who define social roles to make self-fulfilling prophecies by predicting that someone cast into a certain role will emit behav-ior consistent with that role. (pp. 15–16)

Fourth, *institutions and organizations designed to treat or care for people with mental retardation create or reinforce behavior that further distances people with mental retardation from the broader community.* In *Asylums*, Goffman (1961) describes how people confined to "total institutions" such as prisons, mental hospi-tals, and other institutions develop ways of thinking and acting that appear bizarre and maladjusted when viewed from the outside, but that are perfectly reasonable and rational when viewed in the context of institutional life. Similarly, Biklen (1977) reports on the process of "colonization," adaptation to institutionalization, that occurs in institutions for people with mental retardation. Bercovici (1981, 1983) notes that many so-called community programs enmesh residents or clients in a subculture with its own set of prescribed behavior:

> . . . many dehospitalized mentally retarded persons are not, and do not perceive them-selves to be, living in the normal community, contrary to the assumptions that are gen-erally held. The data indicate that these persons may be seen, instead, as inhabitants of a physically segregated and perhaps culturally distinct social system. (Bercovici, 1981, p. 138)

Some social scientists go so far as to suggest that the social processes that cast people who are different into deviant roles, stigmatize them, and exclude them from social life are inherent in society. Combining a labeling perspective with sociological functionalism (Durkheim, 1938; Parsons, 1951; Merton, 1957; for a functionalist perspective on institutions, see Bachrach, 1981), Erikson (1966) argues that social groups place people in deviant roles as a means of maintaining cultural identity:

> Deviant forms of behavior, by marking the outer edges of group life, give the inner structure its special character and thus supply the framework within which the people of the group develop an orderly sense of their own cultural identity. (p. 13)

Commenting specifically on people with mental retardation, Edgerton (1967) and Evans (1983) suggest that the labeling and stigmatizing of the mentally retarded may well be inevitable in society. While the labeling approach to deviance has contributed significantly to our understanding of people with disabilities in society, it has too often been interpreted in terms of the inevitability of rejection of people with obvious differences. The labeling and exclusion of people with disabilities have become so taken-for-granted that instances of acceptance have been glossed over or ignored.

PERSPECTIVE AND METHOD

This article is based on qualitative research methods (Taylor and Bogdan, 1981, 1984) and specifically participant observation and open-ended interviewing. By qualitative methods, we mean research procedures that produce descriptive data: people's own written or spoken words and observable behavior. In contrast to most other forms of research, qualitative research is open-ended and inductive. That is, qualitative researchers are concerned with how people act and talk in their natural settings and allow concepts, insights, and understandings to emerge from the data themselves. Glaser & Strauss (1967) use the phrase "grounded theory" to refer to theories derived inductively from patterns in the researcher's data. Qualitative research methods, also referred to as field work, have a rich history in sociology and anthropology and have been used in the study of mental retardation by Edgerton (1967), Bercovici (1983), Bogdan & Taylor (1982), Bogdan, Taylor, de Grandpre, & Haynes (1974), Langness & Levine (1986), Taylor & Bogdan (1980), Jacobs (1969, 1980), and others.

What we call the sociology of acceptance grows out of field research we and others have conducted at agencies, programs, and homes for people with mental retardation, and especially severe and multiple disabilities, over the past two years. As part of an ongoing study of community living, we have made two- to four-day site visits to programs nominated as innovative or exemplary, according to predefined criteria, through a national search. We have compiled field notes on site visits made to 16 community living, foster care, or family support programs operated by state, regional, or private agencies in 10 American states.

Our purpose in this ongoing study is not to find "perfect" programs, but to understand how services are organized and what daily life is like at programs that have the reputation of being exemplary. Some programs have lived up to their reputations and others have not.

While we have been interested in ideological, administrative, and economic aspects of the programs we have visited, we have also looked at the nature of day-to-day life for a number of individuals served by the programs. Our research design called for observations of the living situations of individuals and interviews with them (whenever possible), staff members, and/or families.

This chapter also draws on data collected through evaluation of four state or private agency programs over the past year and our previous studies of integrated school programs (Taylor, 1982; Bogdan, 1983). In addition, we have utilized data collected through indepth interviewing of family members, agency staff, and citizen advocates conducted by researchers in an advanced graduate seminar (Lutfiyya, 1987; Racino, 1987; Teelucksingh, 1987; Traustadottir, 1987; Traustadottir & Bjarnason, 1987; Walker, 1987; Zollers, 1987).

As we began to analyze and reflect on our data, we came upon instances of relationships between people with severe disabilities and typical community members that could not be explained by current theories of deviance or the mental retardation literature on friendships (see, for example, Landesman-Dwyer, Berkson & Romer, 1979; Kaufman, 1984). Researchers have described instances of relationships between people labeled mentally retarded and nonretarded people—for example, Edgerton's (1967) perceptive description of "benefactors" in *The Cloak of Competence*—but have not explored how these relationships fit with prevailing theories and concepts.

The concept of "accepting relationships," as defined and described below, captures the essence of the relations we observed and heard about. In Glaser & Strauss's (1967) terms, this concept is "grounded" in the data we have collected.

By focusing attention on accepting relationships, we are not suggesting that most mentally retarded people are surrounded by a network of caring community members. Many of the people whose lives we have studied are, in fact, isolated and cut off from the wider community (also see Bercovici, 1983). Indeed, some of our data provide negative instances of acceptance, instances in which staff and others talk about people with mental retardation in stereotyped fashion and socially distance themselves from them. At the same time, however, the many examples of relationships between nondisabled and severely disabled people we have observed lead us to conclude that they are not a unique or exceptional circumstance, but representative of a larger pattern of relations deserving of serious study. It is these examples to which this article is directed.

As in the case of our research with people labeled mentally retarded (Bogdan & Taylor, 1982), we are interested in understanding relationships from the vantage point of the people involved in them (also see Langness & Levine, 1986). Others might approach these relationships from a different perspective; for example, in terms of "denial" or "cult of the stigmatized" (Goffman, 1963, p. 31). Yet any relationship between people can be described in terms of the illusions held by the partners. In this article, we present the perspectives of typical people involved in relationship with people with mental retardation on their own terms.

ACCEPTING RELATIONSHIPS

A sociology of acceptance perspective can be applied to the study of how individuals and groups commonly referred to as deviant come to be accepted into a society or a community. One of the few studies of acceptance of people with a demonstrable disability into a community is Groce's (1985) *Everyone Here Spoke Sign Language*. In this anthropological/historical account of towns on Martha's Vineyard in Massachusetts, Groce documents how the community unselfconsciously accepted deaf people as full-fledged, undifferentiated members. While a fully developed sociology of acceptance might look at acceptance on a societal, cultural, or community level, in this chapter we are concerned with accepting relationships on a personal level.

An accepting relationship is defined here as a relationship between a person with a deviant attribute, in this case mental retardation, and a nondisabled person, which is long-standing and characterized by closeness and affection and in which the deviant attribute, or disability, does not have a stigmatizing, or morally discrediting, character in the eyes of the nondisabled person. Accepting relationships are not based on a denial of the disability or difference, but rather on the absence of impugning the disabled person's moral character because of the disability.

What draws typical people into relationships with people with severe disabilities? What motivates people who form and maintain close relationships with disabled people; people like families who decide to keep their children at home, foster and adoptive families, volunteers and citizen advocates who become involved in the lives of people with disabilities for the long term, and staff members who go beyond their role to form personal relationships with the people they serve?

People who are involved in accepting relationships eventually take them for granted, something that does not require an explanation. In fact, asking people about why they have the relationships may evoke expressions of bewilderment, impatience, or even disgust. This tells them that the person asking the question regards the relationship as something abnormal, that needs to be explained.

While people may not always be able to articulate why they have developed a relationship with a person with an obvious disability, by their actions, way of talking, and explanations given when pressed, they point to a range of sentiments or motivations for entering into accepting relationships. Four major orientations can be distinguished, based on the sentiments held by the typical person towards the person with the disability.

Family

When we asked a 28-year-old married man why he maintains a close relationship with his 18-year-old mentally retarded bother, his immediate and impatient response was: "He's my brother." A sense of family remains a strong sentiment that binds people together. Most people care about and remain close to their disabled spouses, children, parents, aunts and uncles, and siblings.

That the birth and rearing of a child with severe disabilities can be traumatic and stressful for families is widely accepted in the field of mental retardation. Despite the hardships—socially imposed and otherwise—that may be undertaken in caring for a child with disabilities, families can and often do come to accept their disabled members. Common membership in the family supersedes the individual's differences.

For families, acceptance is often based on a sense of commitment and obligation to a family member. The family would not be the same family without the disabled family member. As Al, who with his wife became the foster parent of his institutionalized great-nephew, stated, "He's family." Writing on her decision to keep her disabled child at home, Park (1982) recalls that she agreed with a friend who asked, "Well, you couldn't have done anything else, could you?" A 10-year-old commented on his eight-year-old mentally retarded brother: "I guess he'll live with my mom til . . . he can't live with her anymore and then I'll have him come live with me."

Many families come to view their disabled member in terms of his or her positive characteristics and contribution to the family as a whole. Turnbull, Brotherson, & Summers (1985) report:

> In analyzing our interview data, a major ideological function of families was strikingly apparent—the development of a set of beliefs that helped families adjust to their child's handicap and turn what could be a very negative situation into a positive one. (p. 128)

Similarly, Teelucksingh (1987) describes how parents attribute a positive meaning to their children's disabilities. One parent states, "Her presence in the world has taught people a lot. That's her contribution." Another says, "Even the most handicapped child can teach us something. That might be his purpose."

As a basis for accepting relationships, the sentiment of family can also unite nondisabled and disabled people who are not related by birth. People with the most severe disabilities can be accepted by adoptive and foster families and treated as full family members. Some of the most powerful examples of acceptance we have observed were found among foster families of children and adults.

Consistent with the philosophy of "permanency planning," some state and regional agencies in the United States are aggressively recruiting foster and adoptive families for children with the most severe disabilities, including multiple disabilities, severe and profound mental retardation, and complex medical involvements

(Taylor, Biklen, & Knoll, 1987; Taylor, Racino, Knoll, & Lutfiyya, 1987). Agencies like Michigan's widely heralded Macomb–Oakland Regional Center have been successful in finding surrogate families for practically every child placed out of the natural home. As one Macomb–Oakland administrator has stated:

> There's somebody for everybody. Foster parents aren't interchangeable, though. Some aren't good with kids with behavior problems, but they're good with medically fragile kids. You have to match the kid with the family. The toughest kid will be taken in by someone who likes him.

While families may have a range of motivations for becoming foster or adoptive parents, a person with a disability often comes to be regarded as a central part of the family. A foster parent of several children with severe disabilities, who could not have children of his own, explains:

> We couldn't have children of our own. This gives us our family . . . We treat the kids like kings and queens. But that's the only way. Children should always get the best. These kids are no different.

Another foster parent, who has two children with severe disabilities, one of whom has hydrocephaly and one of whom is self-abusive, describes how one of her foster children fits into the family:

> Billie loves my natural son, John. He just turned 15. He gives Billie a lot of attention. He plays with him and roughhouses with him on the floor and Billie loves it . . . My natural son really loves Billie too . . . He's the little brother he never had . . . Billie understands a lot more than people give him credit for. He understands "No." He has a good personality. He's cute. He giggles. He's a kid . . . There's a lot of rewards. I wanted more kids. Now I have Billie and Susie. I wouldn't have thought I'd like it so much . . . For other families, what it would take is to get to know the kids. Take them in and get to know them.

In families that have taken in adults with mental retardation, acceptance does not seem to occur as naturally. Many "foster" families treat disabled adults as boarders and do not talk about them as though they are full family members. However some, while perhaps overprotective, do view adults with mental retardation living in their homes as a part of the family. One family member states:

> They tell me I can take them back to the state school. I won't do it. I think it would be just traumatic for either of them. They are family to us. We go for all nine yards. It would be like taking one of our kids back . . . Bonnie being here is good for the family and good for Bonnie. We bring them to all family gatherings. My sister said we could hire a babysitter and leave all the foster children home. We said that where we go, they go . . . The family accepts them as part of the family.

As natural and adopting (including foster) families come to accept mentally retarded and disabled family members, the disability gradually becomes less salient in their eyes. They begin to define the disabled person in terms of other qualities and attribute to the person characteristics that are not readily apparent to outsiders who do not have the same type of relationship with the person. A comparison of the perspectives of a special education teacher and a foster parent regarding a six-year-old girl with severe multiple disabilities provides a striking example of this. The teacher describes the young girl, Julie, as follows:

> A truck ran over her head when she was six months old ... She has no purposeful movement ... Julie is susceptible to upper respiratory infections and requires total care. We aren't sure whether she can respond to anything. She is unresponsive.

In the following exchange with an interviewer, Julie's foster mother presents a dramatically different picture of her:

Interviewer: What's Julie like?
Foster mother: She's pleasant, nice. She's good company ... She hears very well.
Interviewer: Have you seen any changes in Julie since she's lived here?
Foster mother: She laughs. She didn't do that before ... She's doing pretty good.
Interviewer: What does Julie need?
Foster mother: A lot of loving.
Interviewer: It is difficult taking care of Julie?
Foster mother: No, not at all. You don't have to chase her around the house.
Interviewer: What else do you do with Julie?
Foster mother: A lot of holding and talking. I talk to her like she knows what I'm saying ... We take her to church, the grocery store, everywhere we go.
Interviewer: Julie's teacher told me she will probably go to school full day next year.
Foster mother: I don't want her going a full day. I like mornings with her. I don't know what I'd do without her.

Some residential agencies adopt a family model as a service ideology. Agency-operated facilities are seldom characterized by the sentiment of family as found in actual families. Since staff may maintain social distance between themselves and residents and separate their own personal lives from their work roles, the term "family" as used in residential programs is likely to represent what Bercovici (1983, pp. 142–143) refers to as "fictive kinship roles," rather than the commitment and bond characteristic of families.

Religious Commitment

For some people, a commitment to spiritual values is the underlying motivation for the establishment of relationships with people with mental retardation. In contrast to family sentiments, in which relationships endure in spite of or without regard to the disability, relationships based on religious sentiments are established precisely because of the person's disability. In other words, the disability is the basis for forming the relationship.

People who develop accepting relationships based on religious sentiments—for example, some people who take mentally retarded people into their homes, some citizen advocates, members of L'Arche communities—often refer to a "calling." For example, a foster parent states, "The Lord calls you to do things." A person living with a number of retarded people explains her reason for "life-sharing," "It's a calling and it's a commitment to individuals."

In accepting relationships built on religious sentiments, the relationships are not merely an expression of charity, which has been the basis for many philanthropic efforts on behalf of people with mental retardation, but of a commitment to people who have suffered or been wounded. Some people see Christ in suffering people. One person describes her beliefs:

> The Lord appears to us through these people. He appears to us through all people, but is also through these people, no matter what their wounds are. The Lord appears to us and will be a blessing to us. We have a prayer in French that says: "Blessed are those that are rejected."

Humanitarian Concern

Similar to religious commitment, some people explain their relationships to people with mental retardation in terms of humanitarian concern or secular motivations. Here, the sentiments range from doing good works to attacking social injustice. One person describes how she became a foster parent: "It is a fulfillment for me, a way of doing something good." Another foster parent explains, "Some day I will need help, someone to care for me . . . If I do a good job now, maybe somebody else will do the same for me."

Though accepting relationships cannot be bought or sold, paid human service workers sometimes develop attachments to people they serve. In contrast to traditional definitions of professionalism that emphasize detachment, their involvement with people with disabilities extends well beyond the requirements of their jobs. For example, staff members sometimes invite their clients to their homes and to social events. At some agencies, staff members are expected to form meaningful ties with their clients. These agencies typically subscribe to an ideology in which human service work in the community is viewed in terms of liberation and civil rights. A staff member at one agency relates how he was moved by the situation of one of his clients:

> We got [a person] directly out of the institution. He had lived there for 25 years . . . Here's a man who is 38 years old and can fit all of his possessions in the back of a station wagon . . . It was real depressing. But if nothing else is ever done in his life, that one move is just so dramatic . . . I think more dramatic than anything you or I have probably experienced in our lives.

Another staff member explains why it is important to integrate people into the community:

> By working on things that help people become part of the community, I feel I'm working on some of my own personal goals to create a better society. All of us do things that are not liked or wanted. If I can help build a society of acceptance it ultimately helps me too.

Feelings of Friendship

Many relationships between people with mental retardation and typical people are based on feelings of friendship. Here the relationship is described not in terms of abstract values—family, religious, humanitarian—but in terms of liking and enjoying the company of the person with a disability.

As McCall, McCall, Denzin, Suttles, & Kurth (1970) note, a defining characteristic of friendship is voluntariness. Friends choose to be together in the absence of obligation.

Friendships between disabled and nondisabled people are typically rooted in other kinds of relationships. Relationships based on family, religious, or humanitarian sentiments often evolve into friendships. For example, while a person may initially become involved with a mentally retarded person because of a religious calling, he or she may come to like and feel close to the person as a result of prolonged contact.

Many of the friendships we have observed and heard about grew out of professional, neighbor (Perske, 1980) or volunteer relationships. While the staff–client relationship cannot be defined as friendship, since it is not voluntary in the sense described above, staff members often come to like the people they work with and choose to spend time with them outside of their work roles. Some of the closest friendships we found involved staff members who decided to maintain a relationship with former clients after they left their jobs.

Becoming friends with a mentally retarded person is a process in which the person essentially becomes "delabeled" (for a discussion of delabeling from the perspective of a person who has been defined as retarded, see Edgerton, 1986). While the disability or label may be prominent in the eyes of the other person during the initial stages of the relationship, that aspect of the disabled person becomes less salient over time.

People who describe themselves as friends of retarded people often point to what they have in common. One person states:

> I really like spending time with him. Why? Because we both have active imaginations, we're artistic, share the same sense of humor, love chocolate, and like good coffee on Sunday mornings. We both like to cook good meals and listen to jazz. Ken and I have similar interests. That's why we're such good friends. You can really become good

friends with anyone if you look for similar interests and do things that you have in common. It's easy to like someone.

The director of an agency, who had developed a relationship with one of the clients, expresses the same sentiment as she discusses her decision to leave her job:

> Joan and I are genuine friends . . . I like her. We have similar interests in music, watching people. We are both physically slow, not athletes, and we don't like physically aggressive activities. We enjoy each other. I, we will keep in touch with each other when I leave my job here.

Similarly, people who have become friends of people with mental retardation focus on their positive qualities. Examples include: "She has a really good sense of humor," "He's a lot of fun," "He really appreciates everything you do for him," "She's really honest," "He doesn't play games like most people."

In short, when people are friends of people with mental retardation, they describe the relationship as reciprocal rather than one-sided.

DISCUSSION

A sociology of acceptance perspective has the potential not only to advance our theoretical understanding of people labeled mentally retarded and mentally ill in society but to provide professionals and others in the field with practical guidance for their efforts. By drawing attention to the labeling and exclusion of people with mental retardation or mental illness, sociocultural perspectives on deviance provided a theoretical underpinning for trends such as deinstitutionalization, normalization and integration. Yet the sociology of deviance directs attention to what not to do rather than to what should be done.

The sociology of acceptance has two major implications for practice in the field of mental retardation. The first has to do with the nature of ordinary people, if not the society. Though prejudice and discrimination toward people with disabilities may run deep on a cultural and societal level (Bogdan & Biklen, 1977; Biklen & Knoll, 1987), it does not follow that communities and typical people will always reject people with disabilities. Our data strongly indicate that a significant number of ordinary community members are willing to accept people with severe disabilities if given the opportunity. Perhaps the culture and society are changing or perhaps there will always be people who are able to transcend cultural values and social pressures. Whether or not rejection of people who are different, and specifically those with severe disabilities, is inevitable in society as a whole is a question that cannot be answered here. However, for many people, familiarity breeds acceptance, not contempt. In terms of future directions for research, we propose the following:

- More historical and anthropological studies of societies and cultures that have accommodated people with disabilities (for example, Groce, 1985).

- Case studies of communities and organizations (for example, churches and community associations) that include and even welcome people with disabilities.

- Examinations, from a critical perspective, of whether laws and policies benefitting people with disabilities (for example, Section 504 and Public Law 94-142 in the United States) represent a change in societal perspectives on people with disabilities.

- Studies that look beyond the field of disabilities to understand the sentiments of people who have challenged cultural prejudices or governmental oppression to accommodate people who have been rejected or excluded (for example, Germans who assisted Jews during the Nazi regime).

- Comparisons of human service agencies that generate acceptance among their staff with those that do not.

The second implication relates to our knowledge and understanding of how relationships are formed. Recent years have seen the publication of compelling arguments on the importance of relationships in the lives of people with severe disabilities and on the tendency of human service systems to usurp community responsibility (Strully & Strully, 1985; McKnight, 1987; O'Brien, 1987). As a field, we have begun to appreciate the importance of personal relationships and the limitations of human services. Yet we know very little about how people come together and how professionals can help people to become part of their communities. We need to know who forms relationships with people with severe disabilities, why and how they form them, and how we can support those relationships or at least know when to stay out of their way. A sociology of acceptance is a modest step towards providing this understanding.

REFERENCES

Bachrach, L. L. (1981). A conceptual approach to deinstitutionalization of the mentally retarded: a perspective from the experience of the mentally ill. In: R. H. Bruininks, C. E. Meyers, B. B. Sigford & K. C. Lakin (Eds.), *Deinstitutionalization and Community Adjustment of Mentally Retarded People* (Washington, D. C., American Association on Mental Deficiency).

Becker, H. S. (1963) *Outsiders: studies in the sociology of deviance* (New York, Free Press).

Bercovici, S. (1981). Qualitative methods and cultural perspectives in the study of deinstitutionalization. In: R. H. Bruininks, C. E. Meyers, B. B. Sigford & K. C. Lakin (Eds.), *Deinstitutionalization and Community Adjustment of Mentally Retarded People* (Washington, D. C., American Association on Mental Deficiency).

Bercovici, S. M. (1983). *Barriers to Normalization* (Baltimore, Md., University Park Press).

Biklen, D. (1977). The politics of institutions, in: B. Blatt, D. Biklen & R. Bogdan (Eds.), *An Alternative Textbook in Special Education* (Denver, Colo., Love Publishing).

Biklen, D. & Knoll, J. (1987). The disabled minority, in: S. Taylor, D. Biklen & J. Knoll (Eds.), *Community Integration for People with Severe Disabilities* (New York, Teacher's College Press).

Bogdan, R. (1983). "Does mainstreaming work?" is a silly question, *Phi Delta Kappan*, 64, pp. 427–428.

Bogdan, R. & Biklen, D. (1977). Handicapism, *Social Policy*, April, pp. 14–19.

Bogdan, R. & Taylor, S. J. (1982). *Inside Out: the social meaning of mental retardation* (Toronto, University of Toronto Press).

Bogdan, R. & Taylor, S. J. (1987). Toward a sociology of acceptance: the other side of the study of deviance, *Social Policy*, Fall, pp. 34–39.

Bogdan, R., Taylor, S., De Grandpre, B. & Haynes, S. (1974). Let them eat programs: attendants' perspectives and programming on wards in state schools, *Journal of Health and Social Behavior*, 15 (June), pp. 142–151.

Braginsky, D. & Braginsky, B. (1971). *Hansels and Gretels* (New York, Holt, Rinehart & Winston).

Dexter, L. A. (1967). On the politics and sociology of stupidity in our society, in: H. S. Becker (Ed.), *The Other Side* (New York, Free Press).

Durkheim, E. (1938). *The Rules of Sociological Method* (New York, Free Press).

Edgerton, R. B. (1967). *The Cloak of Competence* (Berkeley, Calif., University of California Press).

Edgerton, R. (Ed.) (1984). *Lives in Process* (Washington, D. C., American Association on Mental Deficiency).

Edgerton, R. (1986). A case of delabelling: some practical and theoretical implications, in: L. L. Langness & H. G. Levine (Eds.), *Culture and Retardation* (Dordrecht, Reidel).

Erikson, K. (1966). *Wayward Puritans* (New York, Wiley).

Evans, D. P. (1983). *The Lives of Mentally Retarded People* (Boulder, Colo., Westview Press).

Glaser, B. G. & Strauss, A. (1967). *The Discovery of Grounded Theory: strategies for qualitative research* (Chicago, Ill., Aldine).

Gleidman, J. & Roth, W. (1980). *The Unexpected Minority* (New York, Harcourt, Brace, Jovanovich).

Goffman, E. (1961). *Asylums: essays on the social situation of mental patients and other inmates* (Garden City, N. Y., Doubleday, Anchor Books).

Goffman, E. (1963). *Stigma* (Englewood Cliffs, N. J., Prentice-Hall).

Groce, N. E. (1985). *Everyone Here Spoke Sign Language* (Cambridge, Mass., Harvard University Press).

Hobbs, N. (1975). *Issues in the Classification of Children*, Vols. I & II (San Francisco, Jossey-Bass).

Jacobs, J. (1969). *The Search for Help: a study of the retarded child in the community* (New York, Brunner/Mazel).

Jacobs, J. (Ed.), (1980). *Mental Retardation: a phenomenological approach* (Springfield, Ill., Charles C. Thomas).

Kaufman, S. (1984). Friendship, coping systems and community adjustment of mildly retarded adults, in: R. Edgerton (Ed.), *Lives in Process* (Washington, D. C., American Association on Mental Deficiency).

Kitsuse, J. I. (1962). Societal reaction to deviant behavior, *Social Problems*, 9, pp. 247–256.

Landesman-Dwyer, S., Berkson, G. & Romer, D. (1979). Affiliation and friendship of mentally retarded residents in group homes, *American Journal of Mental Deficiency*, 70, pp. 25–30.

Langness, L. L. & Levine, H. G. (Eds.), (1986). *Culture and Retardation* (Dordrecht, Reidel).

Lemert, E. (1951). *Social Pathology* (New York, McGraw-Hill).

Lutfiyya, Z. (1987). Field memo: sociology of acceptance, unpublished document, Center on Human Policy, Syracuse University.

McCall, G. J., McCall, M. M., Denzin, N. K., Suttles, G. D. & Kurth, S. B. (1970). *Social Relationships* (Chicago, Aldine).

McKnight, J. L. (1987). Regenerating community, *Social Policy*, winter, pp. 54–88.

Mercer, J. (1973) *Labeling the Mentally Retarded* (Berkeley, Calif., University of California Press).

Merton, R. K. (1948). The self-fulfilling prophecy, *The Antioch Review*, 7, p. 2.

Merton, R. K. (1957). *Social Theory and Social Structure* (New York, Free Press).

O'Brien, J. (1987). Embracing ignorance, error, and fallibility: Competencies for leadership of effective services, in: S. J. Taylor, D. Biklen & J. Knoll (Eds.), *Community Integration for People with Severe Disabilities* (New York, Teacher's College Press).

Park, C. C. (1982). *The Siege: the first eight years of an autistic child* Boston, Atlantic-Little, Brown).

Parsons, T. (1951). *The Social System* (Glencoe, Ill., The Free Press).

Perske, R. (1980). *New Life in the Neighborhood* (Nashville, Tenn., Abington).

Racino, J. (1987). *Field memo: sociology of acceptance*, unpublished document, Center on Human Policy, Syracuse University.

Scheff, T. J. (1966). *Being Mentally Ill* (Chicago, Ill., Aldine).

Strully, J. & Strully, C. (1985). Friendship and our children, *Journal of the Association for Persons with Severe Handicaps*, 10, pp. 224–227.

Tannenbaum, F. (1938). *Crime and the Community* (New York, Columbia University Press).

Taylor, S. J. (1982). From segregation to integration: strategies for integrating severely handicapped students in normal school and community settings, *The Journal of the Association for the Severely Handicapped*, 8, pp. 42–49.

Taylor, S. J. & Bogdan, R. (1980). Defending illusions: the institutions struggle for survival, *Human Organization*, 39, pp. 209–218.

Taylor, S. J. & Bogdan, R. (1981). A qualitative approach to community adjustment, in: R. H. Bruininks, C. E. Meyers, B. B. Sigford & K. C. Lakin (Eds.), *Deinstitutionalization and Community Adjustment of Mentally Retarded People* (Washington, D.C., American Association on Mental Deficiency).

Taylor, S. J. & Bogdan, R. (1984). *An Introduction to Qualitative Research Methods* (New York, Wiley).

Taylor, S. J., Biklen, D. & Knoll, J. (Eds.), (1987). *Community Integration for People with Severe Disabilities* (New York, Teacher's College Press).

Taylor, S. J., Racino, J., Knoll, J. & Lutfiyya, Z. (1987). Down home: community integration for people with the most severe disabilities, in: S. J. Taylor, D. Biklen & J. Knoll (Eds.), *Community Integration for People with Severe Disabilities* (New York, Teacher's College Press).

Teelucksingh, B. (1987). *Field memo: modes of acceptance*, unpublished document, Center on Human Policy, Syracuse University.

Thomas, W. I. & Thomas, D. S. (1928). *The Child in America* (New York, Alfred A. Knopf).

Traustadottir, R. (1987). *Field memo: accepting relationships within natural families*, unpublished document, Center on Human Policy, Syracuse University.

Traustadottir, R. & Bjarnason, D. (1987). *Field memo: accepting relationships within natural families*, unpublished document, Center on Human Policy, Syracuse University.

Turnbull, A. P., Brotherson, M. J. & Summers, J. A. (1985). The impact of deinstitutionalization on families: a family system approach, in: R. H. Bruininks & K. C. Lakin (Eds.), *Living and Learning in the Least Restrictive Environment* (Baltimore, Md., Brookes).

Vail, D. (1967). *Dehumanization and the Institutional Career* (Springfield, Ill., Charles C. Thomas).

Walker, P. (1987). *Field memo: relationships*, unpublished document, Center on Human Policy, Syracuse University.

Wolfensberger, W. (1972). *Normalization* (Toronto, National Institute on Mental Retardation).

Wolfensberger, W. (1975). *The Origin and Nature of our Institutional Models* (Syracuse, N.Y., Human Policy Press).

Zollers, N. (1987). *Field memo: religious commitment*, unpublished document, Center on Human Policy, Syracuse University.

17

On the Origins of Negative Attitudes
Toward People with Disabilities

Hanoch Livneh

In the past quarter of a century several attempts have been made to categorize the different sources of negative attitudes toward individuals with disabling conditions. Among these attempts, the works of Gellman (1959), Raskin (1956), Siller et al. (1967), and Wright (1960) are often singled out. In addition, a plethora of theoretical and empirical work has been directed toward the narrower goal of advancing and supporting a specific cause (often referred to as *root* or *base*) for negative attitudes toward disability [see Goffman (1963), Meng (1938), Parsons (1951), and Schilder (1935)].

The main objective of the current chapter is twofold: to integrate the major approaches in the domain of attitudinal sources toward people with disabilities, and to offer a new classification system by which these attitudes can be better conceptualized and understood.

Of the four main classifications, earlier attempts by Raskin (1956) and Gellman (1959) were more narrowly conceived. Both offered a fourfold classification system for the roots of prejudicial attitudes toward those who are blind (Raskin) and those who are disabled in general (Gellman). Raskin perceived these attitudes to be determined by psychodynamic, situational, sociocultural, and historical factors. Gellman, on the other hand, viewed the prejudicial roots as stemming from social customs and norms, child-rearing practices, recrudescence of neurotic childhood fears in frustrating and anxiety-provoking situations, and discrimination-provoking behavior by persons with disabilities.

Wright (1960), in a comprehensive literature review, discussed attitudes toward atypical physique according to the following categories: general requiredness of cause–effect relations (i.e., phenomenal causality between certain "sinful behaviors" and disability as an "unavoidable punishment"), negative reaction to

From *Rehabilitation Literature*, 43 (11–12) (1982), 338–347. Reprinted with permission. Published by the National Easter Seal Society, 2023 W. Ogden, Chicago, IL 60612.

the different and strange, childhood experiences, and prevailing socioeconomic factors. Siller et al. (1967), based on their extensive attitudinal study, reported the existence of 13 aversive content categories toward those with disabilities, utilizing both empirical and clinical findings. Their discussion, however, often confuses components of attitudinal correlates (such as functional limitations or attribution of negative qualities) with attitudinal sources (for example, aesthetic-sexual aversion, fear it could happen to self).

The present chapter attempts to deal exclusively with attitudinal sources. In other words, only approaches—both theoretical and empirical—which can be perceived in terms of cause (attitudinal source or root) and effect (negative or aversive reaction or attitude) relationships will be dealt with. Also, the classification system of the different attitudinal sources combines both process (psychodynamic mechanisms) and content (sociocultural factors) related formulations. It was felt that any attempt to separate the two would be rather arbitrary.

SOCIOCULTURAL CONDITIONING

Pervasive social and cultural norms, standards and expectations often lead to the creation of negative attitudes toward the disabled population. Among the frequently mentioned contributing factors are:

1. Emphasis on concepts such as "body beautiful," "body whole," youth, health, athletic prowess, personal appearance, and wholeness. These highly stressed societal standards are often institutionalized into cultural customs, which are to be conformed to by members of society (Gellman, 1959; Roessler & Bolton, 1978; Wright, 1960).

2. Emphasis on personal productiveness and achievement. Individuals in most Western countries are judged on the basis of their ability to be socially and economically competitive (Hanks & Hanks, 1948; Safilios-Rothschild, 1968).

3. Prevailing socioeconomic level. The importance of socioeconomic factors in creating an atmosphere within which attitudes toward individuals with disabilities are often nourished was emphasized by Safilios-Rothschild (1968). The level of societal development (Jordan and Friesen, 1968), the rate of unemployment, beliefs concerning the origins of poverty, and the importance attached to the nation's welfare economy and security are all contributing factors affecting attitudes toward people with disabilities.

4. Society's delineation of the "sick role" phenomenon. Whereas the occupant of the "sick role" is exempt from normal societal obligations and responsibilities, the length of a disabled person's remaining in this role is associated with negative attitudes (Parsons, 1951, 1958; Thoreson & Kerr, 1978).

5. The status degradation attached to disability. The social deviance and inferred stigma of having a physical disability bears heavily on society's attitudes toward those affected (see Davis, 1961; Freidson, 1965; Goffman, 1963; Safilios-Rothschild, 1970; Wolfensberger, 1972, 1976; Worthington, 1974; and

Yamamato, 1971). The cultural values held by members of society are often based on the perception of any form of "imputed deviancy," including disability, as a sign of marginal status. The person with a disability is, therefore, viewed as an "outsider," an "offender," or as "different" (Barker, 1948; Gove, 1976; Kutner, 1971). Wolfensberger (1972, 1976) regards the devalued or deviant status as a negative role imposed on the stigmatized person and views the sources of this deviancy as stemming from physical, behavioral, and attribution-based characteristics. Yamamato (1971) goes as far as to suggest that society needs the deviates as a symbol of evil and intangible dangers.

CHILDHOOD INFLUENCES

The importance of infancy and early childhood experiences, in terms of both child-rearing practices and early parental influences (verbal and behavioral) is often stressed (Gellman, 1959; Wright, 1960). The impact of early experiences and their related emotions and cognitions have a major role in influencing the growing child's belief and value system. Parental and significant others' actions, words, tone of voice, gestures, and so forth are transmitted, directly or indirectly, to the child and tend to have a crucial impact on the formation of attitudes toward disability.

Rearing practices which emphasize the importance of health and normalcy, and which threaten any infringement of health rules with sickness, illness, and long-term disability, result in aversion toward individuals affected (Gellman, 1959; Wright, 1960). Childhood stages of development (oral, anal, phallic, genital) are wrought with anxiety-laden premises regarding the etiology of certain illnesses; therefore, the association with ongoing disabilities and disabled persons, as past transgressors, is readily made.

PSYCHODYNAMIC MECHANISMS

Several mainly unconscious psychological processes have been advanced in the literature as explanatory mechanisms for the attitudes manifested by the "nondisabled" toward the "disabled." Although most of these mechanisms are apparently sown during early childhood (Gellman, 1959; Siller, 1967; Yamamato, 1971) and may, therefore, be regarded as related to childhood experiences, it was felt that due to their significance in creating and maintaining these attitudes such a separation is warranted.

1. Requirement of mourning. The person with a disability is expected to grieve the loss of a body part or function. He or she "ought" to suffer and slowly adjust to such a misfortune (Dembo, Leviton, & Wright, 1956, 1975; Kutner, 1971; Sussman, 1969; Thoreson & Kerr, 1978; Wright, 1960).

The nondisabled individual has a need to safeguard his or her values, by wanting the disabled individual to suffer, and show the appropriate grieving, so as to protect one's own values of the importance of a functioning body (Dembo, Leviton, & Wright, 1956; 1975). Any attempt on the disabled person's part to deny or reject the "suffering role" is met with negative attitudes. The mechanism of rationalization is clearly operative in this case.

2. Unresolved conflict over scopophilia and exhibitionism. Psychoanalytic thought stresses the importance of vision in early psychosexual and ego development (Blank, 1957). The significance of sight, both in terms of pleasure of looking at and being looked upon in the pregenital stages, is stressed in the psychoanalytic literature. Any resolved conflicts related to these developmental stages may be triggered as a consequence of the approach/fascination–avoidance/repulsion conflict often associated with the sight of a disabled person.

3. Negative attributes resulting from the "spread phenomenon." Attributing to those with disabilities certain negative characteristics frequently results when the mechanism of "halo effect" or "spread phenomenon" is in operation (Wright, 1960). The generalization from one perceived characteristic (e.g., physical disability) to other, unrelated characteristics (e.g., emotional or mental maladjustment) is referred to as "spread" and explains the too often pervasive negative correlates of a pure physical deviance (Kutner, 1971; Thoreson & Kerr, 1978).

4. Associating responsibility with etiology. The attribution of personal-moral accountability to the cause of a disabling condition results in negative attitudes. If an individual can be held responsible for an imputed deviance, certain social management approaches are then suggested (punishment, control, "rehabilitation," correction, and so forth), which are frequently embedded with negative connotations (Freidson, 1965; Safilios-Rothschild, 1970; Yamamato, 1971). Again, the operation of a rationalization mechanism is evident here.

5. Fear of social ostracism. Siller et al. (1967) suggest this category as an extension of the "guilty by association" phenomenon. The non-disabled person fears that an association with disabled persons may be interpreted by others as implying some psychological maladjustment on his or her own part. The internalization of others' values and beliefs, which tends to weaken one's ego boundaries, coupled with projection onto others of unwanted personal attributes, are the main operating mechanisms.

6. Guilt of being "able-bodied." Guilt of "enjoying" one's body intactness in addition to possible injustices directed toward persons with disabilities (e.g., the belief in the disabled person's responsibility for the condition, lack of involvement in charitable activities) may result in attempts at atonement or further dissociation from the presence of disabled individuals (Siller et al., 1967; Wright, 1960).

DISABILITY AS A PUNISHMENT FOR SIN

The triad of sin, punishment, and disability can be conceived as a component of the earlier discussion of psychodynamic mechanisms operating in the creation of aversive reactions toward disability. Due to their importance in elucidating the roots of negative attitudes toward people with disabling conditions and the various versions of their interrelatedness which are advanced in the literature, it seems justifiable to treat these concepts under a separate heading.

1. Disability as a punishment for sin. Alexander's (1938) concept of "emotional syllogism," when applied here (Siller et al., 1967; Wright, 1960); stresses the consequential appropriateness between physical deformity and a sinful person. The source of the disabled person's suffering is attributed to either a personally committed evil act or to an ancestral wrongdoing (Sigerist, 1945).

2. The individual with a disability as a dangerous person. Meng (1953) (reported in Barker et al. 1953) attributed fear and avoidance of those who are physically disabled to three unconscious mechanisms: (a) the belief that a disability is a punishment for a transgression and, therefore, that the disabled person is evil and dangerous; (b) the belief that a disability is an unjust punishment and that, therefore, the person is motivated to commit an evil act to balance the injustice; and (c) the projection of one's unacceptable impulses upon the disabled person, which results in perceiving the latter as evil and dangerous (see also Siller et al. 1967; Thoreson and Kerr, 1978). Thus, whereas in the previous section suffering was perceived as being a punishment for an evil deed, in the present section physical deviance is viewed as the cause, the consequence of which is felt to be a sinful and evil act ("a twisted mind in a twisted body").

3. The nondisabled person fearing imminent punishment. If the notion of disability as a punishment is warranted, then the nondisabled person who anticipates, often realistically, retribution for past personal misdeeds avoids the person with disabilities because of guilt of not being punished or the fear of imminent punishment by association (Gellman, 1959).

4. Vicarious self-punishment offered by the punished disabled person. An extension of the above formula was offered by Thurer (1980). The sinning disabled person, in fiction or reality, is perceived to be an easy target for one's own projections. Because the disabled individual was punished for the sin committed and since the nondisabled person unconsciously identifies with the sin, he or she is also punished, albeit vicariously, and the felt guilt is, therefore, lessened. The externalization of one's inner conflicts upon a punished target assists in controlling them. The result is, therefore, the repelling–gratifying conflict of feelings that ensues as a result of seeing, hearing, or reading about a disabled individual.

ANXIETY-PROVOKING UNSTRUCTURED SITUATIONS

The role of unfamiliar situations in creating anxiety and confusion was stressed by Hebb (1946) and Heider (1944). Similarly, upon initial interaction with a disabled person, the nondisabled person is often faced with an unstructured situation in which most socially accepted rules and regulations for proper interaction are not well-defined. These ambiguous situations tend to disrupt both cognitive-intellectual processes as well as the more fundamental perceptual-affective mechanisms.

1. Cognitively-unstructured situations. The nondisabled person interacting with a disabled individual faces uncertain social outcomes engendered by the new and, therefore, cognitively vague situation (Heider, 1958). The unfamiliarity presents an incongruent cognitive gestalt which disrupts the established basic rules of social interaction and may cause withdrawal from such a situation (Yamamato, 1971) or create strain in this interaction (Siller et al., 1967). The often reported findings in the literature—that the lack of factual knowledge and information about disabling conditions tends to lead to negative attitudes (Anthony, 1972; English, 1971a, 1971b; English & Oberle, 1971)—also support this contention.

2. Lack of affective preparedness. There is an apparent fearful and negative reaction, on a visceral level, to the different and strange (Hebb, 1946; Heider, 1958; Siller et al., 1967). Strange and mutilated bodies trigger a conflict in the observer, because of incompatible perceptions (Hebb, 1946). People tend to resist the strange because it does not fit into the structure of an expected life space (Heider, 1958) and because of a lack of affective readiness (Worthington, 1974, Yamamato, 1971). Siller et al. (1967) perceived it to exemplify their negative atypicality category, which creates in the observer a feeling of distress. Lack of experiential contact and exposure to persons with disabilities is a contributing factor to the origination of such an attitude (Anthony, 1972; English 1971a, b).

AESTHETIC AVERSION

The impact of a purely aesthetic-sexual aversion, triggered by the sight of a visibly disabled person, has been stressed by several authors (Heider, 1958; Siller & Chipman, 1964; Siller et al., 1967). These feelings of repulsion and discomfort are felt when nondisabled persons come in contact with certain disabilities [such as amputations, body deformities, cerebral palsy, skin disorders (Richardson et al., 1961; Safilios-Rothschild, 1970; Siller, 1963)]. The importance of aesthetic-sexual aversion as a basis for negative attitudinal formation was also reported in Siller et al.'s (1967) study, in which the felt aversion referred to the direct and conscious reactions experienced on sensory and visceral levels. The role played by aesthetic attractiveness was also demonstrated by Napoleon et al. (1980) as a predisposing factor in judging a person's degree of mental illness.

THREATS TO BODY IMAGE INTEGRITY

The concept of body image, as the mental representation of one's own body, was originally coined by Schilder (1935). Several related formulations were proposed regarding the importance of the body image concept (i.e., self-image, body cathexis, body satisfaction) as an explanatory vehicle in understanding attitudes toward people with disabilities.

1. Threat to the body image. Schilder (1935) argued that, via the mechanism of identification, seeing a person with a physical disability creates a feeling of dis-

comfort because of the incongruence between an expected "normal" body and the actual perceived reality. The viewer's own unconscious and somatic body image may, therefore, be threatened due to the presence of the disabled individual (Menninger, 1949).

2. Reawakening of castration anxiety. The psychoanalytic concept of castration anxiety, as applied to explaining the formation of negative attitudes toward persons with disabilities, stresses the stirring up of archaic castration fears in the presence of analogous situations [such as direct loss of a leg or an eye or an indirect loss of a certain body function (Chevigny & Braverman, 1950; Fine, 1978; Maisel, 1953; Siller et al., 1967; Wright, 1960)].

3. Fear of losing one's physical integrity. Profound anxiety about becoming disabled plays a crucial part in forming prejudicial attitudes toward those who are. When faced with a disabled person, the nondisabled individual becomes highly anxious because the original fear of potential bodily harm is rekindled (Safilios-Rothschild, 1968, 1970). Roessler and Bolton (1978), capitalizing on Gellman's (1959) original discussion, believe that nondisabled persons, being fearful of disablement and loss of self-control, feel intense discomfort which arouses additional anxiety when in contact with a visibly disabled person. The result is avoidance of disabled persons and attempts at segregating and isolating them. Similar ideas were advanced by Siller et al. (1967), who viewed the fear that the disability could happen to oneself as a basis for an aversive attitude toward people who are disabled.

4. Separation anxiety. Although somewhat related to castration anxiety and fear of losing physical integrity, separation anxiety, in the sense of object loss, is another unconscious source leading to negative attitudes toward disability (Siller et al., 1967). The loss of a body part or function may trigger, in the viewer, narcissistic concerns and unresolved infantile anxieties, which often evolve around possible separation from parental figures (Siller, 1964a).

5. Fear of contamination or inheritance. The fear that social interaction with disabled people may lead to contamination provokes aversive attitudes (Siller et al., 1967). This refers to avoiding those with disabilities on both superficial interactive levels (social intercourse) and more in-depth relationships (marriage, having children).

MINORITY GROUP COMPARABILITY

The view that attitudes toward the disabled population parallel those manifested toward minority groups, in general, was advocated by Barker (1953) and further elaborated on by Wright (1960). This view holds that disabled people, as a marginal group (Barker, 1948; Sussman, 1969), trigger negative reactions in the nondisabled majority. Being perceived as marginal, or as a member of a minority group, carries with it the same stereotypic reactions of occupying a devalued and inferior status shared by ethnic, racial, and religious groups (Chesler, 1965; Cowen et al. 1967, 1958; Yuker, 1965). The resulting attitude can, therefore, be categorized as being discriminatory and prejudiced in nature, and as advocating isolation and segregation of disabled persons from the remaining population (Safilios-Rothschild, 1970; Wright, 1960).

DISABILITY AS A REMINDER OF DEATH

The parallelism between reactions toward those who are disabled and feelings associated with dying (anxiety, fear, dread) was suggested by several authors (Endres, 1979; Leviton, 1972; Livneh, 1980; Parkes, 1975; Siller, 1976). The contention is that the loss of a body part or a physical function constitutes the death of a part, which in the past was integrally associated with one's ego (Bakan, 1968). The anxiety associated with death is, therefore, rekindled at the sight of a disabled person. The disabled groups, both literally and symbolically, serve as a denial of our primitive, infantile omnipotence (Ferenczi, 1956) and as a reminder of our mortality.

PREJUDICE-INVITING BEHAVIORS

Gellman (1959) and Wright (1960) discussed the effect of certain provoking behaviors, by persons with disabilities, on discriminatory practices toward them. These provoking behaviors may be categorized into two general classes:

1. Prejudice by invitation (Roessler & Bolton, 1978). Specific behaviors by disabled individuals (being dependent, seeking secondary gains; acting fearful, insecure, or inferior) create and strengthen certain prejudicial beliefs in the observer. Wright (1960) similarly traced these behaviors to the physically disabled person's expectations of being treated in depreciating ways, and as a result set themselves up in situations in which they will be devalued.

2. Prejudice by silence. Lack of interest on the disabled person's part or lack of effective public relations campaigns or self-help groups representing the interests and concerns of specific disability groups to combat the public's ignorance is a way of fostering stereotypic and negative attitudes on the latter's part.

THE INFLUENCE OF DISABILITY-RELATED FACTORS

Several disability-connected variables were reported in the literature as affecting attitudes toward disabled persons. The association of these variables with certain negative perceptions was both empirically studied (Barker, 1964; Siller, 1963) and theoretically discussed (Freidson, 1965; Safilios-Rothschild, 1970).

Among the major reported variables can be found:

1. Functionality versus organicity of disability. Barker (1964) found that a dichotomy exists between the public's perceptions regarding certain personality

traits attached to functional (alcoholism) or organic (blindness, cancer) disabilities. Siller (1963) concluded that those disabilities having the least functional implications were also those reacted to least negatively. Similar conclusions were reached in the context of occupational settings where employers preferred physically disabled individuals (for example, those with paraplegia) to the more functionally impaired persons [such as those who were mentally retarded or emotionally disabled (Barker, 1964; Rickard et al., 1963; Safilios-Rothschild, 1970)].

2. Level of severity. Usually the more severe a disability is, the more negatively it is perceived (Safilios-Rothschild, 1970; Shontz, 1964; Siller, 1963). Severity is, of course, related to level of functional limitation involved.

3. Degree of visibility. Generally, the more visible a disability is, the more negative an attitude it tends to trigger (Safilios-Rothschild, 1970; Shontz, 1964; Siller, 1963).

4. Degree of cosmetic involvement. Generally, the more the cosmetic implication inherent in the disability, in terms of aesthetic characteristics (see also "Aesthetic Aversion"), the less favorably it is reacted to (Siller, 1963).

5. Contagiousness versus non-contagiousness of disability. Safilios-Rothschild (1970) discussed the influence of contagious disabilities on the degree of prejudice directed toward them. The more contagious a disability is, the more fear of personal contraction is aroused and the more negative, therefore, is the ensuing reaction.

6. Body part affected. The importance of the body part affected by the disability, in terms of both personal and social implications, was suggested by Safilios-Rothschild (1970) and Weinstein et al. (1964).

7. Degree of predictability. The factor of imputed prognosis or probability of curability was studied and discussed by Freidson (1965), Safilios-Rothschild (1970), and Yamamato (1971). On the whole, the more curable and therefore predictable the disability is, the less negatively it is perceived.

The final category to be briefly discussed includes the association of certain demographic and personality variables of the nondisabled population with negative attitudes toward disabled persons. Because this category has been the target of extensive empirical research in the past years and since most of these studies are correlational rather than causal in nature, discussion will only revolve around their main findings. It should be noted that although the conclusions drawn by the studies' authors are only suggestive and cannot be generalized beyond their participating populations, most authors regarded the respondents' personal variables under study as determinants of attitudes toward disability due to their enduring and deeply ingrained qualities (such as sex, intelligence, self-concept, anxiety level).

DEMOGRAPHIC VARIABLES ASSOCIATED WITH ATTITUDES

Several major reviews of studies investigating demographic correlates of negative attitudes toward people with disabilities (English, 1971a; McDaniel, 1969; Ryan, 1981) have reached these conclusions concerning the following variables:

1. Sex. Females display more favorable attitudes toward individuals who are physically disabled than males (Chesler, 1965; Freed, 1964; Siller, 1963, 1964b; Yuker et al., 1966).

2. Age. There appear to be two inverted U-shaped distributions when age-related differences toward persons with disabilities are measured (Ryan, 1981). Attitudes are, generally, more positive at late childhood and adulthood, and less favorable attitudes are recorded at early childhood, adolescence, and old age (Ryan, 1981; Siller, 1963; Siller & Chipman, 1964; Siller et al., 1967).

3. Socioeconomic status. Higher income groups manifest more favorable attitudes toward the emotionally and mentally disabled than lower income groups (English, 1971a; Jabin, 1966); however, no differences were found regarding physical disabilities (Dow, 1965; English, 1971a; Lukoff & Whiteman, 1964; Whiteman & Lukoff, 1965).

4. Educational level. In spite of age-confounding research difficulties, most studies concluded that educational level is positively correlated with more favorable attitudes toward persons with disabling conditions (Horowitz et al., 1965; Jabin, 1966; Siller, 1964b; Tunick et al., 1979).

PERSONALITY VARIABLES ASSOCIATED WITH ATTITUDES

Research on the association of several personality traits and characteristics in the nondisabled population with respect to negative attitudes toward disabled people was summarized and reported by several authors (e.g., English, 1971a; Kutner, 1971; McDaniel, 1969; Pederson and Carlson, 1981; and Safilios-Rothschild 1970). Major findings include the following:

1. Ethnocentrism. Chesler (1965), Cowen et al. (1967, 1958), Lukoff and Whiteman (1964), Noonan (1967), Whiteman and Lukoff (1965), and Yuker (1965), following Wright's (1960) formulation of the comparability between attitudes toward persons with disabilities and attitudes toward ethnic and religious minorities, in general, found that high ethnocentrism was related to lack of acceptance of the disabled population.

2. Authoritarianism. Jabin (1966), Lukoff and Whiteman (1964), Noonan et al. (1970), Tunick et al. (1979), and Whiteman and Lukoff (1965) reported a positive correlation between accepting attitudes toward disabled persons and low authoritarianism [see also Dembo et al.'s (1956) theoretical discussion].

3. Aggression. Meng's (1938) original hypothesis suggested that the projection of one's aggressive and hostile desires upon those with disabilities will lead to

the belief that disabled persons are dangerous and, as a result, to prejudicial attitudes toward them. Jabin (1966), Siller (1964b), and Siller et al. (1967) confirmed this hypothesis in independent studies, concluding that less aggressive individuals express more positive attitudes toward this group.

4. Self-insight. Siller (1964b) and Yuker (1962) reported findings which suggested a moderate relationship between the need for introspection, as a measure of insightfulness, and empathetic understanding of people who are disabled.

5. Anxiety. The degree of manifest anxiety was found to be associated with attitudes toward disabled persons. Jabin (1966), Kaiser and Moosbruker (1960), Marinelli and Kelz (1973), Siller (1964b), Siller et al. (1967), and Yuker et al. (1960) demonstrated that a high level of manifest anxiety is positively correlated with rejection of disabled individuals.

6. Self-concept. Several studies (e.g., Epstein and Shontz, 1962; Jabin, 1966; Siller, 1964b; Yuker, 1962; and Yuker et al., 1966) reported a relationship between positive self-concept and a more accepting attitude toward disability. It seems that persons who are more secure and confident in their own selves also tend to feel more positive and accepting of disabled persons.

7. Ego strength. Similarly to self-concept, ego strength was found to be related to attitudes toward people with disabilities. Siller (1964a, 1963) and Siller et al. (1967) reported on the relationship between ego weakness and rejection of the disabled, while Noonan et al. (1970) found a trend in this direction, albeit not statistically significant.

8. Body- and self-satisfaction. Several studies (Cormack, 1967; Epstein and Shontz, 1962; Fisher and Cleveland, 1968; Leclair and Rockwell, 1980; and Siller, 1964a) concluded that lack of satisfaction with one's own body (low "body-cathexis" score) is related, and probably a contributing factor, to the development of negative attitudes toward physically disabled persons. Siller (1964a), Siller et al. (1967); and Yuker et al. (1966) expanded the body-cathexis concept to successfully argue that a positive perception of one's self is related to the acceptance of disabled individuals. People with positive and secure self-concepts tend to show more positive and accepting attitudes toward those with disabilities, while people with low self-concepts often reject them (see also section on "Threats to Body Image Integrity").

9. Ambiguity tolerance. The ability of nondisabled persons to better tolerate ambiguity was found to be positively correlated with acceptance of physically disabled persons (Feinberg, 1971).

10. Social desirability. The need for social approval and acceptance by others was positively associated with acceptance of people having disabilities (Doob & Ecker, 1970; Feinberg, 1967; Jabin, 1966; Siller et al., 1967).

11. Alienation. Alienated individuals tend to be more hostile toward, and rejecting of, disabled persons (Jabin, 1966).

12. Intelligence level. English (1971a) tentatively concluded, from his review of related studies, that there may be a relationship between the non-disabled intellectual capacity and acceptance of disability.

SUMMARY AND CONCLUSIONS

The present chapter has attempted to outline a classification system according to which a number of sources or negative attitudes toward people with disabilities was categorized and discussed.

The major categories included were (a) conditioning by sociocultural norms that emphasize certain qualities not met by the disabled population; (b) childhood influences where early life experiences foster the formation of stereotypic adult beliefs and values; (c) psychodynamic mechanisms that may play a role in creating unrealistic expectations and unresolved conflicts when interacting with disabled persons; (d) perception of disability as a punishment for a committed sin or as a justification for committing a future evil act, which triggers unconscious fears in the nondisabled person; (e) the inherent capacity of unstructured social, emotional, and intellectual situations to provoke confusion and anxiety; (f) the impact of a basic aesthetic-sexual aversion, created by the sight of the visibly disfigured, on the development of negative attitudes; (g) the threat to the conscious body and unconscious body image triggered by the mere presence of physically disabled individuals; (h) the devaluative and stereotypical reactions fostered by the marginality associated with being a member of a minority group; (i) the unconscious and symbolic parallelism between disability and death as a reminder of man's transient existence; (j) prejudice-provoking behaviors, by persons with disabilities, that result in discriminatory practices toward them; (k) disability-related factors (e.g., levels of functionality, visibility, severity) which may contribute to specific negative attitudes; and (l) observer-related factors, both demographic (sex, age) and personality-connected (ethnocentrism, authoritarianism), which may foster the development of negative attitudes.

The classification system suggested suffers one major drawback. There is a certain degree of overlap among several of the categories (e.g., castration anxiety, viewed here as a threat to body image, may well be conceived as belonging to the childhood influences category: or anxiety provoked by unstructured situations may be regarded as just another psychological-operated mechanism if viewed phenomenologically rather than environmentally based). It should be noted, however, that due to the often highly abstract and conjectural nature of several of these categories, at present there is no escape from resorting to a certain level of arbitrariness when attempting to adopt such a classification model.

No attempt was made in the present discussion to suggest the matching of certain attitude-changing techniques (informative, experiential, persuasive) with the categories discussed. Several excellent articles have been written on strategies to combat negative attitudes toward people with disabilities and toward minority groups in general (see Allport, 1954; Anthony, 1972; Clore and Jeffery, 1972; English, 1971b; Evans, 1976; Finkelstein, 1980; Hafer and Narcus, 1979; Kutner, 1971; Safilios-Rothschild, 1968; and Wright, 1980, 1960).

It seems to this author that due to the complexity of the interacting factors that contribute to the creation of negative attitudes toward this group, any attempt at change, in order to be successful, must first be cognizant of the fact that since attitudes are learned and conditioned over many years, any experimental study of short duration, hoping to change attitudes, is futile at best. Attempts to modify the prevailing negative attitudes have been generally unsuccessful (Roessler & Bolton, 1978). They will probably continue to follow such an inevitable course as long as researchers and clinicians look for quick and easy results and solutions.

REFERENCES

Alexander, Franz G. Remarks about the Relation of Inferiority Feelings to Guilt Feelings. *Internatl. J. Psychoanalysis.* 1938. 19:41-49.

Allport, Gordon W. *The Nature of Prejudice.* New York: Addison-Wesley, 1954.

Anthony, William A. Societal Rehabilitation: Changing Society's Attitudes toward the Physically and Mentally Disabled. *Rehab. Psych.* 1972. 19:117-126.

Bakan, David. *Disease, Pain and Sacrifice: Toward a Psychology of Suffering.* Chicago, Ill.: Univ. of Chicago Press, 1968.

Barker, Roger G. The Social Psychology of Physical Disability. *J. Soc. Issues.* 1948. 4:4:28-38.

Barker, Roger G. Concepts of Disabilities. *Personnel & Guidance J.* 1964. 43:4:371-374.

Barker, Roger G.; Wright, Beatrice A.; Meyerson, Lee; and Gonick, Mollie R. *Adjustment to Physical Handicap and Illness: A Survey of The Social Psychology of Physique and Disability* (rev. ed.). New York: Social Science Research Council, 1953.

Blank, H. Robert. Psychoanalysis and Blindness. *Psycho-Analytic Quart.* 1957. 26:1-24.

Chesler, Mark A. Ethnocentrism and Attitudes toward the Physically Disabled. *Personality & Soc. Psychol.* 1965. 2:6:877-882.

Chevigny, Hector, and Braverman, Sydell. *The Adjustment of the Blind.* New Haven, Conn.: Yale University Press, 1950.

Clore, Gerald L., and Jeffery, Katharine M. Emotional Role Playing, Attitude Change, and Attraction toward a Disabled Person. *J. Personality & Soc. Psychol.* 1972. 23:1:105-111.

Cormack, Peter A. The Relationship between Body Cognition and Attitudes Expressed toward the Visibly Disabled. *Rehab. Counseling Bul.* 1967. 11:2:106-109.

Cowen, Emory L.; Bobrove, Philip H.; Rockway, Alan M.; and Stevenson, John. Development and Evaluation of an Attitudes to Deafness Scale. *J. Personality & Soc. Psychol.* 1967. 6:2:183-191.

Cowen, Emory L.; Underberg, Rita P.; and Verrillo, Ronald T. The Development and Testing of an Attitudes to Blindness Scale. *J. Soc. Psychol.* 1958. 48:297-304.

Davis, Fred. Deviance Disavowal: The Management of Strained Interaction by the Visibly Handicapped. *Social Problems.* 1961. 9:2:121-132.

Dembo, Tamara; Leviton, Gloria L.; and Wright, Beatrice A. Adjustment to Misfortune—A Problem of Social Psychological Rehabilitation. *Artificial Limbs.* 1956. 3:2:4-62.

Dembo, Tamara; Leviton, Gloria L; and Wright, Beatrice A. Adjustment to Misfortune—A Problem of Social Psychological Rehabilitation. *Rehab. Psychol.* 1975. 22:1-100.

Doob, Anthony N., and Ecker, Barbara P. Stigma and Compliance. *J. Personality & Soc. Psychol.* 1970. 14:4:302-304.

Dow, Thomas E. Social Class and Reaction to Physical Disability. *Psychol. Reports.* 1965. 17:1:39-62.

Endres, Jo Ellen. Fear of Death and Attitudinal Dispositions toward Physical Disability. *Dissertation Abstracts International.* 1979. 39:7161A (*University microfilm No.* 79-11, 825).

English, R. William. Correlates of Stigma toward Physically Disabled Persons. *Rehab. Research & Practice Rev.* 1971a. 2:1-17.

English, R. William. Combatting Stigma toward Physically Disabled Persons. *Rehab. Research & Practice Rev.* 1971b, 2:19-27.

English, R. William, and Oberle, J. B. Toward the Development of New Methodology for Examining Attitudes toward Disabled Persons. Rehab. Counseling Bul. 1971. 15:2:88-96.

Epstein, Seymour J., and Shontz, Franklin C. Attitudes toward Persons with Physical Disabilities as a Function of Attitudes towards One's Own Body. *Rehab. Counseling Bul.* 1962. 5:4:196-201.

Evans, John H. Changing Attitudes toward Disabled Persons: An Experimental Study. *Rehab. Counseling Bul.* 1976. 19:4:572-579.

Feinberg, Lawrence B. Social Desirability and Attitudes toward the Disabled. *Personnel & Guidance J.* 1967. 46:4:375-381.

Feinberg, Lawrence B. "Social Desirability and Attitudes toward the Disabled." Unpublished manuscript, Syracuse, N. Y., Syracuse University, 1971.

Ferenczi, Sandor. Stages in the Development of the Sense of Reality. In: S. Ferenczi (ed.), *Contributions to Psychoanalysis* (rev. ed.). New York: Dover, 1956.

Fine, Jeffrey A. "Castration Anxiety and Self Concept of Physically Normal Children as Related to Perceptual Awareness of Attitudes toward Physical Deviance." Unpublished doctoral dissertation. New York: New York University, 1978.

Finkelstein, Victor. *Attitudes and Disabled People: Issues for Discussion.* International Exchange of Information in Rehabilitation, Monograph No. 5. New York: World Rehabilitation Fund, 1980.

Fisher, Seymour, and Cleveland, Sidney E. *Body Image and Personality* (2nd rev. ed.). New York: Dover, 1968.

Freed, Earl X. Opinions of Psychiatric Hospital Personnel and College Students toward Alcoholism, Mental Illness, and Physical Disability: An Exploratory Study. *Psychol. Reports.* 1964. 15:2:615-618.

Freidson, Eliot. Disability as Social Deviance. In: M. B. Sussman (ed.), *Sociology and Rehabilitation.* Washington, D. C.: American Sociological Association, 1965.

Gellman, William. Roots of Prejudice against the Handicapped. *J. Rehab.* 1959. 40:1:4-6, 25.

Goffman, Erving. *Stigma: Notes on Management of Spoiled Identity.* Englewood Cliffs, N. J.: Prentice-Hall, 1963.

Gove, Walter R. Societal Reaction Theory and Disability. In: G. L. Albrecht (ed.), *The Sociology of Physical Disability and Rehabilitation.* Pittsburgh, Pa.: University of Pittsburgh Press, 1976.

Hafer, Marilyn, and Narcus, Margery. Information and Attitude toward Disability. *Rehab. Counseling Bul.* 1979. 23:2:95-102.

Hanks, Jane R., and Hanks, L. M. The Physically Handicapped in Certain Non-Occidental Societies. *J. Soc. Issues.* 1948. 4:11-20.

Hebb, Donald O. On the Nature of Fear. *Psychology Rev.* 1946. 53:259-276.

Heider, Fritz. Social Perception and Phenomenal Causality, *Psycholog. Rev.* 1944. 51:358-374.

Heider, Fritz. *The Psychology of Interpersonal Relations.* New York: Wiley, 1958.

Horowitz, Leola S.; Rees, Norma S.; and Horowitz, Milton W. Attitudes toward Deafness as a Function of Increasing Maturity. *J. Soc. Psychol.* 1965. 66:331-336.

Jabin, Norma. Attitudes towards the Physically Disabled as Related to Selected Personality Variables. *Dissertation Abstracts.* 1966. 27:2-B:599.

Jordan, John E., and Friesen, Eugene W. Attitudes of Rehabilitation Personnel toward Physically Disabled Persons in Colombia, Peru, and the United States. *J. Soc. Psychol.* 1968. 74:151-161.

Kaiser, P., and Moosbruker, Jane. "The Relationship Between Attitudes toward Disabled Persons and GSR." Unpublished manuscript, Albertson, N. Y., Human Resources Center, 1960.

Kutner, Bernard. The Social Psychology of Disability. In: W. S. Neff (ed.), *Rehabilitation Psychology.* Washington, D. C.: American Psychological Association, 1971.

Leclair, Steven W., and Rockwell, Lauralee K. Counselor Trainee Body Satisfaction and Attitudes toward Counseling the Physically Disabled. *Rehab. Counseling Bul.* 1980. 23:4:258-265.

Leviton, Don. "Education for Death or Death Becomes Less a Stranger." Paper presented at the American Psychological Association convention, Honolulu, Hawaii, Sept., 1972.

Livneh, Hanoch. Disability and Monstrosity: Further Comments. *Rehab. Lit.* 1980. 41:11-12:280-283.

Lukoff, Irving F., and Whiteman, Martin. "Attitudes toward Blindness." Paper presented at the American Federation of Catholic Workers for the Blind meeting, New York, 1964.

Maisel, E. "Meet a Body." Unpublished manuscript. New York, Institute for the Crippled and Disabled, 1953.

Marinelli, Robert P., and Kelz, James W. Anxiety and Attitudes toward Visibly Disabled Persons. *Rehab. Counseling Bul.* 1973. 16:4:198-205.

McDaniel, James W. *Physical Disability and Human Behavior.* New York: Pergamon Press, 1969.

Meng, Heinrich. Zur sozialpsychologie der Krperbeschädigten: Ein beitrag zum problem der praktischen psychohygiene. *Schweizer Archives fr Neurologie und Psychiatrie.* 1938. 40:328-344. (Reported in Barker, R. G., et al., 1953.)

Menninger, William C. Emotional Adjustments for the Handicapped. *Crippled Children.* 1949. 27:27.

Napoleon, Tony; Chassin, Lauri; and Young, Richard D. A Replication and Extension of "Physical Attractiveness and Mental Illness." *J. Abnormal Psychol.* 1980. 89:2:250-253.

Noonan, J. Robert. "Personality Determinants in Attitudes Toward Disability." Unpublished doctoral dissertation, Gainesville, Florida, University of Florida, 1967.

Noonan, J. Robert; Barry, John R.; and Davis, Hugh C. Personality Determinants in Attitudes toward Visible Disability. *J. Personality.* 1970. 38:1:1-15.

Parkes, C. Murray. Psychosocial Transitions: Comparison between Reactions to Loss of Limbs and Loss of a Spouse. *Brit. J. Psychiatry.* 1975. 127:204-210.

Parsons, Talcott. *The Social System.* Glencoe, Ill.: The Free Press, 1951.

Parsons, Talcott. Definitions of Health and Illness in the Light of American Values and Social Structure. In: E. G. Jaco (ed.), *Patients, Physicians, and Illness.* Glencoe, Ill.: The Free Press, 1958.

Pederson, Linda L., and Carlson, Peter M. Rehabilitation Service Providers: Their Attitudes towards People with Physical Disabilities, and Their Attitudes towards Each Other. *Rehab. Counseling Bul.* 1981. 24:4:275-282.

Raskin, Nathaniel J. "The Attitude of Sighted People toward Blindness." Paper presented at the National Psychological Research Council on Blindness, March, 1956.

Richardson, Stephen A.; Hastorf, Albert H.; Goodman, Norman; and Dornbusch, Sanford M. Cultural Uniformity in Reaction to Physical Disabilities. *Am. Soc. Rev.* 1961. 26:2:241-247.

Rickard, Thomas E.; Triandis, H. C.; and Patterson, C. H. Indices of Employer Prejudice Toward Disabled Applicants. *J. Applied Psych.* 1963. 47:1:52-55.

Roessler, Richard and Bolton, Brian. *Psychosocial Adjustment to Disability.* Baltimore: University Park Press, 1978.

Ryan, Kathryn M. Developmental Differences in Reactions to the Physically Disabled. *Human Develop.* 1981. 24:240-256.

Safilios-Rothschild, Constantina. Prejudice Against the Disabled and Some Means to Combat it. *Intern. Rehab. Rev.* 1968. 19:4:8-10, 15.

Safilios-Rothschild, Constantina. *The Sociology and Social Psychology of Disability and Rehabilitation.* New York: Random House, 1970.

Schilder, Paul. *The Image and Appearance of the Human Body.* London: Kegan Paul, Trench, Trubner, 1935.

Shontz, Franklin C. Body-Part Size Judgement. *VRA Project No. 814, Final Report.* Lawrence, Kansas: University of Kansas, 1964. (Reported in McDaniel, J.W. 1969.)

Sigerist, Henry E. *Civilization and Disease.* Ithaca, N. Y.: Cornell University Press, 1945.

Siller, Jerome. Reactions to Physical Disability. *Rehab. Counseling Bul.* 1963. 7:1:12-16.

Siller, Jerome. Reactions to Physical Disability by the Disabled and the Non-Disabled. *Am. Psychologist, Research Bull.* 1964 a. 7:27-36 (American Foundation for the Blind).

Siller, Jerome. Personality Determinants of Reaction to the Physically Disabled. *Am. Foundation for the Blind Research Bul.* 1964b. 7:37-52.

Siller, Jerome. Attitudes toward Disability. In: Herbert Rusalem and David Maliken (eds.), *Contemporary Vocational Rehabilitation.* New York: New York University Press, 1976.

Siller, Jerome, and Chipman, Abram. Factorial Structure and Correlates of the Attitude towards Disabled Persons Scale. *Educ. and Psychol. Meas.* 1964. 24:4:831-840.

Siller, Jerome, and Chipman, Abram. "Perceptions of Physical Disability by the Non-Disabled." Paper presented at the American Psychological Association meeting, Los Angeles, Sept. 1964. (Reported in Safilios-Rothschild, C., 1970).

Siller, Jerome: Chipman, Abram; Ferguson, Linda T.; and Vann, Donald H. *Studies in Reaction to Disability: XI. Attitudes of the Non-Disabled Toward the Physically Disabled.* New York: New York University, School of Education, 1967.

Sussman, Marvin B. Dependent Disabled and Dependent Poor: Similarity of Conceptual Issues and Research Needs. *The Social Service Rev.* 1969. 43:4:383-395.

Thoreson, Richard W., and Kerr, Barbara A. The Stigmatizing Aspects of Severe Disability: Strategies for Change. *J. Applied Rehab. Counseling.* 1978. 9:2:21-25.

Thurer, Shari. Disability and Monstrosity: A Look at Literary Distortions of Handicapping Conditions. *Rehab. Lit.* 1980. 41:1- 2:12-15.

Tunick, Roy H.; Bowen, Jack; and Gillings, J. L. Religiosity and Authoritarianism as Predictors of Attitude toward the Disabled: A Regression Analysis. *Rehab. Counseling Bul.* 1979. 22:5:408-418.

Weinstein, S.; Vetter, R.; and Sersen, E. "Physiological and Experiential Concomitants of the Phantom." VRA *Project No. 427, Final Report.* New York: Albert Einstein College of Medicine, 1964.

Whiteman, Martin and Lukoff, Irving F. Attitudes toward Blindness and Other Physical Handicaps. *J. Soc. Psychol.* 1965. 66:135-145.

Wolfensberger, Wolf. *The Principle of Normalization in Human Services.* Toronto, Canada: National Institute on Mental Retardation, 1972.

Wolfensberger, Wolf. The Normalization Principle. In: Sheldon A. Grand (ed.), *Severe Disability and Rehabilitation Counseling Training.* Washington, D. C.: National Council on Rehabilitation Education, 1976.

Worthington, Mary, E. Personal Space as a Function of the Stigma Effect. *Environment and Behavior,* 1974. 6:3:289-294.

Wright, Beatrice A. Developing Constructive Views of Life with a Disability. *Rehab. Lit.* 1980. 41:11-12:274-279.

Wright, Beatrice A. *Physical Disability: A Psychological Approach.* New York: Harper & Row, 1960.

Yamamato, Kaoru. To Be Different. *Rehab. Counseling Bul.* 1971. 14:3:180-189.

Yuker, Harold E. *Yearly Psycho-Social Research Summary.* Albertson, N. Y.: Human Resources Center, 1962.

Yuker, Harold E. Attitudes as Determinants of Behavior. *J. Rehab.* 1965. 31:1:15-16.

Yuker, Harold E.; Block, J. R.; and Campbell, W. J. *A Scale to Measure Attitudes Toward Disabled Persons: Human Resources Study No. 5.* Albertson, N. Y.: Human Resources Center, 1960.

Yuker, Harold E.; Block, J. R.; and Younng, Janet H. *The Measurement of Attitudes toward Disabled Persons.* Albertson, N. Y.: Human Resources Center, 1966.

Part IV: The Interpersonal and Attitudinal Impact of Disability—Study Questions and Disability Awareness Exercise

1. How does the media facilitate or impede the communication between persons who are able-bodied and those with handicaps?
2. Are the principles related to the acceptance of relationships between persons with mental retardation and other mental impairments, and persons who are able-bodied, transferrable to other populations, such as persons with chronic mental illness, traumatic brain injury, and people with AIDS?
3. How does the understanding of the origin of negative attitudes toward people with disabilities explain the attitudes related to AIDS and people who have AIDS? How is this understanding helpful in changing those attitudes?
4. Your client, who has facial disfigurement as a result of severe burns, presents concerns to you regarding the best ways for her to handle people who either exclude her from social contact or who intrude on her by "prying" into the causes of her disfigurement and its impact on her. How would you respond to her request for specific suggestions on how to cope with or change this situation?

DONOR OR RECIPIENT?

This experience focuses on complex issues arising for donors of organs for transplant. An intense situation may be created as the person requiring a kidney is someone who is emotionally close to you.

Goals

1. To explore reactions when a person has the opportunity to consider the donation of his or her kidney.
2. To present a situation that is complicated by the needs of a loved one.
3. To examine differing perspectives when the role of a person in need is reversed.

Procedure

1. Leader reads the following statement: "You have just received a phone call from the person you are closest to and love dearly. Stop and reflect on who this person would be in your life now. This person has just received word of having renal failure and is very distressed about his or her health. Due to medical complications the doctors feel that a kidney transplant is critical; without it, the person is in danger of dying."
2. Participants write a one-page statement of their reactions to this information.
3. Group members are selected at random to read their responses.
4. After all members have read their statements an open group discussion takes place.
5. During this discussion particular attention should be paid to the quality of the relationship.
6. The leader introduces the concept of significant others (e.g., if you would be hesitant to donate a kidney to this person, is there anyone whom you might consider as a donor?).
7. Having processed this, the leader moves to the role reversal stage, in which the group members become the person in need.
8. The leader reads the following statement: "You have just been informed by your physician that you have renal failure, unless you receive a kidney within three months you are risking death."
9. The leader asks participants to write a paragraph on the initial reaction to this news.
10. Next the group leader asks the group to write down the name of a person they would ask to donate a kidney to them and to list five reasons why they might ask this particular person.
11. Two group members are selected to role play the situation asking the named person for his or her kidney.
12. What would your response be if a severely disabled family member volunteered to donate a kidney? Did not volunteer? Was in need of a kidney?

Part V

Sexuality and Disability

The sexual realities of persons with disabilities have traditionally been given little recognition by professionals, although currently this is a major area of concern during treatment and rehabilitation. It has been suggested that sexual functioning is a subject area that is frequently avoided by professionals working with clients. Part of this neglect undoubtedly stems from taboos against the discussion of sex. Another reason for avoidance is the lack of education and information about sex as it relates to people with disabilities. The chapters in Part V have been selected to create a perspective focusing on attitudinal and informational problems related to sexuality and disability.

Recognizing that negative attitudes and lack of knowledge about sexuality impede the rehabilitation process, Ducharme and Gill suggest methods for identifying and changing negative attitudes. They further provide strategies to integrate sexual content into comprehensive rehabilitation through sexuality program development, continuing inservice education, and institutional support. Specific suggestions for interventions are also presented.

In Chapter 19, Knoepfler focuses on the relationship between sexuality and psychiatric disability, the impact of specific psychiatric disabilities on sexuality, and suggests educational and therapeutic interventions. This pioneering work, replete with case examples, is a significant contribution to educating rehabilitation practitioners in this important area.

Sexual abuse, a pervasive problem in our culture, does not exclude those who are physically and mentally challenged. General issues about sexual abuse and specific consideration related to abuse in persons who have disabilities are thoroughly and thoughtfully presented by Cole in Chapter 20. Strategies for recognition, prevention, and recovery from sexual exploitation are also provided.

The overall theme of Part V is that a person has many issues to be addressed during life and the living process. Sexuality is a major factor that cannot be ignored and must be part of the treatment and rehabilitation process.

18

Sexual Values, Training, and Professional Roles

Stanley Ducharme
Kathleen M. Gill

Traumatic head injuries affect approximately 7 million people every year. Typically these injuries strike people in the prime of life, with over 25% occurring prior to age 25 (Jennett, 1983), a time of intense turmoil and struggle. Questions of independence and sexuality are the major developmental tasks to be resolved during these years (Ducharme, 1987): Yet in spite of their relative importance, issues of sexuality are seldom addressed in the rehabilitation process. This is even more true where patients with head injury are concerned. For this reason, patients often leave rehabilitation feeling asexual and unattractive. They feel alone in their attempts to get information on sexual functioning and, as a consequence, often avoid intimate relationships.

Sexual dysfunction after head injury is not easily diagnosed. Problems of impotence, loss of sensation, ejaculatory dysfunction, and loss of desire are typical. In this regard, Blackerby (1987) reports that as many as three-fourths of all head-injured patients experience decreased frequency of sexual relations. Generally, he concludes, the incidence of sexual dysfunction increases with the severity of injury and the length of time since injury. The cause of these problems may lie in the patient's physical, emotional, or cognitive realm. In addition to sexual dysfunction, problems such as body-image disturbances, sexual identity, and self-esteem are almost universal among the head-injured population. It is the responsibility of all rehabilitation-team members to facilitate adjustment in these areas. Unfortunately, these problems are not always acknowledged.

In a recent survey of staff members in a Boston-area rehabilitation hospital, Gill (1988) found a conflict between attitudes and behavior. In a sample of 129 rehabilitation professionals, 79% stated that sexual adjustment is as important to patients as any other area of rehabilitation, yet only 9% of staff indicated that they feel comfortable discussing this issue with patients and regularly include the topic in their rehabilitation plans. Of this sample, 51% reported that they discuss the topic only if the patient first asks a question about sexuality. Forty-one percent said they feel uncomfortable because they lack information or expertise in this area. The dilemma is obvious. The patients need information on sexuality, yet the staff members feel inadequate to meet those needs.

STAFF RELUCTANCE

It is interesting to speculate about why staff members avoid discussions about sexuality. A few hypotheses come to mind. First, most people feel anxious regarding sexuality. Second, people with head injuries are stereotyped as asexual or hypersexual and incapable of sexual relationships. Third, there is a fear that talking about sex will lead to an increase in sexual inappropriateness. Staff members often have difficulty trusting in the patient's ability to exercise judgment, good taste, and concern for others.

STAFF ROLE IN THE PHASES OF RECOVERY

The needs of the patient and the goals of the staff fluctuate throughout the recovery process. Factors such as severity of injury, degree of restriction, and preinjury personality all play major roles in the adjustment process.

In cases of minor head injury, cognitive changes in judgment, control, and memory often lead to sexual inappropriateness. In such cases, interpersonal relationships are almost always conflictual. Isolation, social withdrawal, and depression are commonplace. Issues of impotency and lack of sexual desire are typical.

For these patients, staff members must be both educators and counselors. Sexual retraining with behavioral techniques can be helpful and supportive. Couples counseling can also be a source of support and a means of improving communication between partners. Often a better understanding of social situations and related role playing can be a means of developing social skills and facilitating interpersonal relationships. In some facilities, videotaping is used to improve social skills and provide the patient with feedback regarding his or her behavior.

In cases of severe head injury, the sexual behavior is very difficult. In the acute stage, a severely injured patient tends to be self-stimulating. This behavior serves a useful function and should be regarded as appropriate in this context (Blackerby, 1988). It facilitates the patient's waking process.

The responsibility of the staff in these cases is to provide privacy and safety. They should also be providing information and education to the family during this time, so that the patient's behavior and speech are not misunderstood and alienating to family and friends.

In the reentry phase, the patient is often faced with changes in role as well as difficulty reintegrating into the family and community. His or her emotional reaction and feelings of anxiety and depression will often complicate long-term adjustment. Problems in sexual performance may trigger feelings of inadequacy and incompetency. In addition, problems in self-esteem and body image may cause social withdrawal and isolation.

During the reentry phase, staff must show sensitivity and empathy. Education, counseling, social skill development, and family work may all be necessary. As patients struggle to understand themselves and the changes that have occurred, feedback from staff members is essential. As in earlier phases of adjustment, communication between patient and partner is critical, but is almost always a problem. Trained counselors can be very helpful in working on these issues and facilitating communication.

COUNTERTRANSFERENCE ISSUES

To prepare staff members adequately for their roles in sexual rehabilitation, attention must be paid to feelings and attitudes that could interfere (see Table 18.1). Negative societal stereotypes about sexuality and disability prevail among staff members as well as the general public (Romano, 1982). Personal feelings of anxiety regarding sexual topics can cause staff members to overreact to otherwise easily managed patient behaviors such as explicit language, sexual approaches to staff, and disinhibited sexual behavior. Tension and embarrassment may also prevent staff from gathering sexual history information for use in treatment planning or for providing information on sexual adjustment.

Another commonly observed staff reaction is anger. This may result from the heavy demands of working in a rehabilitation setting (i.e., it may be a manifestation of burnout) or from being threatened by sexual topics. It may manifest itself as open, verbal hostility or as limit setting that is overly restrictive in response to sexual content. At other times, anger may manifest itself as denial, overprotection, or the belief that sex education is not relevant for the patient.

Table 18.1.   Staff Values that May Interfere with Addressing Patient's Sexual Concerns

- Anxiety about sexual topics
- Myth of head-injured patients as asexual or hypersexual
- Myth of sex education increasing sexual inappropriateness
- Lack of trust of patients to have a role in their own rehabilitation
- Anger, leading to overly restrictive limit-setting on sexual behavior
- Denial, overprotection, or the belief that sex education is not relevant to the patient
- Lack of empathy
- Moralizing
- Lack of objectivity
- Sexual advances by staff toward patients

Although not necessarily motivated by anger, moralizing is another common error that interferes with staff objectivity. While staff members are not expected to endorse all sexual values represented by clients, they are expected to let clients make their own decisions about sexual behavior, choice of partners, and use of birth-control methods. The stance to be cultivated among care providers is one of self-awareness (Zinn, 1988). Staff are expected to be aware of their own values and reactions in order to maintain a position of objectivity and to label their biases as personal rather than professional issues.

There are certainly classes of sexual behavior that are inappropriate, psychologically or physically harmful, and dangerous. It is critical for staff to prevent public masturbation, sexual assault of staff or fellow patients, or sexual behavior that is likely to communicate sexually transmitted diseases or create problem pregnancy. Furthermore, consistent and direct feedback on less dangerous but socially unacceptable behavior is necessary to ensure adequate adjustment for the head-injured patient (Strauss, 1987). Examples of such restraint might include prohibiting dating between group members for the duration of group treatment and discouraging on-ward romances in the inpatient setting, as well as corrective feedback on inappropriate comments.

In addition to their role in regulating the patient's sexual behavior, most institutions specifically prohibit staff–patient sexual contact in their codes of ethics. Romantic feelings toward patients can be dangerous and unhealthy for all concerned. However, identification and awareness of one's own emotional feelings toward a patient can provide important information and ultimately contribute to an improved patient–staff relationship.

DEVELOPING COMFORT AND CONFIDENCE

A very powerful and direct method of training staff members to understand their own sexual values is by participation in a Sexual Attitude Reassessment (SAR) Seminar. These programs for the disabled and rehabilitation community were originally developed by Drs. Theodore and Sandra Cole at the University of Minnesota School of Medicine in 1973 (Ducharme, 1987). They are now offered in several locations throughout the country and are recommended for both patients and staff. For sex counselors, SAR seminars are required for certification. These workshops provide explicit visual information on the diversity of sexual behavior and values found in our culture. After observing films, role playing, and skits in a large-group situation, individuals are divided into small groups with trained leaders, where they are given the opportunity to process their reactions to the material. The structure works well in providing a safe opportunity for an in-depth exploration of personal issues unavailable in other formats. It also provides a means for developing empathy toward patients, which is necessary for staff to be effective in helping with sexual issues.

PROGRAM DEVELOPMENT

A variety of methods are available for preparing staff members to deal with the sexual concerns of their clients. Program development should always begin with a general-needs assessment. The content of a simple assessment questionnaire should include level of training in human sexuality, attitudes and feelings, knowledge of issues, and experience in working with clients on these concerns (Medlar et al., 1986). Assuring confidentiality of responses by using anonymous reporting and a randomized response method increases the likelihood of collecting accurate data (Cohen, 1987).

Once the needs assessment has been completed, a specific intervention or treatment strategy may be implemented. These strategies may include consultation with a trained behavioral specialist, individual and group psychotherapy programs, an inservice education program, attitude-change exercises, stress-management programs, and establishment of an institutional sexuality committee to oversee policy development and educational and therapeutic programs.

In many settings, the interventions need to be focused on the anxiety of the staff. Two effective methods of managing anxiety and issues of stress are consultation and systematic relaxation training. The consultant serves as a resource person who can respond to staff questions about sexual issues. Ultimately, this individual can help staff members learn how to handle specific situations. The resource person serves as a model for openness and permission giving regarding sexuality. In addition, this individual reduces the sense of isolation that staff members may feel regarding this topic. In general, the consultant's role is to discuss sexual behavior in an open, nondefensive fashion.

Since the majority of rehabilitation staff members will acknowledge anxiety about dealing with sexual issues, they may also be open to methods that will assist them in reducing this anxiety. Systematic muscle-relaxation training is an effective and simple method. A simple relaxation technique can noticeably reduce observable signs of audience tension such as high noise level, nervous laughter, and jitteriness. Participants can use these techniques to prepare themselves for working with patients on high-anxiety topics such as sexuality.

INSERVICE EDUCATION AND CURRICULUM DEVELOPMENT

An ongoing series of lecture and workshop presentations is usually the primary means of on-site staff training. Such presentations should always include opportunities for processing feelings and reactions to the presentation materials. Printed materials and references for further study are generally helpful for those who wish to become more involved in the topic. Explicit or nonexplicit media are often used to supplement the lecture material.

The previously conducted survey should contain a section where staff can indicate questions and concerns that are unique to the setting. These topics can be integrated into a general syllabus that includes anatomy and physiology of the sexual response, effect of head injury on sexual functioning, effects of medication, discussion of sexual concerns with patients (whether to, when, and how), collection of data for a database, documentation, staff–patient interactions, behavior management and counseling, and techniques such as guided imagery and body-awareness exercises (Gill et al., 1987; Schover & Jensen, 1988).

A program evaluation should be conducted at the conclusion of the workshop to assess the extent to which the behavioral objectives (increased awareness of sexual issues, increased comfort in discussing the topic, and practice of intervention skills) have been met. This evaluation will provide a mechanism for refining future presentations. Pretesting and posttesting comparisons are often used to document attitudinal and behavioral change in the desired direction. As a general rule, inservice education is most effective when offered on a regular basis and well integrated into the rehabilitation or postacute program.

INSTITUTIONAL SUPPORT: DEVELOPING AN INSTITUTIONAL SEXUALITY COMMITTEE

Because the topic of sexuality is a controversial one, it is essential to obtain administrative support for the development of sexuality programs. An interdisciplinary sexuality committee composed of staff members with interest and expertise in sexuality issues has as its first task the responsibility to develop a program proposal. This document should outline the procedures to be used in establishing patient, family, and staff education and intervention programs. Despite its clear benefit to the quality of care, the program must address the issues that are important to the administration: reimbursement and improved rehabilitation outcome. If the proposed program is responsible, conservative, and well integrated into the comprehensive rehabilitation program, agency support will be enhanced.

Additional responsibilities of the interdisciplinary committee on sexuality are managing staff resistance and establishing policies and procedures on the most sensitive sexual issues. It is essential that the committee institute policies on such matters as whether to provide a privacy room (Griffith, 1978), public versus private masturbation, partner sexual activity, dissemination of birth-control information and supplies, prevention of sexual assault, prevention of sexually transmitted diseases, and institutional policies relating to the relationship between patient and staff members.

PROFESSIONAL ROLES

Together with the institutional sexuality committee, all members of the rehabilitation team are responsible for assisting the patient with issues of sexuality. Unlike medical rehabilitation, sexual rehabilitation should not be assigned to the duties of any one specific discipline. Under ideal circumstances, the patient should be able to choose the individual with whom he or she feels most comfortable discussing sensitive topics. Although not all staff members need to be experts in this area, all are responsible for affirming the patient's sexuality and handling initial inquiries. Also, all staff members must deal appropriately with inappropriate behavior if the patient is ultimately to develop a healthy sense of self after injury.

Because of the cultural taboos regarding discussions of sexuality, inquiries about sex may at first be disguised or indirect. With some people, talk about relationships, attractiveness, parenting, or social situations may in reality be underlying anxiety about sexuality. With other patients, sexual aggressiveness toward staff members may be motivated by underlying fears of loss of masculinity or femininity. For this reason, behavioral techniques aimed at eliminating unwanted behaviors should always be supplemented with various counseling techniques. Emotional issues always need to be understood and addressed.

The PLISSIT model developed by Annon (1974) provides a useful framework for understanding the various levels of intervention used by staff. In this model, four levels of intervention by staff are postulated: permission, limited information, specific suggestions, and intensive therapy (hence the name PLISSIT). This system allows staff members to rate their own competence and to determine the level of intervention with which they feel most comfortable.

Permission

All staff members are responsible for giving patients permission to discuss sexual concerns. This permission affirms and assures patients that it is a legitimate area of discussion. It encourages patients to experiment with their bodies and to think of themselves in a sexual context. This is an important first step in laying the foundation on which a patient can rebuild an identity that fosters interpersonal relationships and intimacy.

For this level of intervention, staff members do not need to be experts on sexual functioning, but they do need to be comfortable regarding their own sexuality. Feelings of embarrassment, guilt, or shame can easily be communicated nonverbally to patients. Giving a patient permission to discuss sexuality requires that a staff member have effective listening skills, interpersonal sensitivity, and willingness to suspend judgement.

Limited Information

At the second level of intervention, patients are given specific facts regarding their sexual function after injury. This may prevent future anxieties or problems and will help to correct patient misconceptions. In many cases, partners should be included in these discussions to encourage communication and experimentation between the two people.

This level of intervention obviously requires knowledge regarding the consequences of the injury on sexual activities. In addition, it requires that staff members know when to refer a patient for professional counseling (e.g., to a urologist). Staff members need to understand a patient's tolerance and limits for such information and must be able to maintain confidentiality.

Specific Suggestions

This level of intervention requires counseling skills in addition to knowledge of the topic. Therefore, staff at this level should have received specialized training in sexuality and disability and should be familiar with counseling techniques and interventions. Specific suggestions might include areas such as positioning, bladder and bowel care, contraception, and techniques to sustain erections. Knowledge of the patient's (and partner's) emotional condition is essential so that suggestions can be integrated with behavioral assignments that take into account the patient's background and history.

Staff members at this level should be able to establish a therapeutic environment that feels safe to the patient. In addition, this level requires the ability to take a sexual history and be aware of available treatment modalities that might be necessary if problems develop. Naturally, one must also be aware of the disability itself and the unique sexual problems that may result from the injury.

Intensive Therapy

This final level of intervention is intended to be provided by professionals in the mental health field who have had specialized training in sexual counseling. Patients with complex sexual dysfunctions, problem relationships, psychiatric histories, or severe behavioral problems may require this level of intervention. Staff members must be able to identify these patients and to assist in referral with support and encouragement.

Staff members who assume the role of therapist must have prior training and skill development in sex therapy. They must be skilled in various modalities of treatment and have a working knowledge of the legal and ethical issues involved. In many facilities, rehabilitation professionals with appropriate training assume this role and often integrate it with the psychological interventions that are a normal part of the rehabilitation process.

CONCLUSION

Rehabilitation professionals have made considerable progress in integrating sexual issues into the rehabilitation program. For people with head injury, this progress has been somewhat slower and more complex, because of the multifaceted nature of the injury. The sexual myths surrounding people with head injury have been numerous and damaging. Most difficult of all have been the fears, attitudes, and reluctance of many care providers to deal with those issues. However, people with head injuries have the capacity for intimate relationships and sexual expression and have demanded information services in this realm. Staff members in rehabilitation are responsible for teaching, counseling, and supporting personal growth in this critical area of human development.

REFERENCES

Annon, J. S. *The Behavioral Treatment of Sexual Problems*, Honolulu, Hawaii: Enabling Systems; 1974; 1.

Blackerby, W. F. Disruption of sexuality following a head injury. *Natl Head Inj Found Newsletter.* 1987; 7(1): 2,8.

Blackerby, W. F. *Sexual Dysfunction and Adjustment in Head Injury.* Houston, Tex: HDI Publishers; 1988: 10. HDI Professional Series on Traumatic Brain Injury.

Cohen, J. How to ask about sex and get honest answers. *Science.* 1987; 236:382.

Ducharme, S. Sexuality and physical disability. In: Caplan, B. ed. *Rehabilitation Psychology Desk Reference.* Rockville, Md: Aspen Publishers; 1987.

Gill, K. M., Savage, J., Hough, S. Nursing's role in the sexual education of the patient in the rehabilitation setting. Presented at Braintree Hospital Inservice Program; June 1987; Braintree, Massachusetts.

Gill, K. M. Staff needs-assessment data. 1988, unpublished.

Griffith, E., Trieschmann, R. Use of a private hospital room in restoring sexual function to the physically disabled. *Sex Disabil.* 1978; 13: 179-183.

Jennett, B. Scale and scope of the problem. In: Rosenthal, M., Griffith, E. R., Bond, M. R., Miller, J.D., eds. *Rehabilitation of the Head Injured Adult.* Philadelphia, Pa: FA Davis; 1983.

Medlar, T., Faria, J., Unger, L., Kidder, R., McGrath, N. Sexuality and the whole person: Development of a program for use in head injury rehabilitation. Presented at the Braintree Hospital Seventh Annual Traumatic Head Injury Conference; October 1986; Chicago, Illinois.

Romano, M. D. Sex and disability: Are they mutually exclusive. In: Eisenberg, M. G., Griggins, C., Duval, R. J., eds. *Disabled People as Second Class Citizens.* New York, NY: Springer Publishing Co.; 1982.

Schover, L. R., Jensen, S. B. *Sexuality and Chronic Illness: A Comprehensive Approach.* New York, NY: Guilford; 1988.

Strauss, D. Sexuality: Treatment interventions for professionals working with the head injured. 1987, unpublished.

Zinn, W. M. doctors have feelings too. *J. Am. Med. Assoc.* 1988; 259: 3296-3298.

RESOURCES

American Association of Sex Educators, Counselors and Therapists, 435 N. Michigan Ave, Suite 1717, Chicago, IL 60611, (312) 644-0828.

Information and Education Council of the United States (SIECUS), Suite 407, 84 Fifth Ave, New York, NY 10011.

National Head Injury Foundation, 333 Turnpike Rd, Southborough, MA 01772, (508) 485-9950.

National Task Force on Sexuality and Disability, American Congress of Rehabilitation Medicine, 130 S. Michigan Avenue, Chicago, IL 60602, (312) 922-9368.

Sexuality and Disability Training Center, Boston University Medical Center, 88 E. Newton St, Boston, MA 02118, (617) 638-7358.

Sexuality and Disability Training Center, University of Michigan Medical Center, Department of Physical Medicine and Rehabilitation, 1500 E. Medical Center Dr., Ann Arbor, MI 48109, (313) 936-7067.

Sexual Dysfunction Clinic, a service of the Wellness Clinic, Upham House, McLean Hospital, 115 Mill St., Belmont, MA 02178, (617) 855- 2978.

19

Sexuality and Psychiatric Disability

Peter T. Knoepfler

Even though disability secondary to mental illness and to emotional problems affects a much larger group of people than disability caused by physical illness, the study of the relationship between sexuality and psychiatric disability is just starting.

Physical disability is usually readily apparent. The needs and limitations of those with physical disabilities are usually obvious. Anyone can observe disorders of movement or mechanical appliances, which are striking manifestations of physical disability. There are others whose problems are less apparent. People with osteomas, or in the initial stages of illnesses such as arthritis, multiple sclerosis, malignancies, often appear not to suffer from any disability. Most psychiatric disabilities are hidden. When a person has a severe psychosis he/she may appear odd or eccentric, but it is rare that the disability is self-evident. Those with neurotic problems or even incapacitating character disorders show little evidence on casual encounters. This is one of the reasons that the needs of those with psychiatric disability are often overlooked.

It is very anxiety producing for most people to be faced with persons whose hidden limitations resemble their own conflicts. One way to ward off this realization is to blot out and deny the existence of these people. This is one reason that persons with mental illnesses are segregated in places remote from centers of population.

There is a prevailing feeling that disabled persons are not interested in or entitled to enjoy their sexuality. In spite of today's sexual revolution, many people object to nonreproductive sex. The underlying assumption is that persons with disability have no business having children; if there are to be no children, there should be no sex.

These factors make it even more important to increase the awareness of the sexual needs and problems of those suffering from psychiatric disabilities.

This chapter will consider this relationship from two points of view: The relationship of the disability to sexuality, and a survey of psychiatric disabilities and their impact on sexuality.

Psychiatric disability and sexuality can be associated in three ways:

Sexual behavior is the disability. Mr. A. is a man in his twenties who functions well in most areas of his life. His predominant form of sexual expression is being an exhibitionist. Psychiatry considers this form of sexual expression a psychiatric disability.

Sexual behavior is unrelated to the disability. Ms. B. suffers from a severe case of agoraphobia. Sexual behavior in a bedroom does not trigger Ms. B.'s phobia and it is therefore unimpaired.

Sexual behavior is an integral part of the disability. Mr. C. is suffering from a severe depression. While depressed, his sexual desire and interest are impaired. When the depression is treated and relieved, his sexual interest is likely to be reawakened.

We will now survey each major psychiatric disability and study its relationship to sexuality.

The classification used in this chapter follows in general outline the usual nosology. Each subsection has a very brief description of the particular disability. Because the classification of psychiatric disability is not very precise, this brief description will permit the reader to be more aware of the specific condition described.

For example, for many mental health professionals, "schizophrenia" is a disability that leads persons to need hospitalization or placement on large doses of antipsychotic medication. For others, "schizophrenia" also includes persons whose personality structure and defects are those described in schizophrenia even though they are able to function in society and have no need for antipsychotic medication. Even though the diagnostic label is the same, the severity of the two conditions is quite different.

PSYCHOSIS

This is a condition in which a person loses the ability to distinguish reality from fantasy. There are two major functional (nonorganic) types of psychosis.

Affective Psychosis

This is a condition in which there are profound disturbances of mood, either toward depression or euphoria. In some persons these disturbances alternate.

Psychotic depression

In this condition, people suffer a feeling of loss of self esteem, a loss of interest in the world and often a great deal of anger turned toward the self. These persons suffer physiological signs of depression such as: insomnia, anorexia, weight loss, and amenorrhea. They often feel or act suicidal. While in this state, persons find it difficult to make transitions; they feel little sexual desire or excitement. Another stage in the sexual cycle can be postulated. This stage is named transition. It is the stage that bridges a previous activity to a desire for a sexual experience. It requires inner flexibility. For example, a woman caring for a small child all day needs a transition to feel sexual.

> Mr. D. is a 45-year-old man, who became depressed following the death of his wife, who died after a long illness. He became anorexic, lost weight, became constipated, and found it very difficult to sleep. He felt more and more depressed, cried a great deal, felt alone in the world. A feeling of personal worthlessness enveloped him. He began to consider suicide as a way out of his emotional pain. Up to this time, Mr. D. had always had an active and rich sexual life. While severely depressed, he became completely disinterested in anything sexual.

Hypomania and mania

Persons who are in this state feel at one with the universe. They feel very powerful and very excited. They are overactive, need to sleep or eat very little, because they want to do so much. They make rapid transitions and experience desire and sexual excitement in rapid escalation.

> Mrs. E. is a 35-year-old woman who suffered a major disappointment in love. She tried to cope with these feelings by becoming hyperactive; she slept little since she felt terribly busy. She hardly even had time to eat. She felt filled with boundless energy. She started a new career in business and engaged in three sexual affairs almost simultaneously. On some days, she would spend the afternoon in the bed of one man, the late afternoon with another one, and then have her third sexual relationship in the evening with yet another man.

Schizophrenic Reactions

These were originally described and characterized by four primary symptoms: autism, ambivalence, flat affect, and thought disorder. Persons with these conditions frequently experience delusions and/or hallucinations. Sexual thoughts and preoccupations often play a major role in the thought content of most persons. In others, neither their sexuality nor their sexual functioning is affected. The reasons for these differences are unknown. Persons suffering from this set of conditions show wide variations in their symptomatology, therefore it is not possible to make generalizations about the impact of this disability on sexual functioning.

Two additional considerations should be mentioned. First, one of the cardinal deficits of persons suffering from schizophrenic conditions is the impairment of their ability to clearly separate reality from fantasy. They can experience sexual fantasies as real and this can lead them to engage in bizarre sexual behavior.

Mr. F. has heard that the intensity of orgasms in males is increased by partial temporary strangulation. Rather than dealing with this possibility on the fantasy level, he tries to set up conditions to produce temporary strangulation. His plan misfires, his strangulation is permanent. He was discovered having hung himself while masturbating and died of asphyxiation.

Another consequence of the difficulty in distinguishing reality from fantasy is that some persons who had suffered an acute schizophrenic reaction and then have gone into remission is that their emotional equilibrium is very labile and is maintained by extremely rigid control over feelings and fantasies. Any impending loss of control is experienced as a revival of this previous psychosis. Many such persons cannot give up control to experience orgasm. They might request consultation and therapy for their lack of orgasms. If therapy approaches success, and orgasm is nearly imminent, they begin to show incipient signs of psychosis. Basically, for people with these conditions, high levels of excitement lead to a threat of emotional disorganization of their rigidly controlled fragile balance.

Mrs. G. is a 30-year-old woman, who suffered a schizophrenic reaction eight years ago. She was hospitalized and treated with medications; this regimen resulted in a remission of her illness. She finds herself seriously involved with a man, but complains of not reaching orgasm during their sexual relationship. Mrs. G. wants very much to achieve orgasm. She requests sex therapy. Even though Mrs. G. is warned that sex therapy might revive her psychosis, she feels the need to proceed with it. After a few appointments, as she feels close to orgasm, Mrs. G. develops paranoid ideas and feelings of depersonalization. Sex therapy is discontinued and she reverts back into remission.

BORDERLINE CONDITIONS

There are a series of conditions that do not fit clearly into any category. Persons suffering from such conditions are often labeled as having a borderline condition. (Borderline refers to the fact that during ordinary conditions, these persons function well, but even with minor stress develop a temporary psychosis.) One common form of borderline condition is called "narcissistic."

Narcissistic Borderline

In narcissistic borderline conditions, persons have the feeling of being perfect, being endowed with superhuman skills, knowledge and power. They experience themselves as being the center of the universe. They are often also convinced that the ordinary laws of cause and effect do not apply to them because of their superiority.

Ms. H. is the type of person well known to family planning clinics. She is concerned about the fact that she has missed a few periods and comes to the clinic for pregnancy detection. Both physical examination and laboratory tests reveal her to be pregnant. The counselor advises her of this fact. During the dialogue with Ms. H., the counselor becomes aware that Ms. H. experiences herself as special and unique. Being intelligent and well-informed, she knows all the pertinent facts about conception and contraception, but she is convinced that they do not apply to her. If the counselor insists that Ms. H. is pregnant, she becomes guarded, hostile, and paranoid accusing the counselor of plotting against her.

SITUATIONAL REACTIONS

These are personal reactions to situations of stress. Depending on the perception of the severity of the stress, there is often temporary impairment of some or all aspects of sexual functioning.

Mr. I. is a 23-year-old man, who was walking home from a date one evening, when two men accosted him, threatened him with a handgun, robbed him of his money and jewelry. For good measure, one of the men also hit his head with a gun. Even though Mr. I has been a normally functioning male during all his life, his energies are diverted from sexuality, while he attempts to cope with and master this trauma. (He will also probably withdraw from many other activities during this period of coping.)

ORGANIC BRAIN SYNDROME

These are conditions caused by a physical insult to the central nervous system. Disability can be caused by events such as trauma, (e.g., head injury, illness, e.g., multiple sclerosis; chemicals, e.g., LSD, PCP). There will be no discussion of this type of disability in this chapter since the underlying condition is neurological.

CHARACTEROLOGICAL AND PERSONALITY DISORDERS

These disabilities used to be called "psychopathy." They encompass a large and diversified group of disabilities characterized by a very strong inner drive to master anxiety by engaging in action. Many persons in this category tend to act in impulsive ways disregarding consequences. There is often an absence of what is commonly referred to as "conscience." The effect of this disability on sexuality is diverse so that it cannot be classified. These persons will engage in behaviors without taking into account their effect on others or the consequences for themselves.

Mr. J. is a 19-year-old man, who is concerned about his feelings of masculinity. As he was growing up, during adolescence, he had some delay in the onset of puberty and developed minor gynecomastia. His parents set an example by dealing with their own anxieties by drinking too much, driving their cars too fast, or just "doing something" to relieve the inner pressure of anxiety. Mr. J. became friends with a man named Allen and one night dreamed of having a homosexual relationship with him. Mr. J. woke up very anxious, started drinking, and was finally apprehended by the police for exhibiting himself on a busy street of his hometown. Mr. J. illustrates the first category of persons, those for whom their mode of expressing their sexuality is the disability.

Ms. K. is a 28-year-old woman, who comes for treatment of a pelvic inflammatory disease. Her chief complaint is pelvic pain. She mentions that she has been married three times, but none of her husbands satisfied her either emotionally or sexually. She often feels very dissatisfied with life and needs to do something. This "need to do something" has included: multiple casual sexual partners, excessive use of alcohol and valium. When these outlets were not available, Ms. K. would tend to overeat and her weight would fluctuate by more than 50 pounds. She is intolerant of delay, has difficulty in looking forward to or planning for the next month or year. She wants what she wants and she wants it now. Delay is painful and elicits a rage reaction. She tries to cope with these rage reactions by the use of alcohol, valium, and marijuana. Ms. K. illustrates a person who needs to act when she feels under stress and anxious, even when these actions are not in her best interest.

NEUROSES

Persons with these disabilities suffer from anxiety and guilt. Secondary symptoms emerge that try to control the anxiety and guilt. These can include: phobias, neurotic depressions, obsessive-compulsive thoughts or behaviors, psychosomatic conditions, etc. It is these secondary symptoms that constitute the neurotic patterns. This pattern can be either related to or independent of sexual concerns.

ANXIETY

Anxiety is a very painful feeling of fear that occurs in response to fantasized rather than real threats. To illustrate, a car driving towards a person at 80 miles an hour elicits fear (a real threat). Being close to a friend about whom a person has unacceptable fantasies elicits anxiety.

Nonsex-Related Anxiety

Mr. L. is a 36-year-old man, who finds himself beset by feelings of anxiety. He is completely unable to relate these to specific events, only to notice that any change or expected change in life leads to intense feelings of anxiety. During these times, he is so involved with these experiences that he neither has the energy nor the interest for anything sexual. Even nonsex-related anxiety leads to avoidance of transition, excitement, and orgasm phases.

Sex-Related Anxiety

Mr. M. comes from a very orthodox religious background. He was taught that masturbation is a major sin and that those who commit major sins end up in hell. Hell was always described in very explicit, graphic, concrete terms. Whenever Mr. M. feels sexual arousal without an available partner be becomes very anxious, since he is tempted to masturbate. Even though intellectually he no longer believes in his childhood religion, the picture of hell appears in his fantasies. Gradually he permits himself fewer and fewer situations of sexual excitement. Anxiety leads to an inability to make transitions, detracts from sexual excitement and interferes with experiencing orgasm.

GUILT

Many persons suffer from guilt and find it difficult to tolerate the experience of pleasure. Often there are underlying fantasies that make the experience of pleasure seem wrong.

Guilt Unrelated to Sexual Concerns

Mr. N. is a 33-year-old man, who was taught from early childhood that expressing anger is wrong. Since his life has some frustrations and feels angry, he starts to feel guilty and undeserving. He avoids situations that might provide him with pleasure such as dancing (which he loves) and he declines promotions at work. Even though he and his wife engage in regular sexual intercourse, he will at times ejaculate without the emotional pleasure of an orgasm.

Guilt Related to Sexual Concerns

Ms. O. is 23 years old. She was taught that only marital sex leading to reproduction was acceptable, any other sexual activity was evil and a cardinal sin. Ms. O is deeply emotionally involved with her boyfriend. She enjoys being sexual with him, but feels very guilty later. She develops postcoital reactive depressions. Gradually she develops other means to deal with these conflicts.

She will have a few drinks before her sexual activity and forget to use contraception. This enables her to pretend to herself that sex only happened because she felt intoxicated with alcohol. She says to herself that she did not plan to be sexual, since she did not use contraception. She punishes herself by worrying about a possible pregnancy after her unprotected intercourse.

Ms. O. started developing sadomasochistic fantasies. These consist mainly of being tied up by a considerate but insistent lover and then being made love to while tied down. She has decided to share this fantasy with her boyfriend and they have acted out the fantasy in their love making. She noticed that she feels much less guilty and depressed after being sexual under these conditions. She can pretend to herself that she was only a helpless victim, who had intercourse forced on her. Ms. O. finds that she is only able to achieve orgasm under these two conditions.

Persons suffering from this type of guilt will permit the phase of transition and the phase of excitement, and except under special circumstances will deprive themselves of the phase of orgasm.

Secondary Symptoms

Many examples of secondary symptoms exist in people's repertoire. Some examples will be used below:

Phobias

Phobias are rather useful ways to cope with anxiety. Instead of free-floating anxiety, a person can concentrate on avoiding a specific situation.

> Mr. P. has developed a fear of small black dogs with white ears. As long as Mr. P. avoids these specific dogs, his sexual life remains unimpaired.

Phobias can also be sex related

> Ms. Q. has been generally anxious. Gradually she has found that sexual situations lead to feelings of anxiety. She has developed a phobia of seeing, touching, or feeling a penis. Because Ms. Q.'s orientation is heterosexual, this phobia is a major interference in her sexual life.

Reactive depressions

A reactive (or neurotic) depression is a depression in response to a stress. They are much less severe than psychotic depressions and encompass much less of the person's total functioning. They are closely linked to situational reactions.

> Mr. R. is a 23-year-old man who has had an active and rewarding life. He was wooing a female friend and finally convinced her to have intercourse with him. He was trying very hard to please her and developed situational impotence. His girlfriend made fun of him and the size of his penis. Mr. R. reacted with chagrin, anger, and then a temporary reactive depression. During this time, he felt disinterested in many aspects of his life including sex. He was able to discuss these feelings with his girlfriend and his reactive depression lifted.

Obsessive-compulsive symptoms

These symptoms help the person cope with anxiety, as they can imagine that if they think certain thoughts or perform certain rituals that they will be safe from their anxiety.

Nonsex-related obsessive-compulsive symptoms

Mr. R. witnessed his house burning down when he was four years old. As an adult any sign of fire elicits a great deal of anxiety. He has convinced himself that if he checks his stove three times at exactly one minute intervals before going to sleep at night, he will be safe from fire. Mr. R's behavior appears somewhat eccentric to his girlfriend, but does not interfere with his sex life with her.

Sex-related obsessive-compulsive symptoms

Ms. S. feels that her vagina is dirty, smelly, and repulsive. Close physical proximity to others brings about anxiety that she will be rejected because of her smell. Ms. S. developed the ritual of taking a shower and a douche before leaving the house. When she is confronted with sexual situations, she also douches twice before intercourse, uses very heavy perfume and will only participate in any sexual contact in a room heavily suffused with incense. While participating in a sexual encounter, she continually scans her partner's facial expressions and reactions for any signs of disgust to her smell.

This type of obsessive-compulsive symptomatology interferes with the person's ability to make transitions, experience excitement, or relinquish control enough to achieve orgasm.

Psychosomatic conditions

Each person's psyche and body (soma) are intimately interconnected. There are some individuals in whom somatic signs and symptoms occur, which are more clearly triggered by psychological stress leading to anxiety. Both male and female genitourinary systems are susceptible to this type of disability.

Mr. T. is a 38-year-old man, who attended a business convention within the last year. He met a woman and participated in a brief affair with her. Because Mr. T. is married, he has been feeling very guilty about this relationship. He also became quite concerned about the possibility of having contracted a sexually transmitted disease, even though he had no symptoms. He consulted a physician away from his home town and was reassured after a thorough examination and laboratory workup that he had no sign of any illness. He gradually developed some pelvic pain and was finally referred to a urologist. The urologist again found him to be free of any sexually transmitted disease, but diagnosed him as having nonspecific prostatitis. He had to return to the urologist for prostatic massages, which he found both painful and humiliating. It is quite likely that Mr. T's prostatitis is his body's reaction to the guilt for what he considers a serious transgression of his marriage contract.

Ms. U. is a 27-year-old married woman, who has many fears about pregnancy, labor, and delivery. After lengthy discussions, she and her husband agree that they want to try to have a baby in about six months. The patient develops amenorrhea. Both she and her husband have a complete evaluation and are found to be perfectly normal. Ms. U.'s amenorrhea is probably caused by the high level of anxiety triggered by the underlying myths and conflicts about pregnancy, labor, and delivery.

PSYCHIATRIC DISABILITY AND BODY IMAGE

Body image is the person's inner perception of his or her body's appearance. One test of body image is to ask that three pictures be drawn: A picture of a person, a picture of a person of the opposite gender, and a picture of oneself. The comparison of these drawings will provide an idea of the individual's self-concept and body image.

CASE EXAMPLES

Weight

Ms. V. is always concerned that she is overweight. She has a picture of herself as being too fat. Even though she appears normal to people around her, she keeps struggling to keep her weight down to the level she wants.

Ms. W. suffers from anorexia nervosa. One of her main symptoms is that she always feels very fat. She alternates between not eating or eating then making herself vomit. She has amenorrhea and experiences no sexual interest. If Ms. W.'s condition is not treated, she is likely to become cachetic and die.

Protuberances

Our culture is very concerned with the appearance of and the size of protuberances. Many persons' self esteem is dependent on these factors.

Mr. X. would be considered a normal male. He is 16 years old. His friends passed through puberty earlier than he did. Mr. X. is concerned that he does not have the right body for a man. He is worried that he does not have enough body hair and that his penis is too small. (Most men look at their penis from above; due to this perspective the penis appears smaller than it is.) He avoids urinating in public and experiences a great deal of anxiety when he has to undress in a public place like the locker room for P.E.

Ms. Y. is a 23-year-old female, who would be considered to have a normal body. Most of her friends have much larger breasts than she has. She feels inadequate and unfeminine.

Concerns about body image are very important to most people; even minor bodily imperfections, such as a mole, are often perceived as a major handicap. Persons with psychoses often weave these body image conflicts into their disability.

Mrs. Z. is a 42-year-old woman, who was convinced that she had some inherent damage in the back of her throat. She was afraid to eat anything solid for fear of choking on it. She presented with a severe psychotic depression which on further history taking appeared to be reactive to a very stressful series of events. Mrs. Z. had been concerned about being overweight; she went to a therapist using behavior modification and hypnosis for weight control. While under a hypnotic trance, she was given the posthypnotic suggestion to perform fellatio on the hypnotist. She acceded to his demands, but also felt very guilty about betraying her marriage. Over the next few weeks, she developed the conviction of damage to her throat; this permitted her no longer to perform fellatio and to discontinue her contacts with the hypnotist.

INTERVENTIONS

Interventions in areas of sexuality for people with psychiatric disabilities can be divided into two major categories: education and therapy (or counseling).

Education

Education about sexuality is likely to be the most effective measure in minimizing sexual difficulties. This education needs to address two major areas:

Education around facts

It is advisable that a curriculum for sex education include the following subjects: sexual anatomy, physiology, conception, contraception, and sexually transmitted diseases. In addition, information about sexual activities should be included: masturbation, heterosexual and homosexual behaviors and other sexual variations.

The main problem with factual sexual education is that unless attitudinal aspects are addressed, the information will not be usable by the target population.

Education around attitudes

Most people have rather rigid attitudes about sexuality. The attitudes of many persons with psychiatric disabilities are often part of their disability and interfere with learning. During an adequate sex education program more time and energy will need to be devoted to attitudes than to facts. Issues such as values clarification, decision making, respect for one's own and one's partner's needs have to be addressed. Moral values and ethical attitudes congruent with the person's religious background have to be considered. An example of this type of education would be the use or misuse of sex.

Examples of the use of sex

Mr. and Mrs. A. find that touching each other and having a sexual relationship leads to feelings of greater intimacy and to pleasure for both of them. Sex was used as a way of communicating closeness. This would be an example of the use of sex as a way of sharing a physical intimacy with another person.

Example of misuse of sex

Mr. B. needs to pursue and seduce most women he meets. As soon as he has seduced them, he ignores them and forgets them. Mr. B. does not use sex as a way to share with another person, but as a way to reassure himself about his attractiveness and also to exercise power over women.

Education about attitudes requires a great deal of skill and sensitivity in the professional in order to help each person think through the options inherent in these issues. As an educator to those with psychiatric disability this skill and sensitivity has to be even greater, since psychiatric disability can result in rigidities and distortions that need to be addressed.

Mr. C. is a 31-year-old man, who has had a long lasting schizophrenic disability. (One characteristic of such a disability is the impairment in the ability to make abstractions, to understand jokes or metaphors.) As an adolescent, he overheard a person talking about his friends John and Mary. John and Mary were in love. This person added: Mary really "got under the skin" of John. Mr. C. understood this quite literally and since then has avoided physical closeness, because he was afraid that anyone he would get close to might get stuck under his skin.

A sex educator providing services for Mr. C. would have to be quite knowledgeable about psychoses to be able to help this man deal with this attitude. Any mention of physical closeness by the educator would be likely to elicit a great deal of anxiety in Mr. C.

Counseling (or Therapy)

For the psychiatric disability

It is often necessary to treat the psychiatric disability before any effective intervention can be made in the sexual issues.

Ms. D. learned as a child that sex was dirty and evil. During adolescence Ms. D. would masturbate on occasion. Shortly after one such episode, she heard that her grandmother had died. She developed the fear that any sexual activity on her part would lead to the death of a relative. As a result she has refrained from any sexual behavior. Ms. D. has to have her underlying fears treated before her sexual difficulties can be addressed.

Therapy for the sexual dysfunction

Persons with psychiatric disabilities are as subject to sexual dysfunctions as others in the general population. When the psychiatric disability is not a part of the sexual dysfunction, the usual methods of sex therapy can be employed.

> Mr. E. has many phobias. He is afraid of wide open spaces, wild animals, and very aggressive men. Some of the fears interfere with aspects of his daily life. He happens to suffer from premature ejaculation with his wife. Sex therapy for this couple would be prescribed in a similar way as if Mr. E. did not suffer from these fears.

TRAINING OF PROFESSIONALS

From the above discussions, it is clear that persons suffering from psychiatric disabilities and who have sexual concerns present a complicated series of patterns. The first intervention needed is to make a thorough, careful assessment of the contributions of physical problems, psychological problems, and sexual problems. Such an assessment requires skills in the areas of internal medicine, neurology, psychiatry, and human sexuality. Most commonly, this will require a cooperative team approach of professionals whose areas of expertise complement each other to permit such an assessment.

If such an assessment reveals that an educational intervention is indicated, the educator has to have training and expertise in the education of psychiatrically disabled persons and in human sexuality.

If the initial evaluation reveals that the sexual issues are unrelated to the psychiatric disability, therapy of such persons needs to be undertaken by a professional trained as a sex therapist and who has an underlying working knowledge of dealing with psychiatrically disabled persons.

If the assessment shows that the sexual issues are a part of the psychiatric disability, the professionals must be trained and experienced in treating psychiatrically disabled persons (such as a licensed psychologist or psychiatrist) and who also have had training in human sexuality.

Sex educators and sex therapists constitute a new subspeciality in the area of human services. As a result, some individuals considering themselves experts have either mismanaged or exploited persons with sexual concerns. Sex educators and therapists have started professional organizations that work towards ensuring that professionals claiming to be sex educators and therapists have at least a minimum degree of training, education, and expertise in this area. These organizations require as a condition for certification that the professionals subscribe to their code of ethics. Examples of such organizations are: "The Society for Sex Therapy and Research" and "The American Association of Sex Educators, Counselors and Therapists."

20

Facing the Challenges of Sexual Abuse in Persons with Disabilities

Sandra S. Cole

DEFINITION

Child abuse has been defined in the literature to include any act of commission or omission that endangers or impairs a child's physical or emotional health and development. It may be evidenced by an injury or series of injuries appearing to be nonaccidental in nature and which cannot reasonably be explained. The most frequently recognized forms of child abuse are physical abuse (including neglect or lack of adequate supervision), emotional abuse or deprivation, and sexual abuse (Children's Village, U.S.A.).

All children, unfortunately, are candidates to experience sexual abuse. This includes children who were born with or have acquired a disability. They may be living in foster homes or institutions or with their families.

Sexual abuse can consist of visual, physical, or verbal aggression that can be perceived as unwanted sexual activity. This is particularly true of the victim who is below the age of consent. Sexual assault or abuse includes any form of unwanted sexual touching, nonconsensual sexual intercourse, other ongoing sexual exploitation, or perhaps isolated incidences of physical harassment which is experienced as sexual intent.

The Illusion Theatre in Minneapolis, Minnesota defines sexual abuse as occurring when a person is "manipulated, tricked or forced into touch or sexual contact." A helpful definition of sexual abuse to use with children is: forced or tricked touch or sex. This touch can begin anywhere on your body and may mean the person touches your breasts, buttocks, the vagina, or penis. Sexual abuse can also involve oral, anal, or vaginal penetration. Rape is sexual abuse with penetration. For children, a way to discuss penetration is to say that one part of a person's body (finger, tongue, or penis) goes into a part of another person's body (vagina, anus, mouth). Penetration may occur with an object or a body part.

There is also sexual abuse without touch as when someone forces or tricks another person to look at their genitals or forces or tricks an individual into exposing his or her own genitals. Another type of sexual abuse without touch is an obscene phone call, as when a person calls and talks about sex (ways he/she wants to touch a person's body or be touched him/herself).

Sexual abuse of children involves someone too young to give informed consent but who has been involved in a sexual act. The exploitation of an individual who lacks adequate information to recognize such a situation or who is unable to understand or communicate is also labeled sexual abuse (i.e., the mentally or physically disabled, children).

Sexual abuse or assault is a violation of the whole person and is not restricted to "just a sexual act." It results in indignation and an overwhelming sense of violation and invasion that can affect the victim in a physical, psychological, and social way. Frequently the aftermath of the assault or abuse is more severe than the actual event. This is particularly true of disabled individuals who cannot (or do not) access support systems and services that may be available.

It is a crime committed by adults who have forgotten or not adequately learned that it is their responsibility to protect children or to respect the privacy and integrity of another person. These adults instead force or coerce their victims into sexual encounters, the specifics and ramifications of which are beyond their comprehension. For many reasons, these victims cannot resist what they perceive as the authority of the offender.

The effects of these crimes may be short-term, but in many cases there is virtually irreparable psychological harm done to the victim. Sexual exploitation, molestation, and incest are devastating types of abuse. Some explanation will clarify here that victims include children but also frequently include women, adolescents, the disabled (physically or intellectually), and the female sexual partners of aggressive dominant men, especially if fear of abandonment because of children is involved. The societal taboos surrounding this type of abuse have kept it from widespread exposure. Until recently, it has received very little publicity, helping to keep it a hidden form of abuse. The media is now daily recording such events and demanding our attention.

The nature of sexual abuse also makes it difficult to observe and therefore more threatening to report. The guidelines given for its detection are by no means comprehensive. Several publications are now available in the literature to assist and guide the public and professionals in recognizing signs and symptoms of sexual abuse. These symptoms may exist singly or in various combinations of behavior and attitude as well as physical manifestations.

Illusion Theatre (Anderson, 1983) reminds us that it is important to remember that this form of abuse can make a child or individual both a victim and a prisoner. Those who seek help are often accused of lying. This results in embarrassment, fear, shame, and confusion. Society particularly does not want to accept the fact that disabled persons have become victims of abuse, assault, or rape. The assumption that this is unthinkable creates even more difficulty for persons with disabilities to receive specific services which could help to protect them. Many people perceive the disabled as asexual or not eligible to receive the attention of others in a sexual way. These resistant attitudes are pervasive and also exist in agencies, facilities, courts, homes and police stations. Families don't want to hear/believe these things. This disbelief can result in unnecessary questioning and pressure on the victim, adding yet another burden of victimization (Aiello, Capkin, & Catania, 1983).

A PERSPECTIVE

As children we are taught to obey adults and persons in authority. In addition, victims of sexual abuse are often pressured into secrecy about sexual activity by the abuser, leaving the victim feeling helpless and guilty about the behavior. Victims often perceive that they have no place to turn for help and no acceptable way out. Frequently they have been coerced, manipulated, bribed, or threatened. Frequently they are filled with feelings of self-blame, fear, and, for the physically disabled, increased concerns about being repulsive to others.

Children, adults with disabilities, intellectually impaired individuals, and those in institutions can experience feelings of social powerlessness which make them particularly vulnerable to exploitation and they may not be able to exert their will against the will of the offender. In some cases the victim does not fully understand what is happening because of intellectual limitations, a lack of experience, or a lack of knowledge. It is also recognized that powerlessness of children, disabled or otherwise limited individuals is socially legitimized and even supported. Isolation from society is a major contributor to this feeling of powerlessness. Inability to be viewed as adult or credible because of societal myths about their abilities and rights further contributes to potential exploitation.

It is dehumanizing to be objectified because of a disability. It is further dehumanizing to be omitted or disbelieved as ever being a candidate for molestation, exploitation, or assault. In some cases sexual abuse is not viewed as a serious crime because it occurred to someone who is considered "different" or lacking in power and dignity. The perceived damage won't affect society as a whole or in general; therefore, it won't get the full attention of society.

In the last few years, there has been an increase in the media reporting of sexual abuse (*Life*, 1984). Statistics have been presented which speculate that a child is molested every two minutes in the United States. The majority are between the ages of eight and thirteen. Some estimated that for every victim revealed, nine are hidden from authorities. Because of recent events, we now are forced to recognize that thousands of youngsters fall prey to deviant day care workers, teachers, coaches, and others entrusted with their care. Recent television programs have devoted extensive attention to this topic. The parallel here is that the disabled or institutionalized who are dependent on others fall prey to their care providers in the same way as do children to their assailants. At present, society does not really recognize these parallels.

CHARACTERISTICS

Finkelhor (1984) in his recent studies indicates that a quarter of all abuse occurs before the age of seven. Others suggest that over a third of all those who suffer sexual abuse are victimized before the age of nine. These statistics vary depending on different reference sources, and it is difficult to know the exact numbers which occur because each study has its own limitations. But it is important to recognize the fact that probably most assaults and molestation events are not reported or reflected in the statistics at all. A general estimation is that 20% of cases are reported, the rest are silenced. One of the most uncomfortable facts is that perhaps as much as 50% of sexual abuse occurs within the family (*Life*, 1984) (again statistics vary depending on the study).

Sexual abuse is a crime almost always suffered in silence, shrouded in such fear that the offenders are able to continue for years or perhaps a lifetime without being apprehended. It is recognized that the average molester may have abused as many as an appalling total of 70 victims. Many speculations estimate that a typical offender within the family may have committed as many as 80 acts of incest with female children. It is recognized that child molesters also reveal far more sexual assaults than the number for which they were originally charged. Sex offenders can be sentenced ranging from dismissal and forgiveness to forty years in prison.

Facts about family sexual abuse can be disturbing and confusing. Families differ in values surrounding touch and behavior. A distinction must be made between *normal* family practices of affection, touching and interaction, and that which is defined as incest. Touching, communication patterns, behavior and play patterns may change from culture to culture and family to family. Families will react in different ways to hugging, cuddling, and snuggling of children, to levels of nudity permitted in the family and permissible topics of conversation. Families of disabled children frequently are on either extreme—avoidance of touch (affectional deprivation) or excessive touch (overcompensating, especially with touch). This can confuse both child and adult and appropriate boundaries are crossed or blurred.

The Illusion Theatre has created a "touch continuum" (Anderson, 1983)—the difference between good touch and bad touch and what you do when the touch is confusing. "Most touch is good: That means it feels good, warm, fun, or playful. Good touches may include a kiss, hug, or handshake. Some types of touch are bad: That means the touch hurts our feelings or our bodies. Bad touches may include a slap, kick, or punch. Bad touch also includes sexual abuse—where the touch is tricked or forced sexual contact. Some types of touch are confusing: that means we are mixed up about whether the touch is good or bad, but we do know that something doesn't make sense or feel right. The good or fun touches, including tickling, wrestling, or 'touch games' can become confusing if it doesn't feel like a game anymore or we begin to feel uncomfortable, mixed up, or hurt by the touch. Sometimes people are not used to touch, or don't like to be touched. We need to respect people's right not to be touched if they don't want to be. We also need to understand that severe deprivation of touch has some of the same effects on children as abusive touch and leaves them very vulnerable to being manipulated by what seems to be affectionate contact." We need to consider the importance of teaching these principles, particularly to persons with disabilities and their families.

SPECIAL CONSIDERATIONS

Exploitive situations become more complicated when individuals have a developmental or physical disability. In some cases involving sexual abuse, when the offender is identified as a family member or perhaps care provider, the victim may be unaware of being victimized and may lack the information to recognize exploitation or may be confused about what the activity really means or what the intent of the offender is (Ryerson, 1984). In fact, frequently the victim is told that this activity is "special," and in return for compliance and secrecy will be given rewards. Of paramount importance in these situations is recognizing that frequently the individual who is dependent on relatives and care providers for personal care (i.e., hygiene, dressing, grooming) can become very confused and unable to distinguish appropriate affectionate behavior and touch from exploitative touch that is expressly designed for the sexual gratification of the offender—*not* the victim.

This inability to differentiate basic assistance with personal care activities of daily living (ADL) from sexual exploitation renders them ultimately vulnerable. In a recent NIMH study by the Institute for the Study of Sexual Assault (ISSA) (Musick, 1984), which was designed to identify patterns of sexual abuse of patients in psychiatric settings, it was discovered that orderly psychiatric aides, technicians, and nurses (predominantly male staff) were the most frequent offenders. Their victims were patients, mostly female, who were most dependent and needing constant physical contact. "Testing" of the patient that involved gradual escalation of physical contact wherein the victim was assessed for cooperation resulted in staff perpetrator assaults, which included the full range of sexual acts: intercourse, oral copulation, masturbation, and/or sexual battery. The study also reports that, although staff assailants often did not directly force patients, they simply took advantage of them because many were completely helpless, in restraints, medicated, or in some cases physically limited.

The physical effects of sexual abuse may range from almost nonexistent to venereal disease and pregnancy. Violent attacks often result in bruises and lacerations. Although relatively few instances of sexual molestation or rape are committed with intended violence, it is very easy for the larger, more powerful person to cause serious injury to the child or to the physically limited individual whether or not they resist or try to defend themselves.

EMOTIONAL IMPACT OF ABUSE

It is well recognized that the two factors of shame and guilt (either one or the other or both in tandem) are the prime psychological injuries. Both of these devastating repercussions are the result of the internalization of the offense. Victimized individuals frequently view themselves as the cause and as responsible and perhaps ultimately "bad."

Shame is the emotion most experienced out of feelings of defeat and weakness in such situations. There is a sensed loss of self-control with accompanying loss of self-esteem. Victims may be pressured, forced or tricked and still feel themselves to be accessories to the sexual activity even though they do not truly consent and/or perhaps do not fully understand. The adult can completely dominate and manipulate the victim. Following these experiences is a loss of self-esteem. The main dilemma of shame is that it becomes a part of the individual's personality. When this happens, shame manifests itself in the feeling that the individual has no worth to self or society. Thus, another "disability" is added to the existing physical or intellectual disability of victims.

One of the more common fears of victims is that of being abandoned. Children and dependent or limited individuals particularly can feel at risk if they are unsafe in their environment. When adults do not believe them, or if disclosure threatens their safety, they are further victimized. In some cases this can lead to the belief that they are deserving of this punishment and they begin to experience not only a loss of self-esteem but a general discounting from family members or society.

The victim can also feel the devastating psychological effects of guilt. The individual may have enjoyed the attention and "love" given to some degree and may believe they have created the situation or been responsible for the problem. Children and others who are vulnerable are told they will be doing a misdeed if they do not agree to the pressures of the offender, and they are put into the difficult position of having to agree or go against that which they have been taught is authority and must be obeyed. In most cases the offender lets the victim know that there is something wrong about the act itself by the mere fact that the child or individual is sworn to secrecy. In essence, the victim can feel caught in a double bind. This process is also commonly recognized in the workplace and is called "sexual harassment." There is now legislation to protect the victim from molestation and exploitation, including verbal harassment. Those who are not in the workplace deserve the same protection.

Feelings of guilt are further created by offenders in incest situations when they tell the child/victim that to reveal the sexual abuse would be to destroy the family. This sense of culpability can be reinforced by the management of abuse cases when the child, not the parent, is removed from the home. This guilt becomes part of the person as much as does shame and is incorporated into the individual's development. When these incidences remain unidentified and are not appropriately dealt with the psychological impact of the sexual trauma is carried exclusively and alone.

RECOGNITION AND PREVENTION

There is a direct correlation between the results of training professionals to understand and identify sexual abuse and the number of cases reported. However, low statistics of reported cases do not necessarily mean that the situations do not exist. It is generally recognized in our society that the topic of sexual abuse, exploitation, and molestation is a difficult one to discuss, and many people are not comfortable and/or will not believe it occurs. In spite of all this reluctance, it does. David Finkelhor (1979) reports in his book *Sexually Victimized Children* that one in every five female children and one in every ten male children will be sexually abused before the age of eighteen. There is indication that over 80% of the sexual abuse of children is by someone the child knows, not a stranger. However, in a study conducted by the Seattle Rape Relief and Sexual Assault Center over a seven-year period, it was revealed that 99% of developmentally disabled reported victims were sexually abused by relatives and caretakers (residential staff, bus drivers, recreation workers, volunteers, work supervisors, and others serving in care-provider capacities). Only one percent were strangers to the victim. These are dramatic statistics and serve to alert all of us working in the area of rehabilitation health care. As a first step toward prevention, we must begin to realize that sexual abuse is common. The most recent statistics and general unpublished reports reflect that the number and incidence is higher than has been previously documented in the literature. Some therapists and mental health workers with sex offenders report or discuss among themselves the possibility that perhaps as many as one in three girls experiences molestation by the time she is fourteen and that perhaps as much as 50% of the victimization occurs within the family.

Prevention of sexual abuse starts with recognition and acknowledgement that it is happening. Many victims of sexual abuse suffer long-term and permanent effects not only of shame, guilt, fear, and lowered self-esteem, but also health disorders, learning problems, delinquent behavior, and chemical abuse (Anderson, 1983). Efforts aimed at prevention must necessarily involve an intention to stop assaults before they occur. It is essential to identify and change societal beliefs and norms that permit sexual abuse and exploitation to continue. The power structure in our society sets up males as more powerful than females, able-bodied persons as more powerful than the physically disabled, white persons as more powerful than those of color, the wealthy as more powerful than the poor, and adults as more powerful than children. The child or disabled individual is particularly a candidate to be victimized as there is an imbalance of age, size, power, self-control or knowledge.

Children have the right to grow in a safe environment. Because they are vulnerable, they look to adults for protection. As previously mentioned, victims of sexual abuse are often tricked, not forced, by the offender who is likely to be someone the child knows and trusts. It is easy to understand that the child may not believe or even perceive that this person could/would possibly ever hurt him/her. The same rationale can be applied to adult individuals with intellectual or physical disabilities, those who are institutionalized, the elderly.

Prevention efforts must include programs for individuals that inform them of their right to trust their feelings, to say "no," to tell someone, to live in a safe environment, to not permit any touch or behavior which frightens, confuses or hurts them.

The media in the last five years has made great strides toward publicizing this problem which is reaching national health hazard proportions. General information, highly publicized public service events and announcements, docudramas, talk shows, special news reports help increase public awareness and reporting. In an effort to teach individuals some prevention techniques, the books, media, theater companies, and instructions include basic guidelines:

- say "no" if touch or situation is uncomfortable
- tell someone if help is needed
- do not keep secrets if it feels uncomfortable
- ask questions if confused or frightened by touch behavior
- right to privacy and to not permit anyone else to touch their body in any way without permission
- right to be taught appropriate touch behavior
- right to learn alternative ways of expressing affection without intimate or inappropriate touch

INDICATIONS OF SEXUAL ABUSE

Suspicion of sexual abuse is indicated if:

- clothing appears stained or bloody
- there are reports of injury or neglect by the parents
- the child (victim) has a diagnosis of venereal disease of eyes, mouth, anus, genitalia
- the child (victim) reports pain or itching, bruises or bleeding in the genital area
- overadaptive behaviors that meet the parents' needs rather than the child's (victim's)
- there is extreme fearfulness, withdrawal, or fantasy
- the child (victim) exhibits behavioral extremes (passive, overly compliant to rageful and extremely aggressive), stealing or hoarding, habit disorders, or neurotic traits, hyperactivity, running away, lagging in development.
- there is severe emotional conflict at home
- the child (victim) shows fear of intervention

- there is past history of abuse by the parent or parents
- there is an unwanted pregnancy
- there is inappropriate dress
- there is seductive behavior
- sleep disturbances are being manifested
- there are mood swings, feelings of humiliation, anger, nightmares, eating pattern disturbances, fear of sex, development of phobias about the attack

Specialists who work in the field of sexual abuse consistently state that when an individual does take the risk to identify the abuse and report information related to sexual exploitation or activities, it is crucial that he or she is believed. It may be the only time they risk revealing the taboo and may be the only cry for help that will be given.

There is relatively little written on the topic of sexual abuse and individuals with physical disabilities. However, with the statistics that are available, combined with the knowledge of the personal and societal pressures generally experienced by an individual with a disability, it is not difficult to understand that physically disabled persons are potentially at higher risk than the general population. The mere fact that they are in many ways more dependent on the care-providers to assist them in activities of daily living creates multiple opportunities for them to be vulnerable in ways that the able-bodied are not. Not only do they lack privacy, but also they may lack the ability to be spontaneous in protecting themselves. Many individuals are without speech or language abilities and limited in or without mobility. Some may be so totally dependent on others for health care needs for daily living survival that to consider resisting anything from a care-provider or family member may seem too frightening for their own existence. They may also not know in whom to confide for assistance were they to try to identify abusive behavior. They may already have experienced a disenfranchisement from society and would not be willing to risk a further separation. It is understandable that handicappers may predict that their stories might not be believed because their credibility would be pitted against that of an able-bodied person. It is commonly recognized that many sex offenders are viewed as pillars of the community—respected and trusted. Offenders themselves often state that they are aware of the vulnerability of their victims and deliberately plan this abuse since the likelihood of its being reported is minimal.

The emotional reactions and adjustments of someone who has been denied his or her personal integrity by being assaulted are the same as those of someone who has been denied personal integrity by being institutionalized. Because of the denial of freedom, personal decision-making, privacy, economics, independence, and decreased feelings of personal strength, many persons who have been institutionalized share outward characteristics which indicate a history of abuse (Assault Prevention Training Project, 1983). This makes recognition somewhat difficult at times.

An obvious preventive measure is to encourage and assist parents and families in being comfortable with discussing sex and sexuality and in having the skills and information necessary to provide sex education and prevention techniques. Often parents have difficulty doing so. They may not have received any particular education in sexual health and may find themselves limited and perhaps confused in their own knowledge and skills. This leads many families to avoid the issue and to cloak it in further silence. Individuals who live in institutions may experience the same kind of silence from the institutional staff for the same reasons.

Sexual abuse is not restricted to any social or economic class and, contrary to some popular belief, parents with higher levels of education or income are not providing better sex education and abuse-prevention techniques than parents who have less education and a lower income. A family containing a physically disabled member, particularly a child, is often seen closing around that individual in a self-containing way in an effort to protect itself from the community and society. Not only might a family be naturally more protective of a child with a disability but also it might isolate itself in a cautious way from society and its insensitivities. Although it is subtle, it creates yet another barrier for the sexually abused, disabled child who might otherwise reach out. Frequently the only community the disabled child knows is that of the family and the care-providers upon whom she or he is dependent.

Although evidence indicates that most children don't reveal their victimization and, even when they do, that many families try to shroud the incident in silence lest they call attention to themselves and sexually inappropriate behavior or make a false accusation, increased numbers of treatment programs are needed to respond to victims. All children, particularly the disabled, must be taught personal safety lessons, preventing sexual abuse, and protecting the right and dignity of their well-being. Books have been written for children helping them to identify "good" and "bad" touch. Audiovisual materials are being created regularly, materials are being written for families to use together and efforts are being taken to train professionals to recognize and identify the events surrounding sexual exploitation. However, in an effort to adequately prepare children to recognize sexually exploitive situations, they must understand that a normal looking person, or even someone they know, could molest them. Most importantly, they must be given the message that they can tell anything to the parent or a trusted adult and that they will be believed and loved. If we can teach the children to say "no" and to yell for safety, even if a family member, the local school coach or teacher, attendant, scout leader, transporter, or the next door neighbor is the abuser, we will participate in enabling safety for the vulnerable individual.

Reporting is also directly proportional to the number of education programs operating in the community; and although children often know the difference between touch which is given in love and exploitive touch, they are generally reluctant to acknowledge this unless asked *directly* by a trusted individual and in what they perceive to be a safe setting, free from harm.

Linda Sanford (1982), in her brochure for parents entitled "Come Tell Me Right Away," emphasizes that we must tell the children that we believe them, that the offender did something wrong and that it is not the child's fault. We must report to the authorities (professionals are obligated by law to report suspected sexual exploitation within 24 hours). She instructs that we not confront the offender in the child's presence and that we be sure that the child has a physical examination to reassure him/her that his/her body has not been harmed or changed. Most importantly, she stresses that we allow the child to talk about the incident at his or her own pace, that counseling is helpful and that covering up the incident will not make it go away. The same criteria are applicable for other vulnerable persons.

MYTHS

Some of the more common myths about sexual exploitation, particularly as it relates to disability, are that nice girls don't get raped, that society feels compassion toward disabled individuals and therefore would not think to do such a thing, that people who are handicapped are not really sexual or attractive and are therefore not eligible to be sexually assaulted, that rapists/abusers are strangers to their victims, that someone who can't speak or doesn't have full mental capabilities wouldn't really understand what happened to them anyway and also probably can't be believed. Other myths are that the mentally retarded or physically disabled lie about assault or are promiscuous and "ask for what they get." Many disabled individuals may participate in sexual acting out behavior that is then labeled as offensive or inappropriate by caretakers. Usually in these circumstances no effort is made to modify the negative behavior. These same individuals are also candidates to be treated in a trivial manner and kept socially isolated, reinforcing their sexual ignorance and ultimate vulnerability (O'Day, 1983).

RECOVERY

The most difficult step in recovery from sexual exploitation is actually identifying the sexual abuse. Most therapists acknowledge that "telling the secret" is threatening and traumatizing in and of itself and creates feelings of isolation and further vulnerability. When an individual's life has been violated by a parent or an adult who has forced himself or herself as a lover, it results in a loss not unlike that which is experienced with an acquired or traumatic disability. It can be extremely disruptive and create enormous vulnerability. It is common for victims to say "He robbed me of my childhood ... of my dignity," and "I am broken."

Incest continues to be perceived as the most damaging form of sexual abuse because of the ambivalence created between hating and loving the offender-family member. Frequently the offender may have been the more nurturing of the family members, and the victim experiences further isolation and loss by severing this tie.

A recognized common response to sexual abuse of families and of accused offenders is denial, followed by anger toward the victim. This can result in further shame, increased vulnerability and at times panic, retreat, and even rescinding the accusation. When support groups, networks, counseling, and therapy can be provided, the therapeutic process can result in reduced suffering and positive, although difficult recovery. The emotional scarring can be pervasive and can affect a person's feelings of safety and well-being for the rest of his/her life.

At times of crisis intervention, it is important to determine what the victim needs: to assess his/her immediate health needs, to be assured that he or she is not at fault and to validate the feelings of fear, anxiety and revulsion being felt. We must stand by and assist the victim with problem solving skills for further situations and we must let the individual know that he or she has a right to be safe. These simple guidelines are essential to the healing process.

RESPONSES

Reluctance to talk about sexual assault and exploitation, particularly of children and those with disabilities, is common. The reasons tend to be consistent through-out our society. Parents are afraid of unnecessarily frightening the child by giving them information about abuse. They are often reluctant to talk about sex education mainly for feelings of inadequacy and discomfort of their own.

It is generally regarded as inadequate to discuss sexual abuse in isolation from sex education. Without the context and perspective of sexual health, it is difficult and very frightening for an individual to understand abuse.

Common community resistance often appears in the form of denial that the issue is really a problem in "our neighborhood." Communities are reluctant to in-form the individuals about sexual abuse and sexual information for fear that they will try out all of the sexual activities, act inappropriately, make up false reports or be terrorized. Although most parents support sex education and preventive educa-tion for their children, they are most critical of *who* provides it. Interestingly, Finkelhor (1982) reports that "only 29% of the parents give their children informa-tion about sexual abuse despite their awareness of the prevalence of child sexual abuse." Generally, communities struggle over who should teach prevention pro-grams and how much they should contain and cost. Some community groups sug-gest task forces or child protection teams should do the training, others say the schools, others the police, clergy, rape centers, parents, etc. It is generally ac-knowledged that specific, professional training needs to be provided to those who teach these topics.

Another common concern of communities is limited financial resources. Par-ticularly in times when some conservative elements in the community are against sex education, communities are concerned that talking about anything sexual (healthy or otherwise) is inappropriate and will not be supported financially. There are no easy answers to the dilemma of persuading communities to invest in educa-tional programs, but clearly the intervention techniques are necessary if we are to continue to provide all individuals, able-bodied and disabled, with the right to sexual health.

It is also timely and appropriate to routinely provide sex education, including the area of sexual exploitation, to professionals working in the health care and rehabilitation milieu. It is time for us to aggressively address these unacceptable situations and establish clear directions which mandate respect, dignity, and integrity.

REFERENCES

Aiello, Denise, Capkin, Lee, Catania, Holly: Strategies and Techniques for Serving the Disabled Assault Victim: A Pilot Training Program for Providers and Consumers, *Sexuality and Disability*, Volume 6, Number 3/4, Fall/Winter 1983.

Anderson, Cordelia: No Easy Answers, Secondary Curriculum on Sexual Abuse, Illusion Theatre, Minneapolis, MN. Available from Network Publications, Santa Cruz, CA, 1983.

Assault Prevention Training Project: Women Against Rape, P.O. Box 82024, Columbus, Ohio, 43202, 1983.

Children's Village U.S.A.: Child Abuse and You, National Headquarters Woodland Hills, California, no date.

Finkelhor, D.: Sexually Victimized Children, New York Free Press, New York, 1979.

Finkelhor, D.: Public Knowledge and Attitudes about Child Sexual Abuse: A Boston Survey, Paper presented to the National Conference on Child Sexual Abuse, Washington, D.C., 1982.

Finkelhor, D.: Child Sexual Abuse: Theory and Research, New York Free Press, New York, 1984.

Life Magazine: Special Report on Childhood Sexual Assault, December 1984.

Musick, Judith: Patterns of Institutional Sexual Assault, *Response to Violence in the Family and Sexual Assault*, Volume 7, Number 3, May/June 1984.

O'Day, Bonnie—Minnesota Program for Victims of Sexual Assault: Preventing Sexual Abuse of Persons with Disabilities: A Curriculum for Hearing Impaired, Physically Disabled, Blind and Mentally Retarded Students, Network Publications, Santa Cruz, CA, 1983.

Ryerson, Ellen: Sexual Abuse and Self-Protection Education for Developmentally Disabled Youth: A Priority Need, *SIECUS, Where The Action Is*, Developmental Disabilities Project, Seattle Rape Relief, 1825 South Jackson, Suite 102, Seattle, WA 98144, 1984.

Sanford, Linda Tschirhart: Come Tell Me Right Away, Ed-U-Press Inc., P.O. Box 583, Fayetteville, NY 13066, 1982.

Seattle Rape Relief: The Developmental Disabilities Project, 1825 South Jackson, Suite 102, Seattle, WA 98144, no date.

Part V: Sexuality and Disability— Study Questions and Disability Awareness Exercise

1. How is sexuality impacted by the existence of a disability?
2. What are the unique sexual issues people with the following disabilities must address?

    a. Facial disfigurement
    b. Traumatic brain injury
    c. Alzheimer's disease
    d. Down's syndrome
    e. AIDS
    f. Spinal cord injury
    g. Chemical dependency
    h. Severe obesity
    i. Chronic mental illness

3. Should birth-control information be part of a rehabilitation program for persons with a disability?
4. Discuss the issues generated by a rehabilitation center's policy that has rules against intimate sexual contact.
5. The directors of the rehabilitation agency/facility for whom you work is completely opposed to sex education for any of the unmarried clients. They believe that sex is inappropriate outside of marriage and providing sex education promotes sexual activity. How would you respond to their concerns?

I AM JUST LIKE EVERYONE ELSE

Often the perspective on an issue is altered by the vantage point of the person. The following exercise is designed to create different perspectives on the sexuality of persons with disabilities.

Imagine you are the parent of a sixteen-year-old adolescent who has both a physical and emotional disability. When she asked you for birth control information:

1. What would be your response?
2. The response of your spouse?
3. Would there be a difference if the child was a male?
4. Would your response vary if the adolescent had a chronic mental illness, brain injury, multiple sclerosis, AIDS, or was terminally ill?
5. What would you say if your child was dating a person with one of these disabilities and was sexually active.

Part VI

Interventions in the Rehabilitation Process

The primary goal of rehabilitation is to help persons with disabilities to overcome, as much as possible, their deficits; to capitalize on their assets; and to achieve their optimal functioning. Although this assistance may be provided by peers or professionals, a common denominator in the helping process is the ability to assist others to achieve and maintain rehabilitation goals. Therefore, an understanding of therapeutic strategies is important in the fulfillment of team roles and in the implementation of relevant interventions.

In Chapter 21, Livneh reviews existing stage models of psychosocial adaptation to physical disability and provides 50 intervention strategies grouped by stage. The interventions themselves can be classified as environmental or psychotherapeutic. The strategies are based on a comprehensive literature review that allows the reader to locate the appropriate reference for more in-depth study of the intervention strategy. The rationale behind these interventions is to assist the person with a disability to make the transition from one stage to the next and to prepare for the life tasks that need to be addressed and resolved at each of the stages.

In Chapter 22, McDowell and his associates present an overview of recent mind–body techniques that may be useful interventions in helping persons with disabilities. Drawing primarily from the work of Milton Erickson, they provide strategies to develop rapport and describe the therapeutic use of imagery, paradox, and metaphor.

Based on their philosophical view that all life's experiences are opportunities for personal growth, Hulnick and Hulnick, in Chapter 23, present a model in which disability is viewed as an opportunity for reframing emotional and physical disabilities. Central to this model is the belief that even in the most difficult circumstances, individuals have the ability to choose how they will respond. Interventions designed to facilitate personal healing and empowerment are presented, including reframing, self-forgiveness, and positive self talk.

21

A Unified Approach to Existing Models of Adaptation to Disability: Intervention Strategies

Hanoch Livneh

Following the presentation of a unified model of adaptation to disability (Chapter 13), the present section attempts to outline several psychosocial, behavioral, and environmental intervention approaches appropriate for each of the phases of adaptation considered previously. The intent of this section is neither to serve as a panacea for locating solutions to all encountered problems, nor to offer a "cookbook" or "how-to-do-it" manual for these problems. Rather, the goal is to provide a few and generally useful guides to practicing rehabilitation professionals.

Prior to pursuing this discussion, several suggestions regarding the adoption of these intervention strategies should be set forth. First, the rehabilitation practitioner has to be flexible in his or her orientation. The recommended psychotherapeutic and behavioral approaches are only a representative sample of a broader range of methods. There is a need to consider and adopt an eclectic and flexible strategy when dealing with the disabled individual. The choice of specific approaches and methods depends on the client's needs; the degree of observed or inferred psychosocial impact; the onset, nature, and progression of the disability; the client's support system; the practitioner's acquaintance and mastery of different intervention methods and techniques, and so on.

Secondly, the practioner must come to terms with his or her own reactions to loss, grief, and disability (see also Krieger, 1977). Unless the professional is aware of his or her own feelings concerning coping with crisis, loss, and disability, no honest and productive helper–helpee relationship can ensue. Finally, it is important that the practitioner be able to recognize in what stage(s) the client is operating. It is hoped that, based on the previous discussion, this task will be somewhat simplified.

As a general rule, counseling/psychotherapeutic strategies regarded as being more affective—insightful in nature (i.e., client-centered counseling, Gestalt therapy) appear to be useful in the preliminary stages of the adaptation process. Strategies of a cognitive-behavioral-action orientation (i.e., reality therapy, behavior therapy) appear to be more suited to the later stages. This seems to be a consistent conclusion of most authors on this topic (Crate, 1965; Dunn, 1975; Halligan, 1983; Herman, Manning, & Teitelman, 1971; Hohmann, 1975; Kerr & Thompson, 1972; Scofield, Pape, McCracken, & Maki, 1980; Walters, 1981; Weller & Miller, 1977).

INITIAL IMPACT

The following strategies are often recommended when working with an individual immediately following the occurrence of a traumatic event (shock and anxiety stages):

1. Communicating frequently with the client regarding his or her present situation and offering a careful explanation of the ongoing treatment procedures (Weller & Miller, 1977).
2. Supporting and reassuring the client. Supportive measures assist the recently traumatized individual to ventilate his or her feelings (Herman, Manning, & Teitelman, 1971). Patience and tolerance, likewise, should be the key ingredients of the professional's approach.
3. Comforting gently, both physically and verbally. Willingness to stay with the client through the use of empathic listening and attending to his or her physical and psychosocial needs is often advocated (Dunn, 1975).
4. Reflecting on and clarifying client's verbal statements and concerns. The anxious client will manage to gain a more sensible picture of his or her confused emotional and cognitive states when content and feeling clarification is practiced.
5. Performing muscle relaxation procedures and breathing exercises to calm down the client when anxiety seems to be overwhelming.
6. Structuring the situation by telling the client what has happened and what to expect (Dunn, 1975).

DEFENSE MOBILIZATION

During the stages of bargaining and denial, several approaches should be considered. They cover a wide range of interventions, from initially complying with client's denial attempts to more direct confrontation of them. The strategies include:

1. Noncritical listening to and acceptance of the client and his or her verbal messages. Acceptance of the client's expressions of denial in the early stages suggests recognizing his or her need for self-protection. This, in turn, may disarm the client from responding to the helper angrily and resentfully. A neutral, matter-of-fact attitude, neither encouraging denial, nor arguing with the client, is, therefore, useful (Dunn, 1975).

2. Imparting relevant information to the client about his or her impairment when circumstances dictate. Hohmann (1975) suggested giving the client truthful but ambiguous information so as not to destroy his or her hope of recovery or improvement.

3. A progression of intervention methods was advocated by Herman, Manning, and Teitelman (1971). The authors suggested using gentle support in the beginning, followed by education about the disability, and finally resorting to reality confrontation. According to them, reality will then be tested and confronted in gradual doses prior to its ultimate realization. Weller and Miller (1977) suggested, similarly, a need to eventually work with the present reality. Confrontation should be attempted gently through observing and pointing out inconsistencies and discrepancies to the client regarding his or her overt behaviors, verbal and nonverbal messages, and so on.

4. Also useful at this stage are techniques to heighten self-awareness. Several Gestalt therapy techniques (i.e., the "hot" seat, the empty chair, topdog-underdog dialogue, reversals, staying with the feeling, "I have a secret") may provide the client with better insight and awareness of his or her inconsistencies in the affective and behavioral domains.

5. Another technique to circumvent a client's denial may be to channel his or her fantasies toward the future. Dunn (1975) recommended engaging the client in present activities and tasks while presumably waiting for future functional improvements.

6. Finally, reinforcing behavior incompatible with denial is recommended by Dunn (1975). This may include rewarding physical activity, exercises, etc., in cases of mobility impairment.

INITIAL REALIZATION

During the periods of mourning and depression, a number of approaches to help ease the emotional pain are recommended in the literature. As a matter of fact, it seems that most psychotherapeutic interventions are geared toward clients who manifest depressive symptoms. It is conceivable that in the case of depression following a disabling event, which results in bodily or functional loss, the depression may be classified as reactive rather than psychogenic in nature. However, the distinction between reactive (externally-triggered) depression and idiopathic (of unknown origin) depression, which is treated more often in mental health clinics, does not preclude discussing them jointly. Treatment modalities are often arbitrarily applied to either type of depression. The most commonly suggested strategies during this depression period include the following:

1. Encouraging the client to express and verbalize feelings of depression, guilt, shame and the like. This is accomplished through empathic attending and listening, support, and reassurance. The client's expressed feelings should be non-

evaluatively accepted by the practitioner who refrains from moralizing or judging the client for his or her particular feelings (Halligan, 1983; Hohmann, 1975).

2. Reflecting and clarifying client's feelings as an insight-oriented measure toward promoting acceptance or assimilation of the disability and its implications (Herman, Manning & Teitelman, 1971; Scofield, Pape, McCracken, & Maki, 1980). The utilization of person-centered counseling, at this stage, as a vehicle to promote self-regard (Walters, 1981), self-confidence, and a new sense of self based on intrinsic worth (Siller, 1969) is widely advocated.

3. Reinforcing client strengths and assets (Walters, 1981). This goal can be accomplished through guiding the client to awareness of his or her inner resources, rewarding positive self-statements, and encouraging the client to participate in his or her own case by learning self-management procedures (Halligan, 1983).

4. Applying stress management and relaxation training when acute grief responses are observed (Scofield, Pape, McCracken, & Maki, 1980).

5. Not permitting depressive and dependent habits to get well-established (Dunn, 1975). This may be done through the use of kind firmness, initiating physical activities, and breaking down seemingly overwhelming problems into small, manageable units. Attempts at withdrawal should, similarly, be met with firm disregard or nonpermittance (Dunn, 1975).

6. Reinforcing interpersonal and social contacts and skill acquisition by the withdrawn client. This strategy may take the form of teaching new and appropriate interpersonal skills, practicing self-assertiveness skills, or referring the individual to self-help and similar support groups.

7. Setting concrete, short-term and limited goals (Halligan, 1983). Such a task-oriented approach provides the client with the necessary first steps toward developing and acquiring self-reliant behaviors.

8. Interrupting client's irrational beliefs, as evidenced by his or her verbalizations, and associated feelings of hopelessness and despair (Beck, 1967; Ellis, 1973; Halligan, 1983). Rationale-Emotive Therapy methods may be used to identify irrational beliefs about one's own misery as presumed to emanate from the disabling condition (Scofield, Pape, McCracken, & Maki, 1980). The rehabilitation practioner, then, attempts to dispute and confront these negative self-verbalizations, demonstrate how these ideas are misinterpreted and exaggerated, and finally counteracts the client's tendencies to globalize his or her negative perceptions to other, unrelated domains (Beck, 1967; Halligan, 1983).

In addition to appropriately and discretely utilizing several of the above approaches, the following strategies may be helpful in counseling the person who manifests internalized anger reactions:

1. Encouraging the client to appropriately verbalize and ventilate his or her frustrations that seem to be at the root of the felt hostility (Dunn, 1975).

2. Teaching externalization and release of pent-up anger in a socially-sanctioned manner (Herman, Manning, & Teitelman, 1971).

3. Role-playing anger-causing situations. These role-playing exercises may take a similar form to the Gestalt therapy techniques previously outlined (e.g., the empty chair, the "hot" seat, dialogue of inner personality components, attitude and feeling reversals). These techniques serve to help the client become aware of inner conflicts, predisability unfinished business, and unrecognized or underdeveloped needs and wishes.

RETALIATION

When the person engages in hostile, rebellious, and verbally or physically aggressive acts toward agents of the external environment, it is the role of the practitioner to both gain understanding of the origin of these asocial activities and to alter their manifestations. Several procedures often recommended to achieve this quest are:

1. Meeting the aggressive individual with kindness yet firmness and reducing the hostile act by active support (Kerr & Thompson, 1972).

2. Teaching the client how to express his or her hostility or aggressive behaviors in a socially acceptable manner and to channel it into productive and useful activities (Hohmann, 1975). The teaching may involve mastering interpersonal communication skills. The client should also become aware of the need to make an effort to control and socially direct such feelings.

3. Teaching the client a sense of personal and social responsibility for his or her actions (Glasser, 1965; Halligan, 1983). This may include teaching the person tolerance for frequently-occurring daily frustrations, willingness to invoke help from others when needed, and accepting the offered help without excessive resentment or the development of dependency (Halligan, 1983).

4. Teaching relaxation techniques to defuse the dammed anger.

5. Contracting with the aggressive client to decrease his or her acting out and other abusive behaviors.

6. Refraining from moralizing the client as a person and initially avoiding any direct confrontation. This trend of nonconfrontation, however, may have to be reversed if the client's rebellious and aggressive actions continue.

7. Applying behavioral modification techniques to the client's maladaptive, aggressive responses, and teaching, instead, adaptive and socially-beneficial behaviors. Aversive conditioning, negative and positive reinforcement schedules, are useful for achieving this goal.

REINTEGRATION

The person with a disability, who has reached the final phase of the adjustment process, can be assisted through the adoption of a multitude of physical, psychological, social, vocational, and avocational strategies. The individual who appears to be functioning at the acknowledgement stage may benefit from:

1. Accepting the finality and permanency of the disability and the loss of the "old self," on an affective level. Acceptance of this sort is reflected in a change in the perception of the significance of one's body and fosters a new exploration of reality (Dovenmuehle & Verwoerdt, 1963; Halligan, 1983). The need for this type of acceptance has been termed by Wright (1960) "subordinating physique" where value change occurs in deemphasizing the importance of one's own physique following the occurrence of a physical disability.

2. Value clarification training (Scofield, Pape, McCracken, & Maki, 1980). Clarifying one's value and belief system may foster understanding of the importance of the functional limitations imposed by the disability. It may also help the client through acquiring new values, to make the necessary transition from relying on comparative values to developing asset values (Wright, 1960).

3. Working toward the realization of actual functional limitations and existing strengths (Containment of disability effects; Wright, 1960). Present capabilities can, then, be gradually augmented by further training (Russell, 1981).

4. Assuming a sense of personal responsibility and internal control of one's own existence (Halligan, 1983).

5. Setting concrete and time-limited goals followed by rehearsal of alternative outcomes (Russell, 1981).

6. Encouraging the use of humor, especially when frustrating conditions, both externally and internally triggered, are present.

7. Teaching problem-solving and decision-making skills.

8. Discussing and modeling new and appropriate behaviors. This target may be reached by utilizing the real life participation of individuals with similar disabilities in a group role playing or family counseling contexts. Also, the use of films or audiovisual material may supplement the exposure to in vivo role models.

9. Changing and restructuring the environment (i.e., home, work, recreational facilities) to adapt it to the needs of individuals with certain mobility or sensory impairments (e.g., spinal cord injury, blindness).

Finally, for the person whose progress has culminated in reaching the stages of acceptance/adjustment, continuation of the previously discussed methods (see acknowledgement section above) may be augmented by:

1. Actively exploring and solving realistic and practical issues and presenting problems with the client (Moos & Tsu, 1977). The problems should be directly confronted and their solutions implemented by scaling them down into manageable units and allowing the client to be actively involved and in control of the issues.

2. Further redefining of the client's personal, social, and vocational goals and setting appropriate priorities for each.

More specifically, in the personal domain, help is often required in: (a) additional role playing, behavior contracting, and modeling adaptive behaviors, geared toward personal adjustment (Scofield, Pape, McCracken, & Maki, 1980); (b) shaping and rewarding the acquisition of the newly learned behaviors through the use of operant conditioning (e.g., reinforcements, rewards) techniques (Russell, 1981); (c) teaching self-management techniques by the adoption of self-reinforcement procedures (Scofield, Pape, McCracken, & Maki, 1980).

In the social domain, clients should be: (a) encouraged to further develop interpersonal relationships and resocialization skills; (b) involved in a social network. The practitioner may intervene in establishing a support network of family members and friends (Halligan, 1983) and encouraging the client to participate in peer self-help groups.

Vocationally, client assistance may take the form of: (a) teaching prevocational or vocational skills; (b) referring the client to vocational rehabilitation for vocational planning, training or retraining, and placement.

Finally, when intervention geared toward environmental manipulation is contemplated, the practitioner's responsibility lies in: (a) arranging the physical modification and restructuring of the client's home, and, when appropriate, of the work and recreation setting; (b) serving as a liaison between the client and other involved professionals.

It is the responsibility of the rehabilitation professional, at this point, to give the client periodic feedback regarding his or her personal, social, and vocational progress. In addition, clients should be provided with occasional follow-up sessions when needed.

SUMMARY

The intent of the present chapter was to suggest a variety of intervention (i.e., counseling, psychotherapeutic, behavioral, environmental) strategies often discussed in the literature regarding their appropriateness for each observed stage. Several possible interventions were outlined for each of the stages of adjustment. The rationale behind these interventions is not to try and eliminate certain stages, but rather to ease the transition from one stage to the next and to better prepare the individual for the life tasks (physical, psychological, social, etc.) that need to be addressed and resolved at each of the encountered stages.

REFERENCES

Beck, A. T. (1967). *Depression: Cause and treatment*. Philadelphia: University of Pennsylvania Press.

Crate, M. A. (1965). Nursing functions in adaptation to chronic illness. *American Journal of Nursing*, 65(10), 72–76.

Dovenmuehle, R. H., & Verwoerdt, A. (1963). Physical illness and depressive symptomatology. II. Factors of length and severity of illness and frequency of hospitalization. *Journal of Gerontology, 18,* 260–266.

Dunn, M. E. (1975). Psychological intervention in a spinal cord injury center: An introduction. *Rehabilitation Psychology, 22*(4), 165–178.

Ellis, A. (1973). *Humanistic psychotherapy: The rational-emotive approach.* New York: McGraw-Hill.

Glasser, W. (1965). *Reality therapy.* New York: Harper & Row.

Halligan, F. G. (1983). Reactive depression and chronic illness: counseling patients and their families. *Personal and Guidance Journal, 61*(7), 401–406.

Herman, C. D., Manning, R. A., & Teitelman, E. (1971). Psychiatric rehabilitation of the physically disabled, the mentally retarded and the psychiatrically impaired. In: F. H. Krusen, F. J. Kottke, & P. M. Ellwood (Eds.), *Handbook of physical medicine and rehabilitation.* Philadelphia, PA: W. B. Saunders (Chap. 38, pp. 761–768).

Hohmann, G. W. (1975). Psychological aspects of treatment and rehabilitation of the spinal cord injured person. *Clinical Orthopaedics, 112,* 81–88.

Kerr, W. G., & Thompson, M. A. (1972). Acceptance of disability of sudden onset in paraplegia. *Paraplegia, 10,* 94–102.

Krieger, G. W. (1977). Loss and grief in rehabilitation counseling of the severely traumatically disabled. *Journal of Applied Rehabilitation Counseling, 7*(4), 223–227.

Moos, R. H., & Tsu, V. D. (1977). The crisis of physical illness: An overview. In: R. H. Moos (Ed.), *Coping with physical illness.* New York: Plenum Press (Chap. 1, pp. 3–21).

Russell, R. A. (1981). Concepts of adjustment to disability: An overview. *Rehabilitation Literature, 42*(11–12), 330–338.

Scofield, M. E., Pape, D. A., McCracken, N., & Maki, D. R. (1980). An ecological model for promoting acceptance of disability. *Journal of Applied Rehabilitation Counseling, 11*(4), 183–187.

Siller, J. (1969). Psychological situation of the disabled with spinal cord injuries. *Rehabilitation Literature, 30*(10), 290–296.

Walters, J. (1981). Coping with a leg amputation. *American Journal of Nursing, 81*(7), 1349–1352.

Weller, D. J., & Miller, P. M. (1977). Emotional reactions of patient, family, and staff in acute-care period of spinal cord injury: Part I. *Social Work in Health Care, 2*(4), 369–377.

Wright, B. A. (1960). *Physical disability—A psychological approach.* New York: Harper & Row.

22

Extending Psychotherapeutic Strategies to People With Disabilities

William A. McDowell, George F. Bills, and Marc W. Eaton

In *The Handicapped: Special Needs and Strategies for Counseling* (McDowell, Coven, & Eash, 1979), the authors examined various counseling strategies in light of the psychological needs of persons with disabilities. Various theoretical frameworks were used to illustrate topics such as self-concept, body image, frustration, anger, dependency, and motivation. Additionally, the evolving nature of strategies are examined and extended by the suggestion of applications of modern mind-body techniques to rehabilitation counseling with individuals with disabilities. As in the earlier article, emphasis is on counselor versatility, personal development, and observation of the individual needs of the client.

For the rehabilitation counselor, boundaries are no longer clear-cut. "The past 10 years have witnessed an [*sic*] explosion of research findings suggesting that the mind and body act on each other in often remarkable ways" (Gelman & Hager, 1988, p. 88). New understanding of the interrelationship of physiology to psychology provides methods that require the counselor to pay attention to minute differences from individual to individual in order to utilize those differences to promote change. Persons with disabilities need what every individual needs—respect, encouragement, satisfying experiences, and the opportunity to develop his or her abilities (Wright, 1983). Modern mind–body techniques enable the counselor to intervene with the precision necessary to respect the rights and needs of the client.

Thomas, Butler, and Parker (1987) state that counseling is the core of the rehabilitation process. Szymanski (1987) made the point, with respect to persons with blindness and visual impairments, that counseling approaches "do not differ substantially from those with . . . other disability groups" (p. 433). As noted in McDowell et al. (1979), "no evidence exists that different physical disabilities are related to particular personality types" (p. 228). According to Wright (1983), rehabilitation efforts need to be guided by fundamental principles, such as recognition of client assets and the utilization of these assets in therapy. No longer devaluing themselves in terms of disabilities, clients instead appreciate themselves as individuals with "social and emotional concerns which take time to resolve" (p. xii). Wright further suggests clinicians make use of client input to direct rehabilitation efforts; recognize the relationship of the client to the various environmental systems in which that client moves and interacts; and be flexible in order to respond to the individual differences of the client.

We contend that Wright's fundamental principles are current with trends in psychotherapy over the past decade. Individuals "construct" their reality by sorting out their sensory experiences through their cultural, social, and personal frames of reference and respond accordingly (Snyder, 1984; Rossi, 1986; James & Woodsmall, 1988). We will examine techniques developed to utilize the maps and models a client uses to construct his or her reality in order to promote further change. Evidence that frame of reference changes include physiological correlates as well as psychological realms are now being discovered by neurological technologists (Buchsbaum, 1983).

Many mind–body techniques are the results of the innovative work of Milton H. Erickson, M.D. While this article is not specifically about Erickson, references will be made to him by using anecdotes and case examples of his therapy. Physically disabled himself, Erickson developed utilization techniques in order to overcome the limitations placed on him by his disability.

> . . . the interesting thing about Erickson is that he used his own physical handicaps to learn exquisite things about human behavior. One of the things that perplexes some of his followers is that they aren't able to do what he did simply because they were never challenged in the way he had been—polio twice, bedridden for years. He had an uncanny ability to pick up on subtle kinds of nonverbal behavior because he was paralyzed and confined to bed for months and months and spent time observing and studying the nuances of human behavior. (Morgan & O'Neil, 1986)

Mind-body techniques empower clients to develop strengths out of previously held limitations. The counselor observes individual differences to find the necessary ingredients to deliver interventions. Rapport is established, and the counselor extracts information about the client's methods of constructing his or her reality. Imagery, paradoxical techniques, and metaphor are then employed to promote change.

RAPPORT, MAPS, AND MODELS

O'Hanlon (1987) has suggested that Ericksonian interventions create change by utilizing or blocking current patterns of behavior or by establishing new patterns. Such interventions require the therapist to continually reevaluate his or her own maps and models based on observation of individual differences.

The neurolinguistic programming model (Dilts, 1983), as well as strategic, problem-solving, and brief therapy models (Watzlawick, Weakland, & Fisch, 1974; Haley, 1973; Fisch, Weakland, & Segal, 1983; de Shazer, 1985), emphasizes solutions to problems rather than extended, insight-oriented therapy. As with a systems-oriented approach (Satir, 1972), each approach seeks to break down pathological communication patterns by initiating minimal changes in patterns of communication. The rehabilitation counselor must first establish those characteristics that appreciate a particular client's uniqueness.

By developing rapport with clients on the behavioral, content, and cultural levels of communication (Gordon & Meyers-Anderson, 1981), respect for the client is demonstrated and mutual trust is facilitated. Through mirroring various nonverbal behaviors such as posture, facial expressions, breathing rate, and voice tone and tempo, the counselor paces the client's experience at levels normally outside conscious awareness. Noting and utilizing sensory predicates enable the counselor to make predictions about what the client is attending to in the environment and also enable the counselor to "package" directives in accordance with the client's personal learning style (Bandler & Grinder, 1975; Grinder, DeLozier, & Bandler, 1977; Jacobson, 1983, 1986). Erickson often mirrored several patterns of behavior at once, such as posture, voice tone, and breathing rate (Gordon & Myers-Anderson, 1981). He might also use speech patterns characteristic of the individual. In one case he learned to emulate a schizophrenic patient's "word salad" as a way of developing rapport with the client (Bandler & Grinder, 1975). On another occasion he created trust in a person who was a recovering alcoholic and ex-convict by speaking prison slang to emphasize the client's personal responsibility to return for further work (Zeig, 1980).

One of the authors, in developing rapport with a person with a disability, recognized that the client's difficulties of accepting a newly acquired prosthesis for his arm were accurately reflected in sensory-based descriptions of learning to use that prosthesis:

Client:	I don't feel I can see where I'm going with this thing.
Counselor:	You don't feel you can see where you are going . . . What prevents you from getting a handle on your goal?
Client:	I don't know . . . ah . . . it just seems I come up short each time . . . like I see what I want to do, but I'm struggling to find a middle ground.
Counselor:	Yes, I can see what you mean. I feel the same way myself sometimes. What seems to be missing? Sometimes you reach here, sometimes there. How can you practice to be more systematic?
Client:	That's a good question. Maybe I need to think back over what I've done here a few moments before I go on.

By pacing the client's use of kinesthetic and visual predicates, the counselor was able to sufficiently reflect the client's confusion to allow further distinctions to be made that eventually enabled the client to refine his eye–hand coordinations as part of physical therapy.

IMAGERY AND HEALING

The use of the imagination and imagery is one of the oldest techniques of healing known to us. According to Achterberg (1985), shamanism is the oldest and most widespread method in which the imagination is applied in healing, with evidence suggesting that it was used at least 20,000 years ago.

Use of imagination by guided imagery is at the leading edge of contemporary health care, which creates another vital approach to both physical and emotional healing. This approach to healing and health care has been applied in cases of numerous somatic disorders, psychological problems, and problems in rehabilitation, particularly those involving motivation, refinement of newly acquired behaviors, and retraining of injured bodily members. Research (Achterberg, 1985; Rossi, 1986) has disclosed that the imagination, and images that compose it, can profoundly influence biological processes of the body as well as emotional dynamics.

Imagery is an aspect of cognitive functioning during which an individual allows himself or herself to experience through the imagination some aspect of experience. In the mind, an image is formed of an external referent that may or may not be present, but that is customarily absent. An image may be embodied in any sensory mode. Imagery and the use of imagination are not esoteric, recondite experiences that require years of specialized training. In fact, most, if not all people, engage in imagery several times a day as they reflect on the past, attempt to solve problems, plan for the future, or rehearse desired or anticipated actions.

Guided imagery is an approach to healing and wellness in which a counselor or other helping professional, the guide, assists the client in learning how to gain access to images that have some relationship to the problem confronting the client. Employing any of several techniques, the guide assists the client in learning to allow images of personal problems to appear spontaneously, understanding the meaning of the image or images, and implementing what is learned from the images of everyday life to resolve the problem addressed. Guided imagery essentially encourages a journey by the client into the self, with the function of the guide being facilitation of this journey. The guide does not plan it or direct it. The basic purpose of the guide is to orient the individual's focus inwardly, using images experienced by the individual as the dynamics by which this is accomplished.

Guided imagery has been used successfully in treating a multiplicity of somatic disorders, grief and bereavement, and resolution of problems following traumatic physical injury or disfigurement. Other areas in which it has been implemented for rehabilitation purposes include difficulty in resumption of employment after a long absence from work, impaired social interaction and other activities, and decreased physical discomfort associated with physical or psychological trauma or loss.

Rossman (1987) describes two types of imagery: receptive and active. *Receptive imagery* enables a person to become aware of unconscious dynamics influencing behavior, unmet needs, unrecognized aspects of the problem, and possibilities for change. *Active imagery* permits an individual to communicate conscious intentions to the unconscious mind. Remen (1986) discusses two other types of imagery, which she terms *evocative* and *generic*. Using evocative imagery, a guide can assist the individual in going deeper within the self and experiencing emotional and other reactions associated with the image and the individual's problems. Through generic imagery, the guide assumes much of the responsibility for the pace of working with an image, as well as the method by which an image will be encountered.

The efficacy of guided imagery as a form of healing is well documented. Among the authors writing in the area of imagery and its uses in healing are Rossman (1987), Siegel (1986), Ornish (1982), Jaffe (1980), Simonton, Matthews-Simonton, and Creighton (1980), Breseler (1979), Samuels and Samuels (1975), and Oyle (1974).

PARADOXICAL INTERVENTIONS AND REFRAMING

Inherent in the shift to brief techniques in counseling and the adoption of a utilitarian approach is the idea of *paradox*. Defined as a contradiction that follows correct deductions from consistent premises (Watzlawick, Beavins, & Jackson, 1967), paradox is the natural by-product of the communication process.

Directives such as "Be spontaneous," or situations such as a parent shouting "Be quiet," to a hyperactive child, are paradoxical in that they place the receiver of the communication in a "madness or badness" dilemma. In the rehabilitation setting, persistent, although frequently unspoken directives to "be normal," ensnare clients in a bind that demands they either ignore their disabling condition or become preoccupied with real or imagined variances from "normalcy" (Gove, 1976; Amado, 1988). Thus, persons with disabilities are in a double bind: on the one hand, they are told to realize their physical limitations, separate mind from body, and develop either vocational or academic skills; on the other hand, they are reminded of their imperfections through the media, through interactions with others, and through inner unresolved tension in adjusting to their individual body structure. Reaction to paradoxical communication may well be interpreted as rebellion or insanity unless the client is enabled to formulate responses that integrate the two levels of communication implied in the bind.

Therapeutic binds place the client in a situation where their reactions to the bind result in the client achieving useful therapeutic gains regardless of whether they comply or resist (Bandler & Grinder, 1975). Symptom prescription and symptom modification involve paradoxically exaggerating or altering symptomatic behaviors in such a way as to disrupt the symptomatic pattern and change its function (O'Connell, 1983).

Paradoxical techniques recontextualize symptoms through changing the meaning; that is, reframing of the behavior or rediscovering contexts where the behavior might be useful (Grinder & Bandler, 1982). Erickson often used paradoxical techniques as a way of getting clients to accept physical limitation or to redirect them from being preoccupied with some aspect of themselves. Gordon and Meyers-Anderson (1981) share an anecdote in which Erickson utilized a woman's valued criteria concerning childrearing to reframe the meaning of the woman's broad hips and buttocks from "the biggest fanny" to a "cradle of children" suitable for childbearing, thus encouraging her to accept advances from young men and eventually marry and become a mother.

METAPHOR

Stephen and Carol Lankton term metaphor the *saddlemate* of paradox (1983). The use of metaphor as a teaching tool is a time-honored technique. Two main categories of therapeutic metaphors can be identified: (1) those providing a solution or solutions to the client's problem and (2) those that access the client's unconscious resources to induce change (King, Novik, & Citrenbaum, 1983). Telling stories provides a means for packaging meaningful communications in such a way as to focus the client's attention and open them to possible patterns of change. The nature of metaphors is such that the client can access and reaccess the story and continue to discover new meanings in the metaphor in accordance with his or her background and personal resources.

Attention to the structure of the client's problem situation and attention to the client's preferences in sensory systems as a means of representing experience provide the key for creating useful isomorphs of the presenting problem (Gordon, 1978). From such isomorphs, transitions can be constructed that offer alternative patterns of experiencing within the problem situation.

Clients often describe their experience metaphorically. For example, the client who describes a certain individual as "a pain in the neck" or suggests that certain situations "knock the stuffings out of them" are describing their symptom through analogy. These analogies serve as useful building blocks to formulate meaningful communications embedded within stories. King, Novik, and Citrenbaum (1983) describe a metaphor used in treatment with a woman, quite overweight, who revealed the weight gain corresponded in time to her being a victim of sexual assault. The counselor created a metaphor in which the main character within the story wore numerous layers of clothing to protect herself as a result of a past encounter with a rodent along a forest path. After creating rapport through the isomorphic relationship of the client to the main story character, directives were offered that described the behavior and attitudes the client needed to overcome her weight problem. Metaphoric directives were constructed to account for the important gains the client achieved through remaining overweight, and these directives suggested alternative outlets to fulfill these ends.

One of our clients, a bright, articulate, but difficult client to deal with, continually disrupted successful job placement. Further discussions revealed that, as the client would begin to work, he would generate internal dialogues that would distract him from the task at hand and would eventually lead to an aggravated emotional state. Because the client had a musical background, the counselor was able to gain the client's ear by telling a metaphor about two pianos that paced the client's experience of the two internal voices. In the metaphor, one piano, a "little upright" was "very proud of itself becausei . . . it didn't need anybody to tell it what tunes to play or how to play them." The other piano, a concert grand, was often ignored in spite of its finely crafted structure, due primarily to its placement within the concert hall. Resolution of the differences held by the two pianos was achieved through direction of a "creative concert master."

> One day, when the foyer which contained the player piano was being painted, the two pianos were moved into the concert hall together. As the upright reeled off its tiny collection of pieces, rather mechanically reiterating the same monotonous phrases, the grand piano began to resonate discordantly, unable to escape the tiny tones of the upright.

Amidst this confusion entered the concert master. Having been a part of the concert hall staff from the beginning, he was well aware of the differences between the two pianos and, in one quick motion, he sat down at the grand piano and began to accompany the performance of the little player piano. Soon they joined in harmony and both pianos were astounded at their abilities to tune in on one another. What one couldn't do, the other could do with the help of the creative concert master.

The metaphor continued to suggest the possibility of flexibility, balance, and appreciation by integrating the functions of both pianos into a continuing working relationship.

> The player piano learned to accept its need for accompaniment from the grand piano and grew to admire the concert master's ability to explore the extremes in the two pianos' construction. The grand piano appreciated the player piano's knack for condensing difficult material and learned through watching the concert master how to integrate into similarities functional differences between itself and the little upright player piano.

Together the three made beautiful music for some time to follow . . .

CONCLUSION

In *The Republic* (Plato, in Eastman, 1969), Plato tells a parable of a cave where a fire is burning, throwing shadows on the wall. A group of men sit watching the shadows, unaware of the actual entities blocking the light from the fire. The group of men are neither blind nor unintelligent; they are just not aware that what they "see is not all that is." This metaphor is somewhat similar to the "seeing" discussed by the anthropologist Carlos Casteneda (1968, 1971) as he underwent many experimental trials under the tutelage of the sorcerer Juan. In learning to "see" rather than just see, Carlos developed new understanding on how he constructed his reality.

The last decade has given us further insights into the total individual by research and study in mind–body connections. This helps us "see" the expanding ecology of approaches in rehabilitation. This chapter traces mind–body procedures concerning counseling strategies for counseling with persons with disabilities. Much of what is new and innovative in the psychotherapeutic process has its roots in the seminal work of Milton H. Erickson. Through rapport and respect of clients' unique maps, specific interventions such as imagery, paradoxical techniques, and metaphor, the counselor can aid clients through problematic situations and help create the opportunity to develop their abilities to achieve quality life experiences.

REFERENCES

Achterberg, J. (1985). *Imagery in healing: Shamanism and modern medicine.* Boston: New Science Library/Shambhala.

Amado, A. N. (1988). A perspective on the present and notes for new directions. In L. W. Heal, J. I. Haney, & A. R. Amado (Eds.), *Integration of developmentally disabled individuals into the community* (2nd ed.) (pp. 299–305). Baltimore: Brookes.

Bandler, R., & Grinder, J. (1975). *Patterns of the hypnotic techniques of Milton H. Erickson, M.D.* (Vol. 1). Cupertino, CA: Meta.

Breseler, D. E. (1979). *Free yourself from pain.* New York: Simon & Schuster.

Buchsbaum, M. (1983, July). The mind readers. *Psychology Today,* 58–62.

Casteneda, C. (1968). *The teachings of don Juan. A Yaqui way of knowledge.* New York: Ballantine.

Casteneda, C. (1971). *A separate reality: Further conversations with don Juan.* New York: Pocket Books.

de Shazer, S. (1985). *Keys of solution in brief therapy.* New York: Norton.

Dilts, R. B. (1983). *Applications of neuro-linguistic programming.* Cupertino, CA: Meta.

Fisch, R., Weakland, J. H., & Segal, L. (1983). *The tactics of change: Doing therapy briefly.* San Francisco: Jossey-Bass.

Gelman, D., with Hager, M. (1988, Nov. 7). *Newsweek,* pp. 88–97.

Gordon, D. (1978). *Therapeutic metaphors: Helping others through the looking glass.* Cupertino, CA: Meta.

Gordon, D., & Meyers-Anderson, M. (1981). *Phoenix: Therapeutic patterns of Milton H. Erickson.* Cupertino, CA: Meta.

Gove, W. R. (1976). Social reaction theory and disability. In G. L. Albrecht (Ed.), *The sociology of physical disability and rehabilitation* (pp. 57–71). Pittsburgh: University of Pittsburgh.

Grinder, J., & Bandler, R. (1982). *Reframing: Neuro-linguistic programming and the transformation of meaning.* Moab, UT: Real People Press.

Grinder, J., DeLozier, J., & Bandler, R. (1977). *Patterns of the hypnotic techniques of Milton H. Erickson, M.D.* (Vol. II). Cupertino, CA: Meta.

Haley, J. (1973). *Uncommon therapy: The psychiatric techniques of Milton H. Erickson, M.D.* New York: Norton.

Jacobson, S. (1983, 1986). *Meta-cation* (Vols. I, II, III). Cupertino, CA: Meta.

Jaffe, D. T. (1980). *Healing from within.* New York: Knopf.

James, T., & Woodsmall, W. (1988). *Time line therapy and the basis of personality.* Cupertino, CA: Meta.

King, M., Novik, L., & Citrenbaum, C. (1983). *Modern clinical hypnosis for habit control.* New York: Norton.

Lankton, S., & Lankton, C. (1983). *The answer within: A clinical framework of Ericksonian hypnotherapy.* New York: Brunner/Mazel.

McDowell, W. A., Coven, A. B., & Eash, V. (1979, December). The handicapped: Special needs and strategies for counseling. *The Personnel and Guidance Journal, 228–232.*

Morgan, L. B., & O'Neil, A. (1986, October). Ericksonian hypnosis: A dialogue with Charles Citrenbaum, Mark King and William Cohen. *Journal of Counseling and Development. 65*, 86–88.

O'Connell, E. S. (1983). Symptom prescription in psychotherapy. *Psychotherapy: Theory, Research & Practice, 20*, 12–20.

O'Hanlon, W. H. (1987). *Taproots: Underlying principles of Milton Erickson's therapy and hypnosis.* New York: Norton.

Ornish, D. (1982). *Stress, diet, and your health.* New York: Holt, Rinehart and Winston.

Oyle, I. (1974). *The healing mind.* Millbrae, CA: Celestial Arts.

Plato. (1969). The allegory of the cave. In A. M. Eastman (Ed.), *The Norton reader: An anthology of expository prose* (pp. 576–579). New York: Norton.

Rossi, E. L. (1986). *The psychology of mind–body healing: New concepts of therapeutic hypnosis.* New York: Norton.

Rossman, M. L. (1987). *Healing yourself: A step-by-step program for better health through imagery.* New York: Walker and Co.

Samuels, M., & Samuels, N. (1975). *Seeing with the mind's eye.* New York: Random House.

Satir, V. (1972). *Peoplemaking.* Palo Alto, CA: Science and Behavior Books.

Siegel, B. (1986). *Love, medicine, and miracles.* New York: Harper & Row.

Simonton, O. C., Matthews-Simonton, S., & Creighton, J. L. (1980). *Getting well again.* New York: Bantam Books.

Snyder, M. (1984). When belief creates reality. In L. Berkowitz (Ed.), *Advances in experimental social psychology* (pp. 18–34). Orlando, FL: Academic Press.

Szymanski, E. M. (1987). Rehabilitation counseling and AER: A call for articulation. *Journal of Visual Impairment and Blindness, 81*, 433–434.

Thomas, K. R., Butler, A. J., & Parker, R. M. (1987). Psychosocial counseling. In R. M. Parker (Ed.), *Rehabilitation counselor: Basics and beyond.* Austin, TX: Pro-Ed.

Watzlawick, P., Beavins, J. H., & Jackson, D. D. (1967). *Pragmatics of human communication.* New York: Norton.

Watzlawick, P., Weakland, J., & Fisch, R. (1974). *Change: Principles of problem formation and problem resolution.* New York: Norton.

Wright, B. A. (1983). *Physical disability—A psychosocial approach* (2nd ed.). New York: Harper & Row.

Zeig, J. (Ed.). (1980). *A teaching seminar with Milton H. Erickson.* New York: Brunner/Mazel.

23

Life's Challenges: Curse or Opportunity? Counseling Families of Persons With Disabilities

Mary R. Hulnick
H. Ronald Hulnick

It is interesting to go back and reread a similar article we wrote 10 years ago (Prescott & Hulnick, 1979). Most interesting was the realization that our basic approach is essentially the same. Our philosophical orientation that all of life's experiences are, in fact, opportunities for personal growth and learning is unchanged. We are more convinced than ever that counselor empathy is of paramount importance, as is the need to communicate genuine caring to clients, the importance of carefully addressing the issue of personal responsibility, and the value of effectively dealing with judgment of self and others. And we continue to recognize the validity of having a well-developed information and referral network. These, then, are the fundamentals that enhance the effectiveness of any counseling relationship as much today as 10 years ago.

There are, however, changes that have occurred and that are still in process that speak for the value of an update. For one, the language recommended for referring to individuals with disabilities reflects a fundamental shift. The special issue of *The Personnel and Guidance Journal* in 1979 was titled *Counseling Handicapped Persons and Their Families.* The 1989 issue on the same theme is called *Counseling Persons With Disabilities.* The former referred to *handicapped persons,* while the latter speaks of *persons with disabilities.* It is encouraging to see the language focusing on the person rather than the limitation. As counselors, it is essential that we retain a person-centered rather than a problem-centered approach.

PERSONS AS SEPARATE FROM DISABILITIES

Taking this concept a step further in establishing a context for this chapter, we recognize the importance of further refining our language by defining disabled as *differently abled.* Each of us as human beings has unique challenges as well as unique gifts. As we see it, *disability* is a term referring to functional limitation. Such limitation may occur at different levels; that is, there may be a functional limitation in the physical body, the mind, or the emotions. These limitations can be seen as an individual's challenges and are not to be confused with a person's intrinsic worth or value. As a good friend of ours who is a rehabilitation counselor has said, "We all have our challenges. Some of us wear them on the outside and some on the inside. Down deep, we're all whole and complete, and thank God, we're all worthy."

While a particular person may have a physical limitation, he or she may also have a profound sense of the value of himself or herself and others. Another person may be "physically abled" yet have an extremely low sense of self-esteem and be functionally unavailable to give and receive love. Which person is truly more disabled?

And then there are those like our good friend Kathy, who passed away about a year ago. Kathy used her 8-year battle with cancer to transform herself from an extremely angry and judgmental lady into a most beautiful and lovely soul. We will probably never forget her sitting there at her master's graduation during her last days all hunched over in her wheelchair, looking about 20 years older than she was. She spoke from her heart of the need for us all to learn to love one another and of her loving for us. Her sharing was sacred. She achieved this quality of awareness by successfully dealing with all that her "disability" had brought forward. She became the victor over it rather than the victim of it.

Viewing disability in this way is paradoxical, as it is difficult to know whether one's condition is a curse or an opportunity. As we see it, the only difference is in the way we respond to the challenge. As counselors, we have the opportunity to hold a focus that supports individuals and families in meeting challenges with an empowering perspective that sees all people as worthwhile and responsible players fully capable of actively and successfully participating in the game of life.

Thus a counselor's challenge in working with families of persons with disabilities remains the same today as it was 10 years ago. Fundamentally, it is to assist people in learning the mental and emotional skills and attitudes necessary for dealing effectively with life's gifts as well as life's challenges. What has changed is public sensitivity to the issue of disability, as well as a maturing in the counseling field, which has spawned a new generation of skills and techniques enabling us to stand on the shoulders of those who taught us what we knew 10 years ago. Today we know more about assisting clients in the psychological healing process of applying caring and compassion to the places inside that hurt.

CRISIS AS OPPORTUNITY

In the Chinese language, the written character for *crisis* and *opportunity* is the same. In other words, Chinese culture recognizes that opportunity is inherent in crisis. It all depends entirely on how you look at a given situation. We have a saying in our classes: "How you relate to the issue *IS* the issue;" or perhaps more to the point: "How you relate to yourself while you go through an issue *IS* the issue." Are there, then, ways we can incorporate this attitude into our counseling with families who have a person with disability within their structure? We have found several that we would like to share here.

REFRAMING ISSUES AS CHALLENGES

Reframing is a skill made popular by the founders of neurolinguistic programming (Bandler & Grinder, 1979). Essentially, it is a technique for learning another way of seeing any particular situation. This can include recontexting the issues raised by the presence of a disability. For example, families with a person who has a disability often come to counseling with the orientation (view) that they have a "problem" that by definition tends to be perceived as negative. Because they are in pain, the preferred treatment, as initially seen through their eyes, is eradication. Trying to "get rid of" problems is actually an ineffective approach to life's challenges since, as we have said before, the real issue is *not what* is happening but *how we relate to what is happening*.

What counselors can do is caringly assist family members in learning how to shift, or reframe, their view of the situation. In particular, a shift is usually required in the direction of learning new ways for successfully responding to "what is" rather than magically wishing current reality would change (Wright, 1983). We as counselors can caringly demonstrate how a shift of attitude can be very beneficial in successfully coping with what is. We refer to these types of shifts as moving to a position of positive outlook. Positive outlooks are characterized by the following attitudes: "What new learning is in store for me now?" "What are the opportunities and blessings present in this unique situation?" A positive attitude can provide the inspiration necessary to move forward (Egan, 1988).

An effective counselor's initial responsibilities include establishing a safe space for client expression of feelings and concerns while communicating acceptance, understanding, and empathy. Once this quality of relationship is consistently experienced, then there are four empowering questions the client and counselor can gently explore together, which can be very fruitful for family members:

1. "Can you see any way you can use this situation to your advancement?"
2. "What can you learn from all this?"
3. "What can you do that might result in a more uplifting experience for everyone involved?"
4. "How can you relate to yourself right now in a more loving way?"

These questions in the context of a caring counseling relationship provide an exploratory focus that supports both individuals with disabilities, as well as their relatives, in making peace with the realities of their situation in a way that implies true acceptance rather than embittered resignation. Real healing occurs in the presence of genuine caring. The painful challenges in time become parts of valuable lessons experienced as worth learning (Miller, 1988).

Once a situation has been empathically reframed to a more positive context, then more choices become available for coping with both the emotional and logistical challenges that may be involved. When more options are seen, tensions and pressures associated with seemingly burdensome situations are often alleviated.

CLARIFYING MISINTERPRETATIONS OF PERSONAL RESPONSIBILITY

Accepting personal responsibility for both their feelings and actions is probably the most challenging step family members face in coming to terms mentally and emotionally with the advent of a loved one's disability. As a concept, responsibility seems to have several nonconstructive meanings, which often emerge in working with families of individuals with disabilities. For instance, some family members consider themselves and others "responsible" for their actions in much the same way that a driver is responsible for steering a car off the road. If an "accident" occurs resulting in a family member becoming disabled, this is often viewed mentally, and experienced emotionally, by the other family members involved as evidence that they are not only at fault but "bad" as well.

Seen in this way, personal responsibility becomes twisted and is nothing more than a form of self-judgment, self-punishment, and self-abuse. Since we are "at fault," we must punish ourselves in retribution. It is as if somehow this will make things okay. In some way it evens the score. Guilt and a compensatory desire to do more, to atone for not having done enough, are often part of this pattern. Sometimes clients feel somehow they deserve the "disaster" (Miller, 1988).

Another variation on this type of reasoning occurs when someone, although not directly involved in the disabling process, nevertheless feels responsible. They somehow take another's disability as evidence of their own failure or shortcomings. If an experience, such as a loved one developing a disability, violates one of the family member's beliefs, such as "things like this don't happen to good people," then he or she blames and punishes himself or herself. A result of this type of self-destructive behavior is beating oneself up mentally when our loved one is not physically, mentally, or emotionally "normal" in some way. We judge ourselves as wrong for not measuring up to some unhealthy idea of "goodness." This is often reflected by attitudes or statements such as "What did I do to deserve this?" Or, "If I'd only done something different, this wouldn't have happened."

The error in this approach is, of course, that it has a completely negative focus. The process of engaging in this judgmental activity invariably results in the opposite of uplifting and constructive behavior by family members. It rarely results in a greater willingness to approach the situation constructively, since it only erroneously reinforces the experience of personal failure by associating a family member's disability with the pain of self-judgment. Clients sometimes fool themselves by falsely thinking they are making themselves "right" by judging themselves for "wrongdoing."

Encouraging family members to find a more compassionate definition of personal responsibility is imperative.

RESPONSIBILITY—THE WILLINGNESS TO CHOOSE

Seeing issues as opportunities presupposes a constructive definition of personal responsibility. Here responsibility is defined simply as the ability to respond, and, more specifically, to respond differently and more constructively than the way we have been responding if it has not been truly working for us. In this sense, we are talking about the willingness to consciously make constructive choices rather than to unconsciously react with resentment, disappointment, irritation, or anger. When events characterizing an opportunity for personal growth present themselves, such as a family member developing a disability, demonstrating willingness to accept individual responsibility is, for many families, perhaps the most challenging step. Consciously or not, choices are made by all involved. Exploring choices is an important part of the healing process.

At this point, personal responsibility divides into two areas, outer choices and inner choices. Examples of outer choices include "Will I go to the hospital to visit my son who is going through rehabilitation for serious and disabling injuries, or would I be better off going home and going to bed?" "Will I reach out to my son as well as to those who can support me, or will I withdraw and isolate myself nursing my hurt and self-pity?" Choosing these, or other alternatives, is the process of taking responsibility. It is only when a family member has chosen a course of action and is doing it that they have taken responsibility. And, of course, each separate action will have its consequences. When the consequences appear, the choice in how to respond at that time will be the next opportunity for taking responsibility.

Inner choices are similar. "How will I choose to be with myself over the fact that I have a son who's paralyzed from the waist down?" "And how will I choose to be with myself while I go through the process of dealing with the fact that he has a serious physical disability?" "Will I hold myself 'responsible' for my son's disability, judge myself, and suffer guilt and remorse?" "Or will I move into acceptance that he now has this condition, be loving with myself, and outwardly do those things I need to do in order to assist myself and him?" "Will I take good care of myself and honestly share my feelings and needs for support with other family members?"

In these types of emotionally laden situations, willingness to take inner responsibility in the moment would suggest that it is the choice of each family member whether or not to take 100% responsibility for his or her own internal emotional reaction, independent from what seems to have caused it (e.g., their relative's disability). Viewed in this way, situations are simply triggering devices that surface unresolved issues needing healing within (Power, 1988).

For family members, there is a very human temptation to assign responsibility for their feelings and emotional reactions to what is going on outside, to the "because" in life. Often it sounds like, "I am upset because...," and a laundry list of justifiable reasons follows. "I am upset *because* my child or spouse has a disability." Being caught in this stance is a process of self-victimization. Family members may unknowingly be victimizing themselves by blaming their upset on outside events. Are there alternatives? Although upset is always understandable and acceptable, if there are no *justifiable* causes for being upset, how can we constructively proceed?

SELF-FORGIVENESS: COMPASSION FOR ONESELF

In fact, we may or may not be at all responsible for circumstances that life brings to us. There are mixed opinions on this subject, and we think it is important to remember that that is exactly what they are, opinions. Only God knows for sure. It is precisely this vantage point of realizing "Only God knows for sure," which gives counselors a most important tool as family members must be assisted in facing and healing any deep feelings of rage, sadness, loss, and guilt. Emotional suffering is only exacerbated by holding oneself accountable in a negative way for a loved one's disability. Any unwillingness to let go of blame and judgment one has placed against oneself must be challenged. But how?

We have observed many times that there is a sequence that always seems to be present at times of emotional upset. It goes like this. Whenever anger is present and we look beneath the anger, we always find hurt. Anger turns out to be largely a reaction occurring when we feel hurt. And when we look beneath the hurt, we always find caring. We are only hurt when something or someone we care about has been, in some way, desecrated or violated.

This sequence gives us the key for effectively handling these types of situations. It is this. Give a client full permission to express his or her deepest pain. In fact, assist clients by actively encouraging them in expressing it. If the pain is at the anger level, encourage them in safely expressing their anger. This may involve the use of an encounter bat, rolled-up towel or newspaper, or even a tennis racquet or length of rubber hose directed against a soft object such as a mattress or large pillow. Care must be taken to provide guidelines stressing safety, and a willingness to "not hurt oneself or others in the process" should actually be verbalized and committed to by the client.

As a client risks fully expressing his or her anger, he or she will naturally tend to drop down into the hurt that is always beneath. As with anger, this expression should be actively encouraged. To the degree that clients are willing to risk expressing their hurt, this expression will tend to be characterized by deep sobbing, the deeper the better. It is at this point that a counselor has an opportunity for truly making a serious intervention. It is to encourage the client to begin working with self-forgiveness. For what? We need to forgive ourselves not for our anger and not for our hurt, but for any *judgments* we may have placed against ourselves or our disabled loved one. It is simply an act of realizing "Only God knows for sure what any disability is all about." Regardless of what we may think or feel, we must admit the obvious: We really do not know what any human condition is truly about. We just do not know. The act of judging implies that we do know. By forgiving ourselves, we release the judgments we have placed and we pass through the hurt level into the caring that lies just below. By walking across the bridge of self-forgiveness, hurt gives way to peace, and the client is released from his or her self-induced hell. The healing process has begun.

Assisting clients in evoking their own compassion for themselves as human beings is essential. In this way, they can courageously embrace themselves as worthwhile persons with both strengths and weaknesses. By entering into this quality of caring relationship with themselves, they come into greater willingness and ability to work with the realities of their current situation.

Over the years, we have found that it matters little whether one is disabled or is a family member of a disabled person. The process we have just described is effective regardless.

RESPONSIBILITY—THE CARING CHOICE

Once a client is at peace within himself or herself, it is crucial to assist him or her in recognizing that little has changed regarding outside circumstances. We still must respond to the circumstances coming our way (Frankl, 1963). However, being willing to take responsibility from a place of "caring" inside is a much different story from taking responsibility from a place of "anger or hurt" inside. If we are to be victors, we must be willing to face our choices "caringly." This involves nothing more than assisting families with disabilities in acknowledging not only the choices they are currently making but also inviting consideration of potentially more constructive choices they *could* be making that might produce more beneficial results. In this context, it may be useful to remember one definition of insanity is: Doing the same thing over and over while expecting a different result. Clients often recognize the truth of this statement and experience renewed motivation to move beyond the limitations of previous attitudes and actions.

EMPOWERING QUESTIONS FACILITATING
AWARENESS OF CHOICES

We have designed a series of questions for use in assisting family members in looking at both their inner and outer choices in the context of a caring and supportive counseling relationship.

1. "What choices are you making that tend to perpetuate this situation?"
2. "Are you aware of any other choices you might make which would tend to have a different result? Keep in mind that you are only looking at possibilities and you are not committing to doing anything."

3. "Let's look at each choice you have brought forward in more detail. What would it really look like if you were really to do it? Describe yourself in the present tense as if you are actually doing it now."
4. "Has considering these questions resulted in any new possibilities for you?"

In addition to maintaining an empathic attitude, there are two important aspects to keep in mind while doing this process. The first aspect is the importance of emphasizing that families are not committing to actually doing anything other than looking at choices. We have found that parents, spouses, and siblings all tend to be much more creative when they are given permission to freely explore, knowing that they are not committing to actually doing anything other than consider what they bring forward as alternatives.

The second aspect is to encourage family members in detailing each choice "as if" they were actually doing it here and now. We invite and encourage them to enthusiastically describe themselves in the present tense *having, being, and doing* the experience of their choice. Research is clearly showing that the psyche does not seem to differentiate very well between a well-imagined fantasy and physical reality. By imagining doing something in detail, we have found that many family members often then tend to spontaneously take that action in physical reality. Clients sometimes delightedly report finding themselves doing the new actions that are more supportive of themselves as well as of the family member with the identified disability even though no commitment was actually made.

Part of a counselor's challenge is assisting family members in more consistently choosing the attitudes and actions that support them in creating the quality of inner and outer life preferred. Many times this is a process that requires conscious commitment to moving ahead on the part of all involved, as many responses are well-ingrained habits and it takes time to develop the awareness that allows for more conscious constructive choices.

POSITIVE SELF-TALK—A MAJOR FORCE

Often family members are caught in a mental habit of catastrophizing imagined negative consequences of their situation and the health of their relative with the disability. This kind of inner dialogue repeated internally can become a negative self-fulfilling prophecy. Albert Ellis hit the nail on the head (Ellis, 1988) when he discussed how people tend to get themselves into trouble by continuing to indoctrinate themselves with their own limiting beliefs.

These days this concept can be demonstrated easily through the use of an applied kinesiology technique called *muscle-testing*. This method can be especially powerful in working with families where the disability is physical. When we ask family members to hold out their arm and instruct them to resist our downward pull on their wrist, we most likely will find it somewhat difficult to pull their arm down. We then instruct them to visualize a situation where they entered into judgment or negative self-talk about themselves, another, or a situation, and, while continuing the negative dialogue in their mind, we ask them to once again resist our downward pull. Invariably, we find the muscle has weakened considerably, and it is quite easy to pull their arm down.

We then ask them to tell themselves that, while the situation in question might have been difficult, how they handled it really has very little to do with their value or lovableness as a person. In fact, we have them say out loud something like "I know I am a lovable and worthwhile person." While continuing a positive mental dialogue, we again ask them to resist our downward pull, and we find the muscle usually not only has returned to its original strength but also, in most cases, is actually stronger than when we started.

It seems, then, that what we tell ourselves has a tremendous effect not only on our psyche but also on our physical body as well. In a recent article (Rosellini, 1988), the U.S. Surgeon General, Dr. C. Everett Koop, commented on the mind-body relationship: "There is no question that the things that we think have a tremendous effect upon our bodies. If we can change our thinking, the body frequently heals itself" (p. 64). A good friend or ours who knows the validity of this information has put it wisely, "It's foolish not to win in your own fantasies!"

Positive self-talk is a skill that every counselor can readily teach since, in some ways, the mind is easier to work with than the body or the emotions. It is relatively easy to consciously redirect our thoughts once it dawns on us that we can do so. We find that many people have a critical inner dialogue going on in their minds a great deal of the time. The muscle-testing demonstration shows that this is a physically debilitating process. By consciously choosing to redirect this dialogue so both the content and context (attitude) are positive, we facilitate a more nurturing, supporting, and uplifting relationship inside our self, not to mention the physical benefits. Consciously engaging in this process tends to *automatically* result in more positive outcomes in our lives.

Again, we have designed another series of questions to assist clients in learning to do "positive self-talk." Let us assume a client is complaining about having to spend so much time and effort taking care of his wife who has had a stroke. The steps for assisting him in learning positive self-talk follow:

1. Assist the client in identifying his or her current pattern of self-talk regarding the situation: "What are you telling yourself about this situation?"

2. Encourage the possibility of a more positive and nurturing pattern of self-talk: "What *could* you tell yourself right now which would be more self-supporting to you as well as uplifting to your wife?"

3. Encourage the client in taking responsibility for redirecting self-talk into a more positive pattern: "Would you be willing to begin *right now* and tell yourself this positive self-talk?"

4. Give the client permission to do it and support and encourage as he or she does so: "OK, go ahead and do it!"

THEN AND NOW

Ten years ago we implied, and now we are even more sure, that there is really only one issue with which we are all dealing. It is becoming clearer that earth is a school for learning how to become more loving within ourselves as individuals and between each other. Viewed in this way, there really is very little difference between the so-called *disabled* person and the equally so-called *able-bodied* person. They are both simply conditions with which we must deal. And how we deal with them is everything. If we abuse ourselves complaining about our condition, blaming ourselves and others, and generally expressing negativity, then our life, with disability or without, will be a curse. And if we use our life to transform our pain into loving, then our time, disabled or not, will be a blessing. There is a prayer attributed to an unknown Confederate soldier (Cleland, 1980) that seems to sum up what we are saying beautifully:

> I asked God for strength that I might achieve,
> I was made weak, that I might learn humbly to obey.
> I asked for health, that I might do greater things,
> I was given infirmity that I might do better things.
> I asked for riches, that I might be happy,
> I was given poverty, that I might be wise.
> I asked for power, that I might have the praise of men,
> I was given weakness, that I might feel the need of God.
> I asked for all things, that I might enjoy life,
> I was given life, that I might enjoy all things.
> I got nothing I asked for—
> but everything I had hoped for.
> Almost despite myself,
> my unspoken prayers were answered.
> I am among all men,
> most richly blessed.

REFERENCES

Bandler, R., & Grinder, J. (1974). *Frogs into princes*. Moab, UT: Real People Press.

Cleland, M. (1980). *Strong at the broken places*. TX: Chosen Books.

Egan, P. (1988). Personal statement: My life with a disability—continued opportunities. In P. W. Power, A. E. Dell Orto, & M. B. Gibbons (Eds.), *Family interventions throughout chronic illness and disability* (pp. 44–46). New York: Springer Publishing Co.

Ellis, A. (1988). *How to stubbornly refuse to be miserable about anything—yes anything*. Secaucus, NJ: Lyle Stuart.

Frankl, V. (1963). *Man's search for meaning*. New York: Pocket Books.

Miller, J. (1988). Personal statement: Mechanisms for coping with the disability of a child—a mother's perspective. In P. W. Power, A. E. Dell Orto, & M. B. Gibbons (Eds.), *Family interventions throughout chronic illness and disability* (pp. 136–147). New York: Springer Publishing Co.

Power, P. W. (1988). An assessment approach to family intervention. In P. W. Power, A. E. Dell Orto, & M. B. Gibbons (Eds.), *Family interventions throughout chronic illness and disability* (pp. 5-23). New York: Springer Publishing Co.

Prescott, M. R., & Hulnick, H. R. (1979). Counseling parents of handicapped children: An empathic approach. *The Personnel and Guidance Journal, 28,* 263-266.

Rosellini, L. (1988, May). Rebel with a cause: Koop. *U.S. News & World Report,* pp. 55-64.

Wright, B. (1983). *Physical disability: A psychosocial approach* (2nd ed.). New York: Harper & Row.

Part VI: Interventions—Study Questions and Disability Awareness Exercise

1. Discuss the disabilities that create the greatest challenge for intervention strategies.
2. Can traditional psychotherapeutic strategies be extended to all people with disabilities or must some modification take place?
3. Explain how a person's role and identity can affect the disability experience.
4. How are the cognitive interventions presented different from or similar to "the power of positive thinking?"
5. Present a rationale that supports the premise that a disability is a curse; is an opportunity.
6. Discuss how a functional understanding of personal responsibility can facilitate the adaptation to a disability.

TOO MUCH TO HANDLE

You have just been appointed a counselor in an agency that has as its mission the provision of humane, comprehensive, and long-term care for underserved people with disabilities.

Your first case is a 24-year-old person with a history of mental illness who became a quadriplegic when he attempted suicide. In addition, he sustained a head injury. Recently, he was diagnosed as having AIDS, which resulted from his activities while under the influence of drugs and alcohol.

1. Discuss the multiple issues generated by the case.
2. Develop the mission statement for the agency.
3. Resolve if any public agency can meet the needs of this person.
4. What interventions and resources might you use to be of help to this client?
5. Where should the resources come from? How much money should be spent?

Part VII

New Directions

Rehabilitation is changing dramatically. Some would call it evolution, others upheaval or even revolution. The most significant symbol of this dramatic change is the passage of the Americans with Disabilities Act by the U.S. Congress in 1990. This legislation, which goes further than any other in ensuring civil rights and accessibility for millions of American citizens with disabilities, is seen by many as the culmination of significant positive changes in the 1980s and a symbol of hope for the 1990s.

The new directions of the 1990s will result in individuals being served in greater numbers who were underserved in the past. These include persons with head injuries, older persons, and persons with AIDS. Consequently, new moral and ethical concerns have arisen related to changing and emerging clients' needs. Part VII addresses many of these significant concerns from a futuristic perspective.

DeJong and his associates in Chapter 24, focus on the critical, political, and moral issue of who should be responsible for the life-long well-being of persons with head injuries. They present a model in which responsibility is distributed among the individuals who are head injured, their families, and society. In their presentation of an alternative model, the authors suggest that the resources of the community supplement the resources of the individual, family, and society. The model presented can be applied to similar public policy concerns affecting persons having other severe disabilities.

In "Aging and Disability," Zola, in Chapter 25, recommends a universal policy including both persons with disabilities and older persons rather than to continue with the current divisive policies that pit these groups against each other for limited resources. After tracing the changes in the numbers and nature of persons with disabilities, he presents the important point that "except for sudden death everyone with a disability will age, and everyone who is aging will acquire one or more disabilities."

In another issue of important concern, Callahan, in Chapter 26, examines the moral, social, and psychological issues surrounding family care of persons with severe disabilities, with significant focus on the sacrifice of the family's present and future welfare. In this timely article, Callahan presents the ongoing difficulties and dilemmas faced by families who frequently make heroic sacrifices without adequate support and understanding.

In Chapter 27, Williams and Stafford discuss AIDS from the perspective of its impact upon partners, families, spouses, and significant others of persons with AIDS. Placing AIDS in an illness–disability context, the authors relate AIDS to the dynamics and concerns that have occurred when new, chronic, life threatening disabilities are faced by society. These include stigma, lack of knowledge about the disability and limited referral sources. The complexity of the illness and the challenge to health and human care systems is reflected by the issues raised in the proposed counseling research agenda.

Cnaan and his associates, in Chapter 28, discuss a relatively new approach for assisting persons with severe emotional disabilities to readjust to community living—psychosocial rehabilitation. In providing an organized body of knowledge about this model, 13 major principles are given. These principles have much in common with the basic philosophical and practical principles underlying rehabilitation practice with individuals who have physical disabilities, suggesting that significant common elements unify rehabilitation practice.

In the final chapter of this book, Dell Orto presents a perspective on "Coping with the Enormity of Illness and Disability." The theme of this chapter is that while the harsh reality of illness and disability may be impossible to change, the process certainly can be made more bearable.

24

Who Is Responsible For the Lifelong Well-being of a Person with a Head Injury?

Gerben DeJong
Andrew I. Batavia
Janet M. Williams

The increasing prevalence of head injury in American society is both a sign of progress and personal tragedy. On the one hand, it demonstrates the powerful capacities of our medical delivery systems to save and extend the lives of persons who experience a severe head injury. On the other, it signifies personal tragedy for the 290,000 persons each year (primarily between the ages of 16 and 35 years) who sustain substantial head injuries and for their families and friends. To a greater extent than ever before, these individuals are surviving injuries that result in severe disabilities that often are devastating physically, emotionally, cognitively, and financially (NHIF, 1988). Advanced medical technologies, when combined with an attitude of "survival at any cost," create substantial long-term needs and responsibilities, often of indefinite duration (DeJong & Batavia, 1989).

In responding to the new challenges of head injury, we have yet to sort out how these responsibilities should be distributed among the individual, the family, society, and other possible parties (DeJong & Batavia, 1989). Who should bear responsibility for the lifelong well-being of a person with a head injury? How can such responsibilities and the physical, emotional, and financial burdens associated with them be distributed most equitably? In answering these questions, we are saddled with many misconceptions and faulty assumptions about the needs and capacities of persons with head injuries and the capacities of the family and society to meet these needs.

This chapter seeks to provide some direction as to how responsibilities for the lifelong well-being of a head-injured person should be allocated. Those seeking a "cookbook formula" will be disappointed, because the chapter is intended to offer a more realistic understanding of the capacities and limitations of the individual, the family and society in meeting the lifelong needs of persons with head injury. It further explores the concept of the community as a supplement to the resources of the individual, the family, and society. A better understanding of the choices available is essential to the development of more informed public policies affecting the well-being of persons with head injury and other disabling conditions.

SCOPE OF THE PROBLEM

There are few good statistics on head injury in the United States because the most recent data available derive from the 1974 National Head and Spinal Cord Injury Survey and the 1975 Health Interview Survey (Kalsbeek et al., 1980; Kraus, 1980; Frankowski et al., 1985). Extrapolating from these data, the National Head Injury Foundation estimates that each year approximately 500,000 persons are hospitalized with a head injury in the United States. It estimates that some 290,000 of those hospitalized each year experience symptoms that interfere with daily living skills; of these, at least 70,000 individuals per year experience head injuries severe enough to preclude their return to independent living. This chapter is concerned mainly with the needs of this last group of persons, who require daily supervision or assistance, but also considers the needs of the broader group of persons who require occasional assistance.

Although the incidence of 290,000 disabling head injuries per year and 70,000 severely disabling head injuries per year may not seem large, it has a substantial impact that affects a group much larger than the group of people actually injured. First, it is necessary to consider the large number of spouses, parents, other family members, friends, and business associates directly affected by the injury. By including all persons who are adversely affected by a head injury, its impact increases dramatically. Second, the incidence of head injury does not tell the whole story; it is also necessary to consider the prevalence and severity of head injury. Because many of the effects of head injury are largely permanent, the existing pool of severely disabled survivors increases by at least 70,000 each year. The sequelae of a severe head injury are varied but can affect almost every aspect of a survivor's ability to function and live independently. Thus, the total number of persons who depend on substantial health care and personal assistance services as a result of a head injury is significant and is increasing at an alarming rate.

The incidence, prevalence, and severity of a disabling head injury make it more than an individual or family problem: It is also a concern to society. Society incurs some or most of the financial burden for the direct care of a person with a head injury as well as the indirect costs associated with the individual's loss of productivity. The sheer scope of these costs makes head injury a significant public policy issue.

NATURE OF THE PROBLEM

The issue of who is responsible for lifelong needs is not unique to head injury. The issue also arises with newborns facing lifetime impairments; persons with Down's syndrome, who now have nearly normal life expectancies; persons with chronic mental illness; and older dependent persons, whose lives can sometimes be extended artificially for years. However, the nature of a severe head injury makes the issue of allocation of responsibility even more challenging than it is in the context of these other conditions.

First, head injury is different from most other conditions that cause dependency, because injury to the brain is often more pervasive in its effects than other conditions. In its severe forms, head injury may involve all the functional limitations represented by the above-mentioned conditions: limitations in mobility, cognitive ability, emotional stability, and other functional capacities. Head injury, therefore, may be viewed as a test case for many other conditions that result in lifelong needs.

Second, head injury most frequently occurs during one of life's more awkward stages: the transition from adolescence to adulthood, during which individuals typically begin to assert their independence from their families. Many of our views and beliefs about social responsibility, however, are shaped by established traditions of family and societal caregiving for other dependent populations that do not experience dependency at this developmental stage. In specific, our views on social responsibility are shaped in large part by traditions of caregiving for children, who are too young to assert independence, and for older persons, whose capacities for independent living have diminished with age. Because these populations experience dependency at developmental stages in which dependency is expected whereas persons with head injury typically experience dependency at a stage in which increased independence is expected, they do not serve as ideal models to address issues of responsibility for persons with head injury.

One disability that typically occurs at the same general developmental stage as head injury is spinal cord injury. However, spinal cord-injured persons typically do not experience the types of cognitive and emotional problems experienced by many persons with severe head injury. Such cognitive and emotional problems often serve as impediments to independent living, including the ability to hire, train, and otherwise manage personal assistants (DeJong, 1981; DeJong & Wenker, 1983). Thus the independent living model that has been developed primarily by and for persons who have physical disabilities (DeJong, 1979) such as spinal cord injury may not be fully applicable to persons with severe head injury. Of course, the independent living model may still be applicable to persons with less severe head injury.

As a result, traditions of caregiving for these other populations provide only limited direction as to how responsibilities for the lifelong needs of persons with head injury should be distributed. As a society, we are without a reliable moral and analytic compass to direct us on this issue.

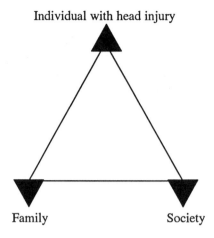

Individual with head injury

Family   Society

Figure 24.1   The unstable triad.

THE UNSTABLE TRIAD

At present, responsibility for the lifelong well-being of persons with head injury usually is distributed among three entities: the individual with a head injury, the family, and society; this triad is depicted in Figure 24.1 (Perlman & Giele, 1982). In this model, *society* is a catchall term referring to a wide range of parties including federal, state, and local government; health and liability insurers; vocational rehabilitation agencies; and various other entities apart from the individual and his or her family.

The triad of responsibility, as conceived here, is a dynamic model in that each entity's ability to address the effects of a head injury has consequences for the other two entities. For example, any shortcoming in an individual's ability to meet his or her needs results in new burdens or new responsibilities for the other two entities in the triad. Likewise, shortcomings in the family's capacity to address the needs of the individual have a direct bearing on the need for societal intervention. Most distressing to families is that the family often must assume the default position in the triad.

The triadic model is useful in depicting how responsibility for the lifelong well-being of a person with a head injury currently is distributed. It is also useful in describing the interdependent nature of human relationships and how that interdependency is altered as a result of a head injury. Like any three-legged stool, however, the triad is inherently unstable if any one of its "legs" (the individual, the family, or society) does not measure up. The triad's stability also is compromised if too much pressure is placed on any of its legs.

Given the complexity of the challenges facing dependent persons who have experienced a traumatic head injury, it appears that the triadic model is not adequate to meet the needs of the head-injured population. As discussed below, more supports (or possibly a different configuration of supports) are needed to make the lives of head-injured persons more stable and secure. Before considering additional elements or a reconfiguration of elements to develop an alternative model, however, it is important to analyze the elements of the triad, to understand better the status quo.

The Individual With a Head Injury

At the apex of the triad is the individual with a head injury, whose needs and capacities drive much of the interaction in the triad. It is essential to recognize that every head injury is different. Consequently, levels of functional capacity and dependency vary dramatically among persons with head injury. Head-injured persons range from totally dependent to fully independent. Furthermore, some head-injured persons have a supportive family, and some have no family; some are employable, and some are not; some have access to financial resources, and some have no resources. Therefore, the extent to which individuals must rely on family and society for support depends largely on their personal conditions and socioeconomic circumstances.

One problem in attempting to fix responsibility for the lifelong well-being of a person with a head injury is our propensity to evaluate responsibility from the vantage of a single point in time. There is a tendency to view the needs and capacities of the head-injured individual as static once the rehabilitation process is largely completed. Although we often anticipate some improved functioning, we do not view the individual's life as a developmental process. Thus one reason for the inherently unstable nature of the triad is that changes occur in the life of the person with a head injury that are not recognized by the other two elements of the triad. For example, a head-injured person whose memory deteriorates significantly over time may not be able to receive the additional assistance he or she needs because the family and society assumed that his or her condition would remain constant.

The Family

In American political discourse, there is currently much discussion about the family as the social unit that is most appropriate to meet certain specific needs of individuals and the one that is most essential to creating greater stability in society. In such discourse, the family often is described as if all families were similar and as if everyone shared a common conception of who or what makes up a family. Although many acknowledge that the character of the American family has changed considerably over the past three decades, many also still ascribe to a single conception of the family's capacity to meet the needs of its individual members.

Persons toward the right of the American political spectrum look to the family as the last bastion of key moral values that have been eroded by a permissive society and a liberal welfare state. Persons toward the left of the political spectrum look to the family as the last hope for a caring social order that has been undermined by an indifferent society and a deficit-ridden government. The fallout from both views is that our collective expectation of what the family can and should do has increased at a time when its capacities have at best remained constant (and probably have decreased).

Families of head-injured persons often have internalized these expectations, even when such expectations may not be realistic, given the overwhelming needs of a family member with a head injury and the diminishing capacities of many families. These expectations create a strong and often unfair presumption about what a family should and can do on behalf of members with a severe head injury. When considering the responsibility of families to address the lifelong well-being of a person with a head injury, it is important to consider the family's caregiving capacities, the family's financial capacities, and certain moral and legal issues.

Caregiving Capacities

A family's caregiving capacities are influenced strongly by living arrangements, the availability of caregivers, competing responsibilities for caregiving, the value systems and motivation of individual family members, and many other factors. These factors are largely subjective and difficult to assess. When considering the lifelong well-being of a family member with a head injury, we also must consider that these factors change over time. Members of the family grow older, siblings move out, members make career decisions, parents sometimes divorce, parents retire, and members die. Families have life cycles, as do individuals. The ever-changing character of the American family makes it difficult to evaluate family caregiving capacity; trying to assess it is like aiming at a moving and sometimes unpredictable target.

Financial Capacities

The costs of medical care, personal care, supervision, residential care, and respite care for a person with a head injury can quickly exhaust the financial capacities of even the most prosperous families. Such costs have been estimated at approximately $4.5 million over the life span of a person with a severe head injury (NHIF, 1988). A family's financial capacity to pay such expenses is, like its caregiving capacity, difficult to assess and likely to change over time. Earnings and family financial obligations change, as do myriad other factors. A monetary settlement or judgment in a court case against a person or organization that caused an injury often means the difference between a family's capacity or incapacity to meet its financial obligations. In the absence of such extensive resources or an insurance policy that pays such costs, the family may have no choice but to impoverish itself in the attempt to meet the eligibility requirements for Medicaid [which, depending on the family's state of residence, may or may not cover many of the expenses (Batavia, 1989)].

Moral and Legal Considerations

In addition to evaluating the financial and caregiving capacities of families with a head-injured member, we also need to address the larger issue of whether families in fact have a moral and legal obligation to provide for the well-being of a family member with a head injury. In American society, the nuclear family is accepted as the unit within which support obligations prevail. When children reach the age of majority and begin to raise families of their own, parents' legal obligations to their adult sons and daughters generally cease. [However, this is not always the case. Some states have imposed a legal obligation on a family to pay for the institutionalization of an adult child with mental retardation (Dept. of Mental Health v. Coty, 1967)]. Moreover, many adults feel that they have a moral obligation to support their aging parents (DeJong, 1982). Thus once a child becomes an adult there often is a moral presumption that caregiving obligations will be reversed.

A difficulty in assessing moral and legal responsibilities with respect to head injury is that head injuries often occur when people are within a few years (on either side) of the age of majority, a time during which moral and legal obligations relative to the person's family of origin are being redefined. Most states currently do not impose a legal obligation on families with an adult son or daughter with a head injury. This obligation, when assumed by the family of origin, is often assumed in the absence of any meaningful alternative.

An even more difficult issue than whether the family currently has a moral or legal responsibility is whether the family *should* have such a responsibility—that is, the issue of fairness. Apart from the assistance that may be available from health insurance or a liability judgment or settlement, should a family have to divert resources earmarked for the education of other family members to meet the needs of a family member with a head injury? Should a family have to impoverish itself to qualify for some form of public assistance? Should a parent have to forgo employment opportunities to meet the extensive personal care needs of a head-injured child? These types of issues are addressed below.

Society

As family capacities are exhausted, the focus moves to the third leg of the triad: society. The attractiveness of society in the triadic model is its ability to spread across a broad population base both the financial risk and the burden of care associated with a severe head injury. Society is able to spread financial risk by taxation and by the mandatory collection of insurance premiums (e.g., health insurance, automobile insurance, workers' compensation, and liability insurance), which is in many respects simply a form of taxation by another name. Society is able to spread the burden of care by using its tax revenues to support the provision of services such as medical care, residential care, and various in-home care services.

Society's financial and caregiving capacities for persons with head injury are limited mainly because American society has chosen through its political process not to meet the new obligations that result from its successes in saving and extending lives. During the past 10 years, the American political climate has turned away from the needs of many of its most vulnerable citizens. American society has not recognized that the political decision to invest massively in medical care and state-of-the-art medical technologies brings with it a moral obligation to care for the people who survive with disabilities as a result of such life-saving interventions. Such an obligation is so substantial in monetary terms that there is little choice in a just society but to spread the financial costs and burdens across society as a whole.

When the burdens and costs otherwise assumed by individuals and families are socialized, however, they also tend to be professionalized. For example, when society assumes responsibility for some of the caregiving services otherwise provided by family members, it expects these services to meet certain standards and to be rendered by trained and competent providers such as home health agencies. These expectations create escalating demands for administration and for highly trained and credentialed personnel. Services rendered by such professionals are relatively expensive and can quickly exhaust society's financial capacities. Moreover, society expects a risk-free system of service delivery, which requires multiple safeguards from abuse and fraud. Although such requirements often are justified, they sometimes do more to serve the interest of professionals and providers than the interests of individuals and families who need these services.

Rehabilitation service programs for persons with head injury have not been immune to the ever-escalating demands for professionalization. These demands are reflected in the standards set by accrediting bodies, in the minimum education credentials and certification requirements of professional organizations, and in the demands for accountability set by third party payers. Continued escalation of professionalization and its associated costs may eventually threaten society's ability to meet its obligations to address the rehabilitative needs of persons with severe head injuries. Society may have to turn to less costly providers to meet its obligations. Whether quality of care would deteriorate under such circumstances depends largely on the nature of the service being provided and the ability of the head-injured consumer (or consumer's representative) to monitor and scrutinize quality.

HOW SHOULD RESPONSIBILITY FOR LIFELONG WELL-BEING BE DISTRIBUTED?

Responsibility for the lifelong well-being of a person with a severe head injury is not the sole responsibility of any one entity in the triadic model. Instead, as we have suggested thus far, the real issue is how the responsibility can be distributed fairly

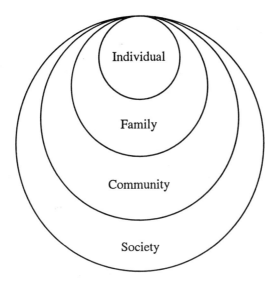

Figure 24.2   Circle of responsibility.

in terms of its burdens and wisely in terms of its potential to further the head-injured person's residual capacities for autonomy and self-direction. As indicated earlier, the concept of an unstable triad is useful in describing how responsibility is presently distributed but is not adequate in attempting to develop a more satisfactory conception of how responsibility for lifelong well-being could or should be distributed.

An alternative to the triad is a model in which the individual with a head injury is placed conceptually in the center of a series of concentric circles representing the family, the community, and society (Figure 24.2). The missing link in the triadic model is the concept of community. By *community* we mean the whole network of friendships, schools, religious organizations, self-help groups, and various business and civic organizations that could conceivably interact directly with the individual and the family in a time of hardship or emergency. Society, as we conceive it here, is more distant and impersonal than community. As implied above, society includes government, third party payers, and other entities that typically intervene indirectly for the collective well-being of individuals, families and communities.

The Role of the Community

Inherently, the line between community and society is a hazy one: Both are collective entities with the purported goal of furthering the broader public interest. A

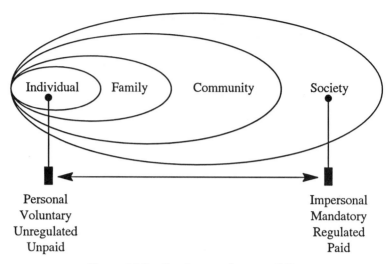

Figure 24.3   Continuum of responsibility.

clear delineation between community and society, however, is not essential for the purpose of determining the most appropriate allocation of responsibility for persons with head injury. However, as a modification of our concentric circle model, we might conceive of a continuum ranging from the individual at the center to the family to various entities whose interests range from the narrowest interests of the community to the broadest interests of society. As depicted in Figure 24.3, activities conducted by those near the center of the circle tend to be more personal, voluntary, and unregulated. Activities conducted by those near the outer portions of the circle tend to be less personal, less voluntary, and more regulated.

Thus, more important than a clear delineation between community and society is the conceptual recognition of an intermediate communal entity (or group of entities) between the highly personalized family and the highly impersonalized society that can provide supplemental assistance in situations that neither the family nor society is well equipped to handle. For example, provision of respite care cannot be addressed by the family, which needs temporary relief from the situation, nor by society, which typically is too removed from the situation to provide humane care. Respite care, and other services such as grocery shopping and housekeeping, may be provided effectively by members of the community.

Currently in distributing responsibility for the lifelong well-being of persons with head injury, we tend to assign responsibility toward either the center or the outer portions of Figure 24.2. The community, as conceived in this model, has thus far played only a small role in meeting the needs of persons with head injury. Although the community may have no enforceable moral or legal obligation to meet the lifelong needs of a person with a head injury, the notion of community is essential to avoid exhausting the capacities of either the family or society.

Because the community in the concentric circle model serves only as a supplement to the resources of the three other entities, issues concerning resources and accountability of the community are far less important than they are for the other entities. The community's resources would derive largely from voluntary financial and in-kind contributions in the community. Because the services provided by the community are voluntary, there is no need to ensure political accountability that community services will be provided. Accountability for the safety of those services that are provided voluntarily by the community would be ensured through the legal system. It should be noted that to encourage voluntary community service a few state jurisdictions have considered imposing a slightly less stringent legal duty of care for volunteers than for nonvolunteers.

The Need to Develop the Community Sector

The main problem with the concentric circle model is that the community sector is not well developed in American life; it is largely supported by philanthropic giving and by voluntary associations. Many commentators on American life have observed that Americans have a great propensity to join groups and to form voluntary associations. Compared to many other nationalities, however, Americans remain relatively individualistic in their outlook and behavior. We have a limited sense of shared community well-being beyond the schools to which we send our children, the churches and synagogues that some of us attend, and the financial contributions that we make to charities. Communal responsibility, when it does exist, tends to be shallow and often does not extend much beyond a narrowly defined set of individual, family, and professional interests.

If the needs of persons with severe head injury are to be met more fully, the community sector will need to be strengthened from both sides (i.e., from both the family and society). The family can contribute by becoming more actively involved in community interests and by offering its services to assist community members who are experiencing hardship. Such involvement already occurs predictably in cases of extreme short-term emergencies such as fires, earthquakes, and other disasters. However, it does not occur sufficiently to address cases of ongoing hardships. There also is much that society, through government intervention, can do to support and strengthen the community sector in American life. Informed public policy at the federal, state, and local levels can do much to boost limited community resources and thereby to encourage community sector growth and development.

The growth and development of the community sector is a goal that is shared by persons along the entire American political spectrum. During the 1988 presidential election, Michael Dukakis used the word *community* rather than *society* many times in discussing the resolution of societal problems such as drug addiction. President George Bush's much-maligned phrase "a thousand points of light" similarly reflects the concept of community as a means to address societal problems. Both were making an appeal beyond mere philanthropy and were groping for a new vision of the community sector in American life. Neither candidate was able to articulate clearly how public policy might strengthen the community sector.

The Need for Surrogacy

One of the most encouraging developments in the community sector of American life is the growth of the self-help movement, a movement in which vulnerable groups have improved their living conditions through their capacities for self-direction and independent living. Through such self-help, persons with disabilities including cerebral palsy, muscular dystrophy, spinal cord injury, and postpolio (to name a few) have realized their potential to live independently and have diminished their need for professional intervention. At the core of the self-help model is the assumption, often negated in the professional-client relationship, that the individual has the capacity for self-direction and decision making. The cognitive impairments associated with severe head injury often challenge this assumption.

If the self-help movement has been essential to the strengthening of the community sector, how can the concept of self-help be made to work on behalf of persons with head injury whose capacities for self-direction are diminished? One promising approach to self-help for head-injured persons is through surrogacy, in which another individual (or group of individuals) acts as a representative on behalf of a person with a head injury. An embryonic example of surrogacy in the context of the self-help movement was a project undertaken by the Boston Center for Independent Living (BCIL) in the early 1980s to address the needs of persons with mental retardation. BCIL developed the concept of an environmental support manager, a person who at times could act on behalf of a person with a cognitive impairment. The environmental support manager supplemented the decision-making skills of the person with the disability and gradually withdrew as the disabled person acquired increased levels of independence.

The concept of surrogacy also can address the varying capacities of the family as its members grow older and move on. Surrogacy can provide an important buffer and an alternative to lifelong parental direction. Surrogacy sometimes is legalized in the form of guardianship, which often is established as a contingency in the event of the parents' death or incapacity. However, guardianship sometimes is merely an extension of parental wishes, and may not address the developmental needs of the head-injured person to develop an identity apart from his or her parents.

IMPLICATIONS FOR PUBLIC POLICY

One test of a sound public policy is its ability to address the needs of diverse groups in an equitable manner. It is important that a public disability policy be as broadly applicable to persons with a wide variety of disabilities as possible but that it not be so broad as to sacrifice the unique needs of any disability group. Thus a public policy for persons with head injury should be applicable (to the extent possible) to other disability groups, such as persons with cerebral palsy, mental retardation, schizophrenia, spinal cord injury, and various other mental and physical impairments. As noted above, because of the all-encompassing nature of severe head injury it may be seen as a test case for a broad scope of other disabling conditions. Therefore, the following discussion of policy options for head injuries may be generalized to a greater or lesser extent to other severe disabilities.

One of the more vexing problems in American public policy on head injury is the difficulty in measuring objectively the financial and caregiving capacities of individuals, families, communities, and society. Sound public policy requires that financial resources and services be allocated efficiently and equitably relative to need and capacity. Head-injured individuals, their families, their communities, and other institutions in society, however, are so variable that objective and equitable criteria are difficult, if not impossible, to specify.

Despite this, there are certain general recommendations that emerge from our examination of the strengths and weaknesses of each of the components of the concentric circle model of social responsibility for persons with head injury. At one extreme, individuals (insofar as they are able to function cognitively) are in the best position to discern their own needs and should be permitted by family, community, and society to define those needs. When an individual cannot assess his or her own needs, the individual's family or an appointed surrogate typically is in the best position to do so on behalf of the individual. However, it is clear that both the individual and the family actually have only a limited capacity to meet the individual's needs.

Society is in the best position to spread the risks and costs of head injury over a broad population base, but it is in a poor position to provide services or even to ensure that they are provided adequately. Members of the community and professional providers often are in the best position to provide services to the individual. Professional providers should be permitted to provide those services that are beyond the technical capability of the individual or the family to provide. The community should provide those services that the individual and the family have the technical capability to provide but that are beyond their physical, emotional, and financial capacities. The individual (or the family or surrogate) typically is in the best position to evaluate the services provided by professionals and the community to determine whether they adequately meet the individual's needs.

Thus public policy should encourage an allocation of responsibility for persons with head injury according to the strengths and weaknesses of each of the elements of the model: the individual, the family, the community, and society. It should also experiment with alternative forms of surrogacy, including surrogacy that does not extend to full legal guardianship. It will be particularly valuable to test and evaluate the efficacy of various forms of surrogacy to help foster the independent living and self-direction goals of persons with head injury. One important and untapped pool of potential surrogates is the growing community of retired citizens, because such individuals often have the time, resources, and experience to serve as responsible representatives of persons with head injury.

Executive and Legislative Policy

One important public policy implication of the foregoing analysis is that government should find ways to stimulate and strengthen the community sector. This can be achieved by the executive and legislative branches of the federal, state, and local governments through modification of tax codes and through budgetary appropriations to support the costs of organization, training, and exchange of information. This has already been done to a limited extent by the federal government through funding of local independent living centers under Title VII of the Rehabilitation Act of 1973, as amended. Even so, independent living centers are located in relatively few communities, generally operate with limited budgets, and have not focused primarily on the needs of persons with head injury.

Additional support for community organizations to meet the substantial needs of disabled persons is sorely needed. In addition to providing essential financial resources, such assistance by government would make the symbolic statement that community activity is valued by society. One proposed legislative approach that would make such a statement is to develop a national volunteer corps in which young people just out of high school would be obligated to perform volunteer community work (for a small living stipend) for a period of 1 or 2 years. One possible service that such volunteers could perform would be to provide needed assistance to persons with disabilities such as head injury.

Stimulation of the community sector also is an appropriate role for grant makers in the foundation and philanthropic communities. One example of this is a recent initiative by the Robert Wood Johnson Foundation to support community organizations that assist persons with disabilities to live independently. As a matter of public policy, government should provide incentives to the philanthropic community as well as to community groups and self-help organizations to stimulate such community sector programs for persons with disabilities.

The stimulation of the community sector is in the interests of both society and the individual. In an era when budget deficits define the public agenda, full-scale reliance on the societal sector is not a realistic option. For society as a whole, the stimulation of the community sector represents a means by which to reduce the total burden on both the family and society and to provide needed services in a personalized manner. For the individual, community sector involvement is likely to foster the head-injured person's residual capacities for self-direction and independent living.

At the same time, we should not be naive about the capacities of the community sector. The needs of persons with severe head injury are complex and require professional intervention at strategic points during the postinjury period. In contrast to the default position assumed by families in the unstable triad (Figure 24.1), society has to be prepared to accept the default position in the allocation of responsibility for the lifelong well-being of persons with head injury. This default position is implicit in figure 24.2, in which society represents the outer ring and fallback position when the individual, family, and community are unable to cope.

Nevertheless, society's role should not be viewed simply as a residual one. As a matter of public policy, government must take an active role in spreading the risks and costs of head injury and in stimulating the community sector. The spreading of risks and costs is best done through expansion of current social insurance programs and, ideally, through the ultimate development of a national health insurance plan that addresses the needs of all persons, including persons with severe disabilities. Society should thereby ensure at least some minimum level of services and benefits to individuals with head injury and their families. It should not limit its involvement to those cases in which families and communities have exhausted their caregiving and financial capacities.

Judicial Policy

As a matter of judicial policy, the financial burden of head injury should be distributed equitably by the courts. Too often, judges and juries award compensatory damage awards (for the costs of compensating the plaintiff for medical expenses, lost work, and pain and suffering) that do not reflect the truly astronomical costs of a head injury. As indicated above, the lifetime costs of a person with severe head injury include the costs of acute medical care, acute rehabilitation, extended rehabilitation, and residential care and are estimated to be approximately $4.5 million (NHIF, 1988).

In cases in which the defendant was reckless or willful in inflicting a head injury as opposed to being simply negligent, the plaintiff should be awarded substantial punitive damages (in excess of compensatory damages) to punish the defendant. Although punitive damages are awarded currently, too often the amount of damages (or an out-of-court settlement) is severely limited. Although this may protect the defendant from impoverishment, it often impoverishes the person who was injured negligently, recklessly, or intentionally. Punitive damages should be awarded in an amount that is sufficient to deter other members of society from engaging in reckless or malicious conduct and should not be unduly limited.

CONCLUSION

The issues before us promise to become more difficult in the years to come as the lifelong needs of a growing head-injured population clash with the limits of family and societal resources. This is one reason why we encourage the nurturing of the currently underdeveloped community sector as a supplement to the resources of the individual, the family, and society. Ultimately, our society's ability to meet the needs of persons with head injury and their families will depend largely on its willingness to spread financial risks across the broad population and on its ability to foster a sense of community and a belief in the importance of mutual obligation. Responsibility for the lifelong well-being of a person with a head injury needs to be perceived as a responsibility to be shared by all sectors.

If the responsibility for persons with head injury were truly a shared obligation, the perceived burden of everyday caring by families would lighten substantially while the increased burden on the community and society would remain manageable. Families of head-injured persons would be strengthened simply by the knowledge that they are not alone and that others are available to assist in meeting the lifelong needs of their family members with head injury. Members of the community and society would be comforted by the knowledge that if they, or one of their loved ones, sustain and survive a serious head injury—a prospect that is not unlikely—they will not face the same nightmare as those who preceded them.

REFERENCES

Batavia AI. *The Payors of Medical Rehabilitation: Eligibility, Coverage and Payment Policies.* Washington, DC: National Association of Rehabilitation Facilities 1989.

DeJong G. Independent living: From social movement to analytic paradigm. *Arch Phys Med Rehabil.* 1979 60:435–446.

DeJong G. *Environmental Accessibility and Independent Living Outcomes: Directions for Disability Policy and Research.* East Lansing, Mich: University Center for International Rehabilitation, Michigan State University 1981.

DeJong G. A legal perspective on disability, homecare and relative responsibility. *Home Health Care Serv Q.* 1982 3:148–160.

DeJong G, Batavia A. Societal duty and resource allocation for persons with severe traumatic brain injury. *J. Head Trauma Rehabil.* 1989 4(1):1–12.

DeJong G, Wenker T. Attendant care as a prototype independent living service. *Caring.* 1983 2:26–30.

Department of Mental Health v. Coty, 38 Ill. 2d 602, 232 NE2d 686 (1967).

Frankowski RF, Annegers JF, Whitman S. Epidemiological and descriptive studies, part I: The descriptive epidemiology of head trauma in the United States. In: Becker DP, Povlishock JT, eds. *Central Nervous System Trauma Status Report.* Baltimore: National Institute of Health 1985:33–44.

Kalsbeek WD, McLaurin RL, Harris BSH III, et al. The National Head and Spinal Cord Injury Survey: Major findings. *J. Neurosurg.* 1980 53:S19–S31.

Kraus JF. A comparison of recent studies on the extent of the head and spinal cord injury problem in the United States. *J. Neurosurg.* 1980 53:S35–S43

National Head Injury Foundation. *The Silent Epidemic.* Southboro, Mass: National Head Injury Foundation: 1988.

National Head Injury Foundation. *Traumatic Head Injury: A Review of Gaps and Problems in Insurance Coverages.* Southboro, Mass: National Head Injury Foundation Insurance Committee 1988.

Perlman P, Giele JZ. An unstable triad: Dependents' demands, family resources, community supports. *Home Health Serv Q.* 1982 3:12–44.

25

Aging and Disability: Toward a Unified Agenda

Irving Kenneth Zola

People who age and people with disabilities have traditionally been split into opposing camps in the eyes of both providers of service as well as their own self-perceptions.

An exclusively special needs approach to either group is inevitably a short-run approach. What we need are more universal policies that recognize that the entire population is "at risk" for the concomitants of chronic illness and disability. Without such a perspective we will further create and perpetuate a segregated, separate but unequal society—a society inappropriate to a larger and older "changing needs" population. It is, however, in the nature of this historical moment that such a change in perspective must take the form of a corrective—a reorientation of the general thinking about disability (Milio, 1981).

Two bases for such a reorientation underlie this chapter. The problems of disability are not confined to any small fixed number of the population. And the issues facing someone with a disability are not essentially medical (Hahn, 1984, 1985; Zola, 1982). They are not purely the result of some physical or mental impairment but rather of the fit of such impairments with the social, attitudinal, architectural, medical, economic, and political environment.

NUMBERS: HOW BIG A PROBLEM IS DISABILITY?

Whether the unit of study be a city, a state, or a country, it is generally estimated that one out of eight people has a disability (National Center for Health Statistics, 1982; Office of Technology Assessment, 1982). Those numbers themselves would be of concern (e.g., 36–40 million people in the United States); but cast as a ratio, the numbers still convey the notion of a statistical minority. Thus a major concern is whether or not such figures are likely to increase (Colvez & Blanchet, 1981).

Recent declines in various mortality statistics (e.g., the total death rate, infant and maternity mortality, condition-specific death rates), increases in life expectancy at birth, and remaining years of life at various later ages cause many to claim that our nation's health is improving. Time series studies of chronic illness and disability, however, provide a different and less optimistic picture.

When Wilson and Drury (1984) reviewed the twenty-year trends (1960–1981) in fifteen broad categories of chronic illness in the United States, they found that the prevalence of seven conditions had more than doubled; two had increased their prevalence from 50 to 99%; five had increased by up to 50%; and only one condition had become less prevalent. The so-called "graying" of the population did not explain this as a similar pattern was observed for persons 45–64. For this latter group—the core of the workforce—chronic conditions translated into activity limitation with a more than doubling (from 4.4% to 10.8%) of the number of males who claimed they were unable to work because of illness or disability.

Looking at two subsets—the young and the old—is particularly instructive. While the absolute number of children (under 17) is not expected to increase, the proportion of those with a disability will. The United States National Health Interview Survey (Newacheck, Budetti, & Halfon, 1986) indicates that the prevalence of activity-limiting chronic conditions among children doubled between 1960 and 1981 from 1.8% to 3.8% with the greatest increase in the last decade. While much of this may be due to the survival of lower-weight newborns with various impairments, the major increase may well be due to shifting perceptions on the part of parents, educators, and physicians where changing educational concerns are making learning disabilities (e.g., dyslexia, etc.) the fastest growing disability in the country (Faigel, 1985). What new learning disabilities will be discovered when computer literacy becomes a *sine qua non* for success in contemporary society is anybody's guess.

All census data affirm that the fastest growing segment of the U.S. population is those over 65. In 1880 they numbered fewer than 2 million (3%) of the total population but by 1980 it was over 25 million (11.3%). By the year 2030 an estimated 20 to 25% of citizens is likely to be over 65 (Gilford, 1988). Put another way, throughout most of history only one in ten people lived past 65; now nearly 80% do. This traditional use of 65 as a benchmark, however, is deceptive, for the most phenomenal growth will occur in the even older age groups, those over 85. Individuals over 85 constituted 1% of the total population in 1980, but are projected to reach 3% in 2030 and over 5% in 2050. By then they could be nearly a quarter of all elderly people (Gilford, 1988). The service implications are worth noting. For while 3–5% of those 65–74 require assistance in basic activities of daily living, over one-third do so by age 85 (Feinstein, Gornick, & Greenberg, 1984; National Center for Health Statistics, 1983). Thus no matter how it is defined or measured the number of people in the United States with conditions that interfere with their full participation in society will inevitably increase.

NATURE: IS DISABILITY THE SAME AS IT ALWAYS WAS?

For years infant mortality has steadily decreased, in large part because of improvements in standards of living and prenatal care. Recently, these improvements have been supplemented by advances in the specialization of neonatology. Though the numbers are as yet small, it is clear that there are increasing numbers of low birth weight and other infants surviving into childhood and beyond with manifest chronic impairments. With advances in medical therapeutics, many children who would have died (from leukemia to spina bifida to cystic fibrosis) are now surviving into adulthood or longer. Diagnostic advances, as well as some life-extending technologies, allow many young people to survive with so-called "terminal" illnesses.

There is a similar trend evident in the young adult group. While trauma still continues to be a major cause of mortality in this group, there is a major turnaround in the survival rates of people with spinal cord injuries. As recently as the 1950s, death was likely in the very early stages or soon after because of respiratory and other complications. Thus in World War I only 400 men with wounds that paralyzed them from the waist down survived *at all*, and 90% of them died before they reached home. In World War II, 2000 paraplegics lived and 1,700—over 85% of them—were still alive in the late 1960s (President's Committee on the Employment of the Handicapped, 1967). Each decade since has seen a rapid decline in the death rate and thus of long-term survival—first of those with paraplegia, then with quadriplegia, and, now in the 1980s, those with head injuries.

At the moment, the situation with the older population may seem less predictable. At the very least, we can speculate that an aging population will be even more "at risk" for what were once thought "natural" occurrences (e.g., decreases in mobility, visual acuity, hearing) and with other musculoskeletal, cardiovascular, and cerebrovascular changes whose implications are only beginning to be appreciated.

Still another unappreciated aspect of most chronic conditions is that although permanent, they are not necessarily static. While we do, of course, recognize at least in terminology that some diseases are "progressive," we are less inclined to see that there is no one-time, overall adaptation/adjustment to the condition. Even for a recognized progressive or episodic disorder, such as multiple sclerosis, attention only recently has been given to the continuing nature of adaptations (Brooks & Matson, 1987). The same is also true for those with end-stage renal disease (Gerhardt & Brieskorn-Zinke, 1986). With the survival into adulthood of people with diseases that once were fatal come new changes and complications. Problems of circulation and vision for people with diabetes, for example, may be due to the disease itself, the aging process, or even the original life-sustaining treatment (Turk & Speers, 1983). Ivan Illich (1976) in particular has drawn public attention to the iatrogenic costs of many medical interventions—costs that may show up only after many years, as one ages, or all too frequently in subsequent generations.

Perhaps the most telling example of a new manifestation of an old disease is the current concern over the so-called post-polio syndrome (Laurie & Raymond, 1984). To most of the public, to clinicians, and certainly to its bearers, polio has been considered a stable chronic illness. Following its acute onset and a period of rehabilitation, most people had reached a plateau and expected to stay there. For the majority, this may still be true, but for at least a quarter, it is not. Large numbers of people are experiencing new problems some 20–40 years after the original onset. The most common are fatigue, weakness in muscles previously affected and unaffected, muscle and joint pain, breathing difficulties, and intolerance to cold. Whether these new problems are the mere concomitant of aging, the reemergence of a still lingering virus, a long-term effect of the early damage or even of the early rehabilitation programs, or something else, is still at issue (Halstead & Wiechers, 1985). Whatever the etiology of this phenomenon, there will likely be many more new manifestations of old diseases and disabilities as people survive decades beyond the acute onset of their original diseases or disabilities (Funne, Gingher, & Olsen, 1989; Sato, 1989). Thus, the dichotomy between those people with a "progressive" condition versus those with a "static" one may well be, generally speaking, less distinct than once thought and indeed be more of a continuum.

Still another source of change is the fit between any impairment and the larger social environment. Simply put, some physical differences become important only in certain social situations (reading and writing difficulties where literacy or speed in literacy is deemed "essential" to success or mobility impairments in a sports-oriented society) or at certain times of life (sexual and reproductive issues are less important for the very young and the very old, and some for only one gender). The life-cycle theorists are quite aware of this and postulate different issues one must contend with and the resulting disablements if one does not. Yet, many of these theories and the resulting social policies are locked into a grid where the "final" stage of life begins around age 65. This might have been at least logical when the general lifespan was much shorter; then, each stage took about ten years (i.e., the seven stages of "man" covering three score plus ten). But what does it imply when the "last" stage is "occupied" primarily by women (Doress & Siegal, 1987) and continues far beyond a decade, with some (Gilford, 1988) estimating it could reach forty years or more. Surely neither society in general nor the individuals involved will tolerate one stage of life that covers nearly half of the lifespan. Later life is clearly an uncharted map that will inevitably bring new challenges requiring different capacities and evaluations (Katz et al., 1983) but also involving new diseases, problems, and disabilities.

CONCLUSION

While building bridges across constituencies is never an easy one, two final considerations, the empirical and the evaluative, make this coalition an overarching necessity. Empirically, we need to remember these facts: barring sudden death, those who are aging and those who have a disability can be only artificially separated at a particular moment in time. For except the possibility of sudden death, everyone with a disability will age, and everyone who is aging will acquire one or more disabilities. As for the evaluative component, the words of Erik Erikson (1964, p. 131) proclaim it: "Any span of the life cycle lived without vigorous meaning at the beginning, in the middle, or at the end endangers the sense of life and the meaning of death in all whose life stages are intertwined."

REFERENCES

Borgatta, Edgar F. and Montgomery, Rhonda J. (Eds.). *Critical Issues in Aging Policy—Linking Research and Values.* Newburg Park, CA: Sage Publishers, 1987.

Brooks, N. and R. Matson, 1987. Managing Multiple Sclerosis. In *Experience and Management of Chronic Illness.* ed. J. Roth and P. Conrad, 73-106. Greenwich: JAI Press.

Colvez, A. and M. Blanchet. 1981. Disability Trends in the United States Population 1966-76: Analysis of Reported Causes. *American Journal of Public Health* 71:464-471.

Doress, P. B. and Siegal, D. L. (1987). *Ourselves growing older: Women aging with knowledge and power.* New York: Simon & Schuster.

Erikson, Erik H. *Insight and Responsibility.* New York: W. W. Horton, 1964.

Faigel, Harris, "When the Learning Disabled Go to College," *Journal of American College Health,* Vol. 43, August 1985, pp. 18-22.

Feinstein, Patrice Hirsch, Gornick, Marian and Greenberg, Jay N. (Eds.), "The Need for New Approaches in Long-Term Care," in Feinstein, Patrice Hirsch, Gornick, Marian and Greenberg, Jay N. (Eds.). *Long-Term Care Financing and Delivery Systems: Exploring Some Alternatives,* Conference Proceedings, January 24, 1984, Washington, DC: Health Care Financing Administration, June 1984.

Funne, K. B., and N. Gingher, and L. M. Olsen. 1989. *A Survey of the Medical and Functional Status of Members of the Adult Network of the Spina Bifida Association of America.* Spina Bifida Association of America. Rockville, Maryland.

Gerhardt, U. and M. Brieskorn-Zinke. 1986. Normalization of Hemodialysis at Home. In *The Adoption and Social Consequences of Medical Technologies.* ed. J. Roth and S. B. Ruzek, 4:271-317. Greenwich: JAI Press.

Gilford, D. M. ed. 1988. *The Aging Population in the Twenty-First Century: Statistics for Health Policy.* Washington, D.C.: National Academy Press.

Hahn, H. 1984. *The Issue of Equality: European Perceptions of Employment for Disabled Persons.* World Rehabilitation Fund monograph no. 24, New York.

Hahn, H. 1985. Disability Policy and the Problem of Discrimination. *American Behavioral Scientist* 28:293-318.

Halstead, L. S. and D. Wiechers. 1985. *Late Effects of Poliomyelitis.* New York: Symposia Foundation.

Illich, I. 1976. *Medical Nemesis.* New York: Pantheon.

Katz, J. 1984. *The Silent World of Doctors and Patients.* New York: The Free Press.

Katz, S., L. G. Branch, M. H. Branson, J. A. Papsidero, J. L. Beck, and D. S. Greer. 1983. Active Life Expectancy. *New England Journal of Medicine* 309: 1218-1224.

Laurie, G. and J. Raymond ed. 1984. *Proceedings of Rehabilitation Gazette's 2nd International Post-Polio Conference and Symposium on Living Independently with Severe Disability.* Gazette International Networking Institute, St. Louis, Missouri.

Milio, N. 1981. *Promoting Health Through Public Policy.* Philadelphia: F. A. Davis.

National Center for Health Statistics. 1983. *Americans Needing Help to Function at Home.* Public Health Service Advance Data No. 92, Department of Health and Human Services pub. no. 83-1250. Washington, D.C.

National Center of Health Services. 1982. *National Health Survey*. Department of Health and Human Services Series 10, no. 146. Washington, D.C.

Newacheck, P. W., P. P. Budetti, and N. Halfon. 1986. Trends in Activity-Limiting Chronic Conditions Among Children. *American Journal of Public Health* 76:178–183.

Office of Technology Assessment, Congress of the United States. 1982. *Technology and Handicapped People*. 11. Office of Technology Assessment. Washington, D.C.

President's Committee on Employment of the Handicapped. 1967. *Designs for All Americans*, 5. President's Committee on Employment of the Handicapped. Washington, D.C.

Sato, H. 1989. Secondary Disabilities of Adults with Cerebral Palsy in Japan. *Disability Studies Quarterly* 9:14.

Turk, D. C., and M. A. Speers. 1983. Diabetes: Mellitus: A Cognitive-Functional Analysis of Stress. In *Coping with Chronic Disease*. ed. T. G. Burish and L. A. Bradley, 191–217. New York: Academic Press.

Wilson, R. and T. Drury. 1984. Interpreting Trends in Illness and Disability. *Annual Review of Public Health* 5:83–106.

Zola, Irving Kenneth, "Medicine as an Institution of Social Control," *Sociological Review*, vol. 20, No. 4, November 1972, pp. 487–504.

Zola, Irving Kenneth. 1982. *Missing Pieces: A Chronicle of Living with a Disability*. Philadelphia: Temple University Press.

26

Families as Caregivers: The Limits of Morality

Daniel Callahan

How are we to understand and live our lives when the moral demands made on us require more than we can give, more than we can make any sense of, and—in our society at least—more than commands much respect and admiration? I raise this disturbing question in the context of a developing trend to return to families and the home the long-term care of the chronically ill and those in need of rehabilitation (Ackford, 1979). The assumption behind the promotion of this trend is that families will, with some modest degree of social support, be able practically to manage such care, and have the moral, psychologic, and spiritual strength to do so.

But is that true? Family care can be a mutually rewarding experience for those who are cared for and those who do the caring, a source of growth and mutual enrichment. The demands it makes can be strenuous and of a kind requiring a new self-understanding for both patient and family; and that can be the occasion of fresh strength and moral achievement (Brody, 1985). But it can also be an occasion of oppression and hostility; the caregiver is often trapped in a way of life not chosen and a future direction not of his or her own. Our secular morality (although perhaps not our religious traditions) provides few resources for living lives of unchosen obligations, those that through mischance lay upon us overwhelming demands to give our life over to the happiness and welfare of someone else.

The idea of a fresh emphasis on family support is both ironic and appealing. Part of the ideology behind medical and technologic progress is that of freeing human life from the inexorability of bodily decay and disability and, at the same time, from the uninvited and smothering social burdens they impose on our individual and communal life. It is then ironic that that progress should lead us back to embracing just those same burdens.

The more understandable and seductive impetus behind this trend is that of the financial pressure occasioned by the growing social burden of disability. An ever-growing proportion of people are kept alive for an ever-longer period of time—but at the price of ever-extended care and rehabilitation to insure their continuing survival and well-being. The full provision of such care by government funds or institutions promises to be insupportable. Too many people need too much care. What is to be done? The popular answer is to widen the scope and acceptability of family care, as a less expensive solution. A supporting motive is a widespread belief that family care is superior care, more kindly and sensitive, more acutely attuned to the needs of individuals, and more compatible with traditional values, notably those of kinship and family integrity.

What kind of moral resources are necessary to carry out such a policy? On the basis of what ethical foundations can society ask people to take on the often heavy, sometimes overwhelming, care of another? Even if people are willing in principle to care for a fellow family member, where can they personally find the necessary moral resources to sustain their commitment, to make moral sense of it? If they can solve that problem, how will society honor and help them, and how will it provide a social meaning to complement and reinforce whatever individual meaning they may bring to bear?

A basic premise of medical progress, and the modernism of which it is a part, is that we need not bow down to the raw deliverances of nature; and one of those deliverances is the way illness makes us a burden upon each other, needy and dependent. Medicine has sought to find a means of liberation from that affliction no less than from the more direct afflictions of the body. But how far are we justified in going to escape the burden that the illness of another can impose on us, and does the fact that the illness may go on much longer than in the past make any difference in thinking about our moral obligations?

It is difficult to find an adequate answer to the question of what we owe each other in times of stress and crisis, and all the more so when the demands made upon us seem to deeply threaten our own happiness and fulfillment. We moralize readily enough about keeping our promises, honoring our commitments, and respecting our contracts. But if doing so begins to threaten our psychologic survival, our basic social freedom, our otherwise legitimate private hopes and plans, then only the most well-rooted, the most cogent reasons, and compelling emotions are likely to sustain us. That goal is not easy in our society. We lack as a people common vision of the wellsprings of moral obligation, a shared understanding of the moral significance of pain and suffering, a clear notion of how we ought to support each other's private griefs and burdens. Nor do we strongly encourage those personal virtues and character traits that enable people to endure in the face of adversity.

The instinct for survival is well imbedded in modern morality (Mailick, 1979). Social morality has become cagey, ready enough to invoke firm rules and principles. Racism, sexism, religious or ethnic discrimination, we well know, admit of no moral wheeling and dealing, no compromise or accommodation. Matters are otherwise with personal morality, where autonomy, choice, survival, and realistic coping are honored—and therapeutic sages well paid to help us escape being trapped in moral corners. After all, what is the point of life if one cannot pursue happiness and have some chance of finding it?

Moreover, quite apart from cultural support, it is an old and hard moral question to know what we should make of demands for self-sacrifice. Most moral rules have common sense and practicality to commend them. Murder, lying, and theft ordinarily have tangibly bad consequences for those who commit such acts. Even our self-interest commends us to avoid them. Matters are otherwise when we are morally asked to give up our lives, or personal hopes, for the sake of another. Only under special circumstances can that seem to make any sense at all from the viewpoint of self-interest, even of the most benign sort. It is not for nothing that almost all Western moralities have been careful to distinguish between duty and supererogation (Urmson, 1958). They all recognize that a morality designed to apply to a whole community cannot require that everyone be a saint or a selfless paragon of altruism. The notion that we might, as a matter of social policy, burden families with the heroic duty of caring for the chronically ill or those in need of a course of rehabilitation that may fail and render them chronically ill or disabled, ought at least to raise a red flag of warning.

What can we realistically ask of people? What can they realistically ask of themselves? If we have an obligation to care for each other as family members when the need arises, what are the limits of that obligation? If it is perhaps reasonable to demand by means of persuasion and social pressure that we discharge our obligations toward our family members, it may not be equally reasonable to always give those obligations legal sanction. Indeed, wisdom might suggest that we make such obligations morally attractive rather than coercive, if only for the sake of those fated to receive the care (who may be presumed to prefer care graciously, rather than grudgingly, given). We need to discover not only what might be morally required, but where the borderline of duty ends. We need also to discover, if possible, how we are to make that duty emotionally satisfying; that is, how to make it productive of meaning and coherence, not of merely arid self-denial and the austere pleasure of doing one's duty for its own sake.

That is by no means an easy task, and it is helpful to look at the realities of family care to understand just how problematic it can be in some circumstances given our present moral resources (Jarrett, 1985). The problem itself is not easy to talk about; it invites undue optimism or undue pessimism. That many families do exceedingly well cannot be denied; both the family and the patient find new personal resources and adapt well. Far from being simply a burden, the patient himself can often make a significant contribution to the family providing the care. That frequent outcome, however, invites an overly optimistic, sometimes rationalizing, attitude; there can be a subtle implication that those who fail to flourish do so because of some character flaw. But it is possible both to recognize that some families and patients do exceedingly well while others, through no apparent fault, find the situation more than they can bear.

I want to put to one side for the moment all those aspects of care that can be satisfying and those circumstances where it works out well enough. I want to focus, instead, on those features of care that impose the sharpest moral demands on the caregiver; in essence, those features that seem to pose a direct and fundamental threat to the welfare and happiness of the person who gives the care, where the caregiver may become—by the sacrifice demanded and extracted—as much a victim of the illness or disability as the person who is cared for.

How might we best think of the moral situation of a family member called on to provide care? Different diseases and conditions modify any general answer, as must different social and familial circumstances. But a common thread is that of a person unfreely and unexpectedly called on to provide a level of care well beyond that ordinarily demanded in family life. I use the term "unfreely" to indicate a lack of initial choice in providing the care. One is drafted by circumstances, and sometimes just as roughly and abruptly as sailors used to be impressed into the British navy. It happens "unexpectedly" in the sense that the family relationship that imposes the moral demand was not originally envisioned as one that would make a radical demand on the self; one feels the victim of capricious and inexplicable bad luck. To marry, as a common vow has it, "for better or for worse, in sickness and in health" suggests that life together may not turn out well; but few actually expect the worst to be realized in marriage. They might well have made another choice had they thought it at all likely. The "worse," then, usually comes as a shock and surprise. That in some cases the person requiring the care is, because of damaging changes wrought by the precipitating accident or illness, no longer the same person as before can only intensify the pain. One is being asked to give of oneself in ways that would otherwise have been unimaginable, and unimaginably unacceptable had it been possible to spell them out in advance.

How do people react to that combination of circumstances? Clearly there are differences between parents caring for a handicapped child, or a young wife caring for a husband recovering from a spinal cord injury, or an elderly husband dealing with the hemodialysis of his wife, or a middle-aged wife helping to rehabilitate a husband struck down by a stroke. Nonetheless, just as those who fall in love, lose a job, or try to cope with the grief of a death will go through many similar feelings even in quite different circumstances, so too there seems to be a striking similarity to the response of caregivers. To be trapped as a caregiver, forced to empty oneself in what is often a one-sided relationship, can be an unendurably great burden. Let me try to sketch a composite portrait of family caregivers [keeping in mind that I am stressing the burdens, not the possible satisfaction (Golodetz, 1969; MacIntyre, 1983; Outka, 1972; Skelton, 1973; Warrington, 1981)].

They are likely, most commonly, to feel anger that an unwanted fate has been visited on them, an anger as often turned inward as toward the person who is ill. Why has this happened to *me*? Will I ever escape? Can anyone possibly understand what this costs me? The anger in turn often generates guilt: sometimes because the anger is aggressively turned toward the ill person—one who may be perfectly blameless but is, nonetheless, the cause of the problem; and sometimes because one feels one has failed oneself, failed by virtue of one's otherwise hidden anger and rebellion, to live up to moral ideals, or to marital commitments, or to what a parent is supposed to owe a child. That others do not notice the failure is beside the point; one's conscience knows and that is enough. One is, at once, on the outside a noble and giving person, gamely and lovingly facing up to adversity; and, on the inside, one who rebels with hostility at the self-giving that is unfairly, even outrageously, demanded. Despite the fact of providing care, the sense of self-worth is severely compromised. Some who suffer in silence and the privacy of their heart come to fear that they will be found out, that as others come to know them better they will be exposed for what they are, not the loving and long-suffering person that appears on the surface, but a petty, self-centered, self-pitying person, full of anger and hostility.

Anger and guilt play on each other, tearing at one's self-image and gnawing away at the bond between the caregiver and the ill person. With great effort, the grosser forms of anger and rebellion can often be brought to heel, only to issue in the slow torture of suffocating irritation and barely repressed irascibility. One lives life on the edge of losing one's temper and one's self-respect.

That such a combination of feelings should on occasion produce fantasies about the death of the ill person is hardly surprising. It is the perfect imaginative solution to the unwanted moral burden of caring for another, at once decisively final in the liberation it promises and utterly acceptable as a social solution. No more ideal a resolution can offer itself to the conscience. But until it happens—and it may not happen for years—the conscience is all the more burdened; it seems almost a form of murder to have such thoughts. But how could one not have them?

If the person cared for were a stranger, matters might be otherwise; some distance would be possible, some saving detachment. In the case of family burdens, what is being drawn upon, and used as a moral noose, is the very love and affection that is supposed to be the mark of such relationships. It is a gross distortion of a bond that is supposed to give us comfort in life. Instead, as a kind of cruel *reductio ad absurdum*, that bond is turned into a yoke that suffocates, making one pay many times over for having hoped for love and joy and having, at one time, perhaps achieved it.

What can it be for a mother—joyous upon the delivery of a child who turns out to be handicapped and requiring great care—to find that she will not have the child she wanted, or the kind of motherhood that is among the more benign of life's aspirations, or the future that had played in her imagination as she waited for her child's birth (Holadays, 1984)? What can it be for the young wife of a stroke victim to find that she must change her ideas of what marriage should be, her ideas of what the social scientists all too coolly call "role expectations" (Carpenter, 1974)? In some cases, the mutuality that was meant to mark their relationship, and at one time actually did so, can barely be recaptured, if at all. Their circle of friends may diminish if her husband cannot negotiate the ordinary demands of a social life; thus to all the other burdens is added that of social isolation. Stigma is sometimes present.

Finally, there is the question of prognosis. Uncertainty of prognosis seems one of the great burdens of rehabilitative care. Will it succeed or will it turn into chronic care? Has the caregiver been sentenced to life imprisonment, or to a short term only? Not knowing the answer to that question can lead to an emotional seesaw of grand proportions, the caregiver tempted one day to see progress in the faintest signs of improvement and no less tempted the next to see no evidence of movement whatever.

At stake here is the possibility of hope. All things may be endurable if the demands are finite in depth and time. But a future that offers no exit at all, even if the burden on a daily basis is not utterly overwhelming, can be an obvious source of sadness and depression. Time is a curious phenomenon in that respect. Our past is always over and gone, and the present transitory and ephemeral. While the wise person is probably someone who knows how to live in and make the most of that transitory present, if the present is unrelenting in its demands, all we have then is our future. No burden can be greater than trying to imagine how one can cope with a future that promises no relief. That is the very meaning of despair and why it is the ultimate human misery. If time is (so it is said) the cure for unrequited love, it might well seem a curse for that requited love that binds us forever to someone as a caregiver.

I have dwelled on some of the details of the moral demands that can be imposed on caregivers because I think it important to understand what is being required of them. Put in the starkest terms, they are being asked by circumstances to sacrifice their selfhood and their own future for the sake of another, and for some undeterminable and possibly interminable period. And they are doing so (at least initially) not because they chose such a fate, but because it was cast on them by virtue of the bonds of love or duty or both. Because at an earlier time they ventured, by a voluntary act, to give of themselves to another, they are now asked to live out some horrible implications of that choice, however unexpected and unwanted they may be. If they do not accept that burden, morality seems to say, they will betray their earlier commitments, and with it, the life of the person who trusted them. If, however, they take up the commitment in its full rigor, they may do so at the cost of their own life and future. Is that fair, and can so much be asked of us?

In trying to deal with that last question, I want first to note what I mean here by moral obligation, and particularly the kind and basis of obligation that seems to present itself in these cases. By moral obligation I mean a justifiable claim made on us to act on behalf of the welfare of another, whether or not so acting is convenient or gratifying; only a higher, more encompassing moral obligation can displace a moral obligation, not claims of unhappiness or inconvenience.

What is the basis of moral obligation in the case of family relationships? It is initially tempting to make many distinctions here. Does it not seem intuitively obvious that there must be some fundamental differences between what a parent owes a child, what a wife owes a husband, what a brother owes a sister, and what a child owes an elderly parent? Should one not distinguish between the kind of contractual relationship that originated a marital bond, and the biologic origins of a parent-child relationship?

Without trying to present a full argument, I want to suggest that the particular nature of the family bond is not nearly so important as a special feature of the relationship. The feature I have in mind is the ultimate neediness and vulnerability of the family member who requires care (Goodin, 1985). The perfect and classical model of such neediness is the dependence of an infant on its parents; its vulnerability is so complete that it cannot even exist unless that is recognized and responded to. But adverse circumstances can make others almost as vulnerable and helpless. It is not necessarily that someone else could not in principle provide the care, just as an anonymous wet nurse can save the life of a hungry child, or a series of hired, indifferent nurses care of the physical needs of an elderly person.

Instead, the important aspect of the vulnerability of ill or injured family members is that they may want and need the kind of care that only someone close to them, an integral part of their lives, can provide. A wife may need her husband, not just any person, to care for her; she is the one who once chose to cast her lot with him and took the trouble over the years to come to know him in a way that is not likely for another. More important, there is no reason why another should care about her welfare as much. What vulnerability most requires is someone who deeply cares, someone who will remain faithful—but faithful to us as a special distinctive person, not as a mere object of moral duty or universal love. All of this is simply to say that at the heart of any significant moral obligation is the vulnerability of another and, in the context of family life and illness, a vulnerability that can only adequately be responded to by a family member. Many exceptions and quibbles can be imagined to qualify that general assertion, but they are not important to my main point.

That point brings me to the heart of the moral problem. If we grant that one family member can desperately need the care of another, and *only* that other can respond to that need in a fully adequate way, does that automatically entail a right (explicit or implicit) on the part of the sick or disabled person to such care, and a corresponding obligation of the family member to provide it? It might at once be responded that even if they initially resist being cared for by those who are not family members, patients can and usually will adapt well enough. Or it might be noted that many of those in need of rehabilitation would prefer to have others provide their physical and health care. I do not want to deny those possibilities, but only want to focus more sharply on those situations where the demands upon family members are not so readily relieved.

I will assume that there is considerable agreement that if the demands are not great or excessive, we do assume the existence of some strong family obligations: parents ought to care for their ill children, husbands for their ill wives, and children for their elderly ill parents. Minimal decency seems to require that (Bluestein, 1982). But the idea of unlimited self-sacrifice encounters heavy, and perhaps increasing, resistance. One line of objection is primarily practical, that if it is true that "ought" implies "can," then the placing of excessively heavy burdens on people is simply unwise. They will collapse under the pressure, and perhaps in the process simply increase the problems of those for whom they are supposed to care. More broadly it could be argued that it would be foolish to advance family care as social policy if the net result would be a sharp increase in divorce, physical and mental abuse, widespread neglect, and other evidence of demands too severe to be widely borne.

I am, however, more interested in noting another line of objection, one that focuses on the morally reasonable demands of self-love and self-interest as a way of establishing the limits of obligation (Urmson, 1958). Contemporary moral philosophers, for instance, show considerable nervousness about extending the scope of moral obligation much beyond explicitly understood and accepted contractual agreements. To count as moral at all, an action must stem from a free choice; autonomy is an underlying requirement. The idea of noncontractual moral obligations thus becomes highly problematic. They violate our autonomy, and they fall into the realm of supererogation, commendable and virtuous and edifying if we freely choose them, but not required in the name of morality. The purpose of drawing such a sharp line is not necessarily to aggrandize the self or lead it into the green pastures of unfettered self-interest. Instead, it stems in great part from the fundamental difficulty philosophers have had in establishing a solid moral basis for involuntary self-sacrifice springing from contextual, not contractual demands. That difficulty stems, I believe, from the essentially individualistic orientation of much contemporary Anglo-American moral philosophy.

Two other intellectual streams offer somewhat different but converging approaches. Feminism has been particularly concerned with combating a culturally reinforced trait of women to all-too-readily embrace self-sacrifice and a selfless life. Since most family caregivers are women, that critique has special importance (Brody, 1985). From another point of departure, Protestant theology since World War II has tried to find a better fit between the central Christian virtue of love of others and the more modern insights into the value and necessity of love of self (Outka, 1972). In particular, it had to take apart the idea that love must, of its nature, be selfless, wholly other-directed. How, many come to ask, can one love another with openness and integrity unless one also loves oneself in some significant way? Can a person who does not love himself love another?

It is far easier to discuss the general problems of moral obligation than to offer specific guidance on setting limits. The most obvious reason is that it is difficult to generalize about the capacity of people to take on heavy moral burdens. Not all people seem equally able to give to others or to be able to greatly affect their emotional capacity to do so, even with the best will in the world. We cannot, therefore, readily establish any set of reasonable expectations of caregivers when heroic, extraordinary caregiving is needed. That kind of caregiving pushes beyond the ordinary bounds of morality.

But that reality suggests a deeper issue about morality itself. Morality in general—but self-sacrificial morality in particular—cannot be sustained by will alone. A presumption of much secular, individualistic morality is that one ought to do one's duty because it is one's duty, and that good reasons for moral behavior are sufficient motivation. One need only make up one's mind to act in a certain way, will to so act, and the actions will follow. But there are too many good-willed but still angry caregivers around to sustain that view. It is psychologically naive. It takes account neither of our emotions (which color our judgment and will from the inside) nor of the social setting of our actions (which influences our judgment and emotions from the outside).

With minor moral rules and moral demands, will alone may sustain us; and, as noted, the following of most moral rules has practical benefits—we get as much as we give. But when we are asked to make sacrifices that seem to promise far more burdens than benefits, much less the more extreme situation of forfeiting a life of our own choosing and direction, then we move beyond what calculating reason can justify or all but the stoutest of wills can will. At that point we are forced to ask how our moral actions give meaning to our life. If the keeping of a moral rule, or the imposition of a heroic demand, seems to threaten our otherwise perfectly legitimate claim to happiness, then some deeper justification than morality alone seems needed. How can we, willingly, be asked to embrace personal tragedy in the name of morality alone? Why should I give up my own happiness for the sake of the care needed by another? There is no good general answer to that question within the compass of a morality of rules, duty, and a will to do the right thing. We can praise those who make great sacrifices, but we cannot readily condemn those who do not. We seem to be at a moral impasse.

Is there a solution? Heroic self-sacrifice, I have come to think, is only possible if understood within the context of an entire way of life, and a way of life set ultimately within some scheme of religious or higher meaning. I suggested above that it is the vulnerability of others that is the source of their claim on us, the fact that we and only we can provide the care they need, a care that responds to them as unique individuals and not merely needy examples of *homo sapiens*. That we are called on to respond to someone else's vulnerability means that, in turn, we become vulnerable also. Something is going to be taken from us as the ineluctable price of self-giving, perhaps something as central as our hopes and our identity.

I can conceive of myself making a radical sacrifice for another if I live in a community that understands the interrelationship of all our mutual needs and vulnerabilities and creates a society to respond to them. It is precisely because life so often fails our expectations that we need each other. It is precisely because the moral demands to give of self can be so outrageous, so utterly devastating, that we need to know others are prepared to do the same for us. It is the isolation of the moral claim to heroic action that is so intimidating in our kind of society. We cannot be sure that others will sustain us, or that others would do likewise for us, if our needs become heavy. Why should we expect any such things if all such sacrifices are thought to be heroic, and thus utterly optional?

In one sense, what I am saying points in the direction of improved systems of social support for those who care for family members. They need the financial and psychologic support of state and federal agencies, and they need responsive, sensitive people to give them help and to give them respite. But that is hardly enough. In another sense, however, we need a different kind of society and a different kind of morality. Even with adequate social support, we are still faced with tragedy, still faced with moral claims that seem to confront us with imperative duties that are, for all that, impossible demands. How are we to give meaning to those demands? Morality alone cannot do so, because morality does not give meaning to life; it cannot lift itself by its own bootstraps. Part of the problem here turns on whether we take the harm done by those injuries and illnesses that lie behind the need for rehabilitation to be that of the injuries themselves or only our social response to them. The aggressive rationalistic and scientific tradition in medicine would look on the injuries themselves as an evil to be eradicated. Another interpretation, however, is that injuries are just chance occurrences of nature; any evil lies exclusively in the failure of the community to respond to the needs of those afflicted by them. Whichever ultimate interpretation we may prefer, however, there will still be, for those families that must provide care, a sense of personal tragedy. Something terrible has happened to them and some meaning must be given to it.

On the whole, it seems to be religious cultures alone that can provide the kind of meaning needed, at least so far in human history. Suffering must be understood to have a point and to be redeemable. The care of another must be transformed from a stark and unpalatable moral demand to a satisfying moral vocation, one honored by the community and returned in kind when the caregiver himself comes, as we all will, to need care. Vulnerability is understood to be part of the human condition, some being visited with greater needs than others, but others being blessed with greater strength. A distinction is still made between duty and moral heroism, but the level of duty is set much higher, there is less nervousness about the boundary line, and heroism is thought to be required of all lives from time to time. A good society is one that finds ways to match needs and strengths, one that cares not only for public injustice visited on minority and other weak groups but also for private injustices that nature and life visit upon individual people.

I said that I think only religious cultures have been able to project, and sometimes embody, that vision of community. For many of us who are not religious believers, we are left with a severe problem. How can we create a secular version of a way of life that fully shares burdens? I am not certain, but until we do, I think we should be wary of asking families to undertake heroic sacrifices. If we must ask them, then it becomes imperative that we find out how we might best reward and sustain them. It seems to me possible that we might find ways to do that.

REFERENCES

Ackford JP: Reducing medicaid expenditures through family responsibility: critique of recent proposal. *Am J Law Med 5*:59–79, 1979.

Bluestein J: *Parents and Children: The Ethics of the Family.* New York, Oxford University Press, 1982.

Brody EM: 'Women in the Middle' and family help to older people. *Gerontologist 21*:471–480, 1985.

Brody EM: Parent care as normative family stress. *Gerontologist 25*:19–29, 1985.

Carpenter JO: Changing roles and disagreement in families with disabled husbands. *Arch Phys Med Rehabil 55*:272–274, 1974.

Golodetz A: Care of chronic illness: 'Responsor' Role. *Med Care 7*:385–394, 1969.

Goodin RE: Protecting the Vulnerable: A Reanalysis of Our Social Responsibilities. Chicago, University of Chicago Press, 1985.

Holadays B: Challenges of rearing chronically ill child. *Nurs Clin N Am 19*:361–368, 1984.

Jarrett WH: Caregiving within kinship systems: is affection really necessary? *Gerontologist 25*:5–10, 1985.

Mailick M: Impact of severe illness on individual and family: overview. *Soc Work Health Care 5*:117–128, 1979.

MacIntyre A: *After Virtue.* Notre Dame, IN, University of Notre Dame Press, 1983.

Outka G: *Agape: An Ethical Analysis.* New Haven, Yale University Press, 1972.

Romano MD: Family response to traumatic head injury. *Scand J Rehabil Med 6*:1–4, 1974.

Skelton M: Psychological stress in wives of patients with myocardial infarction. *Br Med J 2*:101–103, 1973.

Urmson JO: Saints and heroes. *In* Melden AI (ed): *Essays in Moral Philosophy.* Seattle, University of Washington Press, 1958, pp 198–216.

Warrington JM: *The Humpty Dumpty Syndrome.* Winona, IN, Light and Life Press, 1981.

27

Silent Casualties: Partners, Families, and Spouses of Persons With Aids

R. Jane Williams and William B. Stafford

Acquired Immune Deficiency Syndrome (AIDS) was first identified as a specific disease entity by the Center for Disease Control (CDC) in 1981. As of January 1990, the CDC reported that 121,645 AIDS cases were diagnosed. Earlier studies of the effects of serious and chronic illnesses have shown practitioners and counselors that any serious illness fosters "the occurrence of critical and nonnormative [sic] life events ... Such events may interrupt the functioning of an individual and his/her family" (Bander, 1987, p.3). Yet, as late as 1984, reference to the psychosocial effect of AIDS on patients, partners, and families was rare in professional counseling and psychiatric journals, even though nonprofessional journals and the media were offering frequent "human interest" stories about individuals and families coping with AIDS.

From 1984 through 1986, several broad surveys of psychosocial needs relating to persons with AIDS (PWAs) appeared in the counseling literature (Forstein, 1984; Schaffner, 1986). In the past several years research articles and studies on the psychosocial needs of PWAs, and programs designed to meet those needs, have begun to appear more frequently in professional journals (Backer, Batchelor, Jones, & Mays, 1988; Cochran & Mays, 1989). Even as the tremendous emotional and psychological damage AIDS inflicts on PWAs has begun to be recognized, the damage done to spouses, partners, and families of PWAs, extensive and pervasive as it is, remains a largely unrecognized reality in lay and professional circles. The paucity of such research is noted in several of the initial studies (Cleveland, 1987; Greif & Porembski, 1987; Klein & Fletcher, 1987). Research on strategies and outcomes for particular types of support and treatment for partners and families of PWAs is virtually nonexistent.

The literature that does exist is primarily descriptive. The typical focus of the literature is on the plight of the homosexual partner of a PWA, or on the family of either a gay male or substance-abusing PWA. Very little mention has been made of the heterosexual spouse's reactions or needs relating to an AIDS diagnosis of his or her partner. Also overlooked are the needs of children affected by a family member

Reprinted from *Journal of Counseling and Development*, 69, May/June 1991, pp. 423–427. © 1991 AACD. Reprinted with permission.

who has AIDS. Only one article dealt with children's response to AIDS in their families (Belfer, 1986); one additional article dealt with attempts to find and support foster parents for children with AIDS (Gurdin & Anderson, 1987).

The purpose of this article is to provide an overview of the available literature on needs and support of partners, families, and spouses of PWAs. Broad effects of the AIDS diagnosis are noted as well as unique effects on gay male partners, families of intravenous drug abusers, families giving in-home care to their PWAs, and children of PWAs. Suggestions for interventions are noted as found in the literature. Specific suggestions for needed research conclude the article.

PARALLELS WITH TERMINAL ILLNESS AND BEREAVEMENT LITERATURE

The current situation regarding the significant others of PWAs is reflected in recent bereavement research and care. During the past decade, bereavement research has progressed from anecdotal studies to a more quantitative approach. Research is now focusing on quantitative examination of beliefs concerning bereavement (Wortman & Silver, 1989) and early predictors of bereavement coping difficulties (Lund et al., 1985; Owen, Fulton, & Markusen, 1982–1983; Zisook & Shuchter, 1986). Initial findings indicate that the early feelings and behaviors most related to poor coping several years into bereavement included wanting to die, feeling confused, crying, and taking prescription tranquilizers (Lund et al., 1985); that the closeness of the relationship was a factor in the nature and disruptiveness of grief experienced (Owen, Fulton, & Markusen, 1982–1983); and that "grief is often an ongoing, life-long process rather than a crisis that is simply mastered or resolved over a circumscribed period of time" (Zisook & Schuchter, 1986, p. 294).

Examination of the period before a loved one's death and of the stresses attendant to that period in anything but a descriptive way is still rare. Nevertheless, this literature echoes the recognition that "In general, the physical, psychological and spiritual suffering of the terminal patient ... and of the family ... especially [in] the terminal period, plays havoc with the harmonious well-being of the latter" (Godkin, Krant, & Doster, 1983-1984). As with the PWA and significant others, terminally ill persons and their significant others frequently experience social isolation, in part due to this culture's fear of death and the accompanying sense of "contagion," and in part due to the inability of the care giver to exert the energy necessary to reach out to others (Sanders, 1982-1983). The sense of lack of control that is also experienced almost universally in terminal illness is accentuated for significant others in that the disease "belongs" to the dying person, who has much of the decision-making power regarding treatment and care. The family member or significant other is able only to stand by as his or her life is changed irrevocably by their loved one's disease (Kopel & Mock, 1978). Depression, anger, extreme anxiety, deep anticipatory grief, unpredictable mood swings, and ambivalent feelings toward the terminally ill person are also frequently experienced by family members, but these feelings may be withheld from lay or professional support persons out of shame, guilt, or fear of being interpreted as abnormal and mentally unbalanced (Kopel & Mock, 1978; Kübler-Ross, 1969). The need to find meaning in and understand the death of the significant other, as well as to cope with a shaken faith in the world as an ordered and safe place, are primary issues throughout the dying and bereavement process (Kopel & Mock, 1978; Parkes, 1972). Any of the above may be found in the population of significant others of PWAs.

EFFECTS OF AIDS DIAGNOSIS ON SPOUSES, PARTNERS, AND FAMILY

The number of spouses, partners, and family members affected by AIDS has increased geometrically in relation to the increase in the number of PWAs. Few social supports are offered for this population. Spouses, partners, and family members are left to find their own supports or "go it alone" as the unprepared and overburdened system of health care and psychosocial supports scrambles to cope with the enormity of the problems and needs of the PWAs themselves. Additionally, the legacy of the last decade, a societal shift from institutional care to a greater emphasis on self-help, means that in caring for PWAs "services have become the responsibility of families, lovers and friends and an emerging social network of volunteers" (Appleby & Sosnowitz, 1987, p. 3). Without the support of the family, researchers report, the survival of the PWA is further threatened. The family frequently becomes the primary care giver for a PWA unable to care for himself or herself (Greif & Porembski, 1987). Schaffner (1986) reported that if the family or significant other of a PWA deserts the PWA, the PWA is likely to withdraw from social contact and even from medical help. When a PWA is unable to work, the support of family or a significant other may be the only financial stability she or he can depend upon (Schaffner, 1986). Treiber (1986) cited a study (Dobro, Spalinks, Kapila, & Oleske, 1983) that indicated that PWAs with the longest survival rates have been those whose families have been highly supportive of the PWA. Yet, as they support their PWAs, spouses, partners and family all too often find themselves either afraid to ask for help out of fear of exposing themselves to public knowledge of association with AIDS, or abandoned by those who care but are afraid.

Unique Effects on Homosexual Partners

Treatment of gay male PWAs and their partners differs from treatment of persons with other fatal illnesses because of " . . . its newness, severity, the unsolved mysteries of transmission and cure, but above all the social bias against sexually transmitted disease in general and discrimination against homosexuals in particular" (Schaffner, 1986, p. 79). The AIDS diagnosis affects the entire social support network with the most immediately and severely affected being the partner. Geis, Fuller, and Rush (1986) stated that:

> lovers of AIDS victims constitute a population at risk. First, they face all the problems of loss and grief that are present within the general population. Second, they are a population that lacks many of the traditional support systems that help most people deal with grief, namely families and religious bodies. Third, since most AIDS victims are young, they leave survivors who are grieving for untimely deaths. (p. 55)

Geis et al. (1986) noted that anyone involved in counseling gay male partners of PWAs cannot overestimate the high degree of stress and lack of support characterizing their condition. Klein and Fletcher (1987) added:

> those who have lost someone to the ravages of AIDS experience multifaceted repercussions . . . [they] must cope not only with the death of a significant other but also, in the case of gay men, with the possible disclosure of a sexual orientation that carries a social stigma. Partners must confront this discrimination, their own fears relating to AIDS, and possible legal and financial problems. (p. 24)

The fact that a diagnosis of AIDS may alert the families of gay male PWAs and partners that they are homosexual and, simultaneously, divulge a terminal diagnosis for one or both, is one of the most common stressors for partners of gay male PWAs. "A great many gay men have not dealt with their families about their sexual orientation: these families must now deal with the loss of their 'normal' son at the same time that they must deal with his impending death" (Carl, 1986, p. 245). Such a simultaneous disclosure often means the loss of family support for both the PWA and partner at the time when such support may be badly needed emotionally, financially, and physically. Loss of family support may have ramifications that extend to the death of the PWA when the partner may be cut off irrevocably from the PWA's family, preventing the healing possibility of solace gained from the presence, memories, and comfort of the other.

Additional effects on the partner identified by Flaskerud (1987) include guilt about possibly having transmitted the virus to the PWA; fear of getting AIDS from engaging in sexual relations with the PWA; anticipatory grief, mourning, and anger. Existential and spiritual crises at having to face one's own death through the death of a loved one, and the inherent injustice of death at such a young age are also prevalent issues (Flaskerud, 1987; Grant & Anns, 1988).

AIDS, as with any chronic or terminal illness, creates disequilibrium in a relationship through the emotional, physical, and financial dependence of the PWA on the "well" partner. Dealing with the disease daily can drain the partner as he or she is called upon to provide emotional support for the PWA. Yet, AIDS effectively prevents the partner (and the PWA) from receiving such societal support. In addition, there are practical problems, such as travel required for visitation in long-term hospitalizations, insurance issues, and probable loss of time from work for the partner to be a care giver.

AIDS of necessity calls for changes in sexual intimacy patterns for homosexual (and heterosexual) couples. The result is that an avenue of intimacy, communication, and support is summarily closed or, at the very least, changed or threatened. Even everyday intimacies such as holding hands or kissing may be severely restricted by uneasy health care providers during hospitalization. An additional barrier, stated by Carl (1986), is the frequent disregard for couple boundaries and the lack of highly visible role models for permanent committed homosexual relationships.

Although in some areas the situation is changing, the homosexual partner may feel extremely isolated from friends who, having showered concern and energy on the PWA, often overlook the needs of the partner when the PWA dies. In the homosexual community, the partner may become stigmatized as an intimate associate of a person who died of AIDS (Carl, 1986) and may express grief over the loss of future possibilities for intimate relationships due to the knowledge of his relationship with a PWA (Geis, Fuller, & Rush, 1986; Klein & Fletcher, 1986).

Yet another issue for partners of homosexual PWAs results from the general lack of legal status accorded to a committed homosexual relationship. Although the two may be coupled, hospital policies, especially in non-metropolitan areas, often prevent visits by all but legally recognized family in areas such as the intensive care unit or reverse isolation units (Carl, 1986; Flaskerud, 1987). The partner may be excluded from treatment information and decisions that would legally be one's right as a heterosexual spouse "as well as from funeral arrangements or distribution of property" (Carl, 1986, p. 246) that may have been used jointly with the tacit understanding that it belonged to both partners.

All the issues normally associated with chronic or terminal illness of a spouse, including guilt over one's own survival, suppression of preexisting relationship issues in the face of crisis, expectation of loyalty under extreme hardship, physical and emotional fatigue surrounding a prolonged dying process, will necessarily exist for the partner of a PWA.

> One additional factor should be mentioned: the tendency for couples to stay together because of illness, who might otherwise split up. This phenomenon is seen with many other terminal diseases among heterosexuals in marriages. When a spouse chooses to remain because a mate is terminally ill, it can create an additional pressure for the conflicted individual . . . Seldom will the situation change, but the open discussion [between the therapist and clients] of the 'martyrdom' and its implications seems to help. (Carl, 1986, p. 246)

In such cases, the partner may stay for any number of reasons including feeling needed and important to the PWA, shame at leaving one who is dying, hope that in the midst of a crisis the relationship will be seen as valuable and will be healed.

Grief groups for gay men were described by Klein and Fletcher (1987) as one of the few safe places for homosexual survivors to identify, accept, and express feelings without the fears of stigma or reprisal found in a heterosexual population.

Such groups also offer gay male partners of deceased PWAs a place to deal with their devastating loss of hope for emotional intimacy in the future due to the stigma of association with a deceased PWA and fears of being infected oneself with the deadly virus.

Unique Effects on Families of Intravenous Drug Abusers

Greif and Porembski (1987) noted that often the significant other, either parent or partner, is estranged from the drug abuser due to the usual pattern of illegal and irrational behavior that characterizes the drug-abuse life-style. The diagnosis of AIDS, however, and its character as a terminal illness may provide a powerful force for reconciliation between family or partner and drug abuser. Because the family so often is called upon to provide a good deal of the physical and emotional care required in the course of the disease, "the significant other has many feelings of his or her own that need to be considered in any treatment plan involving the PWA" (Greif & Porembski, 1987, p. 151). Greif and Porembski (1987) noted the roller coaster effect often reported by significant others due to repeated opportunistic infections interspersed with recovery, but leading to ultimate deterioration and death. Feelings of helplessness and powerlessness were common as families and partners watched the PWA's condition slowly deteriorate. "This deterioration, combined with a prolonged period of suffering prior to death, left an indelible and haunting scar upon the memories of the significant others" (Greif & Porembski, 1987, p. 153). Often, support systems, previously important to significant others, were not available either because of abandonment due to stigma or, perhaps more frequently, the significant other's hesitancy to share the PWA's diagnosis with those who might then reject the significant other (Greif and Porembski, 1987).

Effects of In-Home Care of a PWA on Families, Spouses, and Children

In a field observation study of 50 family members of gay, bisexual, and I.V. drug-using PWAs, Frierson, Lippmann, and Johnson (1987) found five psychological issues surfacing frequently: (1) fear of contagion, sometimes to obsessive degrees; (2) obsessive concern with cleanliness; (3) refusal to participate in social activities or allow visitors in the home; (4) abstention from sexual contact; and (5) frequently repeated AIDS diagnostic testing. Families having young children were particularly disrupted with fear of contagion, which often translated into negative attitudes about the PWA. Often, families reported conflict between providing a supportive environment for the PWA and perceived responsibility for maintaining the health of other family members. Frierson et al. (1987) reported this to be the most common source of family distress.

Belfer (1986) described the particularly devastating toll of AIDS on uninfected children of PWAs. In addition to facing their parent's death "[t]hese children must contend with the uncertainty of the potential for being infected and/or developing the illness. Perhaps equally stressful is the transmission of the stigma associated with their parents' illness and the implications of their way of life" (Belfer, 1986, pp. 4–5). These children frequently are the object of homophobic reactions and scorn, rather than of the empathy that typically would be offered children whose parents have some other terminal disease. Combining the scorn and isolation with the loss of a parent at highly critical developmental stages of childhood puts these children at high risk and in great need of psychological support and intervention. None of these services is mentioned in the literature at present.

FORMS OF INTERVENTION

Suggestions for interventions with partners and adult family members nearly always center on the use of peer groups to give support, to break down the prevalent feeling of isolation of partners and family members of a PWA, and to enable the kind of sharing that promotes healing (Fuller, Geis, & Rush, 1988; Graham and Cates, 1987; Klein and Fletcher, 1987).

Frierson et al. (1987) and Grant and Anns (1988) reported that those couple and family relationships that have been characterized prior to the AIDS diagnosis as strong, having weathered previous crises, and having exhibited good coping skills with available support systems, as being those relationships in which individuals may need less psychological intervention. These persons can be helped most effectively through reinforcement of existing coping skills.

Additional interventions urged in the literature are (a) the provision of adequate and accurate information to dispel anxiety about prevention and spread of the disease (*Coping with AIDS,* 1986), (b) counseling either within a group, family, or individual setting (Fuller et al., 1988; Geis et al., 1986; Treiber, 1986), and (c) grief work (Flaskerud, 1987; Klein & Fletcher, 1986). The latter was widely reported to be most effective in a group setting where due to the disparity of psychological adjustment levels, new members could gain hope for eventual healing of acute grief from grievers further along in the process.

COUNSELING RESEARCH AGENDA

Research studies that examine psychosocial needs of partners, families, and spouses of PWAs, and programs instituted in an attempt to meet those needs, will not fix the problem, but they most certainly can enable us to hear those who are hurting, and alert us to interventions that can help alleviate suffering.

Longitudinal studies highlighting the progression of psychosocial needs and coping skills of spouses, partners, and families of PWAs at various stages of the disease (initial suspicion of HIV infection, diagnosis, hospitalizations, remission, death) would be helpful to practitioners. The most urgent research questions include:

- Which coping styles increase the ability of the family, partners, and spouses of PWAs to deal with the roller-coaster syndrome of AIDS progression (disease, remission of symptoms, disease)?
- Which measures can help a practitioner assess the level, style, and effectiveness of coping of family, partners, and spouses of PWAs? The development and norming of specific AIDS coping scales seem essential here.
- Is there a similar set of psychosocial needs for the total population of family, partners, and spouses of PWAs, or do psychosocial needs vary according to the particular relationship one has with a PWA (gay partner, parent, heterosexual spouse, other)?
- What is the long-term effect of multiple AIDS-related losses on family, partners, and spouses of PWAs, especially regarding the gay male population and families with several hemophiliac PWAs?

Process and outcome research with various types of intervention groups would help in determining which interventions, if any, are most helpful and why. The central research questions in this area would include:

- Is there a difference between the effectiveness of self-help groups and practitioner-led groups in breaking down isolation and increasing the ability of partners, families, and spouses of PWAs to deal with the disease process as it affects them?
- Are groups whose membership is limited to persons with a specific type of relationship to a PWA (e.g., gay partners, parents) more effective in increasing healthy adjustment to the disease process than groups with a broader membership?
- If a specific type of group is found to benefit spouses, partners, and families, what particular processes, events, sequences, or situations peculiar to that group may be responsible and facilitative to outcome?

Studies of the effect of cross-cultural and gender differences relating to coping with AIDS are desperately needed, as well. Most urgently needed are studies to address the following questions:

- What interactions, if any, occur between minority culture membership and disease stigmatization for family members and significant others of PWAs to increase the probability of dysfunctional coping with the disease process?
- What differences may be evident in the roles adopted by female and male partners and family members in their relationship to PWAs? Do such differences create different supportive needs and varied receptivity to interventions?

The interdisciplinary character of much of AIDS care offers a rich area for investigation of possible interventions using a team approach (medical, psychological, social work, nursing). Research questions include:

- Which particular disciplines (e.g., social work, hospital/hospice chaplaincy, family therapy) that offer specific skills are helpful in working with and planning interventions for spouses, partners, and families of PWAs, and in what situations might practitioners in these disciplines be called in by the treatment team?
- What treatment-team conditions (frequent staff meetings, group support for team members, assignment of one staff person to the partner or family as liaison to other team members) facilitate access of spouses, partners, and family to the highest quality psychosocial care and support?
- Under what conditions do professionals working with PWAs, spouses, partners, and family maintain the highest level of personal and professional efficacy (e.g., receiving individual support from another professional, participating in a support group of other professionals, rotating out of direct AIDS care-giving roles on a periodic basis)?

Research on pediatric AIDS and its effect on parents or hospital staff who become surrogate parents in the absence of biological parents, is particularly lacking and greatly needed given the dramatic increases noted in this age cohort. Research questions for this category include:

- What are the most pressing psychosocial needs for parents and surrogate parents of PWAs? What are the non-psychosocial needs, which, left unfulfilled, affect the ability of this population to deal with the problems attendant with AIDS (e.g., financial, child care, housing)? What level of non-psychosocial support creates optimum ability to provide care of the PWA?
- What models of care for parents of terminally ill children are effective with the specialized problems of parents and surrogate parents of pediatric PWAs?
- What are the differences in needs of pediatric PWAs at various ages (e.g., age 5 years versus age 12 years) and what impact do these needs have on parents and surrogate parents?

Children of PWAs are at particularly high risk for psychological problems because they will likely lose their parents prematurely and need to deal with issues of loss as would any bereaved child. Nevertheless, these children are often handicapped in receiving support due to the culturally attached stigma of AIDS. Research questions essential to this population include:

- What are the longitudinal developmental effects on those children having a parent with AIDS, and how does their development compare to children whose parent is deceased due to another cause? Are there parallels that can be drawn that would indicate directions for interventions for the former?

- What gender and cultural differences affect the needs of children whose parent is a PWA?
- What macro supports are most effective (e.g., in-school support groups, neighborhood-based volunteer networks for families, church- or synagogue-sponsored support for grieving families) and are there specific situations where such support is most crucial?

Counseling involvement with families, significant others, and friends of PWAs is critically important to the ultimate health and wholeness of these survivors. A simple sensitivity to the needs of others who are in relationship to the PWA is essential. Equally important, however, is the development and sharing among professionals of quality interventions that can help these significant others to find and develop a new equilibrium enabling life to be lived most fully in the midst of the crisis of AIDS.

REFERENCES

Appleby, G. A., & Sosnowitz, B. G. (1987). *From social movement to social organization: Voluntary AIDS projects in Conneticut.* Paper presented at the Annual Meeting of the Society for the Study of Social Problems, Chicago, IL. (ERIC Document Reproduction Service No. ED 294 812)

Backer, T. E., Batchelor, W. F., Jones, J. M., & Mays, V. M. (Eds.). (1988). Special issue on AIDS. *American Psychologist, 43*, 835–982.

Bander, R. S. (1987). *AIDS: A challenge to counseling psychologists.* Paper presented at the Annual Convention of the American Psychological Association. (ERIC Document Reproduction Service No. Ed 289 148)

Belfer, M. L. (1986). *Psychological impact of AIDS on children.* Position paper. (ERIC Document Reproduction Service No. ED 271 217)

Carl, D. (1986). Acquired Immune Deficiency Syndrome: A preliminary examination of the effects on gay couples and coupling. *Journal of Marital and Family Therapy, 12*(3), 241–247.

Cleveland, P. H. (1987). *AIDS: A strain on family relations.* Paper presented at the Conference of the National Council on Family Relations, Atlanta, GA. (ERIC Document Reproduction Service No. ED 295 070)

Cochran, S. D., & Mays, V. M. (1989). Women and AIDS-related concerns. *American Psychologist, 44*, 529–535.

Coping with AIDS: Psychological and social considerations in helping people with HTLV-III infection (DHHS Publication No. ADM-85-1432). (1986). Washington, DC: U.S. Government Printing Office.

Flaskerud, J. H. (1987). AIDS: Psychosocial aspects. *Journal of Psychosocial Nursing, 25*(12), 9–16.

Forstein, M. (1984). The psychosocial impact of the acquired immunodeficiency syndrome. *Seminars in Oncology, 11*(1), 77–83.

Frierson, R. L., Lippmann, S. B., & Johnson, J. (1987). AIDS: Psychological stresses on the family. *Psychosomatics, 28*(2), 65–68.

Fuller, R. L., Geis, B. S., & Rush, J. (1988). Lovers of AIDS victims: A minority group experience. *Death Studies, 12*, 1–7.

Geis, S. B., Fuller, R. L., & Rush, J. (1986). Lovers of AIDS victims: Psychosocial stresses and counseling needs. *Death Studies, 10*, 43–53.

Godkin, M. A., Krant, M. J., & Doster, N. J. (1983-1984). The impact of hospice care on families. *International Psychiatry in Medicine, 13,* 153-165.

Graham, L., & Cates, J. A. (1987). AIDS: Developing a primary health care task force. *Journal of Psychosocial Nursing, 25*(12), 21-25.

Grant, D., & Anns, M. (1988). Counseling AIDS antibody-positive clients: Reactions and treatment. *American Psychologist, 43*(1), 72-74.

Greif, G. L., & Porembski, E. (1987). Significant others of I.V. drug abusers with AIDS: New challenges for drug treatment programs. *Journal of Substance Abuse Treatment, 4*(3/4), 151-155.

Gurdin, P., & Anderson, G. R. (1987). Quality care for ill children: AIDS-specialized foster family homes. *Child Welfare, 66*(4), 291-302.

Klein, S. J., & Fletcher, W. (1987). Gay grief: An examination of its uniqueness brought to light by AIDS crisis. *Journal of Psychosocial Oncology, 4*(3), 15-25.

Kopel, K., & Mock, L. A. (1978). The use of group sessions for the emotional support of families of terminal patients. *Death Education, 1,* 409-422.

Kübler-Ross, E. (1969). *On death and dying.* New York: MacMillan.

Lund, D. A., Dimond, M. F., Caserta, M. S., Johnson, R. J., Poulton, J. L., & Connelly, J. R. (1985). Identifying elderly with coping difficulties after two years of bereavement. *Omega, 16,* 213-224.

Owen, G., Fulton, R., & Markusen, E. (1982-1983). Death at a distance: A study of family survivors. *Omega., 13.* 191-225.

Parkes, C. M. (1972). *Bereavement: Studies of grief in adult life.* New York: International Universities Press.

Sanders, C. M. (1982-83). Effects of sudden vs. chronic illness death on bereavement outcome. *Omega, 13,* 227-241.

Schaffner, B. (1986). Reactions of medical personnel and intimates to persons with AIDS. *The Psychotherapy Patient, 2*(4), 67-88.

Treiber, F. (1986). *Acquired Immune Deficiency Syndrome (AIDS): Psychological impact on health personnel.* Paper presented at the Annual Convention of the American Association for Counseling and Development, Los Angeles, CA. (ERIC Document Reproduction Service No. ED 268 396)

Wortman, C. B., & Silver, R. C. (1989). The myths of coping with loss. *Journal of Consulting and Clinical Psychology, 57,* 349-357.

Zisook, S., & Shuchter, S. (1986). The first four years of widowhood. *Psychiatric Annals, 15,* 288-294.

28

Psychosocial Rehabilitation: Toward a Definition

Ram A. Cnaan   *Karlyn W. Messinger*
Laura Blankertz   *Jerome R. Gardner*

INTRODUCTION TO PRINCIPLES AND SUPPORTING THEORIES

Psychosocial rehabilitation (PSR) is a relatively new approach, practiced for about 40 years, for assisting people with emotional disabilities, often the most severely chronically mentally ill, to readjust to community living. Its definition (IAPSRS, 1985) is commonly stated as

> the process of facilitating an individual's restoration to an optimal level of independent functioning in the community ... while the nature of the process and the methods used differ in different settings, psychosocial rehabilitation invariably encourages persons to participate actively with others in the attainment of mental health and social competence goals. In many settings, participants are called members. The process emphasizes the wholeness and wellness of the individual and seeks a comprehensive approach to the provision of vocational, residential, social/recreational, educational, and personal adjustment services. (p.iii)

PSR is based on a number of assumptions, of which two are essential. The first of these is that people are motivated by a need for mastery and competence in areas that allow them to feel more independent and self-confident. Second is that new behavior can be learned and that people are capable of adapting their behavior to meet their basic needs. (Maslen, 1982).

This definition and these assumptions, however, leave ample space for interpretations. Gardner (1985) warns that "the lack of clarity about what psychosocial rehabilitation is, even among its most ardent supporters, will enable others to use this newly popular label for inappropriate services" (p. 5). Although some common threads are clearly present in the programs of most agencies utilizing PSR, the dissimilarities between them are immense. Two clear indications of this lack of clarity and ambiguity regarding PSR are the various names used for this or very much later approaches, such as PSR, psychiatric rehabilitation (Anthony, 1977), and the psychoeducation approach (Walsh, 1987); and the various target populations to which this approach is claimed to be applied, such as people with head injury (Polkow & Volpe, 1985), people with cardiac arrest (Martin & Dubbert, 1982), cancer survivors (Mullen, 1984), war veterans (Blank, 1982), people released from prison (Mir, 1983), the blind (Schultz et al., 1986), and the deaf (Straub, 1983). It is of interest to note that four different journals use the word psychosocial in their title, each with different meanings (*Psychosocial Rehabilitation Journal, Journal of Psychosocial Oncology, Psychosocial Process*, and *Journal of Psychosocial Nursing and Mental Health Services*).

The problem is that as concepts attract popular attention they are interpreted differently by different people. Thus, service delivery principles tend to be idiosyncratic to each of the many PSR-utilizing agencies. Although the basic tenets of PSR are based on community rehabilitation, to be initiated as soon as the pathology and impairment of the acute state have stabilized (Anthony & Liberman, 1986), many try to adapt it for use in long-term mental hospitals (Bell & Ryan, 1984; Manos, Gkiouzepas, & Lavretiadis, 1984). A survey carried out by the International Association of Psychosocial Rehabilitation Services identified over 800 programs claiming to have a psychosocial rehabilitation focus. There is no doubt that this "propagation" of PSR (IAPSRS, 1985), is due in part to its relatively economical mode of hospital care (Bond, 1984). What many of these agencies are providing and how is unclear. There is, however, a clear need to define the principles of PSR and to set limits as to what *is* within this approach and what is not an acceptable component of the approach.

No one person or agency can determine the definite boundaries and principles of any approach. The aim in this review is to present the PSR approach as it is found in the literature. Although the authors are well associated with Horizon House of Philadelphia, their set of principles is not the one utilized at this agency. At Horizon House, a few specific deviations from this model have consciously been made and can easily be justified. Here, however, the extensive literature review is geared towards the configuration of a mainstream model.

In this chapter the basic principles governing the PSR approach will be outlined, illustrating that PSR is not based on exclusive independent theory, but on a set of those principles designed to foster the independence and development of people with emotional disabilities. Numerous theories from the fields of sociology and psychology may be found to be complementary to PSR. Later research will present direct theoretical analysis of PSR. It is also the authors' intention to provide two additional studies covering the implications of the principles and theories of the model for its operational implementation, both in the engagement of human service agencies and in its application to training and direct service work by providers utilizing PSR.

THE MAJOR PRINCIPLES OF THE PSR APPROACH

From an extensive literature review, the following 13 principles have been extracted. There is no logical or accepted hierarchy of these principles. No one of these principles in itself is sufficient to represent the PSR approach. In fact, only agencies that espouse, to a large extent, all or most of these principles can claim to utilize PSR. Almost all human services caring for people with emotional disabilities utilize a few of these principles to a certain degree. However, only PSR calls for a comprehensive application of all or most of the principles listed below. It is well accepted that some principles will be altered by various PSR-utilizing agencies and it is beyond the scope of this chapter to determine what alternatives should be allowed and what must remain intact.

The PSR model as a whole was not envisaged as is by its propounders in the post World War II era. The model was developed incrementally over the last 40 years as a social alternative to the more dominant medical model of treatment of individuals with mental health needs. During this period, various components were added to the model and its modes of application have grown greatly.

Of major significance was the *innovation* of the "clubhouse" of Fountain House. That application has emphasized the long-term character of the service: security, belonging, and contribution to the whole. While this was especially satisfactory in working with those "learned helpless" individuals who had spent extended time in the back wards of state hospitals, it did not attract the younger, more motivated individuals who wanted the challenge of opportunity in place of security. In response to the needs of later clients, the "high expectancy" or "schoolhouse" approach was developed at Horizon House. This application is goal-oriented, time-limited, and sequential in nature and emphasizes the learning of skills that enable the individuals to move on to graduate to independent living.

Operational applications extend across the spectrum of these two approaches. Here, however, the concentration will be on the extracted principles, in the expectation that this effort will be followed by discussions as to how others may see to formalize the PSR methodology.

1. Underutilization of Full Human Capacity

The assumption here is that each person is capable of improving his or her levels of functioning. Thus, each person can and should be assisted to obtain his or her most effective level of functioning. It is also assumed that all people can work toward a series of goals when those goals are personally meaningful (Carling & Broskowski, 1986). Nirje (1969) presented the following philosophical tenets: *Life is a process of growth and change and all persons, even the most severely disabled, are capable of growth and change.* PSR assumes that it is the responsibility of service providers to enlarge clients' expectations of themselves, to help them view themselves as capable of progress, and to support this process of growth (Beard, Propst, & Malamud, 1982). All people, even those of lower intelligence levels or emotional disabilities, are capable of mental growth (Shapira, Cnaan, R. A., &

Cnaan, A., 1986). According to PSR tenets, the client's capability to take advantage of the opportunity for rehabilitative activity is evaluated according to that individual's capacity for progress and change and not according to predescribed deterministic technical or medical standards. The key issue then is *how* to motivate these people towards better use of their potential social, emotional, mental, and instrumental capacity.

2. Equipping People with Skills

It is the presence or absence of skills, not clinical symptoms, that is the determining factor in rehabilitation success (Anthony, 1977; Anthony, Cohen, & Vitalo, 1978). Many people with emotional disabilities have never learned or have unlearned the relevant skills for independent living (Argyle, 1981; Marlowe, 1982; Spivak, 1974; Sylph, Ross, & Kedward, 1977). Along with this are the findings that many people with emotional disabilities lack formal education, and compensatory educational programs are required to allow them to fully benefit from other programs (Barter, Queirolo, & Ekstrom, 1984; Coles, Roth, & Pollack, 1978; Coles, Ciporen, Konisberg, & Cohen, 1980; Katz-Garris, 1982; Unger, Danley, Kohn, & Hutchinson, 1987). Only new learning can equip people with relevant skills for holding a job, living independently, acting in a social network, and utilizing available resources (Liberman et al., 1986; Wallace et al., 1980). Lowell, MacLean, and Carroll (1985) have reported that the lack of independent skills is a predominant factor in causing individuals with histories of hospitalization to be readmitted to an institution. PSR, in fact, assumes that a major factor in rehabilitation is the knowledge of how to function in a variety of settings and situations. Persons with very minimal skills are thus more likely to fail in things that seem routine to others. A primary thrust of this model, then, is teaching people with emotional disability the skills that they lack (Anthony, Cohen, M. R., & Cohen B., 1984). The operational manifestation of this principle is when the client's potential for rehabilitation is being assessed. The assessment focuses on the person as well as on individual skills deficits, existing skills, and strengths with respect to the client's goals. PSR employs methods of "educational therapy" by which improvement of learning and skills also improves psychological and social contact. The learning of skills in turn strengthens an individual's problem-solving capacities and confers protection against exacerbation of psychiatric symptoms (Wallace & Liberman, 1985). PSR further assumes, and studies show, that clients are able to extend their repertoire of skills and to generalize their use to other settings, except in clinical ones (Wallace et al., 1980; Liberman et al., 1986).

3. Self-Determination

Individuals have the right and the ability to participate in making decisions regarding their lives and to do so on a regular basis. While the classical medical and professional models often assume that the staff member knows better than the client, and ought to tell the client what to do, PSR assumes that clients, in fact, do have rights, ability, and knowledge to make decisions (Gardner & O'Hara, 1984). The key issue is not to do things in the best interest of the client but to allow the client, as one would allow any adult individual, to make decisions and live by their consequences.

PSR affirms people's ability to make adequate decisions and to grow by their experience of independence. Even wrong decisions (i.e., those leading to some negative results) are of rehabilitative value, as they educate clients to live by their choices and to improve behavior based on their own initiatives. There are, however, some cases of exception in which a staff member has the responsibility to decide for a client. These are usually cases of emergency or cases in which it is clearly beyond any doubt that clients may hurt themselves or others. The ideal, however, is to teach clients alternative ways of handling stressful situations, while paying them full respect.

The self-determination principle is also extended to the agency level. People with emotional disabilities should participate in the management of the agency, along with staff, in all levels of planning, policy making, implementation, and evaluation (Smith, Brown, Gibbs, Sanders, & Cremer, 1984; Holland, Konick, Buffum, Smith, & Petchers, 1981; Smith & Ford, 1986). Furthermore, self-determination also implies the right to satisfaction with service, that is, clients have the right and the ability to evaluate service, and staff should seek to solicit and accept their evaluation (Tanaka, 1983). As powerful and intelligent consumers, people with social and psychological disabilities should be allowed to refuse services and demand changes in modes of service delivery and/or change in personnel.

4. Normalization

Each individual has the right and is expected to live and function in the setting that is least restrictive and that as closely as possible approximates a regular community setting. The ultimate goal of PSR is independent living in the community, with minimal, if any, support. Efforts are made to prepare people to achieve this goal. Every aspect of care should be provided in a setting as similar as possible to a regular community (Tanaka, 1983). One crucial aspect of the normalization process is a work experience, expected of most adults. Other crucial aspects of normalization are opportunities to get together socially, to live in adequate housing, to shop in regular stores, and to consume leisure services in the community, all normal activities that are expected to be accessible to all (Beardsley, Kessler, & Levin, 1984). Based in this principle is also the conviction that skills must be taught in vivo, that is, in successive approximation toward, and ultimately in, the independent living, work, and learning environment, (Beardsley et al., 1984; Pressing, Peterson, Barness, & Riley, 1983). All of the above is shaped by the client's interests and abilities. Although the current level of knowledge and available resources to motivate each and every client to achieve greater levels of independence is insufficient, the PSR approach strives to integrate as many individuals as possible into the wider community or at least to help them to be served in the least restrictive environment. Lamb and Peele (1984) stated that "normalization of the . . . [person's] environment and rehabilitation to the greatest extent possible should be the goal of treatment . . . . As far as possible, the . . . [person's] conditions should not be allowed to set him or her apart from other citizens in our society" (p. 799).

Another essential part of the normalization principle is that there should be no unnecessary dependency in the client-staff relationships. Clients should be encouraged to live independently even though it adds burden to the staff role (Kultgen & Habenstein, 1984). PSR recognizes that societal prejudice, as well as disengagement, is widespread with regard to those labeled mentally disabled and results in social exclusion of people with emotional disabilities (Breven & Driscoll, 1984). However, as guaranteed in the 1973 Rehabilitation Act, all are entitled to equal opportunity within the normal environment.

5. Differential Needs and Care

People with emotional disabilities have *individual* physical, emotional, social, and intellectual needs, as well as different personal bases of knowledge, skills, experiences, and attitudes that all together form a unique set of preconditions (Dellario, 1982). PSR believes that growth from dependence to independence is a highly individual process, which may last for a longer or shorter period of time for different people. Some people may never be able to be totally independent, while others will reach full independence (Lanoil, 1982). Because of this diversity of people's needs, individualization of the rehabilitation plan is needed. These plans should be based on an assessment of client skills relative to a particular environment to ensure that the actual skills being taught to the specific client are the skills he or she will need in that environment (Anthony et al., 1984; Liberman, 1982). Test and Stein (1977) described the principles of differential care by two complementary guidelines: first, services should be adequate to assume that the person's unmet needs are met, and, second, services should *not* meet needs the person is able to meet on his or her own.

It is recognized, too, that people also differ in terms of their ability to move ahead in rehabilitation. There is no planned, predicted, and gradual manner by which all or most clients progress, but rather, each has a unique track of progress and regression (Black, 1987). Each client, thus, should be assisted according to his or her individual path and speed (Bond, Witheridge, Setze, & Dincin, 1985; Kanter, 1985). This principle attributes a very special responsibility to the practitioner utilizing PSR. There is very little that can be applied, defacto, to all clients as a general category; every day is built on a set of new requirements that cannot be necessarily generalized from one client to the other in a semiautomatic manner. Although attempts have been made to categorize groups of clients (Harris & Bergman, 1987), these are gross categories that encompass multitudes of individual differences. For each client there is a need for a separate plan, separate implementation, and separate evaluation.

6. Commitment of Staff

Levine (1984), in criticizing the importance of neuroleptic drug use in PSR, concludes that the difference between success and failure in utilizing PSR is the level of comprehensiveness of the psychosocial treatment. PSR cannot be effective in small quantities and without staff who are fully committed to the model both in theory and in practice. Genuine concern with the well-being of clients and belief that they are capable of progress must be of paramount importance. Even when clients are losing their determination, staff must be expected to persist in the belief that progress is feasible. The demands on staff in terms of daily crises that are not and cannot be planned for are immense. Staff members use outreach methods, such as telephone calls and home visits, to reduce dropout and to show concern (Brekke & Test, 1987; Unger et al., 1987). The staff member has to create expectations that the client will feel wanted and be obliged to progress through attendance at club and/or rehabilitation activities (Beard et al., 1982). Thus, not everyone can be a staff member in an agency utilizing PSR. Management concern and assistance for workers in these demanding tasks in order to prevent burnout is critical.

7. Deprofessionalization of Service

The human element in staff performance is a crucial part of the rehabilitation process (Anthony, 1977, 1982). Staff members are expected NOT to shield themselves behind a professional front, and all artificial barriers are removed (Smith et al., 1984). The relationships between staff and people with emotional disabilities are personal and based on a one-to-one client-centered approach. Staff members are concerned with all aspects of the lives of clients and are interested in them as human beings with many dimensions, rather than adopting the perspective of one limited area of service (Kultgen & Habenstein, 1984; Smith & Ford, 1986). This type of relationship leads to involvement of staff and clients because clients have a "significant other" to identify with and to test reality against (Bond, Dincin, Setze, & Witheridge, 1984; Lanoil, 1982).

Another key concept in the PSR model is the lack of neutrality of staff members toward clients. Staff members respond to what clients say or do, including in instances regarding non-therapeutic issues, in positive or negative ways. Thus, staff members show concern and care for clients as people through informal interactions in a large number of various daily value-laden negotiations. The PSR deprofessionalization view extends to acceptance and respect for a variety of beliefs and ideas presented by clients and people who are concerned with them, even if these ideas are contradictory to the practitioner's point of view (Smith & Ford, 1986). The exchange of contradictory ideas in a manner of mutual respect provides both parties with appreciation in a socially accepted manner. In a medical professional model, the diagnostic label and prescription for medication can be arrived at without client understanding and/or direct input. In contrast, in PSR, clients are called either members or associates, but not patients (Beard et al., 1982). In PSR, the practitioner is enabled to acknowledge his or her limitations both to clients and their social and kin networks (Yess, 1981; Spaniol, Zipple, & Fitzgerald, 1984). In addition, the intervention cannot be mysterious to the client. The practitioner is constantly trying to demystify the rehabilitation process (Anthony et al., 1982). Such exchange of opinions and information enhances partnership in working toward more realistic rehabilitation goals.

8. Early Intervention

It is essential to PSR that quick (crisis) intervention is given when first warning signs of decompensation or dysfunctioning are observed. This can reduce recidivism and preserves most acquired skills and community ties, including job, housing, and social contacts (Beardsley et al., 1984; Hammaker, 1983). A constant and meaningful relationship with staff and within one's social network is the best precondition for early intervention. When early signs are evident, the people who are close to the person at risk, with the help of staff members, can attend to and assist that person to avoid relapse (Harris & Bergman, 1985; Herz, 1984). Climo (1983) has noted that an understanding of the basic issues of mental health assists staff and significant others in responding to fluctuations in behavior in ways that avoid reinforcing problematic behavior patterns.

Intervention too late may result in hospitalization. Prolonged hospitalization is often associated with delearning of skills required for normal functioning in society and with reinforcement of other characteristics of institutionalization such as passivity and dependence, requiring a renewed process of PSR (Aviram & Segal, 1973; Segal & Aviram, 1976). PSR believes that the role of the case manager, first and foremost, is to prevent hospitalization via crisis intervention at the early stages of problems. For such case management to take place, workers must be in close and trustful rather than remote contact with their clients and must work hand in hand with family and friends (Harrod, 1986).

9. Environmental Approach

The process of rehabilitating people with emotional disabilities cannot be restricted to intrapsychic changes. The immediate environment of each person should be structured to provide support. The emphasis is on the environment and the creation and enhancement of supportive elements within the environment (Easton, 1984). With the help of relatives, employers, and members of one's social network, chances for successful rehabilitation are higher (Anthony, Cohen, M., & Cohen, B., 1983; Livneh, 1983; Unger et al., 1987; Walsh, 1987). In PSR, the practitioner must utilize the environment to assist the client (Anthony & Liberman, 1986; Black, 1987; Finch, 1985; Weinberg & Marlowe, 1983).

Families are clearly the primary caregivers for many people with emotional disabilities. Nonetheless, families frequently do not possess the skills or the resources to adequately assist their disabled family member (Hatfield, Fierstein, & Johnson, 1982; Spaniol et al., 1984). Thus, PSR calls for their inclusion in the caregiving process and their education as to how to help their disabled family member. Strauss and Carpenter (1977) found that the size of a social network was the best predictor for preventing future hospitalization. Harris and Bergman (1985) and Pattison, Lamas, and Hurd (1979) found the size and quality of social networks to be a good distinguishing predictor between people with emotional disabilities and others. Basically, people with these disabilities have fewer ties, are usually restricted to relationships with relatives, and have less frequent contacts and cannot regularly depend on most people in their network. Thus, they suffer from social isolation, have too few supports to assist them in setting limits and expectations, and have too few to depend on in times of need (Easton, 1984; Horne & Otto, 1982). In addition, many employers as well as landlords stigmatize people with emotional disability and discriminate against them in employment and housing. PSR calls on practitioners to advocate against and actively work against such discrimination in order to enhance support for each client with emotional disability who moves into the community (Turner & TenHoor, 1978).

10. Changing the Environment

The aforementioned principle addresses individual efforts of adjustment to the environment by each client. PSR also stresses a broader environmental responsibility. The environment in this respect consists not only of relatives, friends, specific employers and neighbors, but also of broader societal institutions, such as medical services, policies of income support, legislation regarding the rights of exceptional populations, housing and community services, and public attitudes toward people with emotional disability (Anthony, 1972; Mellen, 1985; Turner & TenHoor, 1978). Other models of care, notably the medical model, base their approaches on the "ghettoization" of people with social and psychological disabilities (Aviram & Segal, 1973). PSR advocates normalization (see above) as well as restructuring and reeducating the environment to better absorb and care for people with emotional disabilities. To achieve such goals, change in the environment is sought through public education and other methods to increase community acceptance of exceptional people (Turner & TenHoor, 1978). One of the yet unclear and undetermined issues in PSR is to what extent the environment should be altered. Estroff (1983) has clarified the challenge of this dilemma by claiming that only radical work can justify the term "social" in psychosocial rehabilitation.

11. No Limits on Participation

The PSR approach maintains no limits on length of participation and imposes few selection criteria (Lanoil, 1982). Usually anyone who has been in a mental hospital or who is exhibiting symptoms of difficulties in functioning is accepted by PSR-utilizing agencies, with the exception of those few who need specialized programs, such as alcohol or substance abusers (Bell & Ryan, 1984). Once a person has accessed a PSR program, he or she may be considered part of it for as long as desired. Hogarty, Goldberg and Schooler (1975); Hogarty et al. (1979) and Field and Yegge (1982) found some real effects of psychosocial intervention were apparent after 12 to 14 months. Others have found the length of time until an improvement is evident to be as long as 5 to 10 years or more (Bleuler, 1978; Bond et al., 1984; Kanter, 1985). Liberman and Rueger (1984) and Turner and TenHoor (1978), among others, have recommended that PSR be provided indefinitely, if not for life. This recommendation holds for clients who will most likely be somewhat dependent on help for a long time, if not for as long as they live (Horne & Otto, 1982). Manos and colleagues (1983) showed that ceasing to supply PSR services, even to clients in hospitals, causes significant deterioration in their level of functioning. Some PSR-utilizing agencies do set time limits for participation in some of their programs (Mostly in specific rehabilitation modules), both to motivate clients and to create an in vivo situation of real life demands and formal responsibilities (Beardsley et al., 1984; Bond et al., 1984; Broekema, Danz, & Schloemer, 1975).

12. Work-Centered Process

Although work is an essential and integral element of normalization, its role is of such importance that it is worthy of being seen as a separate principle. The PSR approach believes that work, especially the opportunity to aspire to and achieve gainful employment, is a deeply generative and reintegrative force in the life of every human being. Work must be a central theme in any rehabilitation process, underlining, pervading, and informing all the activities of a PSR-utilizing agency (Beard et al., 1982; Pressing et al., 1983; Connors, Graham, & Pulso, 1987; Anthony et al., 1978). Furthermore, the assumption is that successful involvement in some type of meaningful work is essential to develop independence and self-esteem as well as social contacts with and social recognition from people who are not part of the mental health community (Dulay & Steichen, 1982; Levine & Levine, 1970; Will, 1984). In a society in which work is viewed as vital and a driving ethic, vocational training and placement is a must for social reintegration in the community. Even for people who will remain somewhat dependent on the social services and will not gain full independence, part-time, transitional, or sheltered work is essential for self-esteem and growth (Dulay & Steichen, 1982). Bell and Ryan (1984) have reported that even hospital-based PSR should integrate 20 hours of work per week. PSR calls for professionals to teach not only vocational skills but also job search and job retention skills on an ongoing basis (Liberman et al., 1986). Although this principle is fundamental for PSR, as the word "rehabilitation" implies, in practice it is underemphasized in many small and large agencies claiming to utilize PSR (Taylor & Dowell, 1986) Tessler, Willis, and Gubman, 1986).

13. Social Rather Than Medical Supremacy

The medical model of caring for people with emotional disabilities stresses the word "illness." It approaches the so-called illness with a standard protocol of diagnosis, treatment, and care. Treatment in the medical model is limited to the manifestation of the illness, as diagnosed by the symptoms; stresses medication to reduce symptoms; and assumes that the professional knows what is right for the client (Beigel, 1980; Finch, 1985; Kanter, 1985). PSR, on the other hand, stresses skill-building and social support systems to assist persons to be better equipped to deal with life's stresses. PSR works hand-in-hand with a variety of complementary services to assure that the client's needs will be met, as even these bear psychological advantages (Stockdill, 1985). PSR assumes that psychotic manifestations are reflections of intrapsychic conflict and repetition of negative experiences rather than as a symptom of disease (Carpenter, McGlashin, & Strauss, 1977; Liberman et al., 1986). Rather than working with individuals to bring about insight and subsequent behavioral changes through psychotherapeutic methods, PSR efforts are directed towards the improvement of the life space, station, and venue of the people being served (Dincin, 1981; Easton, 1984). PSR requires an ethos of health, expectation of recovery, challenge, and a practical orientation offering individual autonomy and responsibility (Bell & Ryan, 1984). While the medical model stresses etiologies and past influences, PSR stresses the present with an orientation toward the future. The current level of functioning and the here and now are the focus of PSR. There is a difference between treatment (medical term), which focuses on the client's impairment and rehabilitation (PSR term), which focuses on utilizing the person's strengths and abilities for overall better independent functioning and fulfillment of social roles. In addition, the aforementioned principle of normalization is in contrast with the medical model, based as it is on isolating the sick (the mad), while protecting the general population (Mohelsky, 1985).

CONCLUSION

This chapter is intended to assist the PSR community in understanding the definitions and boundaries of this model. The method of study was content analysis of over two hundred articles, books, and internal documents, in an attempt to extract all the major components of the PSR model that are covered in the literature. It is important to note that claiming to follow the 13 principles discussed is not sufficient. The implementation of the model calls for clear evidence in practice, in clients' records, in functional rehabilitation plans, and in agency-documented regulations and procedures. The definition of this model is necessary if accreditation of this model is ever to be a reality. There are ever-increasing numbers of organizations claiming to utilize PSR while providing a widely varying array of services. If this diversity is ever to be molded into a significant and lasting movement within the field, it will be founded on a clear and well-defined basis.

Spaniol (1986) has noted that, while there has been significant growth in our knowledge of how effective PSR is in helping clients, it should not be a surprise to most professionals in the mental health field that no satisfying empirical studies have been carried out to determine the net quality of PSR vis--vis more traditional models, let alone the competing applications. The absence of agreement and operationalization of the applications is a barrier to progress in this direction.

In striving for understanding, the next step should be an analysis of the accepted and required procedures and practices within appropriate PSR organizations. Such an analysis will pave the way to an empirical process of assessing to what extent clients are being served according to PSR model, allowing the achievement of consistency and competence of care in utilizing the PSR model of care. A careful operationalization of the principles may enable us to weigh the importance of each principle separately to find out how it co-exists in terms of efficiency and to assess accepted levels of deviation from the model.

This presentation of core principles of PSR is recognized as a preliminary step on the road toward the development of a PSR model that allows for variation but is rooted solidly within a theoretical framework that can be measured and evaluated. Without such a base, the dissonance between practices among different providers will continue to expand until the approach is undefinable and indefensible.

REFERENCES

Anthony, W. A. (1972). Societal rehabilitation: Changing society's attitudes towards the physically and mentally disabled. *Rehabilitation Psychology, 13*(2), 117-126.

Anthony, W. A. (1977). Psychological rehabilitation: A concept in need of a method. *American Psychologist, 32*(8), 558-662.

Anthony, W. A. (1982). Explaining psychiatric rehabilitation by an analogy to physical rehabilitation. *Psychosocial Rehabilitation Journal, 5*(1), 61-65.

Anthony, W. A., Cohen, M., & Cohen, B. (1983). The philosophy, treatment process, and principles of the psychiatric rehabilitation approach. *New Direction in Mental Health, 7*(2), 67-69.

Anthony, W. A., Cohen, R. R., & Cohen, B. (1984). Psychiatric rehabilitation. In J. Talbott (Ed.), *The chronic mental patient: Five years later.* New York: Grune and Stratton.

Anthony, W. A., Cohen, M., & Farkas, M. (1982). A psychiatric rehabilitation treatment program. Can I recognize one if I see one? *Community Mental Health Journal, 18*(2), 83-96.

Anthony, W. A., Cohen, M. R., & Vitalo, R. (1978). The measurement of rehabilitation outcome. *Schizophrenia Bulletin, 4*(3), 365-383.

Anthony, W. A., & Liberman, R. P. ((1986). The practice of psychiatric rehabilitation: Historical, conceptual and research base. *Schizophrenia Bulletin, 12*(4), 542-553.

Argyle, M. (1981). The contribution of social interaction research to social skills training. In J. D. Wine & M. D. Smye (Eds.), *Social Competence.* New York: Guilford.

Aviram, V. & Segal, S. (1973). Exclusion of the Mentally Ill: A reflection of an old problem. *Archives of General Psychiatry, 23*(2), 120-131.

Barter, J. T., Queirolo, J. F., & Ekstrom, S. P. (1984). A psychoeducational approach to educating chronic mental patients for community living. *Hospital and Community Psychiatry, 35*(8), 793-797.

Beard, J. H., Propst, R. N., & Malamud, T. J. (1982). The Fountain House Model of Psychosocial Rehabilitation. *Psychosocial Rehabilitation Journal, 5*(1), 47-53.

Beardsley, C., Kessler, R., & Levin, E. I. (1984). Education for young adult chronic client. *Psychosocial Rehabilitation Journal, 8*(1), 44-52.

Beigel, A. (1980). The remedicalization of community mental health. *Hospital and Community Psychiatry, 35*(11), 1114-1117.

Bell, M. D., & Ryan, E. R. (1984). Integrating psychosocial rehabilitation into the hospital psychiatric service. *Hospital and Community Psychiatry, 35*(10), 1017-1023.

Black, J. B. (1987). Reflections on the social in psychosocial. *Psychosocial Rehabilitation Journal, 10*(3), 3-9.

Blank, A. S. (1982). Apocalypse terminable and interminable: Operation Outreach for Vietnam Veterans. *Hospital and Community Psychiatry, 33*(11), 913-918.

Bleuler, M. (1978). *The schizophrenic disorders: Long-term patient and family studies.* New Haven: Yale University Press.

Bond, G. R. (1984). An economic analysis of psychosocial rehabilitation. *Hospital and Community Psychiatry, 35*(4), 356-362.

Bond, G. R., Dincin, G., Setze, P. J., & Witheridge, T. F. (1984). The effectiveness of psychiatric rehabilitation: A summary of research at Thresholds. *Psychiatric Rehabilitation Journal, 7*(4), 6-22.

Bond, G. R., Witheridge, T. F., Setze, P. J., & Dincin, J. (1985). Preventing rehospitalization of clients in psychosocial rehabilitation programs. *Hospital and Community Psychiatry, 36*(9), 993-995.

Brekke, J. S., & Test, M. A. (1987). An empirical analysis of services delivered in a model community support program. *Psychosocial Rehabilitation Journal, 10*(4), 51-61.

Breven, N. L., & Driscoll, J. H. (1984). The effects of post psychiatric disability on employer evaluation of job applicants. *Journal of Applied Rehabilitation Counseling, 12*(1), 50-55.

Broekema, M. C., Danz, K. H., & Schloemer, C. U. (1975). Occupational therapy in a community aftercare program. *American Journal of Occupational Therapy, 29*(1), 22-27.

Carling, P. J., & Broskowski, A. (1986). Psychosocial rehabilitation programs as a challenge and an opportunity for community mental health centers. *Psychosocial Rehabilitation Journal, 10*(1), 39-48.

Carpenter, W. T., McGlashin, T. H., & Strauss, J. S. (1977). The treatment of acute schizophrenia without drugs. *American Journal of Psychiatry, 134*(1), 14-20.

Climo, L. (1983). Helping some state hospital mental patients make small but necessary changes: Transference openings from countertransference traps. *Community Mental Health Journal, 19*(2), 129-136.

Coles, G. S., Ciporen, F., Konisberg, R., & Cohen, B. (1980). Educational therapy in a community mental health center. *Community Mental Health Journal, 16*(1), 79-89.

Coles, G. S., Roth, L., & Pollack, I. W. (1978). Literacy skills of long-term hospitalized mental patients. *Hospital and Community Psychiatry, 29*(5), 512-516.

Connors, K. A., Graham, R. S., & Pulso, R. (1987). Playing store: Where is the vocational in psychiatric rehabilitation. *Psychosocial Rehabilitation Journal, 5*(1), 35-39.

Dellario, D. J. (1982). On the evaluation of community based alternative living arrangements (ALAS) for the psychiatrically disabled. *Psychosocial Rehabilitation Journal, 5*(1), 35-39.

Dincin, G. (1981). A community agency model. In J. A. Talbot (Ed.), *The Chronic Mentally Ill*. New York: Human Sciences Press.

Dulay, J. L., & Steichen, M. (1982). Transitional employment for the chronically mentally ill. *Occupational Therapy in Mental Health, 2*(3), 65-77.

Easton, K. (1984). Psychoanalytic principles in psychosocial rehabilitation. *Journal of the American Academy of Psychoanalysis, 12*(4), 569-584.

Estroff, S. E. (1983). How social is psychosocial rehabilitation? *Psychosocial Rehabilitation Journal, 7*(2), 6-20.

Field, G., & Yegge, L. (1982). A client outcome of study of community support demonstration project. *Psychosocial Rehabilitation Journal, 6*(2), 15-22.

Finch, E. S. (1985). Deinstitutionalization: Mental health and mental retardation services. *Psychosocial Rehabilitation Journal, 8*(3), 36-48.

Gardner, J. R. (1985). Scanning the environment: Psychosocial rehabilitation at the crossroad. *Psychosocial Rehabilitation Journal, 8*(3), 5-7.

Gardner, J. R., & O'Hara, T. J. (1985). The homeless. *Psychosocial Rehabilitation Journal, 8*(1), 17-20.

Hammaker, R. (1983). A client outcome evaluation of the statewide implementation of community support services. *Psychosocial Rehabilitation Journal, 7*(1), 2-10.

Harris, M., & Bergman, H. C. (1985). Networking with young adult chronic patients. *Psychosocial Rehabilitation Journal, 8*(3), 28-35.

Harrod, J. B. (1986). Defining case management in community support systems. *Psychosocial Rehabilitation Journal, 9*(3), 56-61.

Hatfield, A. B., Fierstein, R., & Johnson, D. (1982). Meeting the needs of families of the psychiatrically disabled. *Psychosocial Rehabilitation Journal, 6*(1), 27-40.

Herz, M. I. (1984). Recognizing and preventing relapse in patients with schizophrenia. *Hospital and Community Psychiatry, 35*(4), 344-349.

Hogarty, G. E., Goldberg, S. C., & Schooler, N. R. (1975). Drug and sociotherapy in the aftercare of schizophrenia: A review. In Greenblatt (Ed.), *Drugs in combination with other therapies.* New York: Grune and Stratton.

Hogarty, G. E., Schooler, N. R., Ulrich, R., Mussare, F., Ferro, P., & Herron, E. (1979). Fluphenazine and social therapy in the aftercare of schizophrenic patients. *Archives of General Psychiatry, 36*(12), 1283-1295.

Holland, T., Konick, A., Buffum, W., Smith, W. K., & Petchers, M. (1981). Institutional structure and resident outcomes. *Journal of Health and Social Behavior, 22*(4), 433-444.

Horne, K., & Otto, F. (1982). Adirondack House: The evaluation of psychosocial clubhouse. *Psychosocial Rehabilitation Journal, 6*(2), 2-14.

Huber, G., Gross, G., Schuttler, R., & Linz, M. (1980). Longitudinal studies of schizophrenic patients. *Schizophrenic Bulletin, 6*(4), 592-605.

IAPSRS (1985). Organizations providing psychosocial rehabilitation and related community support services in the United States: A national directory. McLean, VA., IAPSRS.

Kanter, J. (1985). The process of change in the long-term mentally ill: A naturalistic approach. *Psychosocial Rehabilitation Journal, 9*(1), 55-69.

Katz-Garris, L. (1982). Group-oriented therapy with psychiatrically disabled persons. In M. Seligman (Ed.), *Group psychotherapy and counselling with special populations.* Baltimore: University Park Press.

Kultgen, P., & Habenstein, R. (1984). Process and goals in aftercare programs for deinstitutionalized elderly mental patients. *The Gerontologist, 24*(2), 162-173.

Lamb, H. R., & Peele, R. (1984). The need for continuing asylum and sanctuary. *Hospital and Community Psychiatry, 38*(8), 798-802.

Lanoil, J. (1982). An analysis of the psychiatric psychosocial rehabilitation center. *Psychosocial Rehabilitation Journal, 5*(1), 55-59.

Levine, M. D. (1984). A psychologist's reaction. *Psychosocial Rehabilitation Journal, 7*(3), 22-25.

Levine, M., & Levine, A. A. (1970). *Social history of helping services: Clinic, court, school, community.* New York: Appleton Century Crofts.

Liberman, R. P. (1982). Social factors in schizophrenia. In L. Grinspoon (Ed.), *The American Psychiatric Association. Annual Review.* Washington D.C.: American Psychiatric Press.

Liberman, R. P., Mueser, K. T., Wallace, C. J., Jacobs, H. E., Eckman, T., & Massel, H. K. (1986). Teaching skills in the psychiatrically disabled: learning coping and competence. *Schizophrenia Bulletin, 12*(4), 631-647.

Liberman, R. P., & Rueger, D. B. (1984). Drug-psychological treatment interactions: Comprehensive rehabilitation for chronic schizophrenia. *Psychosocial Rehabilitation Journal, 7*(30), 3-15.

Livneh, H. (1983). A meta-model for rehabilitation: Suggestions for a dimensional approach. *Journal of Applied Rehabilitation Counseling, 14*(4), 5-9.

Lowell, W. E., MacLean, N. V., & Carroll, M. (1985). The use of analysis in determining patient selection for rehabilitation programs. *Psychosocial Rehabilitation Journal, 8*(3), 15-27.

Manos, N., Gkiouzepas, J., & Lavretiadis, G. (1984). The value of psychosocial approach in the treatment of long-term hospitalized patients. *Hospital and Community Psychiatry, 34*(5), 456-458.

Marlowe, H. A., Jr. (1982). The social competence deficit model of abnormal behavior: Summarization of empirical studies. In H. A. Marlowe, Jr., and R. B. Weinberg (Eds.), *The management of deinstitutionalization: Proceedings of the 1982 Florida Conference on Deinstitutionalization.* Tampa: University of South Florida.

Martin, J. A., & Dubbert, P. M. (1982). Exercise and health: The adherence problem. *Behavioral Medicine Update, 4*(1), 16-24.

Maslen, D. (1982). Rehabilitation training for community living skills: Concepts and Techniques. *Occupational Therapy in Mental Health, 2*(10), 33-49.

Mellen, V. (1985). A response to the American Psychiatric Association report on the homeless mentally ill. *Psychosocial Rehabilitation Journal, 8*(4), 3-10.

Mir, M. D. (1983). Community participation in social defense. *Social Defense, 19*(4), 33–41.

Mohelsky, H. (1985). Madness as a symbol of the crowd and its implications for psychosocial rehabilitation. *Psychosocial Rehabilitation Journal, 8*(4), 42–48.

Mullen, F. (1984). Re-entry: The educational needs of the cancer survivor. *Health-Education Quarterly, 10*(Special Suppl.), 88–94.

Nirje, B. (1969). The normalization principle and its human management implications. In R. Kugel (Ed.), *Changing patterns in residential services for the mentally retarded.* Washington, DC: President's Committee on Mental Retardation Monographs.

Pattison, E. M., Lamas, R., & Hurd, G. (1979). Social network medication of anxiety. *Psychiatric Annals, 9*(1), 56–67.

Polkow, L., & Volpe, B. T. (1985). The next phase in head injury rehabilitation: Reentry. *Cognitive Rehabilitation, 3*(5), 20–23.

Pressing, K. O., Peterson, C. L., Barness, J. K., & Riley, B. D. (1983). Growing wing: A psychosocial rehabilitation program for the mentally ill patients in a rural setting. *Psychosocial Rehabilitation Journal, 6*(4), 13–24.

Schultz, M. T., et al. (1986). An assessment of the needs of rehabilitation veterans. *Journal of Visual Impairment and Blindness, 79*(70), 301–305.

Segal, S., & Aviram, U. (1976). Community based sheltered care. In P. Ahmad and S. Plog (Eds.), *State mental hospitals: What happens when they close.* New York: Plenum.

Shapira, Z., Cnaan, R. A., & Cnaan, A. (1985). Mentally retarded workers' reactions to their jobs. *American Journal of Mental Deficiency, 90*(20), 160–166.

Spaniol, L. (1986). Program evaluation in psychosocial rehabilitation: A management perspective. *Psychosocial Rehabilitation Journal, 10*(1), 15–26.

Spaniol, L., Zipple, A., & Fitzgerald, S. (1984). How professionals can share power with families: Practical approaches to working with families of the mentally ill. *Psychosocial Rehabilitation Journal, 8*(2), 77–84.

Smith, M. K., Brown, D., Gibbs, L., Sanders, H., & Cremer, K (1984). Client involvement in psychosocial rehabilitation. *Psychosocial Rehabilitation Journal, 8*(1), 35–43.

Smith, M. K., & Ford, J. (1986). Client involvement: Practical advice for professionals. *Psychosocial Rehabilitation Journal, 9*(3), 25–34.

Spivak, M. (1974). A conceptual framework for structuring the housing of psychiatric patients in the community. *Community Mental Health Journal, 10*(3), 345–350.

Stockdill, J. (1985). *Definition of psychosocial rehabilitation.* Transmittal no. 1-NIMH Office of State and Community Liaison of State Mental Health Directors. Rockville, MD: NIMH.

Straub, E. G. (1983). Independent living skills training for multi-handicap deaf adults: A residential approach. *Reading in Deafness,* Mono 6, 150–161.

Strauss, J. S., & Carpenter, W. T. (1977). Prediction of outcome in schizophrenia: Characteristcs of outcome. *Archives of General Psychiatry, 34*(2), 159–163.

Strauss, J., Hafez, H., Liberman, P., & Harding, C. (1984). The course of psychiatric disorder. iii: Longitudenal principles. *American Journal of Psychiatry, 142*(3), 283–296.

Sylph, J. A., Ross, H. E., & Kedward, H. B. (1977). Social disability in psychiatric patients. *American Journal of Psychiatry, 134*(12), 1391–1394.

Tanaka, H. T. (1983). Psychosocial rehabilitation: Future trends and directions. *Psychosocial Rehabilitation Journal, 6*(40), 7–12.

Taylor, A., & Dowell, D. A. (1986). Social skills training in board and care homes for the long-term mentally ill. *Psychosocial Rehabilitation Journal, 10*(2), 55–69.

Tessler, R. C., Willis, G., & Gubman, G. D. (1986). Defining and measuring community care. *Psychosocial Rehabilitation Journal, 10*(1), 27–38.

Test, M. A., & Stein, L. I. (1977). Special living arrangements: A model for decision-making. *Hospital and Community Psychiatry, 28*(8), 108–610.

Turner, J., & TenHoor, W. (1978). The NIMH community support program: Pilot approach to a needed social reform. *Schizophrenia Bulletin, 4*(3), 313-348.

Unger, K. V., Danley, K. S., Kohn, L., & Hutchinson, D. (1987). Rehabilitation through education: A university-based continuing education program for young adults with psychiatric disabilities on a university campus. *Psychosocial Rehabilitation Journal, 10*(3), 35-49.

Walsh, J. (1987). The family education and support group: A psychoeducational aftercare program. *Psychosocial Rehabilitation Journal, 10*(3), 51-61.

Wallace, C. J., & Liberman, R. P. (1985). Social skills training for patients with schizophrenia: A controlled clinical trial. *Psychiatry Research, 15*(3), 239-247.

Wallace, C. J., Nelson, C. J., Liberman, R. P., Aitchinson, R. H., Lokoff, D., Elder, J. P., & Ferris, C. (1980). A review and critique of social skills training with schizophrenic patients. *Schizophrenia Bulletin, 6*(1), 42-68.

Weinberg, R. B., & Marlowe, H. A., Jr. (1983). Reorganizing the social in psychosocial competence: The importance of social network interventions. *Psychosocial Rehabilitation Journal, 6*(4), 25-34.

Will, M. (1984). Bridges from school to working life. *Clearinghouse on the Handicap, 5*, September-October, 585-604.

Yess, J. P. (1981). What families of the mentally ill want. *Community Support Service Journal, 2*(1), 1-3.

29

Coping With the Enormity of Illness and Disability

Arthur E. Dell Orto

No child, adolescent, adult, or family should have to deal with the ravages of illness or disability. To this we all agree. But, unfortunately, life does not always conform to our hopes or aspirations. When severe illness occurs, it seems like an unending nightmare that robs us of our resources, insults our dignity, and often pushes us to the brink of desperation. Sometimes we survive—often not knowing how—puzzled by the abilities that came from nowhere and indebted to the support systems that surprised us with their responsiveness. Other times, however, the results are more disappointing.

The enormity of illness and disability, however, is so pervasive, powerful, and all-encompassing that coping with, challenging, and overcoming it cannot be left to chance. Therefore, it is imperative that all rehabilitation professionals be aware of and in tune with the complexities surrounding the illness/disability experience. To this end, I would like to share some observations with you:

- No one is completely prepared for illness or disability
- Illness changes a family and challenges its resources
- The illness process brings out the best and worst in people
- Disability can deplete resources as well as create them
- Often the only support is the family
- All people do not have families they can rely on
- Not all families are capable of responding to the illness and disability of a family member
- New skills are needed to meet the new challenges created by illness
- Coping with chronic disability is an ongoing developmental process
- Existing health care resources can help as well as hinder adjustment

These points are made as selected examples of issues that must be expanded, explored, understood, and attended to if the family and friends of people with disabilities are to renegotiate a position of survival, development, enrichment, and attainment for themselves and their loved ones.

In my professional and personal life, I have seen families cope with outrageously complex situations. As we know, illness is largely a subjective experience. Some may be able to cope with illness better than others. Unfortunately, there is no choice. If there were a choice, I am certain that many persons living with an illness or disability, as well as their families, could identify other situations that would be more tolerable and less inconvenient.

When discussing the differential impact of disability we must be aware that the resources, problems, hopes, and dreams of people are as different as snowflakes. While the element of individuality is the key to emotional survival, it must be fueled by the commonality that all challenged people and their families share. This commonality is the active ingredient that can enable people to negotiate the perils of the physical and emotional rehabilitation process by recognizing they are not alone and seeing that it can be done. It is more unfortunate when a person's pain and frustration is increased by the *ignorance* of resources and models rather than *lack* of them. One explanation for this lack of awareness is that in the midst of an illness, people are so devastated that they are unable to cope with the hassles of identifying the very systems that are designed to help them.

However, I would not focus on the limitations of the existing resources, but rather create a functional awareness that there are aspects of health care and rehabilitation that must be improved.

A critical element in learning to cope with illness is learning to use resources efficiently and effectively. But what happens when there is nothing? Marilyn Price Spivak founded the National Head Injury Foundation in response to the lack of resources needed to assist her family in coping with the consequences of her daughter's head trauma.

Realistically, however, not everyone is in a position to be a founder of a national foundation. Also, such an accomplishment does not alter the irreversible. When all is said and done, families are faced with the reality of functional or dysfunctional coping. Often, this is a point not understood by the health care system; that is, the *right* and *need* for persons to express grief and loss in a variety of ways. The obligation of parents and health care providers is to ensure that normal or unique grief does not get misinterpreted as a sign of weakness or dysfunction. For example, a parent may express grief or anger in the initial phase of the grieving process and, in turn, may be rejected and isolated by family, friends, and even health professionals due to their inability to respond to these intense feelings.

Such situations point out the need to create resources that are supportive and understanding of the complexities faced by families of persons with unique physical and emotional needs.

As we all know, dramatic changes often occur in a family during the illness and disability experience. One explanation may be that people base their relationships on what they would like their lives to be. The marriage vows, for example, state "in illness and health," but few of us are in a position to comprehensively understand what illness means. Perhaps complete understanding is very difficult, but what can be attained is the development of personal resources to negotiate life, living, and illness. Without a functional, realistic attitude, people tend to create unrealistic goals for themselves and their families. We strive to be always healthy, happy, and satisfied, and are not prepared when these goals become a memory and are replaced with an unanticipated harsh reality.

How can we best maximize our chances for emotional survival when faced with illness and disability? Why should persons with disabling conditions feel isolated? Can we not learn from each other, share mutual strengths, and create an environment that models success? Health care professionals and health care systems must begin to recognize that it is more often *their* limitations and not those of the patients and their families that create problems. It is easy to blame a patient or the family for not doing what we want them to do, but much harder to recognize, accept, and change what we do not do.

Similarly, patients and families can readily blame others when they are not doing all they could to develop coping skills and create functional environments. No, blame is not constructive—but understanding is. We must understand our:

- Strengths
- Humanness
- Problems
- Resources
- Liabilities
- Needs
- Rights
- Vulnerability
- Responsibility
- Options
- Choices
- Dreams

Let us teach each other and pave the way to a better health care environment that minimizes pain, reduces aggravation, supports the family, gives hope to those who are ill and disabled, shares optimism, and deals with reality. Illness has the power to limit those affected by it, as well as fragment the family. Rehabilitation has the potential of putting illness into perspective and creating an option for the family to live as fully as possible. The harsh reality may be impossible to change, but it certainly can be made more bearable!

Part VII: New Directions—Study Questions and Personal Awareness Exercises

1. How does AIDS challenge the rehabilitation and health care system to practice what it preaches?
2. Should the care of a person with a head injury be allowed more resources than a person with any other disability?
3. Should resources be limited when a person reaches a particular age? At what age and how would that decision be made?
4. Should all families and family members be required to be caregivers for a family member with a disability? How can society decide who should or should not be required?
5. Discuss how alcohol and drugs can be major factors and stressors in the disability experience.
6. Are there any situations you can think of that create a disability experience that is so complex that the right to die could outweigh the right for treatment and rehabilitation?
7. Are the principles of psychosocial rehabilitation equally relevant to emotional disability and physical disability?

Personal Awareness Exercises

1. Suppose you had a disability that incapacitated you to a degree, then didn't affect you further for a year; severely incapacitated you for a month and then didn't affect you for three months. There is no continuity in your condition behaviorally or emotionally; you face each situation new, without reference to past experience. Discuss the impact on your social, family, and work relationships.
2. In recent years, hemodialysis patients have been given new hope that they might someday be free from dependence on a machine and benefit from a kidney transplant. Have you thought about donating your kidney for transplant purposes after your death? Present a rationale for your decision.
3. How would AIDS affect your life? The life of your family?
4. A close friend of yours has kidney failure and offers you $50,000 for one of your kidneys. Any response? Discuss how much money you would want to

have or how close the person would have to be before you would consider donating or selling your kidney.

5. Have you become a potential donor of your eyes for transplant after your death? If not, why not? Explore implications of such an action and make a decision after you have all the facts.

6. Would you consider donating one of your eyes to a totally blind person if there were a chance he or she might see again? What if this person were someone you loved very much? What if the person were disabled?

7. List the things that would change in your life if your spouse or loved one had a traumatic brain injury?

8. You are informed that you and your partner can biologically never have a child and you wish very much to adopt. The only children available for adoption to you are children with significant disabilities. Would you adopt one? What would affect your decision? Would the type of disability make a difference?

9. After being a widow(er) for two years, you make the acquaintance of a woman/man to whom you are attracted. After forming a relationship and becoming serious, you decide to marry. At this point, the person tells you she/he has a child who is physically disabled and institutionalized (cerebral palsy, age nine). The child comes home one weekend a month and is to be discharged in one year. Knowledge of the child was kept from you because of the fear of how you would react. Any reaction?

10. Many people express interest and concern with rehabilitation issues. What have you and/or your family actually done to make such concerns an active part in your lives? If little, are there rehabilitation related activities with which you and your family might become involved?

11. Select three disabilities; (1) one which you consider to be mildly severe, (2) one which is moderately severe and (3) one which you consider to be extremely severe. Would your feelings and/or behaviors toward the people you love change if one of them were disabled by any of the disabilities you selected? If so, how? Discuss your reaction. Does this awareness suggest any changes you might consider for interaction with these people? Discuss any changes and be specific.

APPENDIX A

Representative Books Related to the Psychological and Social Impact of Disability

The following books published since 1980 represent contributions to the understanding of the psychological and social impact of disability. The organization of this listing is based on date of publication, with newer books listed first.

Ethical Issues in Disability and Rehabilitation edited by Barbara Duncan and Diane Woods, published by the World Institute on Disability, Oakland, CA, Rehabilitation International, New York, and the World Rehabilitation Fund, New York, in 1990.

> Focusing on decision making as it relates to bioethics, this publication is a report of an international symposium held in 1989 designed to provide a forum for suggestions on how persons with disabilities can become more active and influential in this area. Includes a collection of conference papers and commentary, as well as an annotated international bibliography.

Psychological Aspects of Developmental and Physical Disabilities: *A Casebook* edited by Michel Hersen and Vincent B. Van Hasselt, published by Sage, Newbury Park, CA, in 1990.

> This book provides examples of the types of psychological interventions that can be applied to problems of persons with physical and developmental disabilities. The emphasis is on detailed presentations of 14 individual cases by experts with an emphasis on psychological assessment and treatment. The 14 cases cover a wide range of physical and mental disabilities.

Flying Without Wings, by Arnold Beisser (*), New York, NY. Published by Doubleday, 1989.

> This is Arnold Beisser's personal story of remaking his life after contracting polio in one of the last epidemics of the 1950's. He was completely paralyzed, confined to an iron lung and subsequently, a reclining wheelchair in which he

---

*Adapted with permission from the *Disability Studies Quarterly*, Fall 1990.

can spend limited periods of time. This book could serve as a useful guide for people trying to remake their lives, by helping them to understand that none of us is autonomous.

Psychosocial Interventions with Physically Disabled Persons, edited by Bruce Heller, Louis M. Flohr, and Leonard S. Zegars; published by Rutgers University Press in 1989.

This book, which is the fourth volume in the Mind and Medicine series, addresses significant issues in the psychosocial assessment, treatment, and rehabilitation of persons with physical disabilities. It offers theoretical, research-based, and clinical information written by experts in their field.

Don't Worry, He Won't Get Far on Foot. The Autobiography of a Dangerous Man, by John Callahan (*), New York, by William Morrow, 1989.

Some people might see this book and its quadriplegic, alcoholic, cartoonist on welfare as sick, offensive, and degrading. Others may see it as funny, brilliant, creative, and insightful. Regardless of one's moral and aesthetic stance about this autobiography, the reader will learn much about one man's experiences with parents, religion, alcohol, quadriplegia, hospitals, rehabilitation centers, nursing homes, and the disability welfare system.

Attitudes Toward Persons with Disabilities, edited by Harold Yuker, published by Springer Publishing Co., New York, in 1988.

This volume provides a broad perspective on people's attitudes toward persons with disabilities with coverage by important people in the field. Topics included are basic issues, sources of attitudes, measurement of attitudes, attitudes toward specific groups, and attitude change.

The Meaning of Illness, edited by Mark Kidel and Susan Rowe-Leete, (*) published by Routledge, New York, 1988.

This collection of varied essays arose from two conferences held in 1985 and 1986 in Devon, England, which explored the meaning of illness. In the volume that has been culled from these conferences, an assortment of medical and psychological professionals, as well as articulate and analytical lay people who have experienced illness as patients, explore particular perspectives in an attempt to reframe illness as it has been traditionally defined by Western medicine and culture.

Chronic Illness and Disability, edited by Catherine Chilmen, Elan Nunnaly, and Fred Cox, published by Sage, Newbury Park, CA, in 1988.

Volume two of the five volume *Families in Trouble* series focuses on the problems of families troubled by illness and disability. Family health difficulties are viewed from a total family systems perspective recognizing the rights and responsibilities of each family member.

Women with Disabilities—Essays in Psychology, Culture, and Politics, by Michelle Fine and Adrienne Asch (*). Published by Temple University Press, 1988.

A timely publication that creates a comprehensive perspective of women which facilitates awareness and understanding.

Family Interventions Throughout Chronic Illness and Disability, edited by Paul Power, Arthur Dell Orto, and Martha Gibbons, published by Springer Publishing Co., New York, in 1988.

This book focuses on interventions designed to assist families to cope with the enormity of chronic illness and disability by suggesting interventions that can put the disability into perspective and create options to enable families to live more fully. It further offers knowledge about selected disabilities and chronic diseases, particularly as they impact family dynamics. Useful assessment approaches designed to assist in selecting helping strategies are provided.

Advances in Clinical Rehabilitation, edited by Myron Eisenberg and Roy C. Greziak, published by Springer Publishing Co., New York, beginning in 1987.

A series designed to provide timely and practical information about rehabilitation interventions from a multidisciplinary perspective, each of two volumes to date covers four topical content areas: advances in clinical assessment, advances in rehabilitation technology, selected topics, and advances in rehabilitation research. Disability topics covered include low back pain, brain injury, childhood disabilities, spinal cord injury, thermal injury, and cancer in Volume 1, and brain disorders, disabilities in the elderly, pain, feeding disorders, and aphasia in Volume 2. This is an especially useful book for persons who wish to remain current regarding innovations in clinical rehabilitation that can have immediate positive impact. Volumes are to be released at approximately 18-month intervals.

Disease and Representation: Images of Illness from Madness to AIDS, by Sander L. Gilman (*). Cornell University Press, Ithaca, New York, 1987.

Gilman continues to decode the underlying structures of representation that are part of the Western discourse of disease, the discourse that defines "the diseased" as Other. The "deep structure" of stereotypes is, in this work, only sketchily examined, the main focus is on the ways in which the Western association of disease with chaos and loss of control has been manifested in art, science, and the news media.

Physical Disability—A Psychosocial Approach (second edition), by Beatrice Wright, published by Harper & Row, New York, in 1983.

Relating physical disability to psychology, this book provides the reader with conceptual understanding and practical information regarding the impact of disability. The wealth of concrete examples and nontechnical language make this book of great value to a wide range of readers, both professional and non-professional.

Missing Pieces: A Chronicle of Living with a Disability, by Irving Kenneth Zola, published by Temple University Press, Philadelphia, in 1982.

The personal odyssey of a man who presents what it is like to have a disability in a world that values vigor and health. This book offers a rare insight into the human condition shared by 30 million Americans. A must for those working with the persons who have disabilities.

Ordinary Lives: Voices of Disability and Disease, edited by Irving Kenneth Zola, published by Apple-wood Books, Cambridge, Massachusetts, in 1982.

A collection of engaging stories by men and women who have experienced first hand a chronic disease or disability. The presentations are not about overcoming extraordinary odds but instead about living a full life.

Adjustment to Severe Disability: A Metamorphosis, by Charlene De Loach and Bobby Greer, published by McGraw-Hill, New York, in 1981.

Designed for professionals-in-training, practicing professionals, and parents or families of persons with disabilities. This book focuses on (1) the societal misconceptions that impede the adjustment of persons with disabilities; (2) the effects that those misconceptions have on the attitudes and effectiveness of rehabilitation workers; and (3) existing services, laws, environmental changes, and technical advances that affect persons with disabilities.

The Psychology of Disability, by Carolyn Vash, published by Springer Publishing Co., New York, in 1981.

Based on the author's experiences as a person with a disability and as a rehabilitation psychologist, this book has two primary purposes. The first is to describe the disability experience; the second is to focus on the types of therapeutic strategies used in coping with disabilities. This book is useful for rehabilitation workers, clients, and clients' families.

Annual Review of Rehabilitation, edited by Elizabeth Pan, Thomas Backer, and Carolyn Vash, with the publication of Volumes 1–5, Springer Publishing Co., New York, from 1980 to 1986.

Providing an annual review of the advances in rehabilitation, this publication presented a thorough and critical analysis of the literature in the following areas: administration, rehabilitation process, human resource development, service development, total rehabilitation, demographic groups, disability types, and settings. It was last published in 1986.

The Role of the Family in the Rehabilitation of the Physically Disabled, edited by Paul W. Power and Arthur E. Dell Orto, published by Pro-Ed, Austin, TX, in 1980. This comprehensive collection of original material, selected readings, and personal statements thoroughly describes the knowledge and skills necessary to work effectively with the families of persons with physical disabilities. It describes the manner in which the family influences the adjustment of the disabled family member who is challenged physically, and the role of the family in the rehabilitation process.

APPENDIX B

*Representative Journals Related
to the Psychological and Social
Impact of Physical Disability*

Archives of Physical Medicine and Rehabilitation. Suite 1310, 78 East Adams Street, Chicago, IL.

    Archives is the official journal and published monthly by The American Congress of Rehabilitation Medicine and American Academy of Physical Medicine and Rehabilitation.

Disability, Handicap and Society is written by the Department of Education, Bristol Polytechnic, Red Lane Hill, Bristol, United Kingdom, BS6 6U2.

    A quality international journal that addresses current issues that impact the lives of persons living the disability experience.

Disability Studies Quarterly. Department of Sociology, P.O. Box 9110, Brandeis University, Waltham MA, 02254-9110.

    A valuable resource that provides a comprehensive overview of current literature, reviews, and events designed to meet the needs of consumers as well as professionals.

The Exceptional Parent is published bimonthly by Exceptional Parent, 1170 Commonwealth Avenue, Boston, MA 02134.

    Provides practical information to families of children with disabilities. Emphasis is on relevant programs, approaches, and resources that are useful to a variety of family situations.

Journal of Applied Rehabilitation Counseling is a quarterly journal published by the National Rehabilitation Counseling Association, 633 South Washington Street, Alexandria, VA 22314.

    Concerned with issues of importance to the practicing rehabilitation counselor, the focus is on implications for practice, with less emphasis on technical and research issues.

Journal of Chronic Diseases is published monthly by Pergamon Press, Maxwell House, Fairview Park, Elmsford, NY 10523.

Explores various aspects of chronic illness for all age groups, including long-term medical and nursing care, the impact of the chronically ill on the community, and rehabilitation needs.

Journal of Counseling and Development is published six times per year by the American Association for Counseling and Development, 5999 Stevenson Avenue, Alexandria, VA 22304.

The official journal of AACD, includes articles of broad interest to counselors and counseling psychologists who work in schools, colleges, community agencies, and the government.

Journal of Head Trauma Rehabilitation is published quarterly by Aspen Publishers, 7201 McKinney Circle, Frederick, MD 21701.

It provides information for practicing professionals on the clinical management and rehabilitation of the person with a head injury.

Journal of Rehabilitation is a quarterly professional publication by the National Rehabilitation Association, 633 South Washington Street, Alexandria, VA 22314.

The journal is concerned with the rehabilitation field in general. Articles cover a broad expanse of interests and are usually nontechnical and non-research in nature.

Psychosocial Rehabilitation Journal is a quarterly professional journal published by the International Association of Psychosocial Rehabilitation Services and the Department of Rehabilitation Counseling, Sargent College of Allied Health Professions, Boston University, Boston, MA 02215.

Addressing the comprehensive needs of the psychiatrically disabled, this journal is a state-of-the-art publication that focuses on theory, programmatic models, and skills relative to this population.

Psychosomatics is the quarterly official journal of the Academy of Psychosomatic Medicine, 5824 North Magnolia, Chicago, IL 60660 and is published by American Psychiatric Press, 1400 K Street NW, Washington, DC 20005.

Explores the role of emotional factors in the daily practice of comprehensive medicine.

Psychosomatic Medicine is a semimonthly journal published by the American Psychosomatic Society, 265 Nassau Road, Roosevelt, NY 11575.

This journal is concerned with fostering knowledge concerning psychosomatic problems.

Rehabilitation Counseling Bulletin is a quarterly journal published by the American Rehabilitation Counseling Association, 599 Stevenson Avenue, Alexandria, VA 22304.

This journal focuses on articles illuminating theory and practice and exploring innovations in the field of rehabilitation counseling. It contains a substantial proportion of articles related to psychological issues in disability.

Rehabilitation Education, the official journal of the National Council on Rehabilitation Education is published quarterly by Pergamon Press, Maxwell House, Fairview Park, Elmsford, NY 10523.

This journal publishes a variety of rehabilitation-focused articles that would be of interest to rehabilitation educators and researchers.

Rehabilitation Nursing is published monthly by the Medical Economics Co., Oradell, NJ 07649.

This journal includes a variety of articles that would be of interest to the Rehabilitation Nurse and other allied health specialties.

Rehabilitation Psychology is the journal of the Rehabilitation Psychology Division of the American Psychological Association, 1200 Seventeenth Street, NW, Washington, DC 20036. Published by Springer Publishing Company, 536 Broadway, New York, NY 10012.

This journal publishes original investigations, theoretical papers, and evaluative reviews relating to the psychological aspects of illness, disability, retardation, and deprivation.

Sexuality and Disability is published quarterly by Human Sciences Press, 232 Spring Street, New York, NY 10013.

The purpose of this journal is to provide a forum for clinical and research progress in the area of sexuality as it relates to a wide range of physical and mental illnesses and disabling conditions.

APPENDIX C

Representative Organizations Serving Persons with Handicaps

This appendix contains a partial listing of the many resources serving persons with disabilities.

Alexander Graham Bell Association for the Deaf
3417 Volta Place, N.W.
Washington, DC 20007
(202)337-5220

The Alexander Graham Bell Association for the Deaf is an international organization, founded in 1980, whose goal is to foster supportive environments and programs directed to the preparation of hearing-impaired children and adults to participate independently in the lives of their families, communities, and countries.

American Association of Mental Deficiency (AAMD)
5201 Connecticut Avenue, N.W.
Washington, DC 20015
(202)685-5400

The AAMD is a national organization (founded 1876) of professionals whose objectives are to effect the highest standards of living for the persons with mental retardation and developmental disability.

American Cancer Society, Inc.
1599 Clifton Road, N.E.
Atlanta, GA 30329
800-ACS-2345
(404)320-3333

Founded in 1913, the American Cancer Society's major purpose is to organize and wage a continuing campaign against cancer and its crippling effects, through medical research, professional and public education, and service and rehabilitation programs.

American Coalition of Citizens with Disabilities
1346 Connecticut Ave., N.W.
Room 308
Washington, DC 20036
(202)785-4265

The major purpose of ACCD is to promote the human and constitutional rights of citizens with disabilities through advocacy and legislative programs.

American Congress of Rehabilitation Medicine
20 N. Michigan Avenue
Chicago, IL 60602
(312)236-9512

The American Congress of Rehabilitation Medicine exists for the purpose of providing a scientific forum for communication among the many disciplines concerned with rehabilitation medicine.

American Foundation for the Blind, Inc. (AFB)
15 West 16th Street
New York, NY 10011
(212)620-2032
(800)232-5463

The AFB is a private, national organization whose objective is to help those handicapped by blindness to achieve the fullest possible development and utilization of their capacities and integration into the social, cultural, and economic life of the community.

American Occupational Therapy Association (AOTA)
1383 Picard Drive, P.O. Box 1725
Rockville, MD 20850-0822
(301)948-9626

The AOTA, founded in 1917, is the national membership standard-setting, accrediting, and credentialing organization for the profession.

American Physical Therapy Association
111 N. Fairfax Street
Alexandria, VA 22314
(703)684-4782

The American Physical Therapy Association, founded in 1921, is a membership organization whose purpose is to meet the physical therapy needs of people through the development and improvement of physical therapy education, practice, and research.

American Rehabilitation Counseling Association (ARCA)
5999 Stevenson Avenue
Alexandria, VA 22304-3303
(703)823-9800

The ARCA, a division of the American Association for Counseling and Development is a national professional association dedicated to the advancement of the theory and practice of rehabilitation counseling.

American Speech, Language, and Hearing Association
10801 Rockville Pike
Rockville, MD 20852
(800)638-8255
(301)897-5700

Two major purposes of the American Speech, Language, and Hearing Association are to encourage basic scientific study of the processes of individual human communication with special reference to speech, hearing, and language; and to foster improvement of clinical procedures concerning such disorders.

The Arthritis Foundation
3400 Peachtree Road, N.E.
Suite 1101
Atlanta, GA 30326
(404)266-0795

The Arthritis Foundation is a voluntary health agency seeking the total answer—cause, prevention, cure—to the nation's foremost crippling disease.

Association for Retarded Citizens of the United States
2501 Avenue J
P.O. Box 6109
Arlington, TX 76005
(817)640-0204

The Association for Retarded Citizens of the United States is a membership organization whose major purpose is to promote the general welfare of persons of all ages with retardation through research, placement, and education.

Council of State Administrators of Vocational Rehabilitation
P.O. Box 3776
Washington, DC 20007
(202)638-4634

The Council of State Administrators of Vocational Rehabilitation is composed of the chief administrators of the public vocational rehabilitation agencies for persons with physical and mental handicaps in the United States.

Disabled American Veterans (DAV)
National Headquarters
P.O. Box 1403
Cincinnati, OH 45214
(606)441-7300

The DAV's paramount objectives are to promote the welfare of disabled veterans injured while in the armed services, as well as that of their dependents; and to provide a service program.

Epilepsy Foundation of America
4351 Garden City Drive
Landover, MD 20785
(800)EFA-1000
(301)459-3700

Founded in 1967 after a series of mergers, the Epilepsy Foundation of America is a national voluntary health agency leading the fight against epilepsy in the United States.

Goodwill Industries of America
9200 Wisconsin Avenue
Washington, DC 20014
(301)530-6500

Founded in 1902, Goodwill Industries of America and its member local Goodwill Industries provide vocational rehabilitation services, training, employment, and opportunities for personal growth as an interim step in the rehabilitation process for person's with handicaps and who are disadvantaged.

International Association of Rehabilitation Facilities, Inc.
5530 Wisconsin Avenue, No. 955
Washington, DC 20015
(301)654-5882

In 1969, the Association of Rehabilitation Centers and the National Association of Sheltered Workshops and Homebound Programs merged to form the International Association of Rehabilitation Facilities, Inc., with the purpose of assisting in the development and improvement of services of member facilities in providing services to persons with handicaps.

Muscular Dystrophy Associations of America, Inc.
810 Seventh Avenue
New York, NY 10019
(212)586-0808

Muscular Dystrophy Associations of America, Inc., a nonsectarian voluntary health organization, was founded and incorporated in 1950 to foster research seeking cures or effective treatments for muscular dystrophy and related neuromuscular diseases.

National Association of the Deaf
814 Thayer Avenue
Silver Spring, MD 20910
(301)587-1788

The National Association of the Deaf is a private organization founded in 1880 for the purpose of promoting the social, educational, and economic well-being of the deaf citizens of the United States.

The National Association for Mental Health, Inc.
1021 Prince Street
Alexandria, VA 22314
(703)684-7722

The National Association for Mental Health is a private organization with local affiliate chapters whose aims are to improve attitudes toward mental illness and health and improve the welfare of persons with mental illness.

National Easter Seal Society for Crippled Children and Adults
70 East Lake Street
Chicago, Il 60601
(800)221-6827
(312)726-6200

The National Easter Seal Society conducts a three-point program, in-service, education, and research at the national, state, and local levels; programs serve all types of children and adults with physical handicaps.

National Federation of the Blind
1800 Johnson Street
Baltimore, MD 21230
(301)659-9314

The purpose of the NFB is the complete integration of blind people into society as equal members. This objective involves the removal of legal, economic, and social discrimination and the education of the public to new concepts concerning blindness.

The National Foundation/March of Dimes
Box 2000
White Plains, NY 10602
(914)428-7100

The National Foundation/March of Dimes (founded in 1938) has as its goal the prevention of birth defects.

National Head Injury Foundation
1140 Connecticut Avenue, N.W., Suite 812
Washington, DC 20036
(202)296-6443
(800)444-NHIF (patients & families only)

The National Head Injury Foundation responds to the comprehensive and complex needs of head-injured persons and their families. The foundation emphasizes support, research, education, and program development through its national and state chapters.

The National Multiple Sclerosis Society
205 East 42nd Street
New York, NY 10017
(212)532-3060

The National Multiple Sclerosis Society was founded in 1946. Its major objectives are to support research, to conduct lay and professional services, and to carry out worldwide programs of information and idea exchange regarding multiple sclerosis.

National Paraplegia Foundation
333 North Michigan Avenue
Chicago, Il 60601
(312)346-4779

The National Paraplegia Foundation was founded in 1948 with the objectives of (1) improved and expanded rehabilitation and treatment of those suffering spinal cord injuries; (2) expanded research on a cure for paraplegia and quadriplegia; (3) removal of architectural barriers; (4) increased employment opportunities for persons with handicaps; (5) accessible housing and transportation.

National Rehabilitation Association
633 South Washington Street
Alexandria, VA 22314
(703)836-0850

The National Rehabilitation Association is an organization of professional and lay persons dedicated to the rehabilitation of persons with physical and mental handicaps.

National Rehabilitation Counseling Association
633 South Washington Street
Alexandria, VA 22314
(703)836-0850

The National Rehabilitation Counseling Association was founded in 1958 with the objectives of (1) developing professional standards for rehabilitation counseling;

(2) promoting professional training for rehabilitation counseling; (3) supporting rehabilitation counseling as it contributes to the interdisciplinary approach to the solution of problems.

National Spinal Cord Injury Association
600 West Cummings Pike #2000
Woburn, MA 01801
(800)962-9629
(508)935-2722

Focusing on basic research and community services, this association also provides educational resources related to spinal cord injury.

Paralyzed Veterans of America
801 18th Street, N.W.
Washington, DC 20006
(202)USA-1300

The principal aim of efforts by the Paralyzed Veterans of America is to improve programs of medicine and rehabilitation not only for veterans, but for all those with spinal cord injuries.

Partners of the Americas Rehabilitation Education Program (PREP)
2001 S Street, N.W.
Washington, DC 20009
(202)332-7332

The Partners of the Americas is currently the largest people-to-people program between the United States and Latin America, and is committed to fostering a closer relationship and understanding among our peoples. The purpose of PREP is to increase opportunities and improve programs for persons with handicaps in the Americas.

The President's Committee on Employment of Persons with Disabilities
111 20th Street, N.W., Suite 636
Washington, DC 20036
(202)653-5050

The President's Committee on Employment of Persons with Disabilities was established by the President of the United States in 1947. Since then, every President has given his personal and active support to full employment opportunities for persons with physical and mental handicaps.

Rehabilitation International
25 East 21st Street
New York, NY 10010
(212)420-1500

Rehabilitation International is a network of national agencies and persons in more than 60 countries dedicated to helping all persons with disabilities. Rehabilitation International offers international services to the US rehabilitation community, as well as to draw upon the expertise of the US rehabilitation community for the benefit of persons with handicaps worldwide.

Rehabilitation Services Administration, Department of Education
330 C Street, S.W.
Washington, DC 20202
(202)732-1723

The Office of Special Education and Rehabilitation administers programs of the U.S. Department of Education that deal with the persons with handicaps. The Rehabilitation Services Administration is principally concerned with the rehabilitation of adolescents and adults with handicaps.

United Cerebral Palsy Association, Inc.
1522 K St. NW, Suite 1112
Washington, DC 20005
(202)842-1266
(800)872-5827

United Cerebral Palsy Association is a national voluntary health organization dedicated to a continuing overall attack on cerebral palsy. Its primary function is to seek solutions to the multiple problems of cerebral palsy, with affiliates providing direct services to persons with cerebral palsy in states and communities.

U.S. Department of Veterans Affairs
810 Vermont Avenue, NW
Washington, DC 20420
(202)872-1151

The VA, established in 1930, administers a broad range of programs providing medical care, rehabilitation, education and training, income support, and other benefits for eligible veterans with disabilities and their dependents.

World Rehabilitation Fund, Inc.
400 East 34th Street
New York, NY 10016
(212)340-6062

The World Rehabilitation Fund has as its objective to assist governmental and voluntary agencies throughout the world in expanding and improving rehabilitation services for persons with physical handicaps.

Index

Index

NOTE

The publisher acknowledges the following permissions for the use of previously published materials included in the Third Edition. These citations were inadvertently omitted from the printed book.

Chapter 2. "The interdisciplinary status of rehabilitation psychology" by Joseph Stubbins: Reprinted from *Rehabilitation Psychology, 34*(3), 1989, pp. 207-215. © 1989 Division of Rehabilitation Psychology of the American Psychological Association. Reprinted with permission.

Chapter 3. "Theories and values: Ethics and contrasting perspectives on disability" by Harlan Hahn: Reprinted from *Ethical issues in disability and rehabilitation*, report of a 1989 international conference, pp. 101-104. © 1989 World Rehabilitation Fund, Rehabilitation International and World Institute on Disability. Reprinted with permission.

Chapter 4. "Ethical issues in teamwork: The context of rehabilitation" by Ruth B. Purtilo: Reprinted from *Archives of Physical Medicine and Rehabilitation, 69*, May 1988, pp. 318-321. © 1988. Reprinted with permission.

Chapter 7. "Recovery: The lived experience of rehabilitation" by Patricia E. Deegan: Reprinted from *Psychosocial Rehabilitation Journal, 11*(4) April 1988, pp. 11-19. © 1988. Reprinted with permission.

Chapter 8. "The birth of a handicapped child—A wholistic model for grieving" by Martha Wingerd Bristor: Reprinted from *Family Relations, 33*(1), January, 1984, pp.25-32. © 1984 National Council on Family Relations. Reprinted with permission.

Chapter 9. "Developmental tasks and transitions of adolescents with chronic illnesses and disabilities" by Sherry E. Davis, Constance Anderson, Donald C. Linkowski, Karen Berger, Carl F. Feinstein: Reprinted from *Rehabilitation Counseling Bulletin, 29*(2), December 1985, pp. 69-79. © 1985 American Association for Counseling and Development. Reprinted with permission. No further reproduction authorized without written permission of AACD.

Chapter 10. "Midlife transition and disability" by Paul W. Power, David B. Hershenson, and Nancy K. Schlossberg: Reprinted from *Rehabilitation Counseling Bulletin, 29*(2), December 1985, pp. 100-111. © 1985 American Association for Counseling and Development. Reprinted with permission. No further reproduction authorized without written permission of AACD.

Chapter 11. "Disability and psychosocial development in old age" by Helen Q. Kivnick: Reprinted from *Rehabilitation Counseling Bulletin, 29*(2), December 1985, pp. 122-134. © 1985 American Association for Counseling and Development. Reprinted with permission. No further reproduction authorized without written permission of AACD.

Chapter 13. "A unified approach to existing models of adaptation to disability: A model of adaptation" by Hanoch Livneh: Reprinted from *Journal of Applied Rehabilitation Counseling, 17*(1), Spring 1986, pp. 5-16. © 1986. Reprinted with permission.

Chapter 14. "Denial in rehabilitation: Its genesis, consequences, and clinical management" by Richard Naugle: Reprinted from *Rehabilitation Counseling Bulletin, 31*, March 1988, pp. 218-231. © 1988 American Association for Counseling and Development. Reprinted with permission. No further reproduction authorized without written permission of AACD.

Chapter 16. "On accepting relationships between people with mental retardation and non-disabled people: Towards an understanding of acceptance" by Steven Taylor and Robert Bogdan: Reprinted from *Disability, Handicap, and Society, 4*(1), 1989, pp. 21-36. © 1989. Reprinted with permission.

Chapter 18. "Sexual Values, Training, and Professional Roles" by Stanley Ducharme and Kathleen M. Gill Reprinted from The *Journal of Head Trauma Rehabilitation, 5*(2), 1990, pp. 38-45. Reprinted with permission of Aspen Publishers, Inc.. © 1990.

Chapter 19. "Sexuality and psychiatric disability" by Peter T. Knoepfler: Reprinted from *Sexuality and Psychiatric Disability, 5*(1), Spring 1982, pp. #14-27. © 1982 Human Sciences Press. Reprinted with permission.

Chapter 20. "Facing the challenges of sexual abuse in persons with disabilities" by Sandra S. Cole: Reprinted from *Sexuality and Disability, 7*(3/4) Fall/Winter 1984-1986, pp. 71-87. © Human Sciences Press. Reprinted with permission.

Chapter 21. "A unified approach to existing models of adaptation to disability: Intervention strategies" by Hanoch Livneh: Reprinted from *Journal of Applied Rehabilitation Counseling, 17*(2), Summer 1986, pp. 6-10. © 1986. Reprinted with permission.

Chapter 22. "Extending psychotherapeutics strategies to people with disabilities" by William A. McDowell, George F. Bills, and Marc W. Eaton: Reprinted from *Journal of Counseling and Development, 68*, Nov/Dec 1989, pp. 151-154. © 1989 AACD. Reprinted with permission of the American Association for Counseling and Development. All rights reserved.

Chapter 23. "Life's challenges: Curse or opportunity? Counseling families of persons with disabilities" by Mary R. Hulnick and H. Ronald Hulnick: Reprinted from *Journal of Counseling and Development, 68*, Nov/Dec 1989, pp. 166-170. © 1989 AACD. Reprinted with permission of the American Association for Counseling and Development. All rights reserved.

Chapter 24. "Who is responsible for the lifelong well-being of a person with a head injury" by Gerben DeJong, Andrew I. Batavia, Janet M. Williams: Reprinted from *The Journal of Head Trauma Rehabilitation, 5*(1), 1990, pp. 9-22. Reprinted with permission of Aspen Publishers, Inc.. © 1990.

Chapter 25. "Aging and disability: Toward a unified agenda" by Irving Kenneth Zola: Reprinted from *Journal of Rehabilitation*, Oct/Nov/Dec 1989, pp. 6-8. © 1989 National Rehabilitation Association. Reprinted with permission.

Chapter 26. "Families as caregivers: The limits of morality" by Daniel Callahan: Reprinted from *Archives of Physical Medicine and Rehabilitation, 69*, May 1988, pp. 323-328. © 1988. Reprinted with permission.

Chapter 28. "Psychosocial Rehabilitation: Toward a definition" by Ram A. Cnaan, Laura Blankertz, Karlyn W. Messinger, and Jerome R. Gardner: Reprinted from *Psychosocial Rehabilitation Journal, 11*(4), April 1988, pp. 61-77. © 1988. Reprinted with permission.

Chapter 29. "Coping with the enormity of illness and disability" by Arthur E. Dell Orto: Reprinted from *Rehabilitation Literature, 45*(1-2), January-February 1984, pp. 22-23. © 1984. Reprinted with permission.